The Obama Effect

The Obama Effect

Multidisciplinary Renderings of the 2008 Campaign

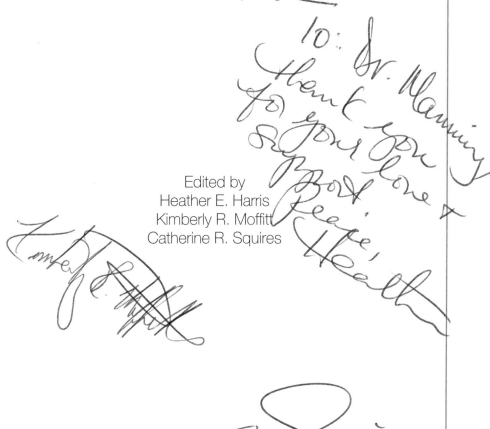

Edited by
Heather E. Harris
Kimberly R. Moffitt
Catherine R. Squires

SUNY PRESS

Published by State University of New York Press, Albany

For information, contact State University of New York Press, Albany, NY
www.sunypress.edu

Production by Ryan Morris
Marketing by Michael Campochiaro

Library of Congress Cataloging-in-Publication Data

The Obama effect : multidisciplinary renderings of the 2008 campaign/edited
    by Heather E. Harris, Kimberly R. Moffitt, and Catherine R. Squires.
        p.   cm.
Includes bibliographical references and index.
ISBN 978-1-4384-3659-3 (hardcover : alk. paper)
ISBN 978-1-4384-3660-9 (pbk. : alk. paper)
    1. Obama, Barack–Influence.   2. Political campaigns–United States.   3. United
States–Race relations–Political aspects.   4. Race relations in mass media.   5. Presidents–
United States–Election–2008. I. Harris, Heather E. II. Moffitt, Kimberly R. III. Squires,
Catherine R., 1972–
E908.3.O33 2011
973.932092–dc22

                                                                        2010032760

10 9 8 7 6 5 4 3 2 1

Table of Contents

Table of Contents

Table of Contents

Section V: Representations

List of Figures

Preface

Desiree Cooper

To quantify the "Obama Effect" is an exercise perhaps as grand and hopeful as the presidential candidacy of Barack Obama itself. The campaign is well over, and we know how it ended: He is the forty-fourth president of the United States. But what effect his rise to power will have and has already had upon history, upon America, and upon the world is anyone's guess.

When scholars converged upon the University of Minnesota in the fall of 2008, it was far from a certainty that the senator from Illinois would become president. But one thing was already certain: America's attitude toward race had shifted in both seismic and subtle ways—ways that needed to be captured and understood before the moment was recast by the hindsight of history.

Traditionally, the mass media have been instrumental in helping us understand life's watersheds, even as we are living them. The media have often been our reflectors and inquisitors, or expositors and agitators. Indeed, it is hard to imagine how the end of the Vietnam War, the success of the civil rights movement, or Nixon's resignation over Watergate would have happened if not for the power of the mass media. "To the press alone," James Madison once said, "the world is indebted for all the triumphs which have been gained by reason and humanity over error and oppression." But when it came to documenting racism in America, African-American journalist Ida B. Wells argued that the press was neither reasonable nor humane. In the late 1890s, she began a one-woman crusade against the lynching of blacks in the South. And while she had once referred to the media as "the great educator," in matters of race she was less charitable: "Somebody must show that the Afro-American race is more sinned against than sinning," she said, "and it seems to have fallen upon me to do so." From publishing runaway slave advertisements, to promulgating dehumanizing images of blacks during the Jim Crow Era, to the contemporary media's invention of the black welfare queen, the media have been key participants in the perpetuation of racist ideology in America.

One effect that the Obama candidacy has had upon the sociopolitical landscape is to subvert the role of the mass media in the national conversation about race. Obama was not just the nation's first biracial candidate, he was the nation's first "new media" candidate. His campaign inspired a genuine melting pot of art and social networking, setting the blogosphere on fire. New media danced on the cusp between reportage and participation. Obama raised a staggering $660 million online, and engaged millions of voters directly through Facebook, YouTube, and text messages.

When Obama easily ran away with the January 26, 2008, South Carolina primary, print and broadcast journalists offered a simple explanation: The black majority had gone to the voting booth in record numbers and voted along racial lines. Obama offered a different explanation. Coming out of South Carolina, he said that his candidacy was not about black versus white, but the past versus the future. Just a year before, that would have been a profoundly cynical statement. But the proof was in the early primaries as Obama swept states like Nebraska, Utah, and Iowa—states that were not only redder than red, but whiter than white. These victories lent credence to the argument that something else was afoot, something that the mainstream media were not registering.

Instead, they were stuck in a snow globe of racialized rhetoric that was sorely out of step with segments of the American public. For example, in early August 2008, candidate Obama was in the Twin Cities for a fundraiser and had stopped by a local café for a three-dollar stack of pancakes. On August 7, the *Minneapolis Star Tribune* Web site said, "Guess who's coming for breakfast?"—an allusion to the 1967 film *Guess Who's Coming to Dinner?*, where African-American actor Sidney Poitier was a white family's surprise dinner guest. Forty years ago, that was groundbreaking. For a newspaper in 2008, it was sadly unimaginative. It spoke to the dearth of positive representations of black men, and to the lack of a progressive racial consciousness in the mainstream media. *New York Times* columnist Frank Rich made a more insightful comparison: "Our political and news media establishments," he wrote on the eve of the election, "have their own conspicuous racial myopia with its own set of stereotypes and clichés. They consistently underestimated Obama's candidacy because they often saw him as a stand-in for the two-dimensional character Poitier had to shoulder."

Obama took the institutional media's racial blunders in stride. At the October 16, 2008, Alfred E. Smith Memorial Foundation Dinner, he remarked that his opponent, Arizona Senator John McCain, had accused him "of being the wed father of two girls." Silence enveloped the room for a tense heartbeat before the audience caught up with the joke. So invested has the media been in the iconography of the black man with countless illegitimate children, it took a while for the audience to realize Obama had said "wed" rather than the expected "unwed." Obama was not just running against his opponents, but against racist media imagery. How qualified was such an institution to cover a political campaign where race was not the subtext, but the story itself? Indeed, it was ill-equipped. The way the media engaged the race question during the campaign was a kindergarten-like tit-for-tat over who was racist and who was not. It openly fumbled the gift that Obama had given us: A chance to talk about race like adults.

There were exceptions. *Chicago Tribune* columnist Dawn Turner Trice began a Web project in the spring of 2008. It became a place where people could ask "dumb" questions about race and explore ideas. For her, one major effect of the Obama candidacy was to create a positive opportunity to engage the questions of race. "This is the first time in modern memory—perhaps ever—that race is the story when we're not in the middle of a negative racial crisis," she said. "There's no riot, no lynching or other hate crime, no travesty of justice.... Instead, we are dealing with race in the context of a person doing what Americans do: Run for president."

How, then, should the racially anorexic media have begun to capture the explosive and paradoxically quiet transformations that Americans were experiencing during 2008? Perhaps by looking at race within their own ranks. Although African Americans comprise 13 percent of the U.S. population, they made up only 5 percent of reporters of America's daily newspapers in 2007. They own no daily newspapers, less than 1 percent of full-power television stations, and 3 percent of radio stations. For a moment, there was hope that one collateral effect of an Obama candidacy would be more journalists of color. But the 2008 campaign coincided with both an economy in free fall and, perhaps more important, a pious mentality on the part of the mainstream press that journalists of color are not a prerequisite for producing objective reporting about race. Instead, there was a general redeployment of the media's few black faces.

What difference does having more diverse staff make when reporting the news? "Well, it certainly changes the questions that are asked and the observations that are made," said the Maynard Institute's Richard Prince on National Public Radio in February 2009. "We saw in the campaign, for example, a lot of cultural miscues because there weren't enough black reporters and editors fostering a dialogue." A case in point: The July 21, 2008, cover of the *New Yorker* depicted then–presidential candidate Obama dressed in traditional Muslim garb. Michelle Obama, the darker and therefore more dangerous half of the duo, was transformed into a version of the blaxpoitation Amazon "Cleopatra Jones," complete with Afro, ammunition, and rifle. A portrait of Osama bin Laden hung over the mantel. In the fireplace burned an American flag.

This image was published at a time when 13 percent of Americans believed that Obama was Muslim and 12 percent were convinced that he had "used a Koran for swearing in to the U.S. Senate," according to a *Newsweek* poll. Had an African American, a Muslim, or an Arab American been in the room when the decision was being made to run the cartoon, hard questions likely would have been raised about the wisdom of satirizing widely held prejudices about blacks, Arabs, and Islam. Perhaps the cover would not have been run at all. At the very least, editor David Remnick would have had a more thoughtful response to the public outrage than what he told the *Huffington Post*: "I ran the cover because I thought it had something to say."

Similarly, could diverse management have prevented Fox News from referring to the future First Lady as "Obama's Baby Mama?" And where was the internal racism radar when the *New York Post* ran a postelection cartoon characterizing the Obama administration as a slaughtered chimpanzee? In response the outcries of racism, the *Post* defended the cartoon as a commentary on the economic stimulus package. In a statement posted on its Web site, the *Post* objected that the cartoon had been "taken as something else—as a depiction of President Obama, as a thinly veiled expression of racism. This was most certainly not its intent; to those who were offended by this image, we apologize." This is a common backhanded apology from media institutions: "We are sorry that communities of color are humorless and hypersensitive." This reveals the appalling ignorance the mainstream media has for the ubiquity of racist iconography, and a stunning unawareness of their complicity in creating and perpetrating those images.

Unfortunately, the media industry will have little time to come to grips with its own culpability in the nation's failure to transcend race. Within six months of President Obama's election, several newspapers—including the 146-year-old *Seattle Post-Intelligencer*—had completely disappeared, while the *Chicago Tribune* and the *L.A. Times* were in bankruptcy. According to the Associated Press, a hundred newspapers in thirty-two states had stopped publishing a print version at least one day per week, including the *Christian Science Monitor*. Meanwhile, almost 75 million Americans were reading their news online, with 3.7 billion page views in January 2009, according to Nielson Online. In the wake of such precipitous decline, Obama has exhibited a stunning ability to expand his new media efforts while controlling his message in the increasingly irrelevant mass media. As Michael Wolff pointed out in the July 2009 issue of *Vanity Fair*, the Obama Administration "created an audience that it could reach through its own distribution prowess," and yet, in the face of the "dwindling life of the establishment media," continues to "talk to the dinosaurs."

Ironically, Obama has utilized—arguably even needed—the mainstream media's intense focus on celebrity news to help recast outdated notions of race. He has been able to use the media effectively to paint himself as cerebral but cool, the First Lady as brilliant, stylish, and motherly, and his daughters as darlings. It will be interesting to see how well these new media images will begin to "normalize" the entire black experience.

The ultimate effect that the Obama presidency will have on enduring, media-fueled, racist archetypes about black men, black families, and black power remains to be seen. That may depend largely on which survives the longest—the Obama presidency or the American press.

Acknowledgments

The journey to this volume began in 2007, with stops at the National Communication Association Convention and a conference at the University of Minnesota. As we write, Barack Obama is the forty-fourth president of the United States of America, and we have an initial sense of the effect of his revolutionary campaign. At this juncture, we are grateful to have grasped the opportunity to capture some of his campaign's innovations in our volume. We also welcome this opportunity to express our gratitude to the many people whose work, participation, support, and tireless commitment contributed to the inspiration and completion of this project.

Acquisitions Editor Larin McLaughlin's easy spirit and insightful guidance was invaluable in shaping our final product. Of course, there would be no final product without the work of our stellar contributors. Their enthusiasm for the volume and their commitment to deadlines made easy work for us. Additionally, the positive feedback from our two anonymous reviewers facilitated the honing of the volume in a way that only an external vantage point can provide.

On a personal note, I, Heather, thank God for love, divine guidance, and assistance in every aspect of my life. To my family, especially my brothers, Wayne and David Harris; my late mother, Euralene (Lynn) Harris; my father, Ralph Harris; my aunt, Eugene Harper; and my cousin, Lorna Ajala, and to my family and friends in Barbados, Canada, and the United States of America, know that I am buoyed by your love for me, and your unwavering enthusiasm for the work I have chosen. To the late Dr. Bradley Niles, and to Dr. Carolyn Stroman, Dr. Lyndrey Niles, Dr. Melbourne Cummings, Dr. Richard Wright, Dr. Anne Nicotera, Dr. Robin Means Coleman, and Dr. Ronald Jackson, your friendship, support, and mentorship enabled me to uncover a research path about which I am passionate. I also thank the Howard University family for honing the skills that led to this project, and the Stevenson University community for its interest in our project. And to my esteemed colleagues, friends, and co-editors, Dr. Kimberly Moffitt and Dr. Catherine Squires, I am grateful for the laughter, the tears, the synergy, the trust, and the excitement and the commitment that we shared in the process of completing this book. What a joy to work with both of you on our volume. Here's one last "Hooray!" Peace.

Acknowledgments

I (Kimberly) embrace fully, give reverence to, and thank my Creator for stimulating my creative and scholarly ability to complete this and other recent works. I also acknowledge my family, both immediate and ancestral, who have shared in my journey to write and chronicle *our* experiences in America. I extend a special recognition to my ninety-nine-year-old (great) "Grandma" Sadie Frazier Moffitt, who died only three days after witnessing presidential candidate Barack Obama become the first male of African descent to become president of the United States! Thank you to my colleagues and friends at the University of Maryland Baltimore County, especially in my home department of American Studies, for continued mentorship, intellectual stimulation and rigor, and support, both emotional and financial, in completing this major piece of scholarship. I must also offer my appreciation to Father Michael Pfleger of the Faith Community of Saint Sabina (Chicago, Illinois) for challenging me—albeit unknowingly—during a sermon at Howard University's chapel service in 2007 to see the possibilities in existence for Obama even though I began this journey as a naysayer who was interested in Obama's protection, not his politics. And finally to my co-editors, Dr. Heather Harris and Dr. Catherine Squires, who have remained dedicated and passionate to bring this project to fruition: I thank you both for making our volume a collaborative effort in the many senses of the word, all while enjoying and learning from your vibrant spirit.

I (Catherine) would like to acknowledge the generous support from many units and individuals at the University of Minnesota who made the Obama Effect Conference a success. The funding from the Cowles Chair of Journalism, Diversity, and Equality, along with contributions from multiple departments in the College of Liberal Arts, provided the means for the event. Sarah Saubert, Jen Keavy, and student staffers of the Minnesota Journalism Center contributed priceless hours and savvy to execute our plans. Faculty colleagues Cindy Garcia and Brian Southwell graciously co-hosted dinners, and members of the School of Journalism and Mass Communication Graduate Student Organization served as panel chairs, greeters, and tech support to make the conference flow smoothly. Special thanks to my graduate research assistants, Sarah Janel Jackson and Deborah Carver, who put in many hours to help get the details nailed down for featured speakers and conference presenters.

I send virtual hugs and high-fives to my Maryland-based co-editors, Dr. Moffit and Dr. Harris, for keeping the faith when my pessimism reared its head. Thanks always to my family, Bryan, Will, and Helena, who allowed me time and space to dash to conference events and to concentrate on our many conference calls as the Obama Effect transformed from a meeting into a book.

Introduction

Catherine Squires, Heather Harris, and Kimberly Moffitt

A wise Latina. "Birthers." A Cambridge cop and a Harvard professor. The Tea Party. These figures interrupted the congratulatory postracial and postfeminist discourses trumpeted in the wake of the historic 2008 victory of Barack Hussein Obama, the forty-fourth president of the United States. The "back-to-the-future" shock of Republican senators grilling (now-Justice) Sonia Sotomayor; the spectacle of angry crowds denying the validity of Obama's Hawaiian birth certificate; and renewed debates over (and denial of) racial profiling reveal a need to revisit and interrogate the assumptions of imminent change that erupted after election night.

The Obama Effect interrogates multiple sites of discourse and citizen inter-action revealed during the campaign to be crucial grounds for rethinking (or reinforcing) social identities and investments. The chapters call upon us to take a fresh look at identity formations of the past and present, to revisit texts and figures that continue to resonate in the Age of Obama (also known as the *postsoul, postfeminist, post–civil rights* era). The essays here chart discourses that were emergent in the 2008 campaign and continue to structure the contours of discussion as President Obama journeys through his first term, a term marked by historic economic woes at home and continued military entanglements abroad. In this time of great uncertainty, the authors in this book provide important questions and reflections to engage both the problems and promises of the election of Obama.

Race and Gender: *Plus ça Change*?

While many observers have disputed the jubilant claims that the election of the first president of African descent marked the "end of race," the events of the summer of 2009 exposed that declaration as naïve and self-congratulatory. Likewise, assertions that Hillary Clinton's run created multiple millions of cracks in the gender "glass ceiling" were exposed as unripe when angry protestors claimed that Obama's health-care plan would increase abortions, and as Michelle Obama's wardrobe remains under a high-powered microscope.

Many of the writers in this book anticipated the durability of long-standing rhetorical strategies and investments in dominant identities. Their analyses remind us that, although muted, frameworks for understanding race, gender, and sexuality that dominated the 1980s and 1990s remain readily available. We have already witnessed how easily pundits branded President Obama himself a racist in the wake of his remarks on the disputable arrest of Professor Henry Louis Gates, Jr., in his own home. And, in a time of severe economic pressures, the past teaches us and the present reminds us how race and gender are still used to attack policies and publics. Today neo-Nazi Web sites warn members to hoard guns for fear Obama is paving the way for militant Black Power; draconian anti-immigrant and anti–ethnic studies laws have passed in Arizona.

Assessing the Obama Effect: Looking Back to Look Forward

The chapters collected here began as conference papers, many of which predicted that, far from ushering in the end of racism or sexism, the 2008 campaign revealed fissures in our sense of national identity. Dina Gavrilos's examination of popular media responses to Obama's allegedly "postracial" persona reveals how this term disguises and reinforces hegemonic racial frameworks. Enid Logan provides insights into how gender/sexism and race/racism worked in campaign rhetoric and young voters' reactions to Hillary Clinton and Obama. Amy Carrillo-Rowe's exploration of mainstream discourses surrounding Obama's relationships to family, friends, and foes underscores how heteronormativity interacts with race.

Frank R. Cooper illuminates the strategic ways in which Obama's more "feminine" style discourages associations with threatening black male stereotypes. Looking at First Lady Michelle Obama, Kimberly Moffitt recalls the ease with which mainstream media attempted to frame her as an angry black woman, reminding us that the same dynamics that undermined previous black women in national politics (such as Anita Hill and Lani Guinier) continue to inflect twenty-first century discussions of the first African-American woman to occupy the White House as a resident rather than as a domestic servant.

Political Participation and Identity in the "Age of Obama": Changing the Game?

The resilience of conspiracy theories regarding the president's birth is put into perspective by the essays that address how Obama's "exotic" background grates against hegemonic norms of American identity. This presents a challenge and an opportunity: Obama's identity has provoked backlash, but also opens the door for wider discussion and appreciation for alternative ways to imagine individual and national identities. Heather Harris delineates how Obama's official Web site was launched with a challenge to and reclamation of the idea(l) of the American Dream. This revised ideal was inclusive of groups that have regularly been jettisoned outside the status quo. Likewise, James Petry examines Obama's progressive take on American exceptionalism, inflected with cosmopolitan visions of America's place in the world and Obama's international family ties.

On a more local level, Sarah McCaffrey analyzes responses to Obama's "race speech" in Philadelphia. Her essay uncovers how admirers and critics of the speech agreed on Obama's willingness to emphasize elements of the painful racial past, but differ on whether his vision of a "racial stalemate" provides sufficient impetus for change. In contrast, Bertram Ashe provides a rubric for understanding and contextualizing complex racial identity formations in the postsoul era, and instructs us to move beyond the simple analyses of Obama's sense of racial self to see how the president's narration of his life story exemplifies how many of his generation experience and (re)define race.

The Obama campaign has been declared a "game-changer" due to its unprecedented and successful merging of Web 2.0 technologies and old-school organizing. Bringing young voters of all colors, genders, and sexual identities into the voting booth, the victory left many observers in awe, predicting that the Obama "machine" would provide powerful coattails to future Democratic candidates. Michael Cheney and Crystal Olsen provide readers with important insights into how this operation transformed itself over the course of the campaign. Beyond the mechanics, Qingwen Dong, Kenneth D. Day, and Raman Deol provide a close analysis of how and why the messages conveyed through Obama's Web site resonated with voters looking for a more personal connection and sense of purpose.

Grace Yoo and colleagues explore how the Obama campaign inspired some women to call themselves "Obama Mamas." Their chosen identity and community defies simplistic renderings of the "gender divide" and "soccer moms" in mainstream media. Finally, Konrad Ng's detailed look at Asian Americans' creative use of the Internet reveals the investment of a social group almost totally ignored in dominant media discussions of the election. These chapters point to the need for continued investigation of how Web 2.0 has various applications and consequences for media, identity, and political participation.

An Obama-nation, or an Abomination?

Since the inauguration, reverence for Obama seems to have faded. As his administration tries to make promised changes, some observers posit that Obama's Web-based machine is not up to the task. Supporters have lamented the seeming inability of the President to employ his personal charisma to win legislative battles, fights that require more than just donations or bumper-sticker displays. In an era of instant communication and celebrity politicians, can the president unleash his "star power" to generate legislative victories? Are Obama voters too disconnected from the world of *realpolitik* to bring the change?

Rebecca Kuehl and Robert Spicer provide some insights into these questions. Kuehl provides a structure for thinking about the power of celebrity in politics, using Oprah Winfrey's relationship to Obama as a starting point for interrogating the utility of celebrity ties for politicians. Spicer explains how media images and discourses framed Obama as a charismatic leader, and illustrates how both supporters and detractors used this image to buttress or undermine Obama's legitimacy. This dynamic is clearly still operating; some observers claim he needs to use his charisma more, others argue he is a charismatic fraud.

These chapters illustrate the seriousness and political utility of identities, and guide us to look beyond the confines of mainstream media (expertly taken to task in Desiree Cooper's preface) that are all too often guided by rigid black/white frameworks. Clearly, the activities of Asian Americans, Latina/os, and "Obama Mamas" are not suited to the black/white paradigm to which dominant media cling.[1] However, the black/white dichotomy continues to vex our discourse and behaviors in the United States. How we might deal with this sticky problem is the question. M. Cooper Harriss considers Obama's approach to race and nation through the lens of comparison to author Ralph Ellison. His essay reveals the similarities in their approaches, and how each complicate and reject simple notions of racial authenticity. Likewise, Suzanne Jones's exploration of *Dreams from My Father* reminds us of Obama's consistent refusal to accept or promote simple understandings of racial identity. To close, the president's brother-in-law, Konrad Ng, provides a focused reminiscence of the campaign and the inaugural in his epilogue, recalling the energies that may yet be harnessed for public policy and social transformation.

This collection helps situate current debates and "whisper campaigns" that surround Obama. Rightfully, many of the chapters maintain that the Obama campaign provided a glimpse of how we could rethink the politics of identity and reinvigorate practices of citizenship. One could argue that this book presents these possibilities as much as it reflects the continued strength of demands for Americans to assimilate to an assumed white norm. Of course, which possibilities we pursue depends in large part on how we imagine our future, a process in which discourses play a large role. One contribution of this volume is providing scaffolding for those visions and discussions, as well as cautions to be vigilant of the ways our past continues to shape our present and future.

---

[1]Readers will note that the chapters here address white, black, and Asian-American identities directly, but Latina/o identities are not thematized. This absence is due to the fact that none of the participants in the original conference presented work on Latina/os and Obama, although as conference organizers, we endeavored to solicit work from a wide range of disciplines and approaches to be as inclusive as possible.

Section I: Rhetoric

White Males Lose Presidency for First Time: Exposing the Power of Whiteness through Obama's Victory

Dina Gavrilos

Barack H. Obama's November 4, 2008, presidential victory presented a racial justice conundrum. On the one hand, it was a stunning historic moment to witness a black man[1] elected U.S. president. Newspapers across the nation proclaimed Obama's election as a symbol of racial progress. Headlines declared: "Obama Elected in Historic Vote: Dream a Reality"[2] (*San Francisco Chronicle*); "Historic Win ... U.S. Elects 1st Black President in 'Victory of Faith Over Fear'"[3] (*Atlanta-Journal Constitution*); "Racial Barrier Falls in Decisive Victory"[4] (*New York Times*); and "Obama Rolls: Red States Turn to Blue as Racial Barrier Tumbles"[5] (*Denver Post*). Indeed, one could not help but feel optimistic and emotionally gripped at the scene of a person of color finally living at what has literally and figuratively been the White House.

On the other hand, those of us interested in racial justice more cynically understand that journalistic discourses proclaiming Obama's victory a racial turning point are politically hyperbolic. The Obama phenomenon is not likely

---

[1]Although Obama is biracial, he was most often characterized as black and self-identified as such. When discussing African-American identities, it is important to acknowledge the cultural and legal legacies of the "one-drop rule" in which any trace of African ancestry tends to supersede other parts of one's racial identity.

[2]Matthew B. Stannard, Justin Berton, and Tom Abate, "Obama Elected in Historic Vote; Dream a Reality: For African Americans Across the Nation, It's a Hallelujah Moment," *San Francisco Chronicle*, November 5, 2008, A3.

[3]Cameron McWhirter, "Historic Win: Barack Obama: 44th President of the United States; U.S. Elects 1st Black President in 'Victory of Faith over Fear,'" *Atlanta Journal-Constitution*, November 5, 2008, 1EX.

[4]Adam Nagourney, "Obama: Racial Barrier Falls in Decisive Victory," *New York Times*, November 5, 2008, A1.

[5]Karen E. Crummy, "Obama Rolls: Red States Turn to Blue as Racial Barrier Tumbles," *Denver Post*, November 5, 2008, A1.

to change—materially or symbolically—the fortunes of those suffering in a society steeped in ongoing, centuries-long racial hierarchies and injustices. While a few news stories indicated a more tempered view of the Obama effect for race relations in the United States—"But does this election fulfill King's dream?"[6]—the prevailing political and cultural mainstream mantra surrounding Obama's election was that racial equality had finally won the day; America was redeemed. Is it possible, though, to move beyond these two political knee-jerk reactions to the Obama phenomenon—beyond a discourse of overinflated hope for social change or tired cynicism? Can we take advantage of Obama's history-making "difference" to raise awareness of persistent problematic racial ideologies rather than to promote racial progress as a fait accompli?

To that end, I want to interpret and then re-interpret the representation of Obama as a national symbol of racial progress—a representation that is not only hyperbolic but downright regressive for the cause of racial justice. Obama's race certainly is historically meaningful. However, I argue that a black man's portrayal as a historic symbol of national racial progress arises from a deeply ingrained yet powerfully unspoken ideology of whiteness—a racial hierarchy that privileges the norms and perspectives of elite white males in political culture. It is extremely telling and proves the point about the invisible power of whiteness that the flip side of this history-making moment was never uttered: that white males lost the presidency for the first time in U.S. history. For more than two centuries, only white males (and, among those, almost exclusively Anglos with stunningly and stubbornly similar cultural, religious and educational backgrounds) had been elected to the presidency of what is proclaimed to be a pluralistic, representative democracy (one that, just as noteworthy, has yet to elect a woman—or a member of one-half the population—as president). The significant, yet silenced, story of political power here is the erased race of all forty-three previous presidents.

In contrast, Obama's race is very visibly marked and appropriated to reinforce status quo political power. This is accomplished by framing Obama's historic racial victory in comforting conservative narratives that buttress the ideological power of whiteness. This racial victory is explained in mainstream media discourses through stories reinforcing the ideology of the American Dream myth of hard work and limitless opportunity for all, and of a race-relations history encompassing slow, steady progress. This chapter delineates why these are problematic ideologies for understanding the profound role of race in power in U.S. culture. Through this critique, I expose the unspoken assumptions about the power of whiteness embedded in dominant cultural understandings of Obama's racial victory and pose alternative ways of seeing this moment.

---

[6]Stannard, Berton, and Abate, "Obama Elected in Historic Vote."

The Ideological Primacy of the American Dream Myth in Obama's Victory

The theme of Obama's life story can be summed in the phrase "only in America could the son of a Kenyan father and Kansan mother ..." This life story embodies the ideologically powerful American Dream narrative that one cannot escape when explaining individual rags-to-riches success in American culture, especially promoted through television and other media forms.[7] Obama himself promotes this theme as a mainstream politician who is not going to position his racial identity in ways that go against dominant cultural and political norms. Together, these discourses paint him as the perfect embodiment of the American Dream—that if one simply works hard and remains optimistic, opportunities for success in America are limitless. The powerfully persuasive pull of this American Dream story lies in its simultaneous glorification of the individual and the nation. Obama's success as an African American is inextricably linked to the story of the nation's success in providing equality and opportunity for all.

From the perspective of racial justice, problematic assumptions abound in tying Obama's individual success to racial progress for African Americans and the nation as a whole. One is the relatively simple observation that marking one individual's achievement as historic for an entire race of people presumes that one individual signifies a restructuring of systemic social and institutional power. One individual cannot symbolically or materially eliminate racial hierarchy or institutionalized racism. The emphasis on individualism in American culture is a problematic lens through which to understand and explain social phenomenon and social injustices.[8] Inspiring and hopeful examples of individual success do not reflect the targeted, discriminatory treatment of various social groups. This individualistic perspective neglects the social, cultural, economic, and political structures that perpetuate a certain social order based on class, race, and gender. As scholar George Lipsitz makes clear, white privilege is a product of a history of federal, state, and local actions and inaction that perpetuate a system of racial hierarchy.[9] The American Dream narrative of Obama's victory masked the ongoing structural and institutional obstacles to success that remain for people of color.

---

[7]Herman Gray, "Television, Black Americans, and the American Dream," *Critical Studies in Mass Communication* 6, no. 4 (1989): 376–86.

[8]For a discussion of the power of individualism in U.S. culture, see Robert N. Bellah, Richard Madsen, William M. Sullivan, Ann Swidler, and Steven M. Tipton, *Habits of the Heart: Individualism and Commitment in American Life* (Berkeley: University of California Press, 1985).

[9]George Lipsitz, *The Possessive Investment in Whiteness: How White People Profit from Identity Politics* (Philadelphia: Temple University Press, 1998).

Moreover, Obama's victory furthered an especially powerful racialized dimension in the American Dream ideology. As an *African-American* success story, Obama makes the American Dream myth even more powerful and powerfully problematic because it is being told via the Other. A person of color's success, by virtue of being symbolically lower in the racial hierarchy, paradoxically signifies *even more powerfully* the potency of the American Dream for all. At the same time, and again paradoxically, a person of color's failure is seen *as yet more proof* of that subculture's endemic moral failings.

Overall, then, representations of African Americans through the ideology of individualism and polarized images (extremely positive and negative) have powerful implications. As Herman Gray writes, "These representations operate intertextually to produce an ideology which explains black middle class success and urban poverty by privileging individual attributes and middle class values and by displacing social and structural factors."[10] Another race and media scholar notes that "when news organizations—however well intentioned—implicitly accent the values and determination of socially and economically successful minority Americans, they feed the mythological notion that the success is equally accessible to all."[11] Similarly, having studied the popularity and appeal of admirable black characters on *The Cosby Show*, Sut Jhally and Justin Lewis argue that such positive representations have, ironically, ushered a new type of racism called "enlightened racism."[12] In this latest version, there is less overt talk of blacks as inherently inferior and an increase in attitudes that blame African Americans who remain poor or struggling in the face of seemingly boundless opportunities for success.

The past few decades, in particular, have witnessed an increased visibility in the rise of minority success stories, especially through the fame of African-American superstars in high-profile industries like sports and entertainment. Scholars who have studied representations of megastar African Americans like Michael Jordan and Oprah conclude that these images reinforce the hegemonic values of the American Dream, glorifying status quo political and economic structures through which they have arisen.[13] Obama is part of this trend, and stands in as the new African-American superstar and role model in the

---

[10]Gray, "Television, Black Americans, and the American Dream," 376.

[11]Christopher P. Campbell, *Race, Myth and the News* (Thousand Oaks, CA: Sage Publications, 1995).

[12]Sut Jhally and Justin Lewis, *Enlightened Racism: The Cosby Show, Racism, and the Myth of the American Dream* (Boulder, CO: Westview Press, 1992): 133.

[13]Mary G. McDonald, "Michael Jordan's Family Values: Marketing, Meaning, and Post-Reagan America," *Sociology of Sport Journal* 13, no. 4 (1996): 344–65; Dana L. Cloud, "Hegemony or Concordance? The Rhetoric of Tokenism in Oprah Winfrey's Rags-to-Riches Biography," *Critical Studies in Mass Communication* 13, no. 2 (1996): 115–37.

political arena. Consequently, the election of a black president makes support for affirmative action or other social policies meant to redress the obstacles still facing discriminated groups seem unnecessary. Some even suggest that Obama's win ushers in a postracial era, one in which racism no longer exists and race does not matter.

Furthermore, Obama's racial victory also became a moment when African-American pride became conflated with national pride. Obama's victory was positioned as a victory not only for an entire race of people but also a nation of people. His victory reinforced the longstanding cliché that "anyone can grow up to be president," which was never true except in the case of certain white males. Like much public discourse on the day after the election, the *St. Petersburg Times* editorial titled "Obama's Victory, and America's" was an example of this conflated national and racial pride:

> Americans on Tuesday turned a page of history, breaking through the partisan politics and racial barriers of the past to embrace the inspiring voice of a new generation. Barack Obama's remarkable rise from modest beginnings to his election as the nation's first black president is a uniquely American success story, and the voters' recognition of his talents and their confidence in his potential sends a positive message to the world.[14]

Obama's victory is being co-opted and framed from a seemingly *unified national* perspective—a flattering view of all Americans moving forward together, fulfilling the nation's destiny as an ultimately righteous nation. Framing Obama's success as part of a national history of racial progress masks the much more successful legacy of white male leaders in various industries to maintain power at the expense of others.

While it is historically, culturally, and sentimentally powerful that an African American has achieved the highest position of political power in the United States, this cannot be celebrated without noting a major contradiction—that *national* structures of power (economic and social policies, cultural ideologies, and political practices) did not help produce of this historic moment but aligned systemically to work against it. The proof of this stubbornly-held power is that it took more than two centuries to see a nonwhite male win. In recent times, thirty-plus years of regressive neoconservative economic and political policies did not make it easier for an Obama to emerge, but harder. If we are to reframe Obama's success in terms of racial justice, we need to proclaim that Obama's victory is not a symbol of the nation's inevitable acceptance of black people or a fulfillment of its ideals of equality and justice. Rather, there are other political

---

[14]"Obama's Victory, and America's," *St. Petersburg Times*, November 5, 2008, 18A.

and economic reasons to which we can point that might explain his success just as well.

Instead of highlighting Obama's success as a symbol of racial "progress," we could reconstruct Obama as one of the most extraordinary individuals to come across the political scene (an ironic, perhaps, racial-justice twist on the cultural ideal of individualism). Rather than pointing to a black man finally crossing a racial barrier, we can paint Obama as an extraordinarily gifted, once-in-a-lifetime politician. This is debatable, of course. But, just as the idea that Obama's success can translate into success for other African-American males is highly questionable, we can pose alternative ways of seeing him. The story of Obama's extraordinary success can start with the hard-to-believe story of a freshman U.S. senator becoming president. He has been described as charismatic and highly intelligent, with the political shrewdness to beat the long-standing Clinton Democratic Party machine.

We need to ask out loud whether the first black president in a society with an entrenched racial hierarchy could be anything but extraordinary. Let's put it this way: Until we have a black president as inarticulate as President George W. Bush, racial progress has not really been achieved.[15] I make this point seriously because of what is often neglected in discussions of the American Dream: The standards for success are actually much higher for nonwhite males in our culture. While white-male normative power can be sustained with a range of skill levels from mediocrity to highly qualified, most African Americans must be, more often than not, extraordinarily above average to be viewed as successes. Re-presenting Obama's success in these terms would help contradict a popular belief that blacks less skilled than whites are hired and promoted for purposes of affirmative action. In fact, American Dream stories featuring high-profile African Americans insidiously communicate a higher standard of excellence for the oppressed group than would be expected for the average (white) person, and thus perpetuate twenty-first-century-style racism. There are so few images of *ordinary* or average African Americans in our culture that African Americans must be supersuccessful to be seen as simply American.

In conjunction with Obama's extraordinary personal talents, we also need to point to the extraordinary times in which Obama's political fortunes emerged. Obama ran for president in a time marked by extremely low levels of confidence in the current president (George W. Bush) and economic turmoil

---

[15]Lest this statement seems too unfair or partisan, I point to Bush's description of his own inarticulate nature: "The way I see it," Bush joked, "I am a boon to the English language. I've coined new words like 'misunderestimate' and 'Hispanically.' I've expanded the definition of words themselves, using 'vulcanizae' when I meant 'polarize,' 'Grecians' when I meant 'Greeks,' 'inebriating' when I meant 'exhilarating.' And instead of 'barriers and tariffs,' I said 'terriers and barrifs.'" (Associated Press, "43rd President is 'Gut Player' Who Eschews Personal Change," MSNBC, http://www .msnbc.msn.com/id/5762240/ns/politics/ [accessed August 3, 2009].)

unseen since the Great Depression. In other words, the first African-American president is not symbolic of postracialism. Rather, large-scale social fear and institutions gone awry are the historical contingencies that allowed Obama's talents to break through the color barrier. Perhaps it was not hope, but utter desperation and fear: Things are so bad, why not give the black guy a chance? This sentiment was smartly captured in a headline from the satirical magazine *The Onion* the day after the election: "Black man given the worst job in the nation."[16]

A common refrain around Obama's victory was that nobody could have imagined a black man as president. But nobody could have imagined the scale of an economic crisis that brought capitalism to its knees, either. Perhaps the sign of the irrelevance of race will be evident when a person of color (or a woman) is elected in ordinary or boom times.

Even if we are to go with the conservative logic of Obama as a symbol of racial "progress," is it not utterly premature to celebrate this on the basis of only one nonwhite man elected as president? With forty-three white male presidents elected in a row prior to Obama, why would we not consider Obama a fluke until subsequent elections also yielded diverse presidential identities? Only in distorted American racial politics would one black man's victory in relation to centuries of white male rule yield such feelings of triumph.

Having pointed to alternative ways of understanding Obama's race and his presidential victory, it is important to acknowledge that Obama does indeed represent a different identity from past presidents and that this can certainly be interpreted as political progress for people of color. It is significant, after all, that an extraordinary gifted black politician *has actually been allowed the opportunity* to make his case for leading the country (and has not been marginalized or murdered in the process). However, there have been millions of African Americans (as well as members of other historically oppressed groups) who have lived and died in obscurity, without an opportunity to explore their talents, much less manifest them. In their name, we should reframe the meaning of this moment, questioning loudly and soberly: How many Obamas did centuries of oppression ignore or destroy?

Rethinking the Telling of History and Racial Progress

The representation of facts and history is not neutral, and the writing of history is a powerful reality-shaping tool. Consequently, the framing of Obama's victory as a historic racial milestone also needs to be unpacked for the problematic ways

---

[16]"Black Man Given Nation's Worst Job," *The Onion*, November 5, 2008, http://www.theonion .com/content/news_briefs/black_man_given_nations (accessed August 3, 2009).

it promotes a white privileged view of history and social change. Indeed, as much as this was touted as a "historic moment," looking back at *centuries* of oppression was not a prominent part of the historic celebration. The racial progress chronicled tended to begin from the contemporary civil rights movement. Much was made about Obama's inauguration, preceded by Martin Luther King Day and taking place at the National Mall, the site of Dr. King's "I Have A Dream" speech. For example, the headline on *ABC News* online declared: "From King's 'I Have a Dream' to Obama Inauguration: On Inauguration Eve, Civil Rights Leaders Reflect on Martin Luther King Jr.'s March on Washington," and *USA Today* stated: "Where King Preached, Obama's the Word."[17] While it is certainly newsworthy to allude to prominent civil rights leader Dr. King upon the inauguration of the first African-American president, the predominant references to the civil rights movement as symbolic bookends of forty-six or so years of racial struggle elides the centuries of oppression experienced by blacks in favor of the relatively recent civil rights historical struggle. This long history of oppression was perhaps too incongruous with the much-needed national pride that was a necessary feature of Obama's victory if it was to be palatable to *all* Americans. The more familiar civil rights movement of the 1960s, with its heroes and memorable moments, provided the visuals that supported the mainstream view of racial struggle: how the March on Washington led progressively, just a few decades later, to this inauguration.

The forward-moving march through time itself is another problematic assumption about history embedded in Obama's story. Obama's victory is seemingly a sign that one of the last great remaining racial barriers in American culture had been crossed. This perspective sees history, and time itself, as moving inevitably, incrementally, and progressively toward racial justice. The ideological premise here is that eventually, given time, one racial barrier after another will fall; first it was sports, then entertainment, and now the highest political office in the land. Combined with the value of individualism, framing progress in terms of individuals crossing inevitable racial barriers avoids a closer examination of the institutional and systemic racial biases that remain.

Thus, this forward-looking view of history is inherently optimistic. It is no wonder that taking into account centuries of oppression does not have much significance in a culture dominated by this future-oriented view of history. Even when acknowledging the past, it is framed from the perspective of the

---

[17]Jennifer Parker, "From King's 'I Have a Dream' to Obama Inauguration," ABC News, http://abcnews.go.com/Politics/story?id=6665595&page=1 (accessed August 3, 2009); Rick Hampson, Larry Copeland, Charisse Jones, and William M. Welch, "Where King Preached, Obama's the Word," *USA Today*, http://www.usatoday.com/news/nation/2009-01-18-king_N.htm (accessed August 3, 2009).

"long journey" or the "long road" that African Americans have tread to reach the White House. The emphasis on "road" and "journey" as metaphors in the story of racial progress implies an inevitable destination, a promised land. It leaves most Americans feeling as though if we wait long enough, justice will inevitably arrive. When tying this supposedly "progressive" view of history to the rhetoric that America, unlike any other, is a nation that espouses ideals of equality and justice and freedom, it is easy to see how ideologically powerful this perspective is. It is more comfortable to be patient and, for whites especially, to feel good on this long journey; after all, the overall goals and intentions are good. Additionally, the implicit rhetoric suggests that, justice for all is such a lofty idea in the first place that some nations do not even strive for it. Consequently, those not experiencing these ideals of equality and justice should not be so greedy as to believe that it can come without a long, hard fight. This ideology of racial progress via historic milestones by great figures also works to squelch desire for urgent, collective action to address social problems. It also sentimentalizes the need to wait for the "right" leader—in this case, Obama—to come along and make change.

Additionally, the myth of racial progress over time implies a linear understanding of time and progress. This view of history deemphasizes what is a more painful understanding of social change. Changing social structures is often an unpredictable, back-and-forth, one-step-forward-two-steps-back process. For example, there is a stark, contradictory picture of race and power coinciding with the first African-American president's term: There is only one black U.S. senator, Obama's replacement and, in total, there are only three other nonwhites and seventeen women out of one hundred senators in 2010—hardly a diverse crop of senators. In addition, on a broader social level, there remain massive disparities between nonwhites and whites in education, jobs, the criminal justice system, and healthcare, among other important areas of collective well-being. The idea that power shifts incrementally, ever forward, toward more inclusivity and just outcomes is not the norm. However, if we remind ourselves that relations of power shift with unpredictable and contradictory rather than progressive results (a Foucaultian view of history), we can remain vigilant about next moves amid potentially regressive social outcomes.

"Historical progress" itself, then, is a myth, arising from the perspective of those in power rather than those who are oppressed. This view of history is from the perspective of those least suffering, for if you are suffering, the road to inevitability can actually be quite an indeterminately long and painful experience.

Instead of talking about milestones reached, then, we could ask: Why did it take so long? What prevented it from happening sooner? Perhaps Obama can be understood as an "unjustly overdue" milestone, emphasizing not national pride, but national humility that it took so long.

The ideological assumptions surrounding Obama as a symbol of racial progress depoliticize his racial difference to service current status quo racial understandings. The implications of framing Obama in this way ultimately lead to an overarching conclusion: Obama's racial victory is framed in ways that reinforce the logic and perspective of whiteness as the norm. But can we salvage this representational moment? Can the power of Obama's highly visible identity—his blackness, his difference—be used for raising awareness about white privilege and power today?

Obama as the Impetus for Unmasking the Power of Whiteness

In recent years, studies of the power of whiteness have described it as a system of privilege and power conferring "unearned assets" to whites who often cannot see these privileges because this white identity is the norm, the lens through which social relations are understood and measured.[18] Whiteness is an invisible and unspoken symbolic and material power precisely because it is so pervasive and taken for granted as the norm. In the early twentieth century, W. E. B. Du Bois described the "psychological wages" of whiteness in the following way:

> It must be remembered that the white group of laborers, while they received a low wage, were compensated in part by a sort of public and psychological wage. They were given public deference and titles of courtesy because they were white. They were admitted freely with all classes of white people to public functions, public parks. ... Their vote selected public officials, and while this had small effect upon the economic situation, it had great effect upon their personal treatment and the deference shown them.[19]

Scholars since have been tracing the economic, political, and social realities that result in the material, psychological, and emotional benefits of being white.[20] Historians have also shown how cultural, political, and economic

---

[18]Peggy McIntosh, "White Privilege: Unpacking the Invisible Knapsack," *Peace and Freedom*, July/August (1989): 10–12.

[19]W. E. B. Du Bois, *Black Reconstruction in America, 1860–1880* (New York: Free Press, 1935/1995), 700–01.

[20]See, for example, Lipsitz, *The Possessive Investment in Whiteness*; McIntosh, "White Privilege"; Paula S. Rothenberg, *White Privilege: Essential Readings on the Other Side of Racism* (New York: Worth Publishers, 2005).

structures have resulted in certain ethnic groups being "awarded" a "white" identity—showing how fluid racial classifications can be.[21]

Racial-justice activists have sought to address the intense denial of the pervasive norm of whiteness, both on a cultural and individual level. This perspective does not promote hatred for white people and does not encourage the passive emotion of guilt among white people for the problems of racism. Rather, if being a person of color has disadvantages, as most honest people would acknowledge, it becomes important to talk about the obvious advantages of not being classified a person of color, as racial-justice activist Tim Wise points out.[22] Only by exposing the flip side of racism (i.e., white privilege) can racial injustices be first acknowledged and then addressed. The denial of the power of whiteness is the most powerful tool in maintaining a racial hierarchy, as Peggy McIntosh relates: "To redesign social systems we need first to acknowledge their colossal unseen dimensions. The silences and denials surrounding privilege are the key political tool here. They keep the thinking about equality or equity incomplete, protecting unearned advantage and conferred dominance by making these taboo subjects."[23]

I think it is possible to redefine Obama's historic significance by making the power of whiteness visible through his "difference." The possibility for a reinterpretation of Obama's identity exists because identities are ongoing social constructions, the result of ongoing discursive battles to define reality and, thus, never "fixed" in meaning.[24] Obama's public image is neither completely of his own making nor solely in the custody of the dominant culture. Even as Obama's historically Other identity has been "fixed" by the dominant and popular media as a symbol of racial progress and the American Dream, and even though the Obama administration must carefully frame his identity in ways that are palatable for mainstream political audiences, we can still seize upon the potential resistance in his historically Othered identity and promote an alternative. This alternative lies in exposing the power of whiteness.

Instead of allowing Obama's identity and difference to be depoliticized, we can use his history-making racial identity to make explicit the implicit power of whiteness; ironically so, since a black man has been elected president and

---

[21]See, for example, David R. Roediger, *The Wages of Whiteness: Race and the Making of the American Working Class* (New York and London: Verso, 1991); Noel Ignatiev, *How the Irish Became White* (New York: Routledge, 1996); Matthew Frye Jacobson, *Whiteness of a Different Color: European Immigrants and the Alchemy of Race* (Cambridge, MA: Harvard University Press, 1998).

[22]Tim Wise, "On White Privilege: Racism, White Denial, and the Costs of Inequality," DVD (Northhampton, MA: Media Education Foundation, 2008).

[23]McIntosh, "White Privilege," 12.

[24]Stuart Hall, *Representation: Cultural Representations and Signifying Practices* (London: Sage Publications, 1997).

race will happen to come up (unlike the erased race of former presidents). As a
first step, then, in talking about Obama's historic win as a black man, should we
not explicitly identify who he beat? Which race lost? Astonishingly—but not
really, considering the unspoken power of whiteness—the race that lost was
never named in this racially historic moment. Considering how much election
coverage is described through "horse race" metaphors, it is astounding that,
with Obama's win, we did not encounter one headline that said, "White Males
Lose Presidency for the First Time Ever." Indeed, prior to Obama's win, we
never encountered a headline indicating the most powerful political trend over
two centuries: "White Male Wins Presidency Again for the 43rd Time." For
political reasons, the dominant culture could not publicly acknowledge this
obvious historical fact and/or did not even "see" it.

Obama's victory can be used to bring to light what has been deemphasized all too much, ironically: that a minority identity has held major political
power in the United States as a result of systemic racial and gendered inequalities. U.S. presidents have not been representative of the majority of the U.S.
population when taking into account women, non-Anglo whites, and poor and
working-class whites, as well as people of color. When taking into account all
of these populations, we can see that political leadership, either in the office of
the presidency or in Congress, has never reflected the majority of people. This
is a remarkable fact for a representative democracy.

Through this election, we can see the stunning invisible power of
whiteness—the absence of any mention of white identity in this historical
racial victory. The legitimacy of a centuries-long streak of white male rule is
so secure and taken for granted that this phenomenon itself is never acknowledged as a historical fact. Historic milestones are achievements of the down-
trodden, whereas status quo trends do not count as history (like centuries-long
white male rule); they are simply facts of life. A black man finally broke the
racial barrier, but we did not explicitly mention who and what was propping
up the barrier for more than two centuries—the election, time and time again,
of white, male, almost exclusively Anglo identities with stunningly and stubbornly similar cultural, religious, and educational backgrounds.

Mainstream political pundits rarely allude to the truly remarkable political trend of the same type of individual winning the presidency over and over.
In any other contest, if the same type of winner emerged time and time again,
people would automatically say the contest was rigged. Certainly, many people
of color are more than aware of racial injustices and of the unspoken power of
whiteness. However, when we discuss race and power on a larger cultural and
political level, we do not acknowledge the unequal playing field. It is much
more comforting to present Obama as a "historic first" that embodies the
promise of the American Dream realized and more "progress" ahead, rather
than focus on how rigged the system has been. Language is power, however,
and how explicitly something is said, what is emphasized or deemphasized,

14

how loudly and boldly it is proclaimed, makes all the difference in how we construct our world.

With his Muslim name, his biracial Kenyan–Kansan parental lineage, and his modest socioeconomic beginnings, President Obama's identity is astonishingly different from past presidents. Obama's identity needs to be reclaimed to service a critical awareness of the broader social power of whiteness. We should invoke Obama's identity in a way that speaks truth, not only *to* power, but *about* power. Obama's highly celebrated, highly visible racial identity should, ironically, force us to see just how invisible the power of whiteness is and has been.

Hermeneutical Rhetoric and Progressive Change: Barack Obama's American Exceptionalism

James T. Petre

On January 20, 2009, Barack Hussein Obama took the oath of office as the forty-fourth president of the United States, becoming the first African American to assume the nation's highest office. His election also signaled a major shift from the policies and attitudes of the Bush administration. Michael Scherer wrote, "The old conservative idea of 'American exceptionalism,' which placed the U.S. on a plane above the rest of the world as a unique beacon of democracy and financial might, has been rejected."[1] I argue that Obama has not rejected American exceptionalism, but has instead reinterpreted the concept in more progressive ways. Obama acknowledges that the United States is not always or inherently "good," and calls on U.S. citizens to see themselves implicated in the world to a degree not seen under his predecessors.

In this essay, I draw upon Leff's conception of hermeneutical rhetoric[2] to analyze U.S. president Barack Obama's reinterpretation of "American exceptionalism" by exploring twelve speeches delivered between 2004 and 2009. By "exceptionalism," I mean seeing one's own country as unique in comparison to other nations in the world. Obama invokes American exceptionalism when he presents an interpretation of what he often calls the United States' "greatness," or "true genius." In doing so, he reinterprets American exceptionalism in arguably progressive ways as a continual struggle for greater inclusion. I explore Obama's interpretation in greater detail following my review of American exceptionalism and hermeneutical rhetoric.

---

[1]Michael Scherer, "Barack Obama's New World Order," *Time*, April 3, 2009, http://www.time .com/time/world/article/0,8599,1889512,00.html (accessed April 7, 2009). Scherer would later acknowledge that Obama did not reject American exceptionalism, but posed a differing interpretation of it. See Michael Scherer, "Obama Too Is an American Exceptionalist," *Time*, April 4, 2009, http://swampland.blogs.time.com/2009/04/04/obama-too-is-an-american-exceptionalist/ (accessed June 28, 2010).

[2]Michael Leff, "Hermeneutical Rhetoric," in *Rhetoric and Hermeneutics in Our Time*, ed. Walter Jost and Michael J. Hyde (New Haven, CT: Yale University Press, 1997), 196–214.

American Exceptionalism

Harold Koh states that "[American exceptionalism] flows through the rhetoric of nearly every American president, from Washington's Farewell Address … to nearly every post–September 11 speech of George W. Bush."[3] Specifically, Koh identifies four "faces" of American exceptionalism: "distinctive rights, different labels, the 'flying-buttress' mentality, and double standards.[4] "Distinctive rights" refers to the United States' being a "rights culture," meaning that there is much greater concern for freedom of speech or religion than other nations.[5] "Different labels" refers to the United States' refusal to accept one set of standards for human rights, while a "flying-buttress" mentality refers to the U.S. practice of *"compliance without ratification"* (emphasis in original).[6] In other words, the United States is often slow to sign on to international agreements out of a desire for an appearance of sovereignty.[7] Finally, "double standards" means "instances when the United States proposes that a different rule should apply to itself and its allies from the one that should apply to the rest of the world."[8] Koh argues that double standards are "the most dangerous and destructive form of American exceptionalism" and have led to problematic policies such as torture and indefinite detainment.[9] This interpretation is particularly troublesome because the unilateralism and double standards of the Bush administration became associated with American exceptionalism writ large.

Toward the close of his essay, Koh points out a fifth face: "exceptional global leadership and activism."[10] He elaborates by stating that if people "too often repeat, 'America is the problem, America is the problem,' they will overlook the occasions where America is not the problem but the solution, and if America is not the solution, there will simply be no solution."[11] He presents his own experience in South Korea during a military coup as one instance in which the United States "did too little," rather than "too much."[12] In this sense, Koh reminds readers that while it is problematic to see the United States only as an

---

[3]Harold K. Koh, "America's Jekyll-and-Hyde Exceptionalism," in *American Exceptionalism and Human Rights*, ed. Michael Ignatieff (Princeton, NJ: Princeton University Press, 2005), 112. Koh traces the concept back to Alexis de Tocqueville.

[4]Ibid., 113.

[5]Ibid., 113.

[6]Ibid., 115.

[7]Ibid., 115.

[8]Ibid., 116.

[9]Ibid., 113.

[10]Ibid., 118–19.

[11]Ibid., 120.

[12]Ibid., 120.

instrument for liberation, it is equally problematic to see the United States only as an instrument for oppression.[13]

I argue that Obama's interpretation of American exceptionalism is centered on this fifth face. Obama's reinterpretation of American exceptionalism represents a progressive restoration of the earlier view, prior to the "new exceptionalists" who influenced Bush.[14] Obama's view evokes the idealism of past presidents such as Roosevelt, Kennedy, and Reagan, but goes further to urge the United States to hold itself accountable as any other nation should. His insistence that the United States match its actions with its ideals could be due in part to the failures of modernization, occurring throughout the Cold War era and beyond.

Following World War II, "America saw itself as the exemplar and apostle of a fully developed modernity."[15] Critics of modernization theory argue that it replicated "the ideologies of colonialism" by equating "modernization" with "Americanization."[16] The failures of modernization theory ushered in a new "Washington consensus" centered on "deregulation, privatization, reduction of state expenditures, fiscal discipline, tax reform, trade liberalization, [and] removal of barriers to foreign investments," and was bolstered by the Reagan presidency.[17] This critique is important because it reminds readers that American exceptionalism was problematic prior to the Bush administration.[18] Rather than a "new" American exceptionalism, Bush's policies constituted a radical interpretation of an American exceptionalism based on the "Washington consensus" of neoliberal economics and interventionist foreign policy.[19] Bush's overreach destabilized this "consensus," and presented the possibility for new interpretations.

American Exceptionalism and Presidential Rhetoric

John Ruggie discusses the influence of Franklin D. Roosevelt on U.S. foreign policy:

> Roosevelt framed his plans for winning the peace in a broader vision that tapped into America's sense of self as a nation: the promise of an international order based on rules and institutions promoting

---

[13]Derek Tam, "Koh Tapped for State Department," *Yale Daily News*, March 24, 2009, http://www.yaledailynews.com/articles/view/28218 (accessed April 7, 2009).

[14]Stanley Hoffman, "American Exceptionalism: The New Version," in *American Exceptionalism and Human Rights*, ed. Michael Ignatieff (Princeton, NJ: Princeton University Press, 2005), 225–40.

[15]Thomas A. McCarthy, "From Modernism to Messianism: Liberal Development and American Exceptionalism," *Constellations* 14, no. 1 (2007): 3.

[16]Ibid., 11.

[17]Ibid., 15.

[18]Hoffman, "American Exceptionalism," 253.

[19]McCarthy, "From Modernism to Messianism," 11.

human betterment ... as well as active international involvement by the private and volunteer sectors.... This first form of American exceptionalism ... became the basis for a global transformational agenda whose effects are unfolding still.[20]

This approach is evident in Roosevelt's rhetoric even prior to U.S. entry into World War II. For example, in his 1941 State of the Union Address, Roosevelt states, "The world order which we seek is the cooperation of free countries, working together in a friendly, civilized society."[21]

John F. Kennedy built on this tradition when he called for a new era of global responsibility in his Inaugural Address: "Let every nation know, whether it wishes us well or ill, that we shall pay any price, bear any burden, meet any hardship, support any friend, oppose any foe, to assure the survival and the success of liberty."[22] However, Kennedy presents an uncritical appropriation of U.S. leadership in the world as a "New Frontier," which was "now envisioned as global, and he introduced domestic and foreign policies intended to capitalize on the persuasive power of the American exceptionalist myth of the frontier."[23] Such an interpretation fails to acknowledge the agency of other nations of the world, and uncritically accepts the United States as an inherent force for good. While Roosevelt also uncritically accepted the United States as a force for good, his emphasis on partnership differed from Kennedy's focus on U.S. leadership.

Ronald Reagan combined an uncritical embrace of U.S. power as morally good with an abundance of religious imagery. Reagan's interpretation fit into the Cold War paradigm as a battle between good and evil, but he particularly emphasized a Puritanical strand of American exceptionalism through his use of words such as "crusade."[24] Reagan refers to 1620 as the beginnings of American democracy,[25] thus challenging Abraham Lincoln's interpretation presented in the Gettysburg Address.[26] Reagan also evoked

---

[20]John G. Ruggie, "American Exceptionalism, Exemptionalism, and Global Governance," in *American Exceptionalism and Human Rights*, 304.

[21]Franklin D. Roosevelt, "The Four Freedoms," speech, Washington D.C., January 6, 1941, http://www.americanrhetoric.com/speeches/fdrthefourfreedoms.htm (accessed July 30, 2009).

[22]John F. Kennedy, "Inaugural Address," speech, Washington, D.C., January 20, 1961, http://www.americanrhetoric.com/speeches/jfkinaugural.htm (accessed April 7, 2009).

[23]William V. Spanos, "American Exceptionalism, the Jeremiad, and the Frontier: From the Puritans to Neo-Con-Men," *Boundary* 2, no. 34 (2007): 48.

[24]Ronald Reagan, "Time to Recapture Our Destiny," speech, Detroit, MI, July 17, 1980. http://www.americanrhetoric.com/speeches/ronaldreagan1980rnc.htm (accessed February 9, 2009).

[25]Ibid., 3.

[26]Leff, "Hermeneutical Rhetoric," 204.

domination in situating U.S. expansion as having "master[ed] a continent."[27] This interpretation grounds Reagan's support for "heroic"[28] expansion and an unapologetic individualism evidenced in his First Inaugural Address when he states, "We will again be the exemplar of freedom and a beacon of hope for those who do not now have freedom."[29] Compared to Roosevelt and Kennedy, Reagan's use of religious imagery is more pervasive, stating that "we are a nation under God, and I believe God intended us to be free."[30] Broadly, Reagan emphasizes leadership over partnership, and the United States is presented as enmeshed in a struggle against an "evil empire."[31]

George W. Bush's American exceptionalism constituted an extreme manifestation of Reagan's. Bush's foreign policy rhetoric was grounded in a unipolar view of the world and a willingness to wage preemptive war. Echoing Hoffman's criticism of Bush's foreign policy, Andrew Rojecki states that "By the onset of the George W. Bush presidency, neoconservatives had evolved a muscular unilateralist approach to foreign policy."[32] This is evident in Bush's Second Inaugural Address when he states, "The survival of liberty in our land increasingly depends on the success in other lands. The best hope for peace in our world is the expansion of freedom in all the world."[33] In his 2002 speech to West Point, Bush states:

> We will defend the peace against threats from terrorists and tyrants. We will preserve the peace by building good relations with great powers. And we will extend the peace by encouraging free and open societies on every continent.
> Building this just peace is America's opportunity and America's duty.[34]

---

[27]Reagan, "Time to Recapture Our Destiny," 6.

[28]See Walter R. Fisher, "Romantic Democracy, Ronald Reagan, and Presidential Heroes," *Western Journal of Speech Communication* 46 (1982): 299–310.

[29]Ronald Reagan, "First Inaugural Address," speech, Washington D. C., January 20, 1981, http://www.americanrhetoric.com/speeches/ronaldreagandfirstinaugural.html (accessed July 30, 2009).

[30]Ibid., 6.

[31]Ronald Reagan, "Remarks at the Annual Convention of the National Association of Evangelicals," speech, Orlando, FL, March 8, 1983, http://www.americanrhetoric.com/speeches/ronaldreaganevilempire.htm (accessed June 28, 2010).

[32]Andrew Rojecki, "Rhetorical Alchemy: American Exceptionalism and the War on Terror," *Political Communication* 25, no. 1 (2008): 71.

[33]George W. Bush, "Second Inaugural Address," speech, Washington, D.C., January 20, 2005, http://www.americanrhetoric.com/speeches/gwbushsecondinaugural.htm (accessed July 30, 2009).

[34]George W. Bush, "Commencement Address at the United States Military Academy at West Point," speech, West Point, NY, June 1, 2002, http://www.nytimes.com/2002/06/01/international/02PTEX-WEB.html (accessed July 30, 2009).

Reagan's view was extended and combined with a doctrine of preemption.[35] Reagan's religious imagery and presentation of the United States as on a "crusade" also continued and increased during Bush's presidency. Although unilateralism was not an invention of the Bush administration, "its specific formulation represented a departure from past policy and an anomaly to a conventional realist-liberal analytic scheme."[36] Despite the Bush policies being an "anomaly," unilateralism is now often conflated with American exceptionalism.

Examining how Roosevelt, Kennedy, Reagan, and Bush use American exceptionalism indicates a procession toward messianism. According to McCarthy, neoconservative influence in the Bush administration was based on two primary principles: military power and moral clarity.[37] While a focus on power and a belief in the need for moral clarity is present in all of the presidents mentioned, the Bush administration showed an increased certainty that the United States and it alone possessed moral clarity, and that the United States and it alone could determine when to use its power.[38]

Barack Obama presents a progressive reinterpretation of American exceptionalism that shares much in common with past Democratic presidents. However, Obama goes further than his predecessors do to remind audiences that the United States' actions must match its idealistic words. A consideration of differing interpretations of American exceptionalism based in different historical contexts brings the relationship between rhetoric and hermeneutics to the fore. Each president presents an interpretation of what makes the United States an exceptional nation, but when they do so, they are not stating an historical fact.[39] Their interpretations are based in particular histories of the United States and interpretations of what those histories mean for the nation.

Hermeneutical Rhetoric

Michael Hyde and Craig Smith point toward "an important relationship between rhetoric and hermeneutics.... the nature of this relationship ... can clarify rhetoric's epistemic function ... [and] such elucidation can provide

---

[35]Bush, "Commencement Address," 2.

[36]Rojecki, "Rhetorical Alchemy," 71.

[37]McCarthy, "From Modernism to Messianism," 18.

[38]George W. Bush, "State of the Union," speech, Washington, D.C., January 29, 2003, http://www.cnn.com/2003/ALLPOLITICS/01/28/sotu.transcript/# (accessed June 28, 2010). This view also fits with Ruggie's description of the New Sovereigntists in "American Exceptionalism," originally described in Peter J. Spiro, "The New Sovereigntists: American Exceptionalism and Its False Prophets," *Foreign Affairs* (November/December 2000): 1.

[39]Leff, "Hermeneutical Rhetoric," 204.

important theoretical directives for rhetorical criticism."[40] According to Hyde and Smith, "The primordial function is to 'make-known' meaning both *to oneself and to others. Meaning is derived by a human being in and through the interpretive understanding of reality. Rhetoric is the process of making-known that meaning* (author's emphasis)."[41] Thus, rhetoric and hermeneutics form a co-constitutive relationship, an intersection and interrelation of interpreting meanings and making meanings known. Rhetoric and hermeneutics dwell in contested sites, as we are always choosing particular interpretations over others. Given this shared focus on "conflicts of interpretations,"[42] it is fitting to explore interpretations of American exceptionalism through this theoretical framework.

Theorizing this relationship between rhetoric and hermeneutics further, Leff reminds us that "all interpretive work involves participation in a rhetorical exchange, and every rhetorical exchange involves some interpretive work."[43] We are always forced to take a position, but these positions are always changing.[44] Leff contends that we are "always arguing at particular moments in specific places, to certain audiences."[45] Thus:

> Hermeneutical rhetoric ... focuses upon interpretation as a source of invention and suggests how traditions can be altered without destroying their identity. It offers a view of community as a locus of deliberating subjects who change themselves and one another by renewing and revaluing moments in their history.[46]

When speakers are providing historical accounts for audiences, they are not simply asserting a fact[47] but presenting an interpretation that is inherently rhetorical.

I use Leff's conception of hermeneutical rhetoric to analyze twelve of President Obama's speeches, delivered from 2004 to 2009, to focus on how Obama's interpretation of American exceptionalism "enters into the production

---

[40]Michael J. Hyde and Craig R. Smith, "Hermeneutics and Rhetoric: A Seen but Unobserved Relationship," *Quarterly Journal of Speech* 65, no. 4 (1979): 347.

[41]Ibid., 348.

[42]Paul Ricoeur, *The Conflict of Interpretations: Essays in Hermeneutics*, trans. D. Ihde (Evanston, IL: Northwestern University Press, 1974).

[43]Leff, "Hermeneutical Rhetoric," 198.

[44]Ibid., 203.

[45]Ibid., 203.

[46]Ibid., 203–4.

[47]Ibid., 204.

of [his] political rhetoric."[48] Specifically, I explore how his interpretation of American exceptionalism draws upon past interpretations, but also contains new elements. I focus on speeches directed toward wide national and international audiences and those containing a detailed interpretation of American exceptionalism.

Barack Obama's American Exceptionalism

Obama often claims that the United States is the greatest country in the world, and this is nothing new in presidential politics. What *is* different is that he interprets "America's true genius" as a capacity for reform. This capacity for reform is grounded in his presentation of U.S. history as a continual struggle for inclusion and extends into the future through a call for hope. Obama operationalizes his American exceptionalism through his suggestion that the United States lead by example. In what follows, I present Obama's American exceptionalism as three interrelated themes: the United States as the greatest country in the world, the greatness of the United States as its capacity for reform, and the United States as leading by example.

The United States as the "Greatest Country in the World"

There are several instances in which Obama argues that the United States is unique or a "shining city on a hill." Importantly, in contrast to his predecessors, Obama personalizes his presentation of the United States as exceptional. For example, Obama declares, "[I]n no other country on Earth is my story even possible."[49] Clearly, this statement evokes American exceptionalism as it is the only place in which a story like Obama's could take place. While not explicitly stating that the United States is the "greatest" country, he implies it by claiming his story could only happen there. Other times, the United States' unique position is stated in more explicit terms: "Where else could they [his parents] have a child who would one day have the chance to run for the highest office in the greatest nation the world has ever known?"[50] Here, the United States is not just the greatest nation at present, but the greatest nation *of all time* because of its capacity to bring people together across different backgrounds. In situating his own candidacy as evidence of American "greatness," Obama implies that electing him reaffirms the greatness of the United States.

---

[48]Ibid., 198.

[49]Barack Obama, "The Audacity of Hope," speech, Boston, MA, July 27, 2004, http://www.american-rhetoric.com/speeches/convention2004/barackobama/2004dnc.htm (accessed October 24, 2006).

[50]Barack Obama, "March 4 Speech," speech, San Antonio, TX, March 4, 2008, http://www.realclear-politics.com/articles/2008/03/barack_obamas_march_4_speech.html (accessed April 24, 2008).

Obama often connects his claim that the United States is a unique place in the world to his own personal story. For example, in Obama's "A More Perfect Union" speech, he states:

> I am the son of a black man from Kenya and a white woman from Kansas. I was raised with the help of a white grandfather who survived a Depression to serve in Patton's Army during World War II.... I've gone to some of the best schools in America and lived in one of the world's poorest nations.... It's a story that hasn't made me the most conventional candidate. But it is a story that has seared into my genetic makeup the idea that this nation is more than the sum of its parts—that out of many, we are truly one.[51]

In this passage, Obama invites audiences to consider how connected we are to each other, within the United States and around the world. His personalizing of this message is an important shift from that of his predecessors, who seldom reference their own personal stories in relation to the American story. It is even less common to find examples in which their personal stories are placed in a global context. Finding common purpose among diverse perspectives is a quality that Obama claims is a fundamental American quality, and it provides a context for his interpretation of the "true genius" of the United States.

A third way in which he argues for the unique greatness of the United States is through his positioning of the United States as a "beacon" or "last best hope." For example, Obama states, "Through hard work and perseverance, my father got a scholarship to study in a wonderful place, America, that shone as a beacon of freedom ..."[52] Here, the United States is not only recognized as the greatest country on Earth by its own citizens, but by people living all over the world. Likewise, in his address to the Chicago Council on Global Affairs, Obama states, "I still believe America is the last, best hope of Earth. We just have to show the world why this is so."[53] While acknowledging he believes the United States is a "last, best hope," he underscores the responsibilities Americans have to live up to this label. After clinching the Democratic nomination, Obama invites audiences to imagine looking back on this accomplishment by suggesting that "this was the moment when we ended a war, secured our nation, and restored our image as the last, best hope on Earth."[54] The use

[51]Barack Obama, "A More Perfect Union," speech, Philadelphia, PA, March 18, 2008, http://www.nytimes.com/2008/3/18/us/politics/18text-obama.html_r=1&pagewanted=print (accessed April 24, 2008).

[52]Obama, "The Audacity of Hope," 2–3.

[53]Barack Obama, "Remarks to the Chicago Council on Global Affairs," speech, Chicago, IL, April 23, 2007, http://my.barackobama.com/page/content/fpccga (accessed April 24, 2008).

[54]Barack Obama, "Remarks in St. Paul," speech, St. Paul, MN, June 3, 2008, http://www.nytimes.com/2008/06/03/us/politics/03text-Obama.html?pagewanted=print (accessed March 18, 2009).

of "restored" implies that the United States is not a "last, best hope" at present. It is important to note that the usage of such claims of the United States as a "last, best hope" is highly problematic in its privileging of U.S. dominance. However, Obama positions the United States as being the "last, best hope" as something to live up to, rather than a self-evident fact. This interpretation situates his claims that U.S. greatness is in its capacity for reform, and that the United States should lead by example.

U.S. Greatness as Its Capacity for Reform

Obama presents an historical interpretation of the unique greatness of the United States as rooted in its capacity for reform. Change—in the form of reform—is grounded in hope for the future. Obama presents this interpretation by explaining the "genius" of the United States. For example, in his 2007 presidential announcement address, he says:

> The genius of our founders is that they designed a system that can be changed. And we should take heart because we've changed this country before. In the face of tyranny, a band of patriots brought an Empire to its knees. In the face of secession, we unified a nation and set the captives free....[55]

Obama presents a history of progress similar to those presented by Kennedy and Reagan. However, he removes almost any reference to expansion or conquest. His attention focuses on occasions in which equal rights, freedom, and justice were expanded, rather than emphasizing military might or frontier mythology. Thus, he portrays the United States and its citizens as striving for greater inclusion, and he invites audiences to continue this history of change by electing him the first African-American president.

Another example of the United States' "true genius" as its capacity for reform is present in Obama's "A More Perfect Union speech":

> The profound mistake of Reverend Wright's sermons is not that he spoke about racism in our society. It's that he spoke as if our society was static; as if no progress has been made; as if this country ... is still irrevocably bound to a tragic past. But what we know—what we have seen—is that America can change. That is the true genius of this nation.[56]

[55]Barack Obama, "Illinois Sen. Barack Obama's Announcement Speech," speech, Springfield, IL, February 10, 2007, http://www.washingtonpost.com/wpdyn/content/article/2007/02/10/AR2007021000879.html (accessed April 24, 2008).

[56]Obama, "A More Perfect Union," 6.

While Obama isn't explicitly invoking American exceptionalism here, it is implied through his claim of "true genius." His interpretation of the "true genius" of the United States as its capacity for reform invites audiences not only to see change as an inherently "American" quality, but to welcome it, and even to work for it themselves by volunteering for the campaign. This capacity for reform is grounded in a hope for a better future.

This clear connection between hope and change is tied to Obama's personal story, the nation's story, and what must happen if the United States (and the world) is to succeed in the future:

> Hope is what led a band of colonists to rise up against an empire. What led the greatest of generations to free a continent and heal a nation. What led young women and young men to sit at lunch counters and brave fire hoses.... Hope—hope is what led me here today.... Hope is the bedrock of this nation. The belief that our destiny will not be written for us, but by us, by all those men and women who are not content to settle for the world as it is, who have the courage to remake the world as it should be.[57]

Obama's interpretation of American exceptionalism as capacity for reform allows him to ground hope and change as bedrocks of American patriotism. He does this by presenting a particular history of the United States that references the Revolution, the Civil War, expansion of immigration, and the struggle for racial equality. Obama draws upon the legacy of manifest destiny by invoking expansion, but it is different from past presidents' interpretations, which focus solely on expansion for prosperity or military greatness. While Obama invokes these themes, he references them less directly and with less romanticism.

Obama implies that the founders intended to create a nation whose capacity for reform signaled its greatness. This challenges the interpretations of commentators who claim that the United States' best days are behind it. In fact, Obama's mere presence on stage as an African American presidential candidate and then president supports his claim that the United States has continually struggled for change; his candidacy and election demonstrate that progress has been made, but his call to hope for better days ahead reminds us that we still have much farther to go. Obama connects his audience with past struggles through a lineage of hope—hope inspired past generations to be great, and this hope will drive the nation to be exceptional again.

---

[57]Barack Obama, "Iowa Victory Speech," speech, Des Moines, IA, January 3, 2008, http://www.newsday.com/news/local/politics/ny-usoba0105-transcript,0,7073760.story (accessed April 24, 2008).

The United States Should Lead by Example

While his predecessors called for the United States to serve as an example for the world, Obama goes further in advocating a U.S. foreign policy that is based on actions matching ideals. Obama challenges a traditional interpretation of world leadership by calling on audiences to see themselves as their "brother's keeper" and their "sister's keeper"[58] in relation to others both within and outside of the United States. In other words, Obama calls audiences toward critical self-reflection by inviting audiences to ask themselves: Are we being good stewards of the world and of one another? Are we acting responsibly toward one another? This is different from Bush's form of American exceptionalism, which assumes that the United States is accountable to no one.[59] Obama doesn't deny that the United States should be a leader, but asserts that the United States should recognize itself as implicated in the world.

Obama states, "We must neither retreat from the world nor try to bully it into submission—we must lead the world, by deed and example."[60] This inclusion of the word "deed" reminds audiences that foreign policy is not about saying one thing and doing another, but is about actually living up to the ideals that we profess. Later in the same speech, Obama asserts, "We cannot hope to shape a world where opportunity outweighs danger unless we ensure that every child, everywhere, is taught to build and not destroy."[61] In this way, the United States is not called to "help" the nations of the world as a heroic act of charity, as Reagan positioned it, or because it is morally right, as Kennedy did, but because it is our responsibility as human beings. Matching words and deeds is the only option for the United States (and the rest of the world) to enjoy peace and prosperity. The emphasis on cooperative security is similar to Roosevelt, but Obama goes further to emphasize equal cooperation in his emphasis of words matching deeds. The United States cannot contradict itself because it affects its own security as well as the security of other nations. This view connects with Koh's critique of double standards.[62]

Obama calls upon Americans to see themselves as implicated in their own actions and to view themselves as others around the world may see them. For example, Obama states:

> There is a young man on my campaign whose grandfather lives in Uganda. He is 81 years old and has never experienced true democracy in his lifetime. During the reign of Idi Amin, he was

---

[58]Obama, "A More Perfect Union," 7.

[59]Bush, "State of the Union," 6–9.

[60]Obama, "Remarks to the Chicago Council on Global Affairs."

[61]Ibid., 5.

[62]Koh, "America's Jekyll-and-Hyde Exceptionalism," 116.

literally hunted, and the only reason he escaped was thanks to the kindness of others and a few good-sized trunks. And on the night of the Iowa caucuses, that 81-year-old man stayed up until five in the morning, huddled by his television, waiting for the results. The world is watching what we do here. The world is paying attention to how we conduct ourselves. What will they see? What will we tell them? ... Can we send a message that the United States of America is, and always will be, the "last best, hope of Earth?" We say; we hope; we believe: Yes, we can.[63]

In this passage, Obama invokes the famous quotation from the 1968 Democratic National Convention protests: "The whole world is watching." At the time of Obama's speech, members of Hillary Clinton's campaign (including Bill Clinton) were accused of "race-baiting," while members of Obama's campaign were accused of being chauvinistic toward Clinton. Obama's reminder invites audiences to avoid the negativity of the campaign. Furthermore, his statement can also be interpreted as a subtle reminder of the election controversies in Florida and Ohio, and to make sure the electoral process runs smoothly this time.

More broadly, by declaring that "the world is watching," Obama invites audiences to recognize how petty negative campaigning may look to people living outside the United States. Obama invites audiences to see the world through the eyes of another, and calls on citizens to see themselves as implicated in the world. Stating, "Yes, we can," invites audiences to envision a world of cooperative partnership, and work to create it. It is also important to note Obama's personalizing of this story. Past presidents have presented general statements to citizens of the world living outside the United States, but Obama positions people of all nations as equal partners in a global family, rather than cases for charity and pity from the United States. For example, Kennedy addressed citizens of the world, but described them as living "in huts,"[64] which suggests a more "primitive" status. Obama's personalizing of this story positions the eighty-one-year-old man as "one of us."

Obama operationalizes this sense of being implicated in the world further in his Inaugural Address. He states: "What is required of us now is a new era of responsibility—a recognition, on the part of every American, that we have duties to ourselves, our nation, and the world, duties that we do not grudgingly accept but rather seize gladly."[65] This speech echoes Kennedy's "New Frontier" speech, and is problematic because it also connotes the legacy of colonial expansion. However, Obama does not explicitly reference a "frontier." Instead,

[63]Obama, "March 4 Speech," 3.

[64]Kennedy, "Inaugural Address," 3.

[65]Barack Obama, "Inaugural Address," speech, Washington, D.C., January 20, 2009, http://www.whitehouse.gov/blog/inaugural-address/ (accessed February 12, 2009).

Obama presents the United States owning up to its worldly responsibilities as a "difficult task," without invoking the legacy of expansion and domination explicitly. Thus, the shift is incremental, but present nonetheless.

Obama follows Roosevelt, Kennedy, and Reagan in his call to lead by example, but differs in his emphasis of responsibility. This strategy contrasts with an uncritical acceptance of American power. Although it is problematic that Obama assumes that the United States has the rightful claim to world leadership, his calls for responsibility and self-reflexivity implicate U.S. audiences in the world, and constitute a progressive interpretation of American exceptionalism.

Implications

While any conception of American exceptionalism is problematic, Obama provides a pragmatic compromise between completely rejecting American exceptionalism (and likely losing an election) or adopting a Manichean style similar to Reagan and Bush. Obama's interpretation of American exceptionalism invites people of all nations to work together to build a better world. However, as president, some of his actions have not met his ideals thus far. For example, Obama issued an executive order to close down the prison at Guantanamo Bay. This action worked to reassure citizens throughout the world that the United States does not exercise double standards on torture. However, the closing of the prison was delayed, and his administration is being criticized for resisting greater transparency.[66] This conundrum points toward the difficulty any president may have in eliminating double standards in the wake of the Bush administration.

On the other hand, one way in which Obama's American exceptionalism continues to enable a more inclusive political culture is evident in his recent speech in Cairo, when he broadened his message of connection to include people throughout the world:

> We have learned from recent experience that when a financial system weakens in one country, prosperity is hurt everywhere. When a new flu virus infects one human being, all are at risk.... That is what it means to share this world in the twenty-first century. That is the responsibility we have to one another as human beings.[67]

---

[66]Lara Jakes, "Obama Revives Terror Tribunals, Dismaying Liberals," *Associated Press*, May 15, 2009, http://www.realclearpolitics.com/news/ap/politics/2009/May/15/obama_revives _terror_ tribunals__dismaying_liberals.html (accessed July 30, 2009).

[67]Barack Obama, "Speech at Cairo University," speech, Cairo, Egypt, June 4, 2009, http://www .nytimes.com/2009/06/04/us/politics/04obama.text.html (accessed July 30, 2009).

While Obama and his administration struggle for a pragmatic compromise between eliminating double standards and responding to military exigency, statements such as these present a dynamic and drastic shift from the rhetoric of the Bush administration.

While it is still too early in his administration to judge how and whether policy will become more inclusive, such an orientation was evident in Obama's response when asked if he believed in American exceptionalism. Obama stated that he does, just as "the Brits believe in British exceptionalism and the Greeks believe in Greek exceptionalism."[68] Obama adds:

> The fact that I am proud of my country, and I think that we've got a whole lot to offer the world, does not lessen my interest in recognizing that we're not always going to be right, or that other people may have good ideas, or that in order for us to work collectively, all parties have to compromise.[69]

Obama's version of American exceptionalism is not free from flaws. It does, however, indicate a shift away from unilateralism and preemption, toward multilateralism and interdependence. It remains to be seen what the results of such a shift will be, in word and in deed.

---

[68]Edward Luce and Delphine Strauss, "Tone Is Key to Obama Message and Impact," *Financial Times*, April 6, 2009, http://www.ft.com/cms/s/0/ebe1070c-22d6-11de-9c9900144feabdc0.html (accessed April 7, 2009).

[69]Luce and Strauss, "Tone Is Key," 1.

Ghosts and Gaps: A Rhetorical Examination of Temporality and Spatial Metaphors in Barack Obama's "A More Perfect Union"

Sarah McCaffrey

"Time and space are modes by which we think and not conditions in which we live."
— *Albert Einstein*

Immediately after proclaiming Barack Obama the president-elect, ABC cut to African-American correspondent Steve Osunsami. Surrounded by a teary-eyed, cheering crowd, the choked-up reporter diverged from journalistic objectivity and shared:

> From a personal note, as a kid, I grew up in a neighborhood that was mostly black and my father used to tell us that there's no way this country would elect a black president. Well, this evening, the country has proved my old man wrong—and we're the better for it.[1]

Despite the progress Obama's election represents, racial tensions were present at every stage of his epic twenty-one-month campaign. Tensions dramatically came to a head when the media and public learned about inflammatory comments made by Obama's former pastor, Reverend Jeremiah Wright. On March 13, 2008, *Good Morning America* aired clips of Wright fierily preaching that "blacks should not sing 'God Bless America' but 'God damn America'"[2] and calling 9/11 a case of "'America's chickens ... coming home to

---

[1]Soledad O'Brien, Juan Williams, Eugene Robinson, and Jim Vance, "An Emotional Election Night for Journalists of Color," *Tell Me More*, National Public Radio, November 10, 2008, http://www.npr.org/templates/player/mediaPlayer.html?action=1&t=1&islist=false&id=96810103&m=96810097 (accessed August 12, 2010).

[2]Brian Ross and Rehab El-Buri, "Obama's Pastor: God Damn America, U.S. to Blame for 9/11," *ABC News*, March 13, 2008, http://abcnews.go.com/blotter/Story?id=4443788&page=1 (accessed August 12, 2010).

roost.'"[3] Given that Wright served as Obama's minister for nearly twenty years, and "married Obama and his wife Michelle [and] baptized their daughters,"[4] Obama's close ties to Wright led many to assume he shared Wright's views. Wright's notorious comments "threatened to capsize Obama's front-running campaign with the speed of a Wall Street bankruptcy."[5]

Often dubbed by members of the media and public as his "Race Speech," "A More Perfect Union" marks an instance where Obama directly addresses a national audience about the politically risky topic of race in America. Every major television network aired Obama's speech, and it was the most viewed video on YouTube in the following week with over 1.6 million hits.[6] By November, the speech had over 5.3 million hits.[7] Faced with "the most serious controversy of his political career"[8] and without the assistance of a speech-writer, Obama crafted "A More Perfect Union." According to David Axelrod, "Obama wrote the 40-minute speech himself, staying up until 2 a.m. [the night before speaking] to finish it."[9] Deemed by *New York Times* columnist Nicholas Kristof "the best political speech since John Kennedy,"[10] "A More Perfect Union" deserves the attention of a rhetorical critic in order to learn what, exactly, Obama's "Race Speech" says about race.

Theoretical Framework

Before delving into an analysis of "A More Perfect Union," I closely examine the starkly different reactions of two African-American critics—Mark McPhail and William Fletcher, Jr.—to Obama's speech. William Fletcher, Jr., is the

---

[3]James Carney, Amy Sullivan, Jay Newton-Small, and Lori Reese, "Why Obama Has a Pastor Problem," *Time Magazine* 171, no. 13 (March 31, 2008): 38–41.

[4]Ross and El-Buri, "Obama's Pastor."

[5]Carney, Sullivan, Newton-Small, and Reese, "Why Obama Has a Pastor Problem."

[6]"Obama's Speech on Race Tops YouTube," National Public Radio, March 20, 2008, http://www.npr.org/templates/story/story.php?storyID=88650809 (accessed August 12, 2010).

[7]Nikki Schwab, "In Obama-McCain Race, YouTube Became a Serious Battleground for Presidential Politics," *US News & World Report*, November 7, 2008, http://www.usnews.com/articles/news/campaign-2008/2008/11/07/in-obama-mccain-race-youtube-became-a-serious-battleground-for-presidential-politics.html?PageNr=1 (accessed August 12, 2010).

[8]Susan Page and Kathy Kiely, "In a Gamble, Obama Takes Aim at America's 'Racial Stalemate,'" *USA Today*, March 19, 2008, http://www.usatoday.com/news/politics/election2008/2008-03-18-obama_N.htm (accessed August 12, 2010).

[9]Page and Kiely, "In a Gamble."

[10]Nicholas D. Kristof, "Obama and Race," *New York Times*, March 20, 2008, http://www.nytimes.com/2008/03/20/opinion/20kristof.html.

executive editor of the *Black Commentator*.[11] Mark McPhail is a professor and is the author of *The Rhetoric of Racism Revisited: Reparations or Separation?* In "Barack Obama's Address to the 2004 Democratic National Convention,"[12] David Frank and Mark McPhail argue opposing positions within one unified article to disagree collaboratively, producing a "'contact of the minds.'"[13] I capture a similar collaborative spirit by tracing Fletcher and McPhail's diverse reactions to "A More Perfect Union." I then use textual analysis in order to explain how "A More Perfect Union" supports both McPhail's and Fletcher's conflicting readings. I hold that Fletcher's and McPhail's different interpretations highlight the multifaceted ways in which Obama uses temporality and spatial metaphors to discuss the charged topic of race. Fletcher's and McPhail's contrasting interpretations illustrate the complex relationship Obama constructs between the past and the present and, spatially, between the current racial situation of the United States and its harmonious, "more perfect" potential, as well as the divides of misunderstanding between races.

In "A More Perfect Union," Obama conflates the past and the present, highlighting their inextricable nature and showing the ways in which past ghosts of structural and attitudinal racial inequality and oppression still manifest in the present. The present moment is the fulcrum of action for changing the future and remedying the injustices of the past. Through his use of temporality and spatial metaphors, Obama imbues the present moment with a sense of urgent importance and empowerment, situating himself as a figure capable of narrowing the racial divides and connecting the current state of the Union with the ideals upon which it was founded; he becomes the bridge to the "more perfect union."

In "Dimensions of Temporality in Lincoln's Second Inaugural," Michael Leff asserts that examining the role of temporality in Lincoln's speech allows for a unique and important perspective. Reading Lincoln's use of tenses, Leff finds that time "is more than a device for separating the gross structural units of these discourses."[14] Leff explains that Lincoln's temporal movement "seems essential to [the speech's] rhetorical economy; it frames the action of

---

[11]"About the Editorial Board," *The Black Commentator*, http://www.blackcommentator.com/about_us.html.

[12]In the article, Frank and McPhail "write together separately" (571). Frank offers substantial praise for the way in which Obama's convention speech promotes racial healing and equality. McPhail, on the other hand, portrays the convention speech as problematic, expressing concern that Obama invites the erasure of race.

[13]David A. Frank and Mark Lawrence McPhail, "Barack Obama's Address to the 2004 Democratic National Convention: Trauma, Compromise, Consilience, and the (Im)possibility of Racial Reconciliation," *Rhetoric & Public Affairs* 8, no. 4 (Winter 2005): 573.

[14]Michael Leff, "Dimensions of Temporality in Lincoln's Second Inaugural," *Communication Reports* 1, no. 1 (Winter 1988): 26–31.

the various argumentative and stylistic elements, [and] blends them into a unified field of textual action..."[15] He continues by explaining that the entire economy of Lincoln's speech "seems designed to achieve this elision of temporal perspectives."[16]

One of Leff's key findings is that Lincoln's use of temporality enables him to build up the importance of the present, portraying it as linked to the sacred rather than to the secular. The temporal motion of Obama's speech also constructs the present as a time of integral importance. The need to "perfect the Union" and undo the injustices of past structures that enabled racism, slavery, and oppression merges with his call to bridge the spatial gap between the imperfect present and a more perfect, prosperous future; it is this melding of past and present that opens the door for contradictory assessments of his approach to race relations.

McPhail and Fletcher Respond to "A More Perfect Union"

Though he labels Obama's 2004 Convention speech an "old vision of racelessness,"[17] Mark McPhail commends "A More Perfect Union" for its frank discussion of the multifaceted topic of race.[18] He emphatically praises the speech:

> [Obama] spoke to something we cannot speak of in this country and he did so with really, really honest rhetoric. What he did was courageous. It was heartfelt and it was sincere, and that was something I felt was missing from just about everything I'd seen up until now that seemed very much motivated by the self-interest and opportunism, by American politics.[19]

---

[15]Ibid., 26.

[16]Ibid., 30.

[17]Ibid., 571.

[18]In Frank and McPhail's "Barack Obama's Address to the 2004 Democratic National Convention," McPhail holds that "[w]hile King understood the salience and centrality of race, Obama invites the erasure of race instead of its re-signing..." (582). Frank, on the other hand, deems Obama's 2004 speech "a prophetic multiracial narrative" (574) and argues that Obama's rhetoric of consilience and unity holds the unique potential to bring together and promote understanding between people of different races; he explains, "Obama's speech drew from his multiracial background to craft a speech designed to bridge divides between and among ethnic groups" (577).

[19]McPhail as quoted in Jonathan Tilove, "Deepening the Meaning of Martin Luther King Jr.," *San Diego Union Tribune*, March 23, 2008, http://www.signonsandiego.com/uniontrib/20080323/news_lz1e23tilove.html (accessed August 12, 2010).

McPhail favorably compares the speech to Martin Luther King, Jr.'s, famous "I Have a Dream" speech. But McPhail additionally praises Obama's speech for serving as "the wake-up call from the dream"—the dream that America has transcended racial inequality and division. "A More Perfect Union" "wasn't about transcendence," explains McPhail, "it was about transformation. It's hard. It's painful. It's going to hurt. But it's good medicine."[20] McPhail further explains his view of the speech by writing:

> In that speech Obama confronted the nation's ability to deal with race, speaking openly of the traumatic history and "stain" of slavery. … [H]is courage, sincerity, and eloquence offered a persuasive and provocative example of rhetoric's potential to remedy and heal the negative differences and divisions of American race relations.[21]

Though McPhail praises Obama for his uniquely sincere discourse about race in the 2008 speech, Fletcher argues that Obama does *not* do enough to acknowledge and validate the frustrations and anger of African Americans in the United States. Fletcher deems Obama's speech "problematic," explaining that Obama

> … attributes much of the anger of Rev. Wright to the past, as if Rev. Wright is stuck in a time warp, rather than the fact that Rev. Wright's anger about the domestic and foreign policies of the USA are well rooted—and documented—in the current reality of the USA.[22]

Fletcher argues that Wright's anger "should not have surprised anyone. It is both anger *and* hope that are critical for a genuine movement that wishes to transform this country."[23] Rather than labeling the speech "courageous," Fletcher holds that Obama takes an easy approach by pushing racism into America's past and downplaying contemporary attitudes, policies, and practices. These opposing readings raise the critical questions: How do these theorists come to such different conclusions? Does Obama avoid fully acknowledging the responsibility of current governmental systems and structures, or does he courageously delve into the intricacies of racial oppression, a move few politicians or speakers dare to make?

---

[20]Ibid.

[21]Mark Lawrence McPhail, "The Politics of Complicity Revisited: Race, Rhetoric, and the (Im)possibility of Reconciliation," *Rhetoric & Public Affairs* 12, no. 1 (2009): 122.

[22]William Fletcher, "Obama Race Speech Analysis," *Black Commentator*, March 20, 2008, http://www.blackcommentator.com/269/269_cover_obama_race_speech_analysis_ed_bd.html (accessed August 12, 2010).

[23]Ibid.

The disparity between these two points of view stems, in part, from the ways in which Obama uses temporality, history, and spatial metaphors to discuss race in the contemporary United States. What McPhail deems a strength—the racial history lesson Obama provides—Fletcher sees as Obama suggesting that Wright is caught in a "time warp." Situating racial issues in a historical context allows Obama to acknowledge the very real presence of racial oppression in the United States and also to shift blame away from his audience and away from contemporary governmental systems. Examining how Obama uses time and space as strategic tools in "A More Perfect Union" reveals his attempt to appeal simultaneously to different segments of his audience, and how the complexity of that approach paradoxically contributes to its failure to appeal to all.

The Function of Temporality in "A More Perfect Union"

McPhail commends Obama's March 2008 speech because in it, Obama focuses on the "very real, concrete aspects of this country's racial history" to demonstrate how racial inequality is inseparable from the founding of the United States. In his speech, Obama recounts an extensive history of U.S. racial oppression, highlighting the real inequality between African Americans and white Americans in the United States. Obama states, for instance, that "many of the disparities that exist in the African American community today can be directly traced to inequalities passed on from an earlier generation."[24] Obama makes his audience face America's cruel past laws and actions, asserting:

> Segregated schools were, and are, inferior schools; we still haven't fixed them, fifty years after *Brown v. Board of Education*, and the inferior education they provided, then and now, helps explain the pervasive achievement gap between today's black and white students.[25]

He continues by recognizing "legal discrimination" where:

> ... blacks were prevented, often through violence, from owning property, or loans were not granted to African-American business owners, or black homeowners could not access FHA mortgages, or blacks were excluded from unions. ... [H]istory helps explain the income gap between blacks and whites, and the concentrated pockets of poverty that persist. ...[26]

---

[24]Barack Obama, "A More Perfect Union," Delivered in Philadelphia, PA. March 18, 2008, <http://www.npr.org/templates/story/story.php?storyId=88478467>.

[25]Ibid., para. 28.

[26]Ibid., para. 29.

By referring to tangible institutions and practices, Obama reaches out to his African-American audience; they are not imagining racial disparity and oppression—these barriers are real, identifiable, and not their fault. African Americans struggle to achieve equality because U.S. social and political structures unquestionably impede their ability to do so.

Obama's willingness to speak critically of his country is, as McPhail suggests, "honest" and "courageous." At the opening of "A More Perfect Union," Obama literally provides a history lesson and argues that racial oppression was inextricably tied to the creation of the United States. Obama explains that "statesmen and patriots who had traveled across an ocean to escape tyranny and persecution finally made real their declaration of independence at a Philadelphia convention that lasted through the spring of 1787."[27] Rather than glorifying the Constitution, Obama makes the markedly bold assertion that the document was "stained by this nation's original sin of slavery."[28] Obama's willingness to speak critically of the Constitution—especially as a politician seeking his party's nomination—explains why McPhail differentiates Obama's speech from all other political rhetoric.[29]

Given the bravery it takes for a presidential candidate to make the politically dangerous assertion that racial oppression was inherent in the founding of the nation, upon first glance it seems strange that Fletcher would not echo McPhail's sentiments. Instead, Fletcher criticizes Obama for dismissing Reverend Wright's anger. Fletcher deems Obama's "history-lesson" approach "problematic." Though on the one hand Obama's approach is brave, it does allow Obama to avoid addressing the contemporary acts, attitudes, and policies that perpetuate old and create new forms of racial injustice. When describing the root of Wright's anger, for instance, Obama ties it to "the reality in which Reverend Wright and other African Americans of his generation grew up."[30] Obama continues by explaining that Reverend Wright and his contemporaries "came of age in the late 'fifties and early' sixties, a time when segregation was still the law of the land and opportunity was systematically constricted."[31] Obama goes so far as to use the word "memories" to describe the source of Reverend Wright and other African Americans' anger. Obama states, "For the men and women of Reverend Wright's generation, the *memories* of humiliation and doubt and fear have not gone away, nor has the anger and the bitterness

---

[27]Ibid., para. 1.

[28]Ibid., para. 2.

[29]McPhail as quoted in Jonathan Tilove, "Deepening the Meaning."

[30]Obama, "A More Perfect Union," para. 31.

[31]Ibid., para. 31.

of *those years*."[32] Obama's assertion that Wright's anger stems from *memories* explains Fletcher's specific accusation that Obama speaks as if Wright is "stuck in a time warp."

Obama's reliance upon history enables him to legitimize anger felt by African Americans without labeling white Americans "racists." Though Obama's inclusive strategy of reaching out to diverse factions of his audience is crucial given his position as a presidential candidate, Obama does not do enough to link Wright's anger to the "current reality of the USA."[33] When the speech moves into the present, Obama's tone becomes increasingly positive. Rather than mentioning the racism that exists today, Obama uses his campaign's success in South Carolina to demonstrate that even the contemporary South has largely moved beyond its racist past. "In South Carolina, where the Confederate Flag still flies," Obama declares, "we built a powerful coalition of African Americans and white Americans."[34] Obama praises South Carolina for its ability to rally behind an African-American candidate rather than condemning the fact that the Confederate flag still flies. He rarely turns attention to current racist systems and instead emphasizes the successes of the present.

Obama also acknowledges attitudinal racism. He admits that even his own white grandmother has uttered racist remarks, explaining that as much as she loves him, she is a woman "who once confessed her fear of black men who pass her on the street, and who on more than one occasion uttered a racial or ethnic stereotype that made [him] cringe."[35] Obama's willingness to admit his grandmother harbors such feelings is part of the "courage" to which McPhail refers; again, he riskily asserts that race relations are not entirely harmonious. In addition, Obama acknowledges the complexity and intricacies of race; racism becomes something that Obama experiences, as an African-American man, and something his own family are guilty of perpetuating.

The story of Obama's grandmother demonstrates courage but also serves as another example of Obama's placing racism in the past. Even though Obama affirms that racist attitudes still exist, he locates those feelings in a woman of an older generation. The anecdote about Obama's grandmother differs starkly from the story he shares about Ashley, a twenty-three-year-old white woman who leads his campaign in South Carolina. Despite a challenging life of family sickness and strife, Obama explains that Ashley did not blame anyone, but instead "sought out allies in her fight against injustice."[36] Obama recounts that

---

[32]Ibid., para. 32, my emphasis.

[33]Fletcher, "Obama Race Speech Analysis."

[34]Obama, "A More Perfect Union," para. 9.

[35]Ibid., para. 22.

[36]Ibid., para. 57.

at a roundtable discussion, Ashley asked the others why they came. One of the members, an elderly African-American man, stated, "I am here because of Ashley."[37] The moment of connection between Ashley and the elderly black man transcends race, gender, and generation. Ashley and the younger generation embody a desire for unification and change. In contrast to Wright, whom Obama criticizes for speaking "as if our society was static,"[38] the elderly black man crosses racial and generational divisions in order to help Obama bring about change.

Fletcher's and McPhail's different interpretations of how Obama temporally frames issues of race is indicative of the complex way in which Obama collapses and conflates the past and present. From the very beginning of the speech, Obama blurs the division between past, present, and future. In the second sentence, Obama invokes words from the Constitution's preamble: "We the people, in order to form a more perfect union," and follows them by stating, "Two hundred and twenty-one years ago, in a hall that still stands across the street";[39] Obama brings together the past and present by referring to a hall 221 years in the past that is also within view, physically present in the moment of his speech. The location of the speech is intrinsically connected to the past and to the inception of the United States.

Leff argues that it is in the first paragraph of Lincoln's "House Divided" that he "introduces the temporal markers that define his perspective,"[40] and notes that the first line is key in spatially and temporally orienting the audience.[41] Similarly, Obama's first line blends past together with present and uses temporal markers to familiarize his audience with a concept important to the temporal structure and content of his speech—the notion that past and present are inextricably linked. In addition, Obama advocates that African Americans embrace "the burdens of our past without becoming victims of our past,"[42] includes William Faulkner's statement—"The past isn't dead and buried. In fact, it isn't even past,"[43]—and claims that past structures of oppression "helped create a cycle of violence, blight, and neglect that continue to haunt us."[44] With

---

[37]Ibid., para. 58, 59.

[38]Ibid., para. 41.

[39]Ibid., para. 1.

[40]Leff, "Dimensions of Temporality in Lincoln's Second Inaugural," 27.

[41]Michael C. Leff, "Rhetorical Timing in Lincoln's 'House Divided' Speech," *The Van Zelst Lecture in Communication*, Delivered at Northwestern University (1983).

[42]Obama, "A More Perfect Union," para. 39.

[43]Ibid., para. 27.

[44]Ibid., para. 30.

Faulkner's quote, Obama questions the entire notion that there is a tangible division between past and present, implying that the past is an active poltergeist that haunts and influences the present.

This notion that the past—segregation, slavery, legalized oppression—is "not past" and continues to "haunt" the present underscores McPhail's assertion that Obama courageously addresses issues of race while providing a "wake-up call from the dream." Though some suggest he transcends race, by recounting a history of racial injustice, Obama highlights the ways in which contemporary U.S. society is still undoubtedly tied to its past practices of racial oppression. Fletcher interprets Obama's conflation of past and present as a "time warp" because Obama alludes to past ghosts rather than critiquing current systems. Such a move dissociates blame from his audience and contemporary U.S. society and accounts for Fletcher's criticism that Obama "attributes much of the anger of Rev. Wright to the past." Fletcher would have liked to see Obama not only discuss the history of racial inequality, but also more fully attend to the reasons *why* Wright feels such anger toward the United States today.

Though Obama portrays the present as haunted by past specters, he also frames the present moment as having the unique potential to serve as a site of action and change. At the beginning of "A More Perfect Union," Obama primarily refers to the past and the creation of the U.S. Constitution.[45] However, each paragraph also looks forward to the future. Obama states, for instance, that the founders of the Constitution left the question of slavery "to future generations,"[46] explains that the Constitution should "be perfected over time,"[47] and expresses that "words on a parchment" would not end injustice and that "future generations" must work to "narrow that gap between the promise of our ideals and the reality of their time."[48] Obama creates a sense of movement and suggests that something was set in motion 221 years ago that continues today.

Obama then positions his campaign as an integral component of the ongoing movement to perfect the union. Obama asserts that one of his campaign's goals is to "continue the long march of those who came before us, a march for a more just, more equal, more free, more caring and more prosperous America."[49] Obama imbues the present moment with unique importance, stating, "I chose to run for president at this moment in history because I believe deeply that we cannot solve the challenges of our time unless we solve them together."[50]

---

[45]Ibid., para. 1–4.

[46]Ibid., para. 2.

[47]Ibid., para. 3.

[48]Ibid., para. 4.

[49]Ibid., para. 5.

[50]Ibid., para. 5.

The present becomes not only an amalgamation of past struggles, but also an important moment for realizing the unfulfilled promises and potential of the Constitution; Obama is not running for president now because it happened that way, but rather because he *chose* this particular moment.

America's past history of racial injustice, the anger experienced by all races, the recent racial turmoil surrounding Reverend Wright—all have helped lead to the current moment, and, as Obama says, "This is where we are right now. It's a racial stalemate."[51] By spending so much of his speech in the recent and distant past, Obama builds toward discussing the present, creating a feeling that there is something particularly revolutionary about "now," that the moment of his speech is a turning point for American society, for equality, and for change. Obama emphasizes the significance of the current moment by repeating the phrases "at this moment" and "this time." He says:

> At this moment, in this election, we can come together and say, "*not this time.*" ... *This time* we want to talk about how the lines in the emergency room are filled. ... *This time* we want to talk about the men and women of every color and creed who serve together, and fight together.[52]

Obama conveys that not only are change and perfection possible, they are more feasible right now than ever before.

Gaps and Chasms: The Role of Spatial Metaphors

A key metaphor that permeates "A More Perfect Union" is that of a gap, space, or divide separating two entities from one another. Obama primarily uses spatial language when he describes the gap between the actual condition of the United States and its "more perfect" potential. This gap manifests itself in the form of numerous chasms between the actual and potential—gaps of achievement, of wealth, of misunderstanding—that exist between racial groups in the United States. By using spatial metaphors, Obama simultaneously validates the severity of social, economic, and racial struggles while conveying that they are challenges he believes can be overcome.

Obama claims that the U.S. Constitution, though containing honorable promises of equal citizenship, liberty, and justice, was not sufficient in delivering "men and women of every color and creed their full rights."[53] Given the disconnect between the promises set forth in the Constitution and the actual condition of the United States, Obama explains that future generations have the

---

[51]Ibid., para. 37.

[52]Ibid., para. 47–50, my emphasis.

[53]Ibid., para. 4.

responsibility of fighting to "narrow that *gap* between the promise of our ideals and the reality of their time."[54] Obama also uses spatial imagery to describe the current inequity between African Americans and white Americans in the United States. He explains, for instance, that the legacy of segregated schools helps account for "the pervasive achievement *gap* between today's black and white students."[55] In addition, Obama says that the history of racial oppression "helps explain the wealth and income *gap* between black and white."[56]

Obama is particularly interested in identifying a "chasm of misunderstanding" that exists between racial groups in the United States and looking at what factors threaten to expand the divide.[57] He asserts that wishing "away the resentments of white Americans" and labeling them "racist," "widens the racial *divide*, and blocks the path to understanding."[58] In addition to condemning or avoiding addressing white anger, Obama claims that criticizing or washing away black anger and avoiding exploring the roots of racial inequality also "serves to widen the *chasm* of misunderstanding that exists between the races."[59]

Obama acknowledges the inequality between racial groups and likens such divisions to large, tangible, physical spaces. It is important to note that Obama does not depict the condition of the United States or of the racial and social tensions and inequalities that plague the union as hopeless or dismal; the state of the nation is not in "shambles" or "ruin." Though "gaps" and "divisions" are not necessarily positive, by portraying challenges in such a way, Obama conveys a message of hope that we can come together and "perfect" our union. Gaps and chasms can be manageably dealt with by crossing from one side to another. Though separated from the ideal, Obama still sends the optimistic message of possibility of reaching the more perfect union by finding a path through the gap. In fact, by suggesting that from its inception to the present the United States has always been divided from a *more* perfect union, Obama implies that the union is already perfect. Rather than trying to take the union from "fair to great," Obama envisions transforming it from "perfect" to "more perfect." On the one hand, using the term "more perfect" allows Obama to veil the criticism of the United States that McPhail deems unprecedented. On the other hand, implying the union is already perfect leads to Fletcher's critique that Obama is hesitant to provide contemporary criticism of the United States.

---

[54]Ibid., para. 4, my emphasis.

[55]Ibid., para. 28, my emphasis.

[56]Ibid., para. 29, my emphasis.

[57]Ibid., para. 33.

[58]Ibid., para. 36, my emphasis.

[59]Ibid., para. 33, my emphasis.

When Obama discusses bridging the divide between contemporary reality and the "more perfect union" and moving into the future, he often uses the metaphor of a path. He explains that wishing away the resentments of whites "blocks the *path* to understanding."[60] Obama notes that he has never claimed that any presidency—including his own—has the power to overcome racial divisions. Obama, however, expresses his optimism by explaining:

> I have asserted a firm conviction—a conviction rooted in my faith in God and my faith in the American people—that working together, we can move beyond some of our old racial wounds, and that in fact we have no choice if we are to continue on the *path* of a more perfect union.[61]

In addition, he says, "In the white community, the *path* to a more perfect union means acknowledging that what ails the African-American community does not just exist in the minds of black people,"[62] and that for the African-American community, "the *path* means embracing the burdens of our past without becoming victims of our past."[63]

The existence of a "path" to the more perfect union conveys Obama's confidence that it is possible to bridge the contemporary gaps and move beyond where we are now, a "racial stalemate we've been stuck in for years."[64] Obama's path imagery is also important because it grants agency; his audience members are not bystanders, but are literally walking with one another into the future.

The imagery of gaps and paths allows Obama to send the message that he would be a good candidate to lead the process of perfecting the nation. A crucial part of the speech comes when Obama provides his own multifaceted narrative and demonstrates his unique position to reach across the chasms. Creating an inclusive ethos and linking himself to an array of racial, social, and economic groups, Obama proclaims:

> I am the son of a black man from Kenya and a white woman from Kansas. I was raised with the help of a white grandfather who survived a Depression to serve in Patton's Army during World War II and a white grandmother who worked on a bomber assembly line at Fort Leavenworth while he was overseas. I've gone to some of the best schools in America and lived in one of the world's poorest

---

[60]Ibid., para. 36, my emphasis.

[61]Ibid., para. 38, my emphasis.

[62]Ibid., para. 42, my emphasis.

[63]Ibid., para. 39, my emphasis.

[64]Ibid., para. 37.

nations. I am married to a black American who carries within her the blood of slaves and slave owners—an inheritance we pass on to our two precious daughters.[65]

Obama's persona is multiplicitous and plural. He refers not only to the racial groups to which he belongs but also to different social classes, occupations, and even time periods. Not only does Obama share and extol the diversity that defines him, he also embodies both sides of numerous binaries. He is both black and white, a product of both the heartland of the United States and of Kenya, Harvard graduate and member of a family that fought through the Great Depression. It is only from America's shameful past of slavery that Obama has his two "precious daughters" who carry the blood of "slaves and slave owners."[66] Obama also explains that he has "brothers, sisters, nieces, nephews, uncles, and cousins, of every race and every hue, scattered across three continents."[67] The persona Obama creates is instrumental because Obama comes to embody his call to narrow the spaces between the "promise of our ideals and the reality of their time" as well as the gaps of misunderstanding and inequality between the races. His story is "a story that has seared into my genetic makeup the idea that this nation is more than a sum of its parts—that out of many, we are truly one."[68] The nation's motto, *E Pluribus Unum*—out of many, one—is inscribed into Obama's genetic code.[69]

Conclusion

Proposing that both McPhail and Fletcher are "right" does not come close to capturing the complexities surrounding how "A More Perfect Union" sustains such diverse readings. Though Obama clearly conveys hope about the United States' ability to build a path to a more perfect union, Obama's path involves facing past ghosts, delving into the history of racial oppression, reexamining typically romanticized moments as the signing of the Constitution, a document Obama deems stained with the sin of slavery. Obama's willingness to speak about race in such open and strong terms as a candidate absolutely reflects courage, as McPhail suggests; it absolutely makes Obama's speech something special, something that stands apart from most political rhetoric.

---

[65]Ibid., para. 7.

[66]Ibid., para. 7.

[67]Ibid., para. 7.

[68]Ibid., para. 8.

[69]Ibid., para. 8.

Fletcher likely agrees that Obama's speech reflects bravery, but directs our attention to its problematic aspects. Holding Obama to his own value of exploring sources of anger, Fletcher points out that

> ... we live in a society that is so much in denial of the actual conditions of the oppressed both inside and outside our borders; that has come to accept torture; ... that was angry about, yet threw up its hands in the face of the Katrina disaster; ... that witnesses major banks and corporations disembowel communities and face few consequences... .[70]

Forging a path to a more perfect union must involve facing contemporary practices that block the path. Fletcher's and McPhail's disparate positions elucidate that Obama's approach of historicizing racism is, in fact, both extraordinarily important and courageous, as well as an approach of convenience and avoidance; the history lesson Obama provides acknowledges current racial inequities without having to take contemporary U.S. citizens and government to task. Leff and Utley explain that "the persona of the rhetor often functions as a means of constituting the self in relation to a complex network of social and cultural relationships."[71] "A More Perfect Union" relies upon Obama's carefully constructed persona. Obama develops his inclusive persona in such a way that allows him to affirm concerns of some audience members—such as those who agree with the views of Reverend Wright—while not alienating other factions.

It is crucial to remember that Obama's speech emerged as a direct response to the heated controversy surrounding Reverend Wright, and an often-unmentioned reality of "A More Perfect Union" is that it is a political *apologia*. Obama's speech resonates with many of the traits Sharon Downey ties to contemporary *apologia*.[72] Downey quotes Ellen Reid Gold's observation that "candidates' ability to free themselves rhetorically from political nettles is often seen as analogous to [their] ability to lead the country."[73] Obama seizes the opportunity to create a unifying, inclusive persona that embodies the qualities of a leader; in some ways, "A More Perfect Union" might more aptly be deemed Obama's "Leadership Speech" than his "Race Speech." Obama's calculated approach leaves him largely, though not entirely, beyond reproach, and the voting public came to see him as the right figure to walk with them down the path in search of the more perfect union.

---

[70]Fletcher, "Obama Race Speech Analysis."

[71]Michael C. Leff and Ebony A. Utley, "Instrumental and Constitutive Rhetoric in Martin Luther King Jr.'s 'Letter From Birmingham Jail,'" *Rhetoric & Public Affairs* 7, no. 1 (2004): 37.

[72]Sharon Downey, "The Evolution of the Rhetorical Genre of *Apologia*," *Western Journal of Communication* 57 (1993): 53.

[73]Downey, "Evolution of the Rhetorical Genre," 60.

Section II: New Media

Media Politics 2.0:
An Obama Effect

Michael Cheney and Crystal Olsen

The presidential campaign of Senator Barack Obama defied and redefined the conventional wisdom of politics and media in the political campaign process. Characterized in different ways, the term "Obama Effect" probably does the best job of incorporating and encapsulating the wide range of areas where the campaign transformed and is still transforming the political process. The chapters in this volume provide the reader with the range and depth of the Obama Effect in a campaign that lasted less than two years and yet continues to transform the way we think about society and politics today. For this chapter, we will focus on the role that new media interacting with social organizing played in the campaign of Senator Obama, something we will label as "Media Politics 2.0." This chapter will outline the basic concepts involved in Media Politics 2.0 and then look at the evolution of the Obama campaign's use of Media Politics 2.0 as they transformed what began in early February 2007 in Springfield, Illinois, and continued through the Inauguration.

Whether it was large crowds at various campaign speeches or impressive fund-raising totals or passionate supporters going to the polls in record numbers, the media noted that Obama's presidential campaign was not a conventional campaign. Regularly, stories were reported that tried to account for this transformation that candidate Obama brought to the political process. While not to prejudge future books or articles on the topic, many of the past articles and books failed to grasp the full meaning of the campaign.[1] They were not focused on reporting the broad scope of the Obama campaign and the ways it transformed the way politics in the twenty-first century, but rather focused on narrow, almost microscopic aspects of the process, leaving the larger story untold. By way of example, in a primary campaign issue, the *National Journal* had as its cover headline "How the Obama-Clinton Race Is Fundamentally Changing the Way Candidates Run for the Presidency."[2] The publication

---

[1] One notable exception is R. Harfoush, *Yes We Did It!* (Berkeley, CA: New Riders Press, 2009).

[2] *National Journal*, April 19, 2008.

offered up a number of articles that attempted to address the headline. But each article, in its own way, missed the larger scope of the Obama campaign.

One article had the suggestive title "New Media as the Message."[3] The article noted that during the Super Bowl pregame show in 2008, an advertisement for Senator Barack Obama asked viewers to text the letters HOPE as a show of support. As the article points out, this was an example of how the Obama campaign has tried to leverage and use new media in order to engage voters.[4] What was not suggested was how this activity—what we will later call a *tactic*—allowed the Obama campaign to gather cell-phone numbers for supporters for future use by the campaign. The author noted:

> ... [I]n an around-the-clock media environment fixated on all things political, Obama has experimented with new tools for communication in a media climate so diffuse that it's difficult for any candidate to shape a message let alone hold it for a few hours. He and his team have exploited the elite media's enthusiasm for the history-making features of his campaign, while also making adroit use of technology to push information to supporters using a network that some describe as "off-line..."[5]
>
> [C]ampaigns understand that the quirky electronic new-media platforms can easily spark coverage or help candidates play defense against rivals.[6]

The article focused primarily on the success the campaign had on the campaign messages not being filtered by mainstream media, but rather going directly to individual voters and supporters.

The assessment of the Obama campaign by people involved with politics at the national level is telling in what they address and do not address. One observer noted, "Hillary Clinton would've been the nominee, but for the Internet, and she would have secured the nomination—as the campaign expected—by Super Tuesday."[7] Another authority moved a little closer to the full story when she noted that the Obama campaign "... may change what we talk about, how we talk about it, and that's potentially a seismic change that has nothing to do with the Obama candidacy."[8] What the article did not

---

[3]A. Simendinger, "New Media as the Message," *National Journal,* April 19, 2008, 40–44.

[4]Ibid., 40.

[5]Ibid., 41.

[6]Ibid., 41–42.

[7]Ibid., 43.

[8]Ibid.

directly address was how the Obama campaign created a community of supporters, those who were willing to take information from face-to-face and online sources, integrate it into their daily lives, and use it in their work for the campaign. The emphasis in almost all of the campaign coverage about social media was largely on the technology and tactics of using new media and not the overarching strategy that was being used.

Media Politics 2.0 and Twenty-First Century Campaigns—Theory, Strategy, Tools, Tactics

As journalists, pundits, and consultants discussed Campaign 2008, there were changes in the ways campaigns were being run during this campaign cycle. Most campaigns still operated in a top-down fashion where the campaign controlled not only the message, but also the manner in which supporters and volunteers were engaged. Here, the message of the day would go out and everyone involved in the campaign would follow that message. In many campaigns, individuals were defined in terms of how the campaign wanted to categorize them—pigeonholing them—which resulted in a one-dimensional approach. The Obama presidential campaign was different, however. Whether one was a volunteer, a donor, or a potential voter, one could participate on one's own terms. The campaign saw a wide range of initiatives by the supporters that were not suggested or even approved by the campaign. As but one example, YouTube videos about Obama proliferated and were encouraged. In contrast, other campaigns tried to channel such activities into contests, which were then monitored by the campaign. In short, the Obama campaign was a two-way, interactive communication environment, and supporters and volunteers felt empowered to strike out in new and creative fashions.

Media Politics 2.0—the Basics

As one looks at where the Obama campaign started and where it went, as compared to the competition, the key difference was that the Obama campaign learned how to communicate with and organize individuals in a new, twenty-first-century approach.

Theory

The understanding of how social media work is a fairly recent area of inquiry in the scholarly literature. Two of the more productive areas of research and insight into understanding social media and politics are information theory and attachment theory. Both predate social media, but can help provide insights into how social media work as they have moved to integrate online communication into the literature.

Information Theory

In the early years of communication scholarship, information theory provided scholars with a beginning model of communication. The Shannon–Weaver model of communication was the first and remains one of the most formative models of communication.[9] Based on work in information theory, it went a long way toward identifying and categorizing the communication experience. Subsequent scholarship took this framework and moved out into other disciplines to understand communication more fully. In studying the new communication environment of the Internet and social media, information theory can provide us with a new beginning model of what many call the Media 2.0 communication environment. One of the pioneers of understanding this new-media environment is David Weinberger, who synthesizes a great deal of thinking in his work *Everything Is Miscellaneous*.[10] This book provides a solid grounding for us to understand this new age of information and communication. In the early chapters, Weinberger outlines the ways information has been organized and categorized.

For Weinberger, the first order of data is the individual unit—voters, supporters, and volunteers. As this level, there is no structure and all of the items are viewed as being chaotic or miscellaneous, much like the clutter one might find in a kitchen drawer. To move from chaos to structure, Weinberger argues that we need a second order of data to make sense of this miscellany, which involves some sort of organizational system. Probably the best example would be an index or a table of contents for material in a book. For people who are running political campaigns, this second-order data largely is defined as voter lists and contributor lists. Each list is organized around a particular dimension—such as location, level of support, or past volunteer activities—one-dimensional relationships, and only rarely are the names cross-referenced. As Weinberger notes, we have years of experience in organizing, and the structures we use to organize have become second nature to us, blinding us to the restrictions the structures impose on our thinking.

Third-order data, according to Weinberger, is data that has multiple associations. A simple example could be a digital camera. A digital camera can be associated with many different attributes or associations—the cost for the item in a certain range, the manufacturer, the pixel resolution, and even color, which could be listed and then cross-referenced—something not readily possible

---

[9] W. Weaver and C. Shannon, *The Mathematical Theory of Communication* (Urbana: University of Illinois Press, 1963).

[10] D. Weinberger, *Everything Is Miscellaneous* (New York: Times Books, 2007).

until the emergence of the Communication 2.0 environment with its use of relational databases.

In third-order data, there is ongoing categorizing or tagging of data—be it with personal tags, such as "Dad's camera," or with public tags, such as "best value." Tagging platforms such as Digg, del.icio.us, and Technorati provide revealing profiles of associations and relationships for a particular item, article, or person. Third-order data and the new relationships and associations that can be created become possible because of the movement from physical space to digital representation. The recent work *The Chaos Scenario* gives a wide-ranging account of how the digital has transformed all aspects of society. While not using the terms *second-order* and *third-order data*, the underlying assumptions are the same.[11]

Political campaigns that push to create third-order data systems can connect and relate individuals in myriad ways, giving the campaign a far more interactive and synergistic environment than the traditional first- and second-order data worlds that most candidates continue to use to define individuals.

Attachment Theory

As information theory can help explain *how* individuals can be related or associated to each other through third-order data relations—Obama supporter, small-business owner—attachment theory can help explain *why* individuals might choose to associate with others in the new-media environment. Attachment theory can address a wide range of relationships—from parent–child to sibling to friend to other face-to-face to online relationships. Attachment theory argues that individuals develop an internal way of modeling the world at birth that shapes how they believe relationships function.[12] While attached to a caregiver at birth, in adolescent and adult life, individuals develop new and shifting relationships, which in turn influence their view of the world.[13] While face-to-face—"offline"—relationships have been studied for many years, online relationships are only of late beginning to be studied. In one of the more insightful studies, Buote and colleagues argue in the review of literature of the challenge to understand online communication:

> The many opportunities to communicate in an asynchronous and anonymous nature while using the Internet may provide an opportunity for some individuals to differentially affect friendships as a function of attachment style. For example, less socially skilled

---

[11]B. Garfield, *The Chaos Scenario* (Nashville, TN: Stielstra Publishing, 2009).

[12]B. L. Weimer, K. A. Kerns, and C. M. Oldenburg, "Adolescents' Interactions with a Best Friend: Associations with Attachment Style," *Journal of Experimental Child Psychology* 88 (2004): 102–20.

[13]J. Bowlby, *Attachment and Loss: Vol. 1., Attachment* (New York: Basic Books, 1972).

individuals may be able to utilize asynchrony as an opportunity for reflection, planning, and as a result may be able to present themselves more effectively. Alternatively, the absence of immediate feedback (both verbal and behaviorally) may be detrimental to relationship building.[14]

Their assessment mirrors that of other scholars studying social relationships online. Bargh and colleagues suggest that the literature supports a reading that the online environment provides a venue that allows for opportunities to connect in ways otherwise not possible—this bridging of time and space that is a key feature of online relationships.[15]

In the most recent work by Buote and colleagues, the authors conclude that:

> Friendships were equally high in quality, intimacy and self-disclosure ... providing convergent evidence that online friendships present a positive and beneficial alternative to offline friendships.[16]

Going further, they conclude that:

> Online sources may provide a starting point to navigate friendships. Initiating an online friendship might seem less risky and easier to initiate, as there is less cost associated with this type of friendship. Further, the potential for asynchronous and anonymous interactions allows the opportunity for self-presentation strategies and reflection and thought before engaging in online conversation. Similarly, newer developments in Internet communication ... may provide alternative ways for less socially skilled individuals to express themselves.[17]

The opportunity to develop more relationships and more robust relationships is what social media offer—a way for individuals to engage in new contexts—such as a presidential campaign with a dynamic candidate—with new people with whom they have this and other dimensions in common. (As is well-documented, the Obama campaign attracted a much larger than expected number of first-time participants—from voters to volunteers to donors.)

---

[14]V. M. Buote, E. Wood, and M. Pratt, "Exploring the Similarities and Differences between Online and Offline Friendships: The Role of Attachment Style," *Computers in Human Behavior* 25 (2009): 562.

[15]J. K. Bargh and K. McKenna, "The Internet and Social Life," *Annual Review of Psychology* 55 (2004): 573–90.

[16]Buote, Wood, and Pratt, "Exploring the Similarities and Differences," 566.

[17]Ibid.

By approaching social media as a communication environment for creating multiple associations on different dimensions (third-order data) and an environment where individuals can navigate from fairly passive—"lurker"—relationships to ones that are more active—one can see the outline for the Obama campaign's success.

Strategy, Tools, and Tactics

The theory behind social media is just that—a theory. Without the strategy, tools, and tactics to energize the campaign's supporters, the idea of an interactive and synergistic base of supporters, volunteers, and contributors would have been nothing more than an idea. As noted in the earlier discussion of press coverage about the Obama campaign, there was a tendency by many reporters, pundits, and commentators to focus on individual aspects of the campaign and not to embrace a full explication of what made the campaign successful.

Strategy

Strategy in Media Politics 2.0 is the overall direction a campaign chooses to go. It organizes and drives the entire campaign forward and can address a full range of levels in the campaign. One level of strategy might be that the Obama campaign would contest every state in the quest to reach the required number of delegates. Then, tools and tactics would be called upon to realize that goal. For strategies to work in Media Politics 2.0, they must have interactive and synergistic tools and tactics that amplify the relationships. So a strategy to win a caucus state by reaching likely attendees might involve the volunteers going door-to-door. As these volunteers go door-to-door, they learn more about the issues on the minds of the citizens, and these in turn are added to the presentation made by the volunteer. This information also gets passed back to the main campaign office, resulting in ideas and concepts that might be used in future communications. Every bit of data that is collected can then be used in multiple ways and is understood to have value, maybe even in areas that are unanticipated.

Tools

The Obama campaign used a full range of technologies that are usually associated with new-media communication. The technologies that drive the new-media environment include computers, Web sites, cell phones, video cameras, GPS devices, and so forth. There are new and hybridized versions of these coming onto the market each year, and they bring new and compelling technologies that can restructure how we communicate. With these technologies, the goal of a Media Politics 2.0 campaign is to find ways for individual users to connect, converge, and create communalities with these technologies. And as will be illustrated, the Obama campaign has taken no technology off the table.

(Even video games have become a venue for the Obama campaign to offer its message.)

A second tool, which was equally critical and worked in synergy with the new-media technologies, was the social organizing theory of "public narrative."[18] The early use of face-to-face canvassers who were trained in the public narrative concept through Camp Obama was an equally important part of the campaign. The three-story model, which will be covered in the next section, works in both interpersonal-communication environments and social-media environments.

Tactics

Throughout any political campaign, there are myriad choices about what to do or not do—individual actions taken toward implementing and realizing a particular strategy. A tactic might be to send an e-mail to all supporters asking for a financial contribution before the end of the reporting period. Another tactic might be to have student canvassers identify local supporters to take over the role of precinct chair or organizer. And another tactic might be not to respond to a particular ad or comment. Individual tactics merge in particular tools to address particular strategies. With a background in theory of social media and a framework of strategy, tools, and tactics of Media Politics 2.0, the focus of this chapter now turns to the particulars of the Obama campaign.

Media Politics 2.0—The Obama Campaign Strategy

An overarching strategy of the Obama campaign was to build a state-of-the-art database of third-order data that would identify voters, volunteers, and contributors; tag the nature of their relationship—tagging that might be done by the individual, by a campaign volunteer, or by peers; and work to develop interactive and synergistic relationships that blended together the virtual world of third-order data with the face-to-face interactions that research shows brings voters to the polls. With this grand strategy in place, campaign architects set about building up the tactics that fit within that strategy and doing so in new and unexpected ways, relying on both online and face-to-face means of communication. There are a number of tactics that might be examined that worked to build this database, but we will limit ourselves to three: BarackObama.com (the Web site and its offshoots); the on-ground

---

[18]The best explication of "public narrative" comes from the work of Marshall Ganz. See Marshall Ganz, "What Is Public Narrative?," 2008, http://grassrootsfund.org/docs/WhatIsPublic-Narrative08.pdf (accessed August 12, 2010).

operations of Camp Obama and canvassing, with an example from Iowa; and the use of social media sites such as Facebook and YouTube.

BarackObama.com

The Web site of Barack Obama was a source of strength for the candidate from the very start of his campaign, and set him apart from his Democratic and Republican rivals. Only six days after his announcement in Springfield, Illinois, on the steps of the Old Capitol, the Web site BarackObama.com was fully functional.

On February 16, his Web site contained more than the basic candidate information—biography, issue stances, news links, donation links, and volunteer signups—one would expect from a modern presidential campaign. Instead, it further integrated new media, social media, and conventional media. For example, the first version of Obama's presidential candidate Web site included a blog for staff on the new-media team, "Barack TV" for videos of speeches and video biographies, an "Obama Store" to buy official memorabilia from the campaign, and links to Facebook (a social media site originally aimed at the college-aged generation), PartyBuilder (a social media site supported by the DNC), a voter registration Web site, YouTube (a site where users can post video media), and Flickr (a site where users can post pictures).

From the outset, My.BarackObama.com (an offshoot of the main site), or "MyBo," was an integral part of the campaign, indicating that Obama's strategy was new-media/social-media-centric. What was truly revolutionary about MyBo was that it was a social-media site designed for the Obama campaign to be used by fieldworkers, volunteers, supporters, and those simply interested in the campaign alike. It allowed its users to contact each other, join groups related to the user's interests, plan events, and donate funds, just to give some examples.

As the primary race progressed, the Obama Web site developed along with the growing campaign. In terms of the content of the site, there was a substantial jump in the number of new-media and social-networking links given at the bottom of the page, indicating an increase in Obama-relevant material on these sites between February and October 2007. The number of links jumped from five to nine in that period of time. There was also a significant design change in one area. A new heading/dropdown menu called "States" was also added, which brought significant change to the Web site. This dropdown menu is related to the pictures of the United States right below it, where one could see the different states with upcoming primaries and caucuses such as Iowa, Nevada, New Hampshire, and South Carolina. Each of those states was included in the dropdown menu and has a specialized version of BarackObama.com dedicated to it, with information and resources specific to the state.

This indicates a significant change, because states were continually being added, allowing any person to receive information specific to his or her state without signing up as a supporter. This is noteworthy because it increased personalization and built relationships with the potential voter without demanding commitment, which encourages trust. Building relationships and trust is a quintessential feature of Media Politics 2.0 that the Obama campaign executed brilliantly.

Perhaps the most significant design change to the Obama Web site came between October 2007 and February 2008. Besides the aesthetic changes and size of the main page, there were several noteworthy changes to the site's content. Most important were the addition of the "Make a Difference," "Know the Facts," and "Obama Everywhere" boxes. The "Make a Difference" box contained links to find local events, make calls, register to vote, and volunteer more accessible on the main page of the Web site, instead of reserving those functions for MyBo. The "Know the Facts" was a link to www.FactCheck.BarackObama.com, a rapid-response site meant to counter false claims and attacks of the sort that derailed John Kerry's 2004 presidential bid. The "Obama Everywhere" box contained all of the links to outside new-media and social-media Web sites with Obama-related content, which in February 2008 totaled sixteen, compared with the five original links on the site. The title describes the growth of the campaign as well as the growth of new media into the campaign.

David Axelrod, Obama's chief strategist, told *Newsweek* in April 2008 that the campaign was planning to expand its research and rapid-response team in order to combat anticipated attacks on Obama's ties with Bill Ayers and Antoin Rezko. "I don't think people should mistake civility for a willingness to deal with the challenges to come," stated Axelrod.[19] Karen Tumulty of *Time* magazine indicates that "for more than a year, Obama relied on conventional means to confront the blogosphere's superheated rumor mill—to little effect. The 'fact-check' feature on his Web site, for instance, only seemed to spawn more, and wilder, rumors."[20] So, by June 2008, "Know the Facts" had grown into its own Web site called "Fight the Smears," a comprehensive "Web-based rumor clearinghouse."[21]

The campaign had also developed the "Obama Action Wire" and "Obama Rapid Response" sites as branches of BarackObama.com used to address specific

---

[19]Mark Hosenball, "Obama: Can't 'Swift Boat' Me," *Newsweek*, April 28, 2008, http://www.newsweek.com/2008/04/19/obama-can-t-swift-boat-me.html (accessed August 12, 2010).

[20]Karen Tumulty, "Will Obama's Anti-Rumor Plan Work?," *Time Magazine*, June 12, 2008, http://www.time.com/time/politics/article/0,8599,1813663,00.html (accessed August 12, 2010).

[21]Ibid.; see also Anita Hamilton, "Maligned Online? How to Retaliate Against Web Attacks," *Time Magazine*, September 19, 2008, http://www.time.com/time/business/article/0,8599,1842104,00.html (accessed August 12, 2010).

allegations as they arise.[22] The use of these proactive Web sites in correcting negative political banter is an extremely good example of Media Politics 2.0 in the Obama campaign as new media is used as a tool to combat negative smears more actively than any candidate ever has, and to inform and interact with supporters and contributors on these matters. Tumulty states in her article that "as long as there have been rumors in politics, there has been one widely accepted way for a candidate to deal with them. Basically, it's not to."[23] Because of the Obama campaign's proactive, Media Politics 2.0 response, this may not be the case in future campaigns.

In addition to putting together an excellent main Web site and effective rapid-response/action web sites that engage voters like never before, the Obama campaign has succeeded in building a massive database that will make Obama "a power broker in the party for years to come," with or without the White House.[24]

On-Ground Campaigning—Building the Database

The Obama campaign was not the first to use the Internet to garner support; the history of presidential politics has earlier examples of the ways technologies and tactics of new media have been used to connect with voters. However, what sets Obama's 2008 presidential campaign apart is that they were able to turn widespread online support into record-breaking amounts of cash, volunteers on the ground, and eventually votes in the ballot boxes.

In 2000, Senator John McCain used the Internet to raise funds at a time when his traditional approaches to fund-raising were coming up short of the funds needed to carry on the campaign. In 2004, the campaign of Governor Howard Dean set a standard for an effective and robust use of new media with tactics to use the technologies to raise funds and assemble supporters. Nevertheless, the campaign came up short, largely due to a lack of volunteer education and a disorganized fieldwork operation in Iowa.

Obama's campaign strategists understood that for the campaign to execute their new-media/social-media-centric strategy, merging online support with time-tested fieldwork operations was crucial. As Exley states, "The Dean

---

[22]J. McCormick, "Web mobilizes rapid response—Obama targets media when attacks aired," September 17, 2008, 1.

[23]Tumulty, "Will Obama's Anti-Rumor Plan Work?"

[24]C. Stern, "Obama's 'Gigantic' Database May Make Party's Power Broker," *Bloomberg News*, April 28, 2008, http://noir.bloomberg.com/apps/news?pid=newsarchive&sid=aW_Qty8aiVTo (Accessed August 28, 2010.)

campaign had Internet gurus; the Obama campaign has community organizing gurus."[25] "Camp Obama" was created to turn inspiration into organization.

Camp Obama

As Dean's campaign shows, online support doesn't necessarily transfer into numbers on the ground or quality volunteers. Camp Obama was designed to turn those people with interest in the candidate into trained field organizers and knowledgeable volunteers, with the same type of education Barack Obama received as a community organizer in Chicago. A nearly weeklong program was implemented in May of 2007 at the Chicago campaign headquarters, only three months after Obama's announcement that he would be a candidate for the Democratic presidential nomination. Initially, the camp ran four days a week for seven weeks with about fifty people each week. The campaign received more than 1,200 applications for those original 350 spots.[26] Most of those people trained during this period became field organizers in early states, such as Iowa, New Hampshire, and South Carolina, and were eventually sent throughout the country for the extended primary season and general election.

As the campaign progressed, so did the Camp, training nearly a thousand volunteers in Super-Tuesday states in three-day sessions during July and August 2007.[27] Trainees left organized into teams by Congressional district and charged with building an organization that reached all the way to the precinct level.[28] Eventually, those graduates were holding their own two- or one-day "mini-camps" across the United States.

Steven Rose states in his October 2008 *Huffington Post* article that "if Barack Obama becomes President it will be because of grass roots organization"[29]— organization that was cultivated by Camp Obama. He goes on to say that "you

---

[25]Zack Exley, "Obama Field Organizers Plot a Miracle," *Huffington Post*, August 27, 2007, http://www.huffingtonpost.com/zack-exley/obama-field-organizers-pl_b_61918.html (accessed August 12, 2010).

[26]D. Bellandi, "Camp Obama Focuses on Election Win," *Associated Press*, June 2, 2007, http://www.boston.com/news/nation/articles/2007/06/02/camp_obama_focuses_on_election_win/ (accessed August 12, 2010).

[27]Exley, "Obama Field Organizers Plot a Miracle."

[28]Zack Exley, "Stories and Numbers: A Closer Look at Camp Obama," *Huffington Post*, August 29, 2007, http://www.huffingtonpost.com/zack-exley/stories-and-numbers-a-clo_b_62278.html (accessed August 12, 2010).

[29]Stephen C. Rose, "Barack Obama's End Game Will Be on the Ground," *Huffington Post*, October 17, 2008, http://www.huffingtonpost.com/stephen-c-rose/barack-obamas-end-game-wi_b_135528.html (accessed August 12, 2010).

organize not by getting adherents, but by finding ever more organizers, proven people who can canvass, call, plan and execute events, get voters to the polls on election day,"[30] a skill that made graduates of Camp Obama an indispensable resource for the campaign. Through this "camp," the campaign taught the participants everything from canvassing and campaigning to how the Iowa caucuses work and how to organize supporters.

In an interview with National Public Radio in June of 2007, Hans Riemer, the national youth vote director for the Obama campaign, commented on the purpose of Camp Obama:

> Barack Obama is inspiring a new generation of people to come in, and a lot of people have not been involved in the political process before. ... We are training them, teaching them how to be effective, showing them what their role is in our strategy to win the election. ... We're taking people from raw enthusiasm to capable organizers.[31]

Much of the training program used in Camp Obama was based on Obama's own community-organizing experiences in Chicago during the 1980s and early 1990s, which were rooted in the teachings of Saul Alinsky, the pioneer in "community organizing" who was, coincidentally, a Chicago native. Jocelyn Woodwards, director of Camp Obama, stated in a September 2007 interview that she wanted her participants to "stop thinking about Barack Obama and be Barack Obama"[32] by connecting their interests to his. At the core of the Alinsky model is the concept of "agitation," or making someone angry enough about the bad state of his or her life that he or she agrees to take action to change it, which ties into the participant's personal stories, which they are encouraged to share at Camp and when talking to people in the community.

As part of exercises at Camp Obama, leaders and participants would discuss Obama's story as it is laid out in his book *Dreams from My Father*. The "story of self," his challenges and choices, his "story of us," where Obama pivoted to connect his own story with the challenges and choices that now face Americans as a people, and the "story of now," where Obama laid out what we have do to make the world a better place right now were the three stories used by Camp Obama participants to develop an approach to social organizing.

---

[30]Ibid.

[31]David Schaper, "'Camp Obama' Trains Campaign Volunteers," National Public Radio, June 13, 2007, http://www.npr.org/templates/story/story.php?storyId=11012254 (accessed August 12, 2010).

[32]Abdon M. Pallasch, "'Ruthless' for Obama," *Chicago Sun-Times*, September 4, 2007, http://www.suntimes.com/news/elections/540781,CST-NWS-camp04.article (accessed August 12, 2010).

Then the campers would begin developing their own stories of "self," "us," and "now" as they related to the campaign.[33]

These three stories are the pillars around which Marshall Ganz developed his theory of "public narrative." He argues that "public narrative is a leadership art through which we translate values into action: engaging heart, head, and hands" and is built from "the experience of challenge, choice, and outcome."[34] Narrative, as he describes it, allows us to "communicate the emotional content of our values." And, through the shared experience of our values, "we can engage with others, motivate one another to act, and find the courage to take risks, explore possibility, and face the challenges we must face."[35]

Social Media

The elements of face-to-face information-gathering, where one had a personal relationship with the volunteer, and Web-based information-gathering, where one provided personal data to the Web site, were fused for an extra level of collaboration with the use of social media. New-media/social-media sites like Facebook, MySpace, and YouTube were used extensively by the Obama campaign and their supporters to connect with the new-media-conscious of America and were an integral part of Media Politics 2.0 and the Obama campaign strategy.

For example, nearly every major speech or interview given by Barack Obama was uploaded to YouTube, a video clip–sharing site. His "A More Perfect Union" speech had nearly 8.2 million views as of August 2010.[36] The campaign has its own user account, which has uploaded more than 1,850 video clips with total views of nearly 22 million, and is now being used during the Obama presidency to advocate his agenda.[37] This user account is connected to BarackObama.com and can be subscribed to by YouTube users. Video clips, from personal video blogs to cell-phone-captured on-the-ground views of speeches and glad-handing, could be uploaded by any person in the world with an e-mail address, adding to the exposure.

Facebook and MySpace were essential organizing tools for the campaign, especially when targeting the younger twenty-something supporters who

---

[33]Exley, "Stories and Numbers."

[34]The best explication of "public narrative" comes from the work of Marshall Ganz. See Ganz, "What Is Public Narrative?"

[35]Ibid.

[36]"Obama Speech: 'A More Perfect Union,'" March 18, 2008, http://www.youtube.com/watch?v=pWe7wTVbLUU (accessed August 12, 2010).

[37]http://www.youtube.com/user/BarackObamaDotCom

had driven the meteoric rise of this campaign. "Students for Obama" groups across the nation had been able to organize online as well as on the ground as registered student organizations. With Facebook, for example, supporters of Obama on a certain campus could search "Obama" and would be met with people, groups, events, and even applications that connected them with other supporters and even the campaign itself. The first search result for groups was often the local Students for Obama (SFBO) chapter, which they could join online, and members could be updated with events and messages on a regular basis. The official Obama application, which came directly from the campaign, could be added to a user's profile page and gave them connectivity to other supporters and materials put out by the campaign, such as the YouTube videos previously mentioned. These new and social media were essential in gathering and organizing support for the campaign.

In the closing weeks of the campaign, the Obama campaign launched a new application to further fuse the individual relationships among individuals, their friends and community, and the Obama campaign—the Obama application for the iPhone. With this application, the contact data on each user's iPhone was reorganized to better facilitate a supporter's involvement and support for the campaign. Something as simple as taking a supporter's contact list and restructuring it according to state-by-state divisions allowed the campaign to send a message to each supporter and ask that the supporter call friends in particular states to canvass for Obama. While the individual numbers were not recorded, the Obama campaign did want to collect the states and the number of calls one made and use this for some of their paid canvassing. (As part of the interactive nature of the campaign, the iPhone app was actually developed by an Obama supporter and shared with the Obama campaign, which quickly released the app through the Apple iTunes store. This is but one of a series of innovations that were credited to the Obama campaign that actually had their origins in the work of the Obama supporters, examples of the unconventional, two-way, interactive communication environment between supporters and the campaign).

Conclusion

In this chapter, we focused on the role that new media interacting with social organizing played in the campaign of Senator Barack Obama and in the Obama Effect. As can be seen throughout this chapter, Obama's campaign redefined the conventional wisdom of politics and media in the political campaign process. Obama and his team successfully created the first "Media Politics 2.0" campaign as it evolved from what began in early February 2007 in Springfield, Illinois, through the Inauguration. The campaign developed a solid infrastructure of third-order data, trained fieldworkers, and volunteers on public narrative, as well as new- and social-media presence, and used strategy, tools, and tactics synergistically—all of which are integral parts of Media Politics 2.0. While books and articles have reported on individual successes of the campaign (such as its impressive use of new media) most of them have missed the bigger picture—that it was the fusion of the online and on-ground campaigns that truly made the campaign successful. Into this mix, add a candidate whose vision and speeches spoke to a world of diverse and robust relationships captured by the Obama campaign, and you have a model for the twenty-first-century campaign.

The Webbed Message: Re-Visioning the American Dream

Heather E. Harris

A multicultural and arguably marginalized worldview enabled a junior senator from Illinois to create a multicultural and multimedia message that resonated with the American populace during the 2008 electoral campaign in a way that had never been done. Then-Senator Barack Obama's message, transmitted primarily and innovatively via the Web, was one that sought to reignite the imaginations of Americans in a dream in which they could all partake with their eyes wide open regardless of their ethnicity, gender, class, able-bodiedness, religion, political perspective, or sexual orientation. His "webbed" message connected, inspired, and mobilized previously disconnected segments of Americans by imploring them to re-envision and to work for a truly "United" States that would critically challenge and change the dominant narratives and practices of the last two-hundred-plus years. Christopher Hayes described the campaign as "[p]olitics without division; progress without anyone's interests being threatened."[1] This chapter reflects on how that computer-mediated message was thematically conveyed via BarackObama.com using Douglas Kellner's critical cultural-studies framework in which he addresses the meanings of cultural artifacts in media at the level of production, the text, and the audience's response. He asserts that analysis of these levels of culture provides insights into the societies, politics, and economies from which they emerge.[2] Furthermore, James Lull concurs with Kellner's view that the manifestation of ideology is central to understanding the cultural artifacts under examination.[3] According to Kellner, "Ideologies of class, for instance, celebrate upper-class life and denigrate the working class. Ideologies of gender promote sexist representations of women, and ideologies of race utilize racist representations

---

[1]Christopher Hayes, "Obama's Media Maven," *The Nation*, February 19, 2007, 20.

[2]Douglas Kellner, "Cultural Studies, Multiculturalism, and Media Culture," in *Gender, Race, and Class in Media: A Text-Reader*, ed. Gail Dines and Jean M. Humez (Thousand Oaks, CA: Sage, 2003), 9–20.

[3]James Lull, "Hegemony," in *Gender, Race, and Class in Media*, 61–66.

of people of color and various minority groups. Ideologies make inequalities and subordination appear natural and just, and thus induce consent to relations of domination."[4]

The innovation of the Web as a campaign tool captured the attention of presidential hopefuls in 2004, most notably former Vermont governor Howard Dean. Yet none used it to the extent or with the success of Team Obama. In fact, Obama's Web site may have been an outgrowth and modification of the successful site developed for his 2004 senatorial race. According to Andrew Romano, the introduction of Web 2.0, MySpace, Facebook, and LinkedIn, for example, provided an advantage unavailable in the past and increased the likelihood of a successful outcome for the candidates in their quest for the White House. He added that during the campaign, BarackObama.com was considered on par or more advanced than the Web sites of his competitors.[5] Furthermore, David Mark explained that the 2004 senatorial campaign may have proved to be an excellent practice run, since 2008 was considered the first election in which the use of the Internet was viewed as critical for the candidate's success.[6]

Additionally, in order not to be impacted by the offline/online disconnect experienced by his predecessors, especially in places like Iowa, the Obama team incorporated offline practices such as, but not limited to, the neighbor-to-neighbor practice used by President George W. Bush in 2004.[7] While Gary Rawlins[8] and Roy Mark[9] asserted that Obama's team was able to capture a large percentage of the eighteen-to-thirty-year-old demographic, it was also necessary for his team to connect with Americans who were accustomed to, or who preferred, other forms of media for their information. This was particularly true among the Iowa caucuses who favored television to the Web.[10] Consequently, it was the grassroots-based, volunteer, offline/online mélange that contributed to the rewriting of U.S. election campaigning in the twenty-first century. [11]

---

[4]Kellner, "Cultural Studies," 11.

[5]Andrew Romano, "Netroots Renewed," *Newsweek* 149, no. 21 (May 21, 2007): 30.

[6]David Mark, "04 Illinois Democratic Senate Candidates," *Campaigns and Elections* 24, no. 6 (June 2003): 40. Andrew Noyes, "Panelists Say Internet Political Impact only Likely to Grow," *Congress Daily* (March 4, 2008): 10.

[7]Chris Cillizza, "Obama Campaign Aims to Turn Online Backers into an Offline Force," *Washington Post*, March 31, 2007, 1.

[8]Gary Rawlins, "Check it Out," *USA Today*, April 7, 2008, 4B.

[9]Roy Mark, "Tech's So-So Showing in Politics," *eWeek*, January 14, 2008, 19–20.

[10]Julie Bosman, "The Web, Despite Its Promise, Fails to Snare Iowa Voters," *New York Times*, October 13, 2007, 8A.

[11]Roger Cohen, "The Obama Connection," *New York Times*, May 26, 2008, 1.

… Obama's Web strategy is premised on connecting activists and supporters to one another, not just pushing out tightly controlled messages from campaign HQ. Following the false start of Howard Dean's campaign, the Internet has come of age. All this works because the principles are right. Obama's campaign has at once lowered the barriers to entry into politics and consistently raised expectations of what can be achieved when people are willing to take part.[12]

Essential to maintaining a Web presence during the campaign was funding, and in 2008, it was viral. Walsh[13] reported that about one-third of Americans got their campaign news online. Additionally, those individuals were earning $75,000 or more, and half had earned college degrees. Dan Morrain stated that in terms of money, this translated into a second-quarter fund-raising of over $30 million dollars for the Obama campaign.[14] According to Karen Tumulty, much of the funds came from 258,000 potential voters who clicked the "donate" button on his Web site or texted a friend.[15] The Obama team also modified the bundling technique used by presidential candidate George W. Bush in the 2000 campaign. Yet whereas Bush used CEOs to raise money from their friends and families, Obama used stay-at-home moms, teachers, aspiring athletes, and software engineers. The campaign's fund-raising total amounted to over half a billion dollars in donations.[16]

The Obama team's savvy and effective use of mixed media and its viral fund-raising campaign was built upon a central message. It was a message that elicited overwhelming participation in the campaign, and which undoubtedly figured prominently in his becoming the forty-fourth president of the United States. Obama articulated what at first glance or hearing might be interpreted as a "counternarrative" of a united and inclusive America. Yet closer examination may reveal the current and dominant version as contrary to that to which many citizens aspire for themselves and the nation. His narrative was undergirded by a connected pluralism where it was not necessary to deny one's background in order to participate in politics or the attainment of the American Dream. It is a dream that under the current narrative can often be elusive for those who do not, or cannot, conform to the country's white, male, heterosexual, Protestant,

[12]David Lammy, "The Lessons of Obama," *New Statesman*, June 9, 2008, 15.

[13]Kenneth Walsh, "The Internet," *U.S. News & World Report* 143, no. 2 (July16, 2007): 39–40.

[14]Dan Morrain, "Raising $32.5 Million, Obama Far Outpaces Rivals, Sets Record," *Los Angeles Times*, July 2, 2007, 1.

[15]Karen Tumulty, "Obama's Viral Marketing Campaign," *Time* 170, no. 3 (July 16, 2007): 38–39.

[16]Tahman Bradley, "Final Fundraising Figure: Obama's 750M," ABC News, 2008, http://abcnews.go.com/Politics/Vote2008/story?id=6397572&page=1 (accessed August 30, 2009).

able-bodied, and upper-middle-class criteria for achieving it. Furthermore, Obama's firsthand understanding of multiculturalism uniquely positioned him to move his apparent counternarrative to the center of the American, and world, consciousness. He offered an opportunity for national healing and change, and many Americans from all walks of life responded to his ideas with enthusiasm.

Perhaps due to his varied lenses resulting from his being multiethnic, and multicultural, he chose to see beyond the country's black/white chasm and to address directly Americans from different backgrounds, persuasions, and orientations on his Web site. He simultaneously understood the balance of diversity and oneness in this nation. Regardless of who the potential voter was, the message seemed tailored for her or for him. For example, potential voters saw themselves on BarackObama.com, regardless of whether they were Muslim, differently-abled, Native Americans, or nonnative English speakers. This perspective affirms what Karen Houle describes as a more effective way of knowledge attainment. "… Democracy and diversity are the normative hallmarks of better knowing."[17] Her point of view echoed in the message on the BarackObama.com Web site. The site represented an inclusive platform, due to its multiple lenses, for those who often find themselves disenfranchised due to their differences from the country's dominant groups. Those who engaged the Web site were seen, heard, and provided with opportunities to act for the change they desired by the campaign's organizers. They were empowered and guided through multimedia and motivational messages to move from their periphery spaces to create centers that did not exclude others.

Upon further examination of the overarching message, three major themes were identified: the "Movement"; "Yes, I Am Black, And …"; and Agency. Additionally, because of its inclusionary nature, a common thread of community was found to exist throughout the primary message and its themes. Campaign strategists encouraged community at a number of levels: the parochial, the political, the American, and the global. Each level seemed necessary in order for the change the campaign espoused to occur, and as a result, the Obama team was able to connect American communities that would not normally interact into a web of unprecedented political momentum and power. The first theme examined in this chapter is the "Movement," which encouraged a reclaiming of the American Dream.

The Movement

The campaign appeared to rekindle the passion for the nation's fundamental ideals through its webbed message. BarackObama.com's manifestation of the "Movement" appeared to be an attempt to realize the ideological promises

---

[17]Karen Houle, "Making Strange," *Frontiers: A Journal of Women Studies* 30, no.1 (2009): 174.

of the United States as stated in the country's Declaration of Independence. He encouraged the American electorate to make those truths self-evident in the moment. Though spearheaded by a man with a multiethnic background, his message was not pigeonholed as a continuation of the black civil rights movement. For while his message rests on the foundation of that message, it also rests on the foundation of any American movement that used as its source the American tenants of the pursuit of happiness and justice for all. His movement challenged Americans to believe that change for the better could be attained imminently. According to the Web site, the elements required to realize that change were social responsibility, accountability, increased use of diplomacy on the international stage, and situational leadership. Social responsibility meant the positive change yearned for had to emerge from every level of society. There was a role for everyone in ensuring that they and others were both participants and beneficiaries of the American Dream. Accountability related to spending and transparency in the practices by those agencies and individuals responsible for providing services to the populace. On the diplomatic front, negotiation would take precedence over preemptive strikes and calls to war. Nation-states would be encouraged to present their positions and seek solutions acceptable to both sides. Finally, situational leadership was configured as less partisan and more cooperative on those issues that supported the vision for this new America. In the subsequent theme, "Yes, I Am Black, And …," the campaign's Web site presents the candidate's multiple identities as positives that mirror a diverse and dynamic America.

Yes, I Am Black, And …

Obama presented himself as a nonthreatening everyperson with an understanding of the needs of a diverse American society and world. Whether it was his background, education, or profession, there was an aspect of Obama with which a voter could identify. His ethnic and racial backgrounds, resulting from diverse parents, siblings, and relatives, still often led to the default reading of him as an African-American male. Yet his "Africanness" is qualified by his medium-to-light brown complexion, which may not have been perceived as menacing by some segments of the dominant groups. Furthermore, his even temper and broad and easy smile also assisted in allaying fears of the angry black male in the midst of the predominant pool of apparently rational and white males, and a single white female, New York senator Hillary Rodham Clinton.

Obama's academic and professional credentials may have also bolstered his acceptability, if not his credibility, among the dominant groups in the United States. He did not just graduate from law school; he went to Harvard. He was not merely a student; he was the editor of the *Law Review*. After school, he chose service by becoming a community organizer. While being a community organizer did not win him praise among some members of the dominant groups in society, it was a point at which he was able to relate to members of the working classes. Community organizing was not seen in the same category as "service" to others in need of some form of assistance; however, being a servant of communities and understanding the needs of the people served was critical to Obama garnering the support of populations who may have felt disenfranchised. Now there was someone running for the highest office in the land who understood their plight, and who would work for change in the White House that would include them.

His acculturated multicultural experiences include, but are not limited to, exposure to the multiple cultures in the state of Hawaii, living in Indonesia, traveling to Kenya, and having siblings and relatives who are ethnically and culturally diverse. These experiences undoubtedly contributed to his ability to appeal to an America that most politicians have been unable to reach or uninterested in reaching up until this point in time. He exhibited what Stuart Hall calls the new ethnicities: "… [a] recognition that we all speak from a particular place, out of particular history, out of a particular experience, a particular culture, without being contained by that position …"[18] These ethnicities are fluid and engage differences rather than suppress them because they expand the values and beliefs of the society. Therefore, when Obama brought his ethnicities to the fore simply as a matter of his being, he broadened, intentionally or unintentionally, the perception of what it means to be American, as well as what America can be if it embraces its complex human mosaic.

Agency

"I'm asking you to believe not just in my ability to bring about change in Washington. I'm asking you to believe in yours."[19]

The theme of agency was pivotal in priming potential voters to actually cast their ballots for the change they desired. Individuals did not have to be well-known in political circles to be empowered in the Obama campaign. They were given voice through the ability to pose questions and suggestions to the campaign. They were encouraged to volunteer until they could not volunteer anymore, and they were guided by the Web site to five things they could do for the campaign. They were updated frequently about rallies, lies, and videotape, and they were asked to donate and donate, and donate some more. This was a campaign that seemingly welcomed the active role supporters could play in an American transformation. Leadership came from the top and the grassroots synergistically. It came from young adults, the elderly, expatriates, the

[18]Stuart Hall, "New Ethnicities," in *Black British Cultural Studies: A Reader*, ed. Houston Baker, Manthia Diawara, and Ruth Lindeborg (Chicago: University of Chicago Press, 1996), 169.

[19]http://www.BarackObama.com

differently-abled, naturalized citizens, and the LGBTQI (lesbian, gay, bisexual, transgender, queer, questioning, and intersex) communities, for example. The American populace was called to action in a way that it had not been in the past, and it responded with resoundingly positive action. It was continually reinforced that the change was not contingent solely upon a win for an individual; it was also dependent on what supporters—supporters-turned-voters, it was hoped—would continue to do for the causes they believed in once the election was over and the hard work had begun. It was a call for a participatory rather than a passive democracy. Each person, not just those in government, was encouraged to continuously cultivate the change she or he desired.

Analysis

Beyond the aforementioned, what do the three major themes of the Obama Web site's message reveal when cast within the frame of Kellner's critical cultural-studies lens of production and political economy, textual analysis, and audience response? First, when production and political economy are considered, the themes are examined to determine how the system from which they spring impacts the message. This includes, according to Kellner, "… [w]hat structural limits there will be as to what can and cannot be said and shown, and what sort of audience effects the text may generate."[20] The mode of production in this instance is the Internet; this is a fundamental point. Kellner mentions that media such as radio, television, film, and the music industry tend to have entrenched guidelines as to what is permitted with regard to production, due in part to corporate conglomeratization.[21] I would argue, however, that the relatively novel nature of the Web makes it fertile space for experimentation and hence for a campaign such as Obama's to have existed. His message would have been more difficult to disseminate in more traditional media because of dominant ideological entrenchment in those media. As an outsider, he used what traditional politicians with more financial resources may have viewed as a less traditional type of message resource. The Obama team required a new medium that had not been fully co-opted by major media companies, in order to achieve campaign success, because they initially had neither the money nor the political standing to disseminate their nontraditional message via traditional media. Ironically, this seeming restriction amounted to the campaign's saving grace. It was the new media that enabled him to move from the margins to the center in the presidential campaign. Once momentum had been established on the Web, he was sought out by more traditional media organizations who wanted to understand better his success, and in doing

---

[20]Kellner, "Cultural Studies," 9.

[21]Kellner, "Cultural Studies," 9.

so, they helped to spread his message to even wider and more traditional audiences. Had new media in the form of the Internet not been available and effectively used by the Obama campaign, his message would probably have been quickly suppressed by traditional media organizations because it appeared not to affirm the status quo.

In examining the Obama's webbed message as a text for cultural analysis, James Lull's articulation of hegemony as the management of ideology must be considered. Lull asserts that "… ideological resistance and appropriation frequently involve reinventing institutional messages for purposes that differ greatly from their creator's intentions."[22] Is this in fact the case with the Obama team's webbed message? If the original creators of the message, that of participation in the American Dream, are the founding fathers of the nation, the Obama message is neither new nor counterhegemonic. Rather, it is more likely an expansion of a message primarily intended at the time, and often since, as one for the dominant groups of the U.S. population. What made the Obama message press against the hegemonic boundaries was its inclusion of the masses. The dream was no longer just for some, but for all. What may have bordered on counterhegemonic was the Obama team's subtle acknowledgement of class, race, gender, religion, language, and ability issues as influential in their message of change. The middle class may have been highlighted on television and in debates, yet everyone who makes up the fabric of the nation was considered in the webbed message, whether they lived in the United States or planned to vote from abroad. The message therefore was not counterhegemonic in terms of achieving the American Dream; it was simply inclusive in its goal that the dream of the nation's forefathers be one that is actually attainable for all.

The campaign's volunteers and the record amount of funds raised served as evidence of the success of the Obama team's message to the electorate. He, as much as the message, represented the attainment of the dream. If he won, it would be proof that an individual perceived as a member of one of the nation's most marginalized and disenfranchised ethnic groups could also be an heir to the highest office in the land. Furthermore, his success might then signal that individuals from every sector represented in his webbed message could also attain their dreams. The message not only promised the electorate a new leader, it professed a different kind of leadership. Kellner[23] states that it is important to determine whether the audience is responding to a message that is in line with the dominant, oppositional, progressive, reactionary, or emancipatory ideologies. In the case of Obama team, the message seems to be progressive (an expansion). This is because enough of the dominant ideologies

---

[22]Lull, "Hegemony," 65.

[23]Kellner, "Cultural Studies," 9.

remain in the message for the audience to view it as refreshing without it being revolutionary, as an oppositional message might be perceived.

Through the "Movement," "Yes, I Am Black, And ...," and Agency, the BarackObama.com message undoubtedly affirmed Houle,[24] who stated that democracy and diversity lead to better ways of knowing. The Obama webbed message was democratic and diverse, and it indeed provided different—and, some would argue, better—ways of knowing the potential of the U.S. government to serve its populace and the world regardless of socioeconomic status, race, ethnicity, ability, orientation, religion, and/or political perspective. The campaign leadership consciously connected with and inspired hope among many sectors of the electorate to form an irrepressible momentum for change. It also provided an example of an innovative way of running a successful election campaign in the twenty-first century.

Conclusion

While the Obama message was able to expand the breadth of the ideas offered during the election campaign, those ideas remained framed within the boundaries created by the country's dominant groups and their ideologies. Resistance to the campaign's webbed message ironically was also resistance to the manifestation of the ideals of the American Dream for a greater portion of the population. Given that the "Dream" is seldom lived out by those perceived as different because of class, ethnicity, gender, orientation, and so forth, the Obama message emerged as somewhat threatening. Until the Obama message, the attainment of the "Dream" was a bastion seemingly reserved for the country's elites—albeit with a few members of the other socioeconomic classes realizing the dream against great odds and consternation. The fact that many more of them are not able to reproduce the success of the few tokens is often seen by some members of the dominant groups as reflecting a defect of that individual's class, ethnic group, gender, orientation, and so forth, rather than being a flaw in the ideologies that create and perpetuate many of the social ills that plague the nation. The prominence and presence of the Web site, in addition to the participation of Obama himself, were evidence of him resisting the ideological limitations often ascribed to persons of African descent and/or other ethnic groups in the United States and other parts of the world. Furthermore, he was deliberate in presenting himself and his presence as "normal," and multiculturalism as a practice as opposed to an ideal. Finally, his decision to run for the presidency of the United States and seat himself at the table without invitation was the ultimate act of agency. He led his supporters by example. It now remains to be seen what forms of resistance will emerge from some

---

[24]Houle, "Making Strange," 172.

members of the dominant groups to ensure that Obama's attainment of the American Dream is not repeated by those of his kind, or others who have been ideologically deemed unworthy to hold the highest office in the nation.

On November 4, 2008, American voters cast their ballots for Obama's expanded version of the dream. With their votes, they said there were ready to work for the change they believe in by participating in a movement that stresses community connection, social responsibility, accountability, transparency, and peaceful negotiations between nation-states. They voted to expand the perception of who is American, and what Americans can achieve if they adhere to the highest values of the nation's creed. They voted to build upon the cornerstone of a healing nation. Undoubtedly, four years will be insufficient to determine the full impact of the Obama Effect. Perhaps it will take decades and generations before we are able to see the full harvest of this turning point in American history and its political landscape. "Sow," now we wait.

The Resonant Message and the Powerful New Media: An Analysis of the Obama Presidential Campaign

Qingwen Dong, Kenneth D. Day, and Raman Deol

Barack Obama's presidential campaign is widely viewed as unprecedented and perhaps one of the most highly successful presidential campaigns in U.S. history. Day and Dong believe that "the astounding success of Barack Obama as a presidential candidate is in part due to his powerful rhetoric and use of the new media."[1] Rice and Atkin have asserted that a candidate's message and use of media play a critical role in informing, persuading, and motivating changes in behavior among message recipients.[2] This chapter focuses on the resonance of Senator Obama's campaign messages and the powerful new media used by the Obama campaign for diffusing that message.

The Resonant Message

The Obama campaign maintained a simple, focused theme: "change we can believe in." This campaign slogan resonated with the willingness and reasoned intention of many receivers of the message. The official Web site of the Obama campaign further illustrated the essence of the message: "I am asking you to believe. Not just in my ability to bring about real change in Washington.... I'm asking you to believe in yours." This message initiated receivers' self-efficacy and empowered each receiver to believe in his or her capacity to become politically engaged and "make a positive change in our country." Self-efficacy theory

---

[1]Kenneth Day and Qingwen Dong, "Constructing Presidential Candidate Ethos: The Case of Barack Obama," paper presented at the Western States Communication Association Annual Conference in Denver/Boulder, CO (2008), 12.

[2]Ronald Rice and Charles Atkin, "Communication Campaigns: Theory, Design, Implementation, and Evaluation," in *Media Effects*, ed. J. Bryant and D. Zillmann (Mahwah, NJ: Lawrence Erlbaum Associates, 2002), 427–51.

suggests that individuals who believe in themselves tend to get involved and do well in both the social and political world.[3] Accordingly, the aforementioned message of the Obama campaign called on individuals to believe in themselves and their ability to produce positive change in the United States by becoming involved in political action through working through grassroots networks.

Interpellation and Constitutive Rhetoric

According to Day and Dong, "interpellation and constitutive rhetoric have been powerful tools in the grassroots movement that has been the core of the campaign of Barack Obama."[4] Louis Althusser developed the concept of *interpellation* or *hailing* to describe socially constructed "yous" in the society to which people belonged. Althusser viewed hailing or interpellation as one of the controlling mechanisms for managing capitalist societies, but failed to see it as a rhetorical strategy.[5]

Michel Foucault expanded the interpellation concept with his observation that discursive texts speak to subject positions. This led to an understanding of interpellation as a rhetorical strategy.[6] Day and Dong have pointed out that Foucault's conceptualization of interpellation suggests that discourse can inter-pellate subjects without the obvious mechanism of the use of second-person singular and plural pronouns. "Most, if not all texts speak to a subject position, but interpellation is most obvious in texts that employ 'you' or 'we' or other forms of these pronouns."[7]

The application of these pronouns helped shape the nature of resonating messages experienced by the receivers during the discourse. The use of inter-pellation has been detailed in an analysis of print advertising.[8] For example, an advertisement can aim at receivers by hailing, using the pronoun "you," suggesting that "people like you use [the product]." This approach generates the bonding relationship between the audience and the product: audience members become defined by the products they use. In a way, these resonat-ing messages develop high levels of shared meanings between speakers/senders and listeners/receivers. Day and Dong observed that many of the advertising

[3]Albert Bandura, "Exercise of Personal and Collective Efficacy in Changing Societies," in *Self-Efficacy in Changing Societies*, ed. Albert Bandura (Cambridge: Cambridge University Press, 1995), 1–46; and Albert Bandura, *Self-Efficacy: The Exercise of Control* (New York: Freeman, 1997).

[4]Day and Dong, "Constructing Presidential Candidate Ethos," 8.

[5]Ibid.

[6]Ibid.

[7]Ibid., 10.

[8]Judith Williamson, *Decoding Advertisements: Ideology and Meaning in Advertising* (New York: Marion Bowers, 1994).

hailing techniques could easily be applied to political rhetoric "in which people are told that their support of a candidate is a reflection of who they are."[9]

Charland was interested in the use of interpellation to create constitutive rhetoric.[10] Here, people acquire a rhetorically constructed conception of themselves in the ideology and historical context that envelops them. According to Charland, an effective constitutive rhetoric must not only successfully interpellate subjects but lead to consequences in action."[11] As we demonstrate in this study, constitutive rhetoric played a critical role in activating the grassroots movement that was the core of the Obama campaign.

Leff built upon this notion of interpellation and stated that in order to provoke action in a group, rhetoric creates an "ambiguous notion of agency that positions the orator both as an individual who leads an audience and as a community member shaped and constrained by the demands of the audience."[12] These constraints upon the rhetor are in the form of tradition, as tradition "can function as a mediating force between individual and collective identities," and thus, call to tradition or traditional values can be seen as an indirect mode of interpellation.[13] This allowed the Obama campaign a measure of flexibility in message strategy since there are different sets of tradition and traditional values that can be referenced, some very much to the specific advantage of a political candidate.

The Powerful Media

The Internet is viewed as a revolution in "control transfer," meaning that people tend to control themselves rather than being controlled by institutions.[14] Rice and Haythornthwaite have suggested that there are six core features of the Internet that enhance individual control.[15] These features include interactivity, digital content, making communication flexible the design of the Internet as a distributed, packed-based network, and the interoperability of the Internet so that information can flow freely throughout a network, with broadband capacity and universal access.

---

[9]Day and Dong, "Constructing Presidential Candidate Ethos," 11.

[10]Maurice Charland, "Constitutive Rhetoric: The Case of the *Peuple Québécois*," in *Landmark Essays on Rhetorical Criticism*, ed. Thomas Benson (Davis, CA: Hermagoras Press, 1993), 213–34.

[11]Day and Dong, "Constructing Presidential Candidate Ethos," 12.

[12]Michael Leff, "Tradition and Agency in Humanistic Rhetoric," *Philosophy and Rhetoric*, 36 (2003): 135.

[13]Ibid.

[14]Andrew Shapiro and Richard Leone, *The Control Revolution* (New York: Public Affairs, 1999).

[15]Ronald Rice and Caroline Haythornthwaite, "Perspectives on Internet Use: Access, Involvement and Interaction," in *The Handbook of New Media*, ed. L. A. Lievrouw and S. Livingstone (Thousand Oaks, CA: Sage Publications, 2007), 92–113.

The Obama campaign team conducted an effective campaign by using new-media technologies and the Internet to its advantage. The team developed an appealing, informative, and persuasive Web site to draw people into Obama's candidacy. After registration, each voter constantly received e-mail messages from the campaign team, including messages attributed to Obama, campaign results, solicitations for donations, and recruitment requests to make phone calls before primaries and the presidential election itself.

According to Nielsen Media Research, Obama beat all other candidates in using the Internet to draw supporters into his campaign. Moreover, the Internet played a unique and critical role in helping Obama collect donations and reaching out to those who have been difficult to reach in campaigns using traditional media. Urista, Dong, and Day noted that the two leading online social networking sites (SNS), MySpace and Facebook, both are very popular among young adults.[16] People can customize their own home pages to display their personal interests in elements of pop culture including music, television, and politics. Dye believed that this new medium has created a new generation of individuals whose identities are defined by their connections and the content they produce online.[17] Research has showed that the Obama campaign thrived by using social networking media.[18] Erwin suggested that the campaign built a brand in the same way social networks are built, making its Web site friendly, social, and community-oriented. The campaign linked strangers via the powerful new media, and these strangers were able to share their stories and make donations in response to the resonance-empowered campaign message. Based on the review of literature, this study proposes the following two research questions: (1) How did the Obama campaign generate resonant messages? (2) How did the Obama campaign use the new media in conveying its message?

Method

This study employs a qualitative approach based on a review of literature of the Obama campaign, and a textual and rhetorical analysis of campaign messages and the communication channels that were used to deliver them. This textual and rhetorical analysis approach includes an analysis of key speeches, documents, and

---

[16]Mark Urista, Qingwen Dong, and Kenneth Day, "Explaining Why Young Adults Use MySpace and Facebook through Uses and Gratifications Theory," paper presented at the annual meeting of the National Communication Association in San Diego, CA (2008).

[17]Jessica Dye, "Meet Generation C: Creatively Connecting through Content," *Econtent* (2007), http://www.econtentmag.com/Articles/Editorial/Feature/Meet-Generation-C-Creatively-Connecting-Through-Content-35942.htm

[18]Joe Erwin, "Brand Obama Was Built to Thrive on Social Networking," *Advertising Age* 79 (2008): 18; and Roy Mark, "Tech's So-So Showing in Politics," *eWeek Online*, http://www.eweek-digital .com/eweek/20080114_stnd/?pg=19#pg20, Jan 14, 2008, (accessed June 2, 2008); and Mike Shields, "Obama Cues Web Video as Tuesday Primaries Loom," *MediaWeek*, 18 (2008): 10.

e-mail messages from Obama and his campaign team. This analytical method provides a systematic account of what techniques the campaign used in making campaign messages resonant among the audience or receivers. In addition, the method helps provide a descriptive analysis of how the Obama campaign team used the new media to generate an effective communication campaign.

In terms of analytical procedures, this study first developed a theoretical framework for message analysis. Campaign messages were examined for their use of interpellation and constitutive rhetoric. Second, the authors analyzed campaign messages from various sources, which included e-mails sent to volunteers by the campaign headquarters, speeches by Obama, personal letters to potential voters and volunteers, books and newspapers, and other media outlets. The time line for the analysis of these messages was between the California Primary Election (February 5, 2008) and the Democratic National Convention in Denver (August 30, 2008). Third, the authors synthesized existing literature to provide an analysis of how the Obama campaign used various new media to its advantage in conveying its powerful messages. Fourth, the authors examined networking and other features of the Obama Web site to identify what abilities were made available and how these features were used. Finally, a synthesis of research findings and integrated analysis were used to answer the two research questions.

Results

The results showed that interpellation and constitutive rhetoric were widely used in the Obama campaign messages. These messages made the speaker or the sender turn into an individual siding with the other audience members. Results showed that Obama campaign messages tended to constantly use "you" and "we," which "constitute the listener as a member of the Obama's political activists and a member of a group including Obama himself."[19] The following examples illustrate that the pronoun of "we" is used frequently:

> Qingwen—
>
> A week from tomorrow could be the decisive day in this campaign. **We** started behind in the two biggest states that will vote on March 4th, Ohio and Texas, but as **we** spend time on the ground, **we** are gaining strength. But that's nothing new for **us**. **We** have started as the underdog in just about every state. And thanks to a growing movement of support from ordinary people across the country, **we** came from behind and won the last 11 contests in a row. **We** can do this again.
>
> (e-mail from Barack Obama, February 25, 2008)

---

[19]Day and Dong, "Constructing Presidential Candidate Ethos," 10.

Qingwen—

... **We** knew from the day **we** began this journey that the road would be long. And **we** knew what **we** were up against. **We** knew that the closer **we** got to the change **we** seek, the more **we**'d see of the politics **we**'re trying to end.... And together you and I are going to grow this movement to deliver that change in November.

Thank you,
Barack   (e-mail from Barack Obama, March 5, 2008)

These two e-mail messages from Obama display an obvious interpellation effect with the message receivers feeling that they and the message senders are in the same group sharing the same goal, same feelings, and same results. This constitutive rhetoric allows the speaker and the receiver to become "we" or "us." In the March 5 e-mail, "we" is used nine times in this short paragraph, the repetition of which is an effort to emphasize the resonant effect of the message. Similarly, the ending sentence of the February 25 e-mail in particular illustrates the weight of the interpellation effect: "We can do this again." This simple, brief, and straightforward sentence closely links the sender and receiver. The message with these pronouns constantly appearing in sentences generates a consistently resonant message effect.

Day and Dong observed that when the interpellation technique is used in political rhetoric, interpellation is easy to recognize when the pronoun "you" is employed.[20] In their study, the two authors also found that interpellation messages tend to display obvious "hailing," which allows the receivers/audience to feel not that they are on the receiving side of the message but that they share the position of the speaker/sender. The following example shows that the pronoun "you" is repeatedly used:

Qingwen—

... If **you**'re fed up with these kinds of tired attacks, **you** can do something about it right now.... **You** can see for **your**self exactly what kind of movement this is. When **you** make **your** donation, **you**'ll see the name and town of the person just like **you** who matched **your** gift. **You**'ll also see a note from them with their story and why they gave, if they chose to write one.

You'll double the impact of **your** donation if **you** make a matching fight right now. Will **you** help fight back now?

David
David Plouffe
Campaign Manager
Obama for America (e-mail from David Plouffe, April 14, 2008)

---

[20] Ibid.

The above e-mail message shows how the pronoun "you" is used. This application of "you" in rhetoric generates a strong empowerment effect on the side of the receiver/audience. This emphasis of the pronoun puts the receiver/audience in the position of the subject who joins the sender to become members of the same team, playing a determining role in shaping the discourse. It may be useful to compare the use of "you" and "we" in contrast in the e-mails attributed to John McCain. Consider the following e-mail sent by John McCain on September 26, 2008:

> My Friends,
>
> Tonight, Senator Obama and I participated in the first debate of the general election. It was a spirited debate and I believe the difference between our visions for America were made very clear.
>
> In a few hours, I will return to Washington to resume negotiations with the Administration and Congressional leaders from both parties to forge a bipartisan solution to our economic crisis. I am optimistic we will come to a final agreement soon. All voices must be represented in the final agreement, especially those of taxpayers and homeowners.
>
> We cannot be interested in who would get credit for finding a solution and who would be blamed if an agreement cannot be reached. We must put our country first to solve this economic crisis. Because in the end, that's what leaders do in times of crisis...

While we again find the use of "we" and "you," the e-mail fails to offer a constitutive rhetoric subject position. McCain holds himself and his vice presidential running mate apart from his audience. "We" is understood to be McCain and Palin. While the "you" is an interpellation, it hails an isolated individual being asked to help these leaders succeed. Even in the paragraph that is ambiguous as it begins "We cannot be interested ...," the possible reading that "we" refers to the speaker and the listener is undone by the closing, "Because in the end that is what leaders do ..." McCain stands above and apart from his supporters.

The interpellation effect may be presented in an indirect way with an emphasis on a larger area, joint efforts, common goals, and national interests shared among the senders and receivers. The following two e-mail messages illustrate these interpellation effects:

> Qingwen—
>
> From the beginning, our goal has been to **reach out to people** of all races, ages, and backgrounds and bring them back into the political process. We must use the rare opportunity we have right now to bring people together and make this **a better country for all**

Americans.... If we are going to change this country, the change must come from the bottom up. That means reaching out in **your community,** in **your circle of friends,** and even in **your family.**...

Michelle   (e-mail from Michelle Obama, May 1, 2008)

Qingwen—

My father called on Americans to ask what they could **do for their country**.

Those who answered his call built a movement that transformed our country and brought out the best in **our national character**. Barack Obama has **followed in that tradition**—dedicating himself to public service as **a community organizer** on the South Side of Chicago and then as a state and U.S. Senator. Now, Barack is calling on **a new generation of leaders** to get involved and help transform this country ...

Thank you.
Caroline Kennedy (e-mail from Caroline Kennedy, May 3, 2008)

This example of constitutive rhetoric is constructed through the use of the traditional networks or connections of which the audience is a part. Leff stated that in indirect interpellation, "tradition emerges as the primary resource for rhetorical invention."[21] The above e-mails use tradition and community as focal points of the appeals made, activating existing social networks within the audience's life and bringing them into the message, aligning the receiver with the sender without the obvious use of "you" or "we."

Tradition is called on quite strongly in these two e-mails as interpellation techniques. For instance, in the May 1 e-mail, we see a call to a traditional message of "making this a better country for everyone," which is echoed in Caroline Kennedy's e-mail, which recalls the famous words of her father, appealing to what has become a part of American history and tradition. Community is also used as an interpellation device to call the audience to action. Michelle Obama calls on the audience to reach out to their communities to provide support for Barack Obama, and Caroline Kennedy reminds the audience that Obama is a community member and leader. This call to community places Obama and the audience on equal footing, as people with similar ties and connections, and allows the receiver to identify more closely with him. Interestingly, it seems that only Obama himself directly interpellates his audience as "we" in a constitutive sense within e-mail messages. This suggests possible restraints on constitutive rhetoric.

---

[21]Leff, "Tradition and Agency," 135.

Interpellation can also be used with an assumed audience, not to gain supporters and members, but to build closeness and cohesion among existing group members. This use of interpellation can be seen in the following example:

Qingwen—

This night could not have happened 40 years ago—or even 4 years ago. And it could not have happened without **you. You** believed, against the odds, that change was possible. I felt **your** passion here tonight, and I know it was shared by millions of Americans who are building this movement all across the country. Tonight is **your** night. But tonight is just the beginning.... Thank **you** for everything **you**'ve done,

Barack   (e-mail from Barack Obama, August 28, 2008).

The above use of the "you" is slightly different from the second set of e-mail messages analyzed. The above messages use the interpellation technique of "you," but in a congratulatory sense. This form of interpellation is assuming an audience of "yous" who have helped Obama get as far as he did. This technique not only aligns the receiver with the sender, making them teammates, but also rewards the receiver for having been a part of the team, making this not a message of recruiting or gaining audiences, but recognizing an already engaged audience. For instance, Obama, in the August 28, 2008 message, uses past tense to describe the actions of the audience, such as *believed* and *felt*. This use of the past tense assumes an audience who have already done the actions mentioned, which is highlighted by the last line of the message, which thanks the audience for everything they've done.

The e-mail messages analyzed above all show the use of interpellation, some direct and some indirect. The use of "we" and "you" and tradition all constitute an audience and activate them to action in some way. This use of interpellation is what creates resonant messages. The resonance of these messages lies in the combination and alignment of the sender and receiver in the pronouns and the shared goals, concerns, traditions, and rewards. As the analysis of the e-mail messages shows, Obama and his campaign have used interpellation to build audiences through resonance, which helps answer the first research question, "How did the Obama campaign generate resonant messages?" The study finds that the use of "we" and "you" allows receivers to become part of the rhetoric and thus a part of the sender, making messages particularly resonant. The use of tradition and community allows the receiver to identify with the sender as a person similar to themselves, making indirect interpellation resonant in a different way. The use of assumed audiences allows the receiver to share in the rewards of the campaign, making the results of any action toward the sender more personal and sought-after, creating a third level of resonance.

The second research question is, "How did the Obama campaign use the new media in conveying its message?" It is useful to answer the question by examining features of the www.BarackObama.com Web site that differ from the official John McCain Web site, which over the campaign has come to copy an increasing number of features from the Obama site.

Providing a subscribed mailing list and multimedia messages from the candidate is not a unique feature of the Barack Obama official site, nor is the attempt to sign people up for assistance with the campaign. Current versions of both the Obama and McCain sites have splash pages (an initial page that precedes the home page of the site) that encourage people to provide their e-mail addresses. McCain's splash page even includes a video. Once on the home page of both Web sites, there are links to contribute, links to become involved with the campaign in particular locales, and links to recruit friends.

More social networking–oriented, the Obama site gives the opportunity to register and construct a MyBO (MyBarackObama) page, much like a MySpace or Facebook page, as a representation of oneself on the Internet. The page is more like MySpace than Facebook in that the person's actual identity need not be revealed, and there are options for hiding the page from public eye or searchability. As with other social-networking sites, one is provided with a blog and a messaging system to talk to other people who have registered on the site. The page serves as a convenient means to access any aspect of the campaign that particularly interests an individual at the same time as being a presentation of who he or she is. Here a person constructs his or her identity as an Obama supporter by making a statement of why he or she supports him. Groups to which one belongs that are associated with the campaign appear here, but a surprising number of other things as well—such as how much one has donated to the campaign and the campaign events one has created and/or participated in. One's status is mathematically calculated in a box based on how active one has been in the campaign. Points are scored for events hosted and attended, calls made, doors knocked, number of blog posts, donors to personal fundraising efforts, amount raised, and groups joined. The status score serves both as a reward for activity and as an incentive to become more active.

The McCain Web site, in an initial attempt to copy the Obama site, tried to implement similar features that were far less like Web 2.0. Once logged into the Web site, which was not easy to do, since a login seemed to be offered after a signup attempt recognized the user was already signed up, the user was given the option of going to a "dashboard" that provided scores on different activities as well as a link to create a McCainSpace page. The dashboard on the Obama site is the MyBO page, but on the McCain site, the social-networking page lies deeper in. After much criticism of the limitations of the original page, a much more Facebook/MySpace-like version of this page was released in August of 2008. As many others have reported, we had considerable difficulties even logging into the system.

On the Obama site, those with MyBO pages can search for other people by name or by zip code and build up a friends list as well as communicate with these friends internally on personal messages posted to the Web site. Thus, Obama supporters can "hook up" in their efforts and make friends as a part of their support. The Obama site is also well-connected to the Internet as a whole. The home page provides links for Obama pages on MySpace and Facebook, pictures on Flickr, videos on YouTube, Obama bookmarks on Digg, reports of what Obama is currently doing on Digg, and a list of social-networking sites by different ethnicity and other demographics. For Obama, all these sites reference each other back and forth.

Results indicated that new media use by the Obama campaign was the key to the campaign success. Based on a synthesis of results from existing literature (the Obama campaign team did not provide any interviews for the investigation), the study extracted the following four principles to explain the Obama campaign success in using new media.

1. *New media help convey resonant message.* The Obama campaign maximized the functions of the new media and took advantage of new media's unique features including being personal, interactive, instant, and convenient. These features or characteristics of the new media helped the Obama campaign convey the resonant messages in an effective way. As discussed earlier, Obama and his campaign members tended to send out their e-mail messages frequently to their volunteers and those who would like to learn about the campaign activities. These e-mail messages tended to be very personal (e.g., they addressed the individual by first name) and relational, as shown through the process of the interpellation or constitutive rhetoric. The interactive nature of the Internet offered volunteers and campaign workers an opportunity to communicate with each other. Unlike the traditional mass media, the Internet and cell phone allow a free interaction between senders and receivers, making it possible for generating resonant campaign messages. The instant nature of the Internet made campaign tasks much easier in delivering messages, exchanging messages and sharing feelings toward these messages. Convenience is another characteristic of the Internet that offered various ways for the campaign to convey Obama messages to millions of individuals conveniently. People could be reached through text messages, Web, e-mails, social-networking sites, and many others. These various media provided a convenient exchange between the sender and the receiver.

2. *Social networking use wins the hearts of young adults.* Many analysts believe that one of the key successes in the Obama campaign was its ability to take advantage of social-networking sites such as MySpace and Facebook. Social-networking site users could create a "homepage" that includes their favorite pictures, music, and other materials. These social networking sites have emerged as a global, dominant, online socialization network.

The Obama campaign made new media the core of its campaign. According to Kara Rowland, New Media Director, Joe Rospars played a critical role in moving the campaign forward over the Internet.[22] As a new media strategist with former Vermont governor Howard Dean's 2004 campaign, Rospars is widely viewed as the first successful master of the Internet. In order to take the lead in maximizing the social-networking sites' application, Obama recruited the co-founder of Facebook, Chris Hughes, to develop the centerpiece of the campaign machine.[23] Steve Schifferes observed that Obama's decision to run for President was indeed influenced by the fact that "a page created on MySpace by supporters not connected to any official campaign quickly signed up 160,000 supporters."[24] Studies showed that Obama was far more popular on Facebook than any other candidates including Hillary Clinton or John McCain.[25]

3. *Internet applications enhance fund raising at clicking speed.* Funds are fuel for the campaign machine. In today's presidential election, whoever has sufficient funds can continue the fight and have a likelihood of winning. Traditionally, a candidate had to travel to dozens of cities, taking hundreds of pictures, holding hundreds of hands, to raise even moderate funds. Today, the Internet has changed the fund-raising paradigm. Whoever can take advantage of the new media and craft a resonant message can raise funds at clicking speed.

Schifferes noted that the Internet tends to favor the outsider, providing an opportunity to mobilize support and money online.[26] During the early stages of the election, Obama only had limited name recognition, and his campaign started with inadequate funds. Talbot observed that Hillary Clinton's campaign depended more on conventional tactics like big fund-raisers, while Obama concentrated more on new media for gaining support and financial supports.[27] According to Talbot, Clinton's camp had about 20,000 volunteers working in Texas, while more than 100,000 Texans had registered for social-networking pages on MyBO, a Facebook-like part of the official Obama Web site at www.BarackObama.com.[28] Talbot showed that MyBO and the rest of the Obama site were very successful in raising funds for the campaign, setting a record in the American politics by raising $55 million in donations for

---

[22]Kara Rowland, "High-Tech Campaign Media Race Favors Obama," *Washington Post*, p. 2, July 1, 2008.

[23]David Talbot, "How Obama Really Did It: Social Technology Helped Bring Him to the Brink of the Presidency," *Technology Review*, 111 (2008): 78–83.

[24]Steve Schifferes, "Internet Key to Obama Victories," BBC News, http://news.bbc.co.uk/go/pr/fr/-/1/hi/technology/7412045.stm (accessed June 12, 2008).

[25]Ibid.

[26]Ibid.

[27]Talbot, "How Obama Really Did It," 2008.

[28]Ibid.

a single month. On the contrary, funding shortages forced Clinton to borrow her own funds and limited her campaign activities. Schifferes noted that some observers anticipated that "Mr. Obama will raise $1 billion online during the 2008 campaign, 12 times as much as John Kerry raised through online fund-raising in 2004."

4. *Taking advantage of various features and functions of new media generates the best campaign effects.* Internet use was not new to the 2008 election. However, the success of the Obama campaign was accomplished by taking advantage of each new Internet-based medium to use it to its highest benefits. The Obama campaign tried to use as many of these new Internet-based media as possible since these media tended to be used by those who supported the Obama campaign and tend to cost less—or nothing. These new media included wikis (a collection of Web pages to help create collaborative Web sites), MySpace and Facebook, Web sites, e-mail, blogging, microblogging site Twitter, and text messages.

The Obama campaign found ways to use each medium to its best result. For instance, when Obama announced his choice for vice president, the campaign team asked individuals to sign up to receive e-mail or text messages from the campaign. By doing this, the campaign had access to thousands of communication numbers that were used by the campaign to mobilize ground forces during Election Day. Rowland explained that using text messaging was critical in the election because the general population tended to stop using landline telephones.

Not everyone could donate to the campaign, although it must be noted that the Obama site invited even small donations. The Obama campaign tended to use innovative ways to make sure that everyone had a chance to do something to move the campaign forward. Throughout the election, the Obama team asked its volunteers to call their neighbors and potential voters in other states (battlegrounds such as Ohio, Texas, and Pennsylvania) to persuade those people to vote for Obama. Most of the time, the Obama campaign asked people to take twenty telephone numbers and a script to call people to persuade people to vote for Obama. This involved more people in the election process who were emboldened to put "a foot in the door." These people become a "ground-war" force to win the victory/election.

In summary, this study provides some interesting answers to the two proposed research questions. Results indicate that the Obama campaign successfully created resonant messages through an interpellation process. This constitutive rhetoric empowered individuals who took the same subject position to view the issues, making the campaign messages very effective and persuasive. The results also showed that the Obama campaign successfully used new media to convey its resonant messages because of unique characteristics including personal, interactive, instant and convenient. The new media played a critical role in fund-raising, mobilizing people, and getting people engaged.

Discussion

We have discussed and observed ways in which the presidential campaign of Barack Obama harnessed the media of the Internet and used an effective rhetorical strategy in activating a large base of donors and campaign volunteers. Through using not only e-mails but also the social-networking capabilities of the Internet, a new and very effective set of campaign techniques was developed. Constitutive rhetoric through interpellation was shown to be a consistent mobilizing technique in the messages produced by the campaign.

It would seem likely that the Obama campaign has profoundly changed political campaigning. Although the McCain campaign's efforts to imitate some of the new techniques of the Obama campaign were clumsy, their efforts suggest that these techniques will become common in future campaigns.

Our qualitative assessment of the techniques of the campaign would benefit from more empirically based ethnographic or social-science studies that would attempt to demonstrate effects on those exposed to campaign messages or who became involved in the campaign. It may well be that younger individuals were more influenced by social-networking campaigning since they are more likely to be using these features on the Internet.

Greater involvement of individuals in the political process would seem quite consistent with most visions of democracy. Whether this will benefit the political process in the long term has yet to be seen.

Beyond the Candidate: Obama, YouTube, and (My) Asian-ness

Konrad Ng

Introduction

In August 2008, NPR and ABC political analyst Cokie Roberts criticized then–Democratic presidential candidate Barack Obama, for choosing to vacation in Hawaii, the state of his birth and where his late grandmother and other relatives lived. Roberts argued that Obama should have chosen to vacation in Myrtle Beach, South Carolina, stating, "I know Hawaii is a state, but it has the look of him going off to some sort of foreign, exotic place."[1] The implication, as *New York Times* editorial writer Lawrence Downes noted, was that "Hawaii is elitist while South Carolina is not, and that Mr. Obama was foolishly squandering votes by walking on the wrong beach in the wrong state."[2] Indeed, Roberts's comments suggest that Hawaii, a state that is predominantly Asian, Pacific Islander, and Native Hawaiian in history, culture, and population, is dissonant with mainstream America and that a trip to Hawaii would be a mistake for the first African-American Democratic presidential nominee. I find this episode interesting for its interarticulation of elitism, exoticism, race, and the meaning of American-ness. Throughout the campaign and even into his presidency, Obama faced charges of elitism[3]

---

[1]"Cokie Roberts on Obama's Vacation: 'I Know His Grandmother Lives in Hawaii and I Know Hawaii Is a State,' But It Looks 'Foreign, Exotic,'" *Media Matters for America*, August 10, 2008, http://mediamatters.org/mmtv/200808100001 (accessed August 10, 2008) and "Roberts Again Criticizes Obama for 'Exotic' Trip Home to Hawaii," *Media Matters for America*, August 11, 2008, http://mediamatters.org/research/200808110177 (accessed August 11, 2008).

[2]Lawrence Downes, "A Few Words about Hawaii, U.S.A.," *New York Times*, August 13, 2008, http://theboard.blogs.nytimes.com/2008/08/13/a-few-words-about-hawaii-usa (accessed August 13, 2008).

[3]See "Matthews: Does Obama 'Connect Connect with Regular People' or just African-Americans and College Grads?," *Media Matters for America*, April 2, 2008, http://mediamatters.org/research/200804020001 (accessed April 2, 2008) and "Hardball? Matthews Asked McCain: '[W]e've Had Enough Softball, Senator. ... Is Barack Obama an Elitist?'" *Media Matters for America*, April 15, 2008, http://mediamatters.org/research/200804150008 (accessed April 15, 2008).

and questions about his citizenship. Pundits and political opponents alike questioned his ability to connect with everyday Americans. Obama was called the choice of "wine drinkers," a vernacular description for educated and affluent voters that is used in opposition to "beer drinkers," working-class, less-educated, and less-affluent voters.[4] The claims that Obama was elitist and foreign locate Obama's subjectivity on familiar ground for the meaning of Asian America and the racialization of Asian bodies. Obama's biography, which includes relatives of Asian descent and is plotted through predominantly Asian locales such as Hawaii and Indonesia, and Ivy League schools such as Columbia and Harvard, resonates with the stereotype that haunts the meaning of Asian bodies in America: the myth of the model minority. Far from being a benign stereotype, the racialization of Asian bodies as the model minority holds power over Asian lives, particularly in how the meaning of Asian bodies has been used as a foil for American identity. One can point to the critical work of Lisa Lowe,[5] David Palumbo-Liu,[6] Robert Lee,[7] or Michael Omi[8] to demonstrate how the meaning of Asian America has been a powerful organizing principle to arrange the economic, ideological, domestic, and foreign affairs of the nation-state. Lowe contends that the meaning of American citizenship

> has been defined over [and] against the Asian *immigrant*, legally, economically, and culturally. These definitions have cast Asian immigrants both as persons and populations to be integrated into

---

In May 2009, political commentators Sean Hannity, Laura Ingraham, and Mark Steyn criticized President Obama for being an elitist because he ordered a burger with "spicy mustard" or "Dijon mustard." Please see "Dijon Derangement Syndrome: Conservative Media Attack Obama for Burger Order," *Media Matters for America*, May 7, 2009, http://mediamatters.org/research/200905070031 (accessed May 7, 2009).

[4]See "Chicago Tribune Repeated Obama-Arugula Falsehood, Used Anecdotes to Cast Obama as 'Wine-Track,'" *Media Matters for America*, September 24, 2007, http://mediamatters.org/research/200709240012 (accessed September 24, 2007) and Gail Collins, "Pinochle Politics," *New York Times*, April 10, 2008, http://www.nytimes.com/2008/04/10/opinion/10collins.html (accessed April 10, 2008).

[5]Lisa Lowe, *Immigrant Acts: On Asian American Cultural Politics* (Durham, NC: Duke University Press, 1996).

[6]David Palumbo-Liu, *Asian/American: Historical Crossings of a Racial Frontier* (Palo Alto, CA: Stanford University Press, 1999).

[7]Robert G. Lee, *Orientals: Asian Americans in Popular Culture* (Philadelphia: Temple University Press, 1999).

[8]Michael Omi, *Racial Formation in the United States: From the 1960s to the 1990s* (New York: Routledge, 1994).

the national political sphere and as the contradictory, confusing, unintelligible elements to be marginalized and returned to their alien origins.[9]

Lee argues that images in print, music, and film have depicted Asians in America, "immigrant and native-born, [as] ... a race of aliens."[10] As Michael Omi and Taeku Lee state, "Asian Americans are collectively regarded as the symbolic 'alien' and remain 'perpetual foreigners' despite the very long and continued presence of Asians in America."[11] Palumbo-Liu writes that the notion of Asian Americans as the "model minority" has distinguished Asians as "viable objects for admiration [which is] ... of course a specific mode of containment."[12] The model minority myth effaces the heterogeneity of Asian people, and the linking of achievement to a homogenous concept of race establishes a regulative ideal for discerning cultural authenticity and the "innate" character of Asian communities. The model minority myth has been "deployed to contain and divert civil rights policymaking, to neutralize activism, and to promote a laissez-faire domestic urban policy."[13] That is, the association of Asians as the model minority equates Asian-ness with apathy by suggesting that ideal minorities and immigrants assimilate without cultural and political commotion. Consequently, Asian American concerns can be neglected in political discourse, and the community can be used to disavow the experience, specificity, and activism of other minorities and their concerns. In *Asian American Politics*, political scientists Andrew Aoki and Okiyoshi Takeda note that the politics of recognition and representation have become part of the Asian American political agenda. They contend that "control over one's identity is an important prerequisite for political inclusion and opportunity. Stereotypes have deep roots ... [and] the struggle to eliminate them is an important part of Asian American battle for equality and acceptance."[14] During the 2008 presidential election, the anemic representation of Asian Americans in political and cultural discourse prompted Democratic members of Congress to write letters to Jonathan Klein, president

---

[9]Lowe, *Immigrant Acts*, 4.

[10]Lee, *Orientals*, xi.

[11]Michael Omi and Taeku Lee, "Barack Like Me: Our First Asian American President," *Obama Reflections: From Election Day to Presidency: Social Justice Thought Leaders Speak Out* (Columbus, Ohio State University, Kirwan Institute for the Study of Race and Ethnicity, 2009), 45.

[12]Palumbo-Liu, *Asian/American*, 4.

[13]Ibid., 172.

[14]Andrew L. Aoki and Okiyoshi Takeda, *Asian American Politics* (Malden, : Polity Press, 2008), 154.

of CNN,[15] and Phil Griffin, executive-in-charge at MSNBC,[16] criticizing each network's poor coverage of Asian American and Pacific Islander voters and issues in relation to other constituencies. The letters also affirmed the importance of Asian American and Pacific Islander participation in the political process and the media's responsibility in "recognizing or ignoring these voices."[17] Scholars, critics, and supporters in the Asian American community highlighted Obama's "Asian American-ness" as a unique point of connection. In a reprise of African-American author and poet Toni Morrison's claim that Bill Clinton was "the first black president,"[18] Asian popular culture scholar Jeff Yang mused that "the tropes that surround and define Obama can just as easily be read as those of another community entirely.... Could it be that our true first black president might also be our first Asian American president?"[19] Ethnic studies scholar Michael Omi and political scientist Taeku Lee argued that Obama was the first Asian American president in how his "life experiences have been fundamentally shaped in close association with Asians and Asian Americans."[20] The mistaken belief that Obama was too elite and foreign to appeal to mainstream America "sound[ed] a lot like the conflicted, ambiguous, and unsettled racial position of Asian Americans."[21] As such, in what ways did "model minority" Obama affect the cultural politics of communities beyond black and white? What forms of support did Obama engender among America's "model minority"?

This chapter addresses these questions by studying the new media works created by Obama's grassroots Asian American supporters. I contend that Obama's candidacy motivated these people to engage the representation of race

---

[15]"Members of Congress Write to Jonathan Klein, CNN President," *The Democratic Party*, February 15, 2008, http://www.democrats.org/a/2008/02/members_of_cong_1.php (accessed February 15, 2008).

[16]"Members of Congress Write to Phil Griffin, Executive-in-Charge, MSNBC," *The Democratic Party*, February 15, 2008, http://www.democrats.org/a/2008/02/members_of_cong_2.php (accessed February 15, 2008).

[17]Ibid.

[18]Toni Morrison, "Comment," *New Yorker*, October 5, 1998, http://www.newyorker.com/archive/1998/10/05/1998_10_05_031_TNY_LIBRY_000016504 (accessed July 31, 2008).

[19]Jeff Yang, "Could Obama Be the First Asian American President?" *SFGate*, July 30, 2008, http://www.sfgate.com/cgi-bin/article.cgi?f=/g/a/2008/07/30/apop.DTL (accessed July 30, 2008). Others have since made the same claim: June Shih, a former Whitehouse speechwriter for the Clintons, and news agency *Agence France-Presse* have since made the same claim: June Shih, "Barack Obama—America's First Asian American President?," *Arcof72.com*, January 30, 2009, http://arcof72.com/2009/01/30/barack-obama-americas-first-asian-american-president/(accessed February 1, 2009); Shaun Tandon, "Obama the First Asian American President?," *Agence France-Presse*, April 27, 2009, http://news.yahoo.com/s/afp/20090427/pl_afp/uspoliticsobama100daysasia (accessed April 27, 2009).

[20]Omi and Lee, "Barack Like Me," 44.

[21]Ibid., 45.

in their campaigning for Obama, and this aim reveals the emergence of campaign strategies that reflect a set of objectives beyond rallying around the candidate. Asian American supporters treated cultural representation and political engagement as a synonymous practice in their repositioning of Asian-ness in the American political and cultural imaginary. I explore this critical intersection of race, culture, and politics by examining YouTube videos. For these supporters, YouTube was an opportune way to support Obama and empower Asian American representation. As Henry Jenkins writes about the new media landscape in *Convergence Culture: When Old and New Media Collide*: "As average citizens acquire the ability to meaningfully impact the flow of ideas, these new forms of participatory culture change how we see ourselves ... and how we see our society."[22] With YouTube, grassroots Asian American Obama supporters realized that they could advance support for Obama while simultaneously critiquing Asian American stereotypes. To this end, I focus on three forms of Asian American YouTube engagement: videos that challenged existing representations of Asian-ness; videos that repurposed existing Obama campaign literature to recognize a diverse Asian electorate; and videos with imagery that associated Asian Americans with political agency.

Asian-ness as Polycultural Agency: "La Bamba Obama"

Posted on February 18, 2008, *La Bamba Obama*[23] is a two-minute-forty-seven-second video that features a middle-aged Asian male performing a musical parody of Ritchie Valens's iconic song *La Bamba*. The man exchanges the lyrics of the original song with Spanish words of support for Obama. Though not self-evident, the producer and performer of the video is Bill Ong Hing, a noted professor of law and Asian American studies at the University of California, Davis. *La Bamba Obama* is emblematic of YouTube's "do-it-yourself" (DIY) apparatus. That is, the "*mise-en-scène*" or background—props, actors, acting, costuming, and lighting—of the video is simple: An Asian man wears a "Barack and Roll" T-shirt with an Obama button and sings in Spanish while playing his guitar. There is an "Obama 08" sign hanging in the background. The lighting and sound are basic, using, it appears, natural lighting and sound without any special effects. The cinematography is equally basic. The main character is framed in a medium shot, there is no camera movement, and much of the *mise-en-scène* is in focus.

---

[22]Henry Jenkins, *Convergence Culture: Where Old and New Media Collide* (New York: New York University Press, 2006), 279.

[23]billysoohoo, "La Bamba Obama," *YouTube*, http://www.youtube.com/watch?v=iTtd5n03-FY (accessed February 18, 2008).

In terms of editing, the video is a long take—that is, a continuous scene without cuts. While straightforward, the choice of a long take stands out in how it allows the viewer to make connections between the elements of representation at work in the video. French film theorist Andre Bazin suggests that the long take, when employed in conjunction with deep focus (where the entirety of a frame remains in focus), allows the viewer to let his or her attention wander the space of the scene. As the action unfolds, the meaning of the scene becomes open to interpretation as the viewer must make his or her own sense of the on-screen action and the meaning of the sequence. Bazin states that a long take "affects the relationships of the minds of the spectators to the image, and in consequence it influences the interpretation of the spectacle. … [I]t implies, consequently, both a more active mental attitude on the part of the spectator and a more positive contribution on his part to the action in progress."[24] In *La Bamba Obama*, the long take and relative deep focus of the video prompts viewers to contemplate the representations within and consider how the video is not a simple online spectacle. First, *La Bamba Obama* reveals that Hing's commitment to Obama is serious. While the video may feel lighthearted because of its novelty, Hing's performance is sustained, suggesting that the main purpose of the video is not to entertain per se, but to express his support for Obama. In other words, Hing wants his performance and Asian-ness associated with political agency. Second, Hing's video expresses a polycultural attitude towards Asian cultural identity. By "polycultural," I refer to the argument of cultural theorist Vijay Prashad[25] that identity can be understood as a composition of congruent cultural, political, and ideological lineages. Rather than see identities develop in isolation of each other, a polycultural perspective looks for family resemblances between cultural identities and instances of collaboration. *La Bamba Obama* is a polycultural work. Hing sings, in Spanish, one of the few popular songs of American rock-and-roll that is not sung in English. By making these choices, Hing suggests that Asian American identity is congruent with Latino-American identity. Hing interarticulates his Asian-ness with Latino-ness to offer a moment of collaboration and civic engagement. The fact that his video was posted to the apparatus of YouTube means that *La Bamba Obama* will be viewed, circulated, and discussed. In this sense, the video is simultaneously a rallying point for Obama and an alternative point of discussion for the meaning of Asian-ness and American-ness.

---

[24]Andrew Bazin, "The Evolution of the Language of Cinema," in *Film Theory and Criticism*, 6th ed., ed. Leo Braudy and Marshall Cohen (New York: Oxford University Press, 2004), 49.

[25]Vinjay Prasad, *Everybody Was Kung Fu Fighting: Afro-Asian Connections and the Myth of Cultural Purity* (Boston: Beacon Press, 2001).

Asian-ness as Political Agency and Cultural Representation: Captioned Media for Obama

Captioned for Obama[26] is a YouTube channel created by Captioned Media for Obama, a grassroots group of Obama supporters and organizers. The channel features Obama campaign videos that have been captioned in English, Chinese, Korean, Vietnamese, Japanese, and Spanish. The videos were produced by Captioned Media for Obama to help the Obama campaign reach voters whose first language was not English as well as those voters who are hearing-impaired. Instead of creating new videos, Captioned Media for Obama repurposed existing campaign new-media content to address specific constituencies and provide more campaign resources for use by other grassroots supporters. The group ripped key campaign videos like biographies, major speeches, interviews, and debates to translate and caption. The translations and captioning attempted to address the heterogeneity of Asian languages spoken in America while remaining faithful to the original text.

The campaign's Obama introduction video, which features Obama's defining speech at the 2004 Democratic National Convention, was captioned in Chinese,[27] Vietnamese,[28] and Korean.[29] The Obama biography video featuring Michelle Obama was also captioned in Chinese,[30] Korean,[31] and Vietnamese.[32] The campaign biography video featuring Obama's younger sister, Maya Soetoro-Ng, was captioned in Chinese[33] and Vietnamese.[34] While the videos were available from Captioned Media for Obama, both the video's translator and

---

[26]captionedforobama, *YouTube*, http://www.youtube.com/user/captionedforobama (accessed March 31, 2008).

[27]captionedforobama, "Barack Obama Intro in Traditional Chinese," *YouTube*, http://www.youtube.com/watch?v=jE-AFTmHL4I (accessed April 2, 2008).

[28]captionedforobama, "Barack Obama Intro in Vietnamese," *YouTube*, http://www.youtube.com/watch?v=D-BWNzGQ4D8 (accessed April 2, 2008).

[29]captionedforobama, "Barack Obama Intro in Korean," *YouTube*, http://www.youtube.com/watch?v=LF4s_5eNq5Q (accessed April 3, 2008).

[30]captionedforobama, "Michelle Obama Introduction—With Chinese Subtitles," *YouTube*, http://www.youtube.com/watch?v=9L7oBLOyGFA (accessed April 2, 2008).

[31]captionedforobama, "Michelle Obama with Korean subtitles," *YouTube*, http://www.youtube.com/watch?v=RqaOQNWvpH0 (accessed April 3, 2008).

[32]captionedforobama, "Michelle Obama in Vietnamese," *YouTube*, http://www.youtube.com/watch?v=l0wsMjRUTx4 (accessed April 3, 2008).

[33]captionedforobama, "Maya Ng-Soetoro in Chinese. Barack Obama's Half Sister," *YouTube*, http://www.youtube.com/watch?v=p1wiyrwBE_Y (accessed April 5, 2008).

[34]captionedforobama, "Maya Ng-Soetoro in Vietnamese. Barack Obama's Half Sister," *YouTube*, http://www.youtube.com/watch?v=ElJ6-ZNN3xk (accessed April 5, 2008).

Captioned Media for Obama went uncredited; subtitles were the only element added to the videos. As such, the captioned material could spread as if it came directly from the campaign. By anonymously captioning videos in multiple Asian languages, Captioned Media for Obama crafted the image that Obama recognized and valued a culturally heterogeneous portrait of Asian America. Consider that the grassroots Asian American supporters of John McCain did not produce as many captioned YouTube videos as Captioned Media for Obama. The McCain Asian American grassroots group, Asian Pacific Americans for Change (APA4McCain),[35] created a YouTube channel two days before the general election and offered nine videos of which two were official McCain campaign videos captioned in Vietnamese[36] and Chinese.[37] At the same point in the election, Captioned Media for Obama offered eighty-seven captioned videos. The combined effect of Captioned Media for Obama's work was to associate Asian-ness with political importance and agency; their videos supported Obama's candidacy and in the process of doing so, the repurposed imagery offered an alternative representation and valuation of Asian-ness in America.

Asian-ness as Political Agency and Cultural Representation: United for Obama

United for Obama[38] is a coalition of Obama grassroots supporters from across the country. Many of the group's members include Asian American filmmakers like Eric Byler (*Charlotte Sometimes*, 2003; *Americanese*, 2006), Annabel Park (*9500 Liberty*, 2009), Warren Fu (music-video director and animator), and Mora Stephens (*Conventioneers*, 2005), among others. These filmmakers formed United for Obama to use their skills and networks to "amplify Obama's message on YouTube and offer visible, tangible evidence that this movement [to support Obama] is real and spreading."[39] As Asian American filmmakers, however, their experience in the entertainment industry provided an additional purpose to their work; they are part of an industry where the meaning of Asian

---

[35]Asian Pacific Americans for Change, *YouTube*, http://www.youtube.com/user/APA4McCain (accessed November 2, 2008).

[36]APA4McCain, "Spread the Wealth—Vietnamese version," *YouTube*, http://www.youtube.com/watch?v=5tdLcg6eLJE (accessed November 2, 2008).

[37]APA4McCain, "IAmJoe—Subtitled,"*YouTube*,http://www.youtube.com/watch?v=LlnNf3IpaOY (accessed November 2, 2008).

[38]United for Obama, *YouTube*, http://www.YouTube.com/user/UnitedForObama (accessed January 16, 2008).

[39]United for Obama, *YouTube*, http://www.YouTube.com/user/UnitedForObama (accessed January 16, 2008).

America is contested cultural terrain. That is, Asian identity is defined in and against the normative representations and narrative and aesthetic form of American cinema. Film theorist Peter Feng aptly describes this tension for Asian American film and filmmakers as an attitude of "ambivalent dis-identification." For Feng, ambivalent dis-identification is to be "engaged in a project of signifying on cinematic convention, using cinema to critique cinema, using a mode of communication to convey messages that subvert that mode,"[40] as a way to fill gaps in American history.

Asian American cultural production often highlights the exclusion and misrepresentation of Asian America in the medium of its production. Many of the thirty-one videos by United for Obama embodied this practice. Through aesthetic and narrative choices, the group's YouTube videos expressed support for Obama while associating Asian-ness with political agency and cultural presence. A particular set of videos stands out: the videos of an Asian American actor discussing why the Asian American community supports Obama and how Obama has motivated Asian Americans to be active in politics in spite of the cultural baggage to be otherwise.

In "Kelly Hu, Asian Americans for Barack Obama,"[41] actress Kelly Hu (*Martial Law*, 1998–2000; *The Scorpion King*, 2002; *Undoing*, 2006; *Americanese*, 2006; *Shanghai Kiss*, 2007) hosts an informal Asian American roundtable discussion about the reasons why the participants supported Obama and wanted to become more involved in the political process. Hu opens the video by explaining why her involvement in the election is tied to increasing Asian American participation. She states,

> I think the reason why I decided to get so involved this year in supporting a particular candidate is because I felt that what I did in the last election was just not enough, trying to get Asian Americans to get out and vote, was just not enough.... Obama living and growing up in Hawaii has lived amongst Asian people for such a long time, that I think he really understands us.[42]

Similarly, in "Kal Penn (Harold and Kumar) for Obama,"[43] United for Obama member Annabel Park interviews actor Kal Penn (*Harold and Kumar Go to White Castle*, 2004; *The Namesake*, 2007) at an Obama rally held before

---

[40]Peter X. Feng, *Identities in Motion: Asian American Film and Video* (Durham, NC: Duke University Press, 2002), 14–15.

[41]United for Obama, "Kelly Hu, Asian Americans for Barack Obama," *YouTube*, http://www.youtube.com/watch?v=IW_AXO8wCj0 (accessed January 16 2008).

[42]Ibid.

[43]United for Obama, "Kal Penn (Harold and Kumar) for Obama," *YouTube*, http://www.youtube.com/watch?v=yJvw1-oZCNM (accessed January 16, 2008).

the January 15, 2008, Democratic candidates' debate in Las Vegas, Nevada. Penn begins the video by discussing his feelings toward partisan politics and how he "never campaigned with anyone before"[44] meeting Obama. Penn praises Obama's character and discusses how Obama has solicited feelings of inclusion and support from minority communities. Throughout Penn's interview, cutaway shots of Asian American supporters engaging in the rally are included in the video. With Penn playing the role of community advocate against a backdrop of political activity featuring Asian Americans in action, the video comes together as a strong display of Asian representation and political engagement. In "Yul Kwon with Asian Americans for Barack Obama,"[45] Yul Kwon, the winner of *Survivor: Cook Islands* (2006), reports from a San Francisco Obama canvassing station that was organized by Asian Americans. In the video, Kwon wants "to chart what's going on in the Asian American youth political movement."[46] Kwon interviews several Asian Americans who discuss how Obama's narrative and vision resonates with their life and politics. The video explores why Asian American youth may feel excluded from the political process and how Obama makes Asian American supporters feel empowered as cultural and political citizens. At the end of video, Kwon concludes,

> … [A]nd we hear some of the same common themes from each one of them [the supporters]. They believe that Obama is a unifier. They believe that he has the background, and especially the multiethnic background, to really relate to a lot of different minorities. They believe that he has a message of hope and inspiration that really resonates with people who have historically not been part of the political process and have usually felt disenchanted with the partisan politics of the past. So, for a lot of APAs [Asian Pacific Americans] in this community, it appears that Barack Obama is someone they see as a symbol of hope and someone who can represent their voices within the national debate, and for this country.[47]

In "Ken Leung (Rush Hour, X-Men 3) for Barack Obama,"[48] actor Ken Leung (*Rush Hour*, 1998; *X-Men: The Last Stand*, 2006; *Shanghai Kiss*, 2007) offers a personal testimony about how Obama compels him to be political in a

---

[44]Ibid.

[45]United for Obama, "Yul Kwon with Asian Americans for Barack Obama," *YouTube*, http://www.youtube.com/watch?v=PZ8-s8jf_pc (accessed January 27, 2008).

[46]Ibid.

[47]Ibid.

[48]United for Obama, "Ken Leung (Rush Hour, X-Men 3) for Barack Obama," *YouTube*, http://www.youtube.com/watch?v=2LCde5gFNDA (accessed February 5, 2008).

way that goes against type. Early in the six-minute-forty-seven-second video, which is composed of long takes and tracking shots, Leung states,

> I'm trying to learn how to—how to express myself, politically, and he's moved me to do that and I think that is the biggest impact he has had on me so far. Where he has activated this part of me that has not really existed before. ... You know, I was raised with—my parents are part of a generation that never felt that they were in a position to embrace or own the process, you know, they came to America, just tried to do the best they can and stay to themselves.[49]

Leung's testimony captures the general narrative thread that runs throughout the videos: an Asian American popular culture figure discusses the importance of political engagement as a way to support Obama and improve Asian American representation while Asian Americans are background figures participating in political activities.

In terms of aesthetics, members of United for Obama have made films with the high production values of Hollywood studio films, yet many of the YouTube works embraced the platform's DIY and *cinéma vérité* documentary-style aesthetics. The filmmakers in United for Obama chose "realist" aesthetic techniques that presented the on-screen action as natural grassroots activity as opposed to staged action. The videos were composed of long takes and handheld camera movements to convey the sense that the action was live and unrehearsed. Each video was shot on location and used the available lighting to capture the reality of moment. Each video did not diminish the interruptions of ambient sound so that viewers could also feel the moment. This realist aesthetic prompts viewers to see Obama's grassroots Asian supporters and their campaign activities as authentic, organic, and earnest, and as such, Asian bodies are displayed as natural political agents. Moreover, the DIY style of the videos make a critical distinction between Hollywood cinema, which has misrepresented and underrepresented Asian Americans, and a real life representation and experience of Asian America.

Conclusion

This chapter captures just some of the novel forms of political culture that emerged in support of Obama. Asian American creative expressions for Obama demonstrated a new sense of Asian American film political and cultural engagement that challenged the predominant configuration of elitism, exoticism, and race in the discourse of the model minority. These YouTube

---

[49]Ibid.

expressions offered polycultural stances, repurposed existing Obama campaign materials to value a diverse Asian American electorate, and presented imagery that associated the meaning of Asian America with political agency and cultural presence. Obama and the new-media spirit of his campaign became the black–Asian vehicle for treating cultural representation and political engagement as synonymous practices, and by doing so, presented a new and critical sense of Asian America. It may be tempting to see invigorated Asian American political participation as merely an extension of good citizenship—in other words, a continuation of the model minority—but what these grassroots YouTube activities accomplish is a repositioning of elitism and race in the meaning of American identity. Rather than see the tropes of Asian-ness as elite, foreign, exotic, and thus out of touch with American values, as Cokie Roberts did, the argument is that Asian-ness is visible, active, and central to the American experience. The study of these fresh articulations of political and cultural engagement expressed on behalf of Asian America reveal how new-media technologies are enabling the formation of increasingly more complex political practices and resetting the terms of debate on the status of race in America.

Section III: Identities

Post-Soul President:
Dreams from My Father
and the Post-Soul Aesthetic

Bertram D. Ashe

Three o'clock in the morning. The moon-washed streets empty, the growl of a car picking up speed down a distant road. The revelers would be tucked away by now, paired off or alone, in deep, beer-heavy sleep, Hasan at his new lady's place—don't stay up, he had said with a wink. And now just the two of us to wait for the sunrise, me and Billie Holiday, her voice warbling through the darkened room, reaching toward me like a lover.[1]

—Barak Obama, Dreams from My Father

A twenty-year-old Barack Obama sits alone in the darkness of the small hours, as he and Lady Day "wait for the sunrise." The party is over, his roommate and the guests have gone, and as chapter 5 of *Dreams from My Father* opens, Obama recalls the evening as one in which he not only surveys his postparty house, but also looks critically at his life. One of the things on which he's reflecting is his relationship with Regina, a young student who had angrily left the party earlier. But in a more expansive way, he's also likely ruminating on three additional Occidental College students: Joyce, Tim, and Marcus. Chapter 5 is the culmination of the period of his life I'm calling "The Barry Era," and it focuses intently on these students' sometimes vexed and sometimes voluntary relationship with the black community.

The last section of the chapter begins, "I rose from the couch and opened my front door, the pent-up smoke trailing me out of the room like a spirit. Up above, the moon had slipped out of sight, only its glow still visible along the rim of high clouds. The sky had begun to lighten; the air tasted of dew."[2] A page and a half later, Obama ends the chapter by circling back to Billie Holiday: "For a few minutes more I sat still in my doorway, watching the sun glide into place, thinking about the call to Regina I'd be making that day. Behind

---

[1]Barack Obama, *Dreams from My Father: A Story of Race and Inheritance* (New York: Three Rivers Press, 2004), 92.

[2]Ibid., 110.

me, Billie was on her last song. I picked up the refrain, humming a few bars. Her voice sounded different to me now. Beneath the layers of hurt, beneath the ragged laughter, I heard a willingness to endure. Endure—and make music that wasn't there before."[3]

The entire chapter, then, takes place in a thought bubble hovering above Barry's head as he sits and thinks. That early morning, he's about contemplation, about assessment, and even though the chapter informs and explains to his reader his life at Occidental College and his views on everything from the difference between being ambitious and being a "good-time Charlie,"[4] to the difference between being "educated" and being "trained,"[5] the surface-level narrative action for the balance of the chapter is this: twenty-year-old college student sits alone in the late-night/early-morning hours, thinking about his life. It is Barack Obama, the writer, however, who actually fills the narrative space with his own mature retrospective of what young Barry must have been thinking in that moment. It's true that he kept a journal,[6] and it's certain that he consulted it, but the wisdom and wide-ranging knowledge that he brings to this crucial chapter belies that of the deepest and most self-aware twenty-year-old. And anyway, Barry Obama didn't write *Dreams from My Father*—Barack Obama did. Early in chapter 6, having transferred to Columbia University, Obama will sharply correct his new New York roommate: Instead of answering to "Barry," he will insist on "Barack."[7] In a narrative that widely tracks Obama's search for self, chapter 5 focuses as narrowly as possible on his attempt to find a stable, workable black identity.

I use the words "black identity" advisedly. Genetically, of course, Barack Obama is biracial. By no means am I blithely ignoring this fact. But the familiarity of his identity journey, a journey made by countless post-civil-rights-movement blacks who, like Obama, were born or came of age after the civil rights movement, suggests that while his biracial status was an important factor in his quest for identity, the search itself is one that is less about being biracial and more about being bicultural. Here's the way Obama put it early in that fifth chapter: "Grow up in Compton and survival becomes a revolutionary act. You get to college and your family is still back there rooting for you. They're happy to see you escape; there's no question of betrayal. But I hadn't grown up in Compton, or Watts. I had nothing to escape from except my inner doubt.

---

[3]Ibid., 112.

[4]Ibid., 95.

[5]Ibid., 97.

[6]Ibid.; In his introduction, Obama writes, "much of this book is based on contemporaneous journals or the oral histories of my family ..." (xvii).

[7]Obama, *Dreams from My Father*, 118.

I was more like the black students who had grown up in the suburbs, kids whose parents had already paid the price of escape. You could spot them right away by the way they talked, the people they sat with in the cafeteria."[8] The suburbanite black kids Obama refers to aren't biracial, but they are bicultural, and it is with those young blacks Barry identifies. I won't be talking much, here, about Obama's biracial status as such; I'm more concerned about why and how Obama both lived, as a youth, and represents, as an adult writing about his youth, a peculiar and particular aspect of the post-civil-rights-movement era called the *post-soul aesthetic* (or PSA).

The term "post-soul," as I define it, generally refers to art produced by African Americans who were either born or came of age after the civil rights movement. I limit the post-soul aesthetic to artists or writers of the post-civil-rights-movement era for one important reason: These artists were not adults—or adolescents, for that matter—during the civil rights movement. Mark Anthony Neal, in *Soul Babies: Black Popular Culture and the Post-Soul Aesthetic*, sums it up nicely: "The generations(s) of black youth born after the early successes of the traditional civil rights movement are in fact divorced from the nostalgia associated with those successes and thus positioned to critically engage the movement's legacy from a state of objectivity that the traditional civil rights leadership is both unwilling and incapable of doing."[9] Post-soul artists such as memoirist Obama explore the hazy, ill-defined blackness of the post-civil-rights era, a blackness that stands in marked difference from the raised-clenched-fist, say-it-loud, I'm-black-and-I'm-proud conception of blackness from the 1960s, or even the purposeful sense of presumed monolithic blackness in the 400 years before that.

Obama's memoir in general—and more specifically his fifth chapter—is an example of post-soul "blaxploration" (I'm intentionally signifying the "blaxploitation" term of the previous era).[10] Obama and his fellow post-soul artists and writers are recognized by their embodiment of the "cultural mulatto" archetype, to use a term Trey Ellis coined in his seminal 1989 essay, "The New Black Aesthetic." Here's Ellis's definition:

> Just as a genetic mulatto is a black person of mixed parents who can often get along fine with his white grandparents, a cultural mulatto, educated by a multiracial mix of cultures, can also navigate easily in the white world. And it is by and large this rapidly growing crop of

---

[8]Ibid., 99.

[9]Mark Anthony Neal, *Soul Babies: Black Popular Culture and the Post-Soul Aesthetic* (New York: Routledge, 2002), 103.

[10]For a thorough discussion of blaxploration and the PSA, see Bertram D. Ashe, "Theorizing the Post-Soul Aesthetic: An Introduction," *African American Review* 41, no. 4 (Winter 2007): 609–23.

cultural mulattoes that fuels the NBA. We no longer need to deny or suppress any part of our complicated and sometimes contradictory cultural baggage to please either white people or black. The culturally mulatto *Cosby* girls are equally as black as a black teenage welfare mother. Neither side of the tracks should forget that.[11]

Ellis possesses an unabashed enthusiasm for his conception of the cultural mulatto, but it is important to balance Ellis's upbeat view of the post-civil-rights-movement possibilities of blackness with, say, novelist Reginald McKnight's far less encouraging use of the term "cultural mulatto" in his short story "The Honey Boys," published a year before Ellis's essay: "Black was nothing more than a color to me. I was a cultural mulatto.... My color was a nuisance. I was too black to be white, too white to be black."[12] McKnight's literary photograph of the "cultural mulatto" seems to have had no flashbulb; it's a much darker portrait of this post-civil-rights-movement phenomenon than Ellis's. As Madhu Dubey writes in *The Black Scholar*, "For McKnight, 'mulatto' signifies the tragic plight of 'victims' of the Civil Rights movement, caught between two worlds and burdened by anxieties about their racially ambivalent status."[13]

Obama's blaxploration begins with Barry similarly "burdened" by anxieties about his "racially ambivalent status." Indeed, the set of five characters (including a younger version of himself) Obama discusses in chapter 5 of *Dreams from My Father* illustrate well the three-pronged definition of the cultural mulatto to which Ellis refers in his essay: "Today's cultural mulattoes echo ... 'tragic mulattoes' only when they too forget they are wholly black. Most self-deluding cultural mulattoes desperately fanaticize themselves the children of William F.

---

[11]Trey Ellis, "The New Black Aesthetic," *Callaloo* 12, no. 1 (Winter 1989): 189.

[12]Reginald McKnight, "The Honey Boys," in *Mustapha's Eclipse* (New York: Ecco Press, 1989), 86.

[13]Madhu Dubey, "Postmodernism as Postnationalism?," *The Black Scholar* 33, no. 1 (Spring 2003): 11. Indeed, Trey Ellis himself, writing fifteen years later in a book on interracial friendships, presents a startlingly different take on his own bicultural youth: "Since leaving Detroit, I had metamorphosed from a regular old black kid into what I would refer to, in a 1988 article entitled 'The New Black Aesthetic,' as a 'cultural mulatto.' I was equally uncomfortable in the world of pizza parlors and duckpin bowling alleys of southern Connecticut as I was visiting my grandparents in either Dayton or West Philadelphia. Back in Hamden at my new elementary school, it was not unusual for me to be called 'Oreo,' by some black kid who was bused to school, and 'nigger,' by some 'Italian Stallion' wannabe in the same week. Deracinated and adrift, I was a wreck. After reading Hamlet, I knew that I had found my literary soul mate, and alone at night in my room, I luxuriated in the self-pity of calling myself 'The Melancholy Black Dane.'" Trey Ellis, "Repellent Afro," in Some of My Best Friends: Writings on Interracial Friendships, ed., Emily Bernard (New York: HarperCollins, 2004), 86–87. Clearly, in order for Ellis to write so enthusiastically about cultural mulattos in "The New Black Aesthetic," he must, like Obama, have emerged from his own identity journey sound and intact, but it's also as clear that the difficulties Obama discusses in his book had their analogue with Ellis, as well.

Buckley. However, a minority affect instead a 'superblackness' and try and dream themselves back to the ghetto."[14]

Given these two poles—blacks either unnaturally tending toward attributes traditionally associated with whiteness or pointedly adopting a "superblackness"—the implication is that the optimal PSA standpoint is somewhere in the middle. Indeed, a "healthy" cultural mulatto is one who realizes that the goal is not to stand firm on either pole, falsely conforming to black or white society's ideals, but to enjoy surfing the midrange, riding the always-shifting center of the cultural mulatto teeter-totter. Obama refers to this himself, echoing Ellis's words from "The New Black Aesthetic," when he writes of learning to "slip back and forth between my black and white worlds, understanding that each possessed its own language and customs and structure of meaning, convinced that with a bit of translation on my part the two worlds would eventually cohere."[15] Obama learns, eventually, to feel a sense of multifaceted cultural comfort, even as—especially as—one is fully embodying a bicultural status. Novelist Zadie Smith, for example, writes that the tale Obama tells "is not the old tragedy of gaining a new, false voice at the expense of a true one. The tale he tells is all about addition. His is the story of a genuinely many-voiced man. If it has a moral it is that each man must be true to his selves, plural.... For Obama, having more than one voice in your ear is not a burden, or not solely a burden—it is also a gift."[16]

For healthy cultural mulattos, the idea, in the end, is to *embrace* cultural difference: Lisa Jones, in *Bulletproof Diva: Tales of Race, Sex, and Hair*, employs "difference as pleasure," and almost seems to be envisioning a future, mature Barack Obama as she explains her phrase: Not difference "as something feared or exotic, but difference as one of the rich facts of one's life, a truism that gives you more data, more power, and more flavor."[17] Jones, in her book, articulates a critically informed stance that is, indeed, shared by writers such as Obama, and not just because both of them are biracial. Eventually, as cultural mulattos move through the sort of black identity journey Obama tracks in his book, many do—eventually, self-consciously—adopt a "difference as pleasure" view toward blackness. A hybrid, fluid, elastic sense of black identity marks *Dreams from My Father*, and authorial blaxploration seems a critical part of Obama's goal: the decentering, destabilizing, expansive exploration of black identity.

"Difference as pleasure" is merely a destination, however; the road to get there is marked with painful trial and difficulty. And our readerly access to

---

[14]Trey Ellis, "The New Black Aesthetic," 190.

[15]Obama, *Dreams from My Father*, 82.

[16]Zadie Smith, "Speaking in Tongues," *New York Review of Books* 56 (Feb 26, 2009), 24.

[17]Lisa Jones, *Bulletproof Diva: Tales of Race, Sex and Hair* (New York: Anchor, 1994), 33.

that road is focused and shaped by the writer. Certainly, there's Obama's life-as-lived, breathing and moving, second by second, from his birth through this very moment, as you read this. But more importantly, for our purposes, there's Obama's life as represented through the narrative *Dreams from My Father: A Story of Race and Inheritance*. As with all autobiographical writing, as we read his narrative we straddle an interpretive fence: through the power and skill of his writing we're immersed in the world of young Barry Obama—yet it's always the mature Barack Obama who's constructing that world, who's making that very immersion possible. He gives us a vivid, compelling view into his formative years, but the *way* he does it is indicative of the end-result of those very same years. In other words, his successful maturation into a healthy cultural mulatto—the standpoint from which he writes—greatly informs his tale of how he came to attain that health.[18]

The act of narrative construction, then, is Obama's key blaxploration gesture in *Dreams from My Father*. Like all writers of memoir, Obama's past life lay before him, ready to be compiled and organized into words, paragraphs, and chapters (one can imagine him sitting and reflecting about what to write, in much the same way he describes a scene of such reflection in the epigraph above). The (re)construction of that life, on the page, required him to sift through his youth and the events and people he encountered therein, ordering and structuring those events into narrative, recalling and emphasizing certain experiences—and relaying those experiences in a certain way—while "forgetting" others, deemphasizing them, in order to present a coherent narrative, one that does what all memoirs do: present a constructed version of past reality, from a specific, present-day perspective. That's why, from the beginning of this essay, I've made a distinction between the two Obamas: I call him "Barry" when describing a scene in which the younger Obama appears, but refer to him as "Obama" when talking about how the mature writer is constructing that scene.[19]

[18] *Dreams from My Father* was first published in 1995, during a boomlet of several PSA nonfiction narratives, including *Black Ice*, by Lorene Cary (1991), *Bourgeois Blues: An American Memoir*, by Jake Lamar (1991), *White Bucks and Black-Eyed Peas: Coming of Age Black in White America*, by Marcus Mabry (1995), *The Color of Water: A Black Man's Tribute to His White Mother*, by James McBride (1996), and *When Chickenheads Come Home to Roost: A Hip Hop Feminist Breaks It Down*, by Joan Morgan (1999). Each book wrestled, in its own way, with PSA issues attendant to being born or coming of age in the post-civil-rights-movement era.

[19] Obama speaks directly to this requirement of autobiography in his introduction: "Finally, there are the dangers inherent in any autobiographical work: the temptation to color events in ways favorable to the writer, the tendency to overestimate the interest one's experiences hold for others, selective lapses of memory.... I can't say that I've avoided all, or any, of these hazards successfully. Although much of this book is based on contemporaneous journals or the oral histories of my family, the dialogue is necessarily an approximation of what was actually said or relayed to me. For the sake of compression, some of the characters that appear are composites of people I've known, and some events appear out of precise chronology. With the exception of my family and a handful of public figures, the names of most characters have been changed for the sake of their privacy" (*Dreams from My Father*, xvi–xvii).

These five characters, then, are as much constructs as characters, set in motion by a mature Barack Obama not only to describe his life, but also to execute an incisive bit of blaxploration as he recalls attending Occidental College for the first part of his undergraduate education. Novelist and poet Paul Beatty, one of the most noteworthy of PSA artists, wrote an essay in 1994 called "What Set You From, Fool?" Deep into the essay, he constructed the Beatty Scale of Quintessential African-American Blackness. During the culmination of Obama's Barry Era, I see him metaphorically locating these students on the Beatty Scale. The four categories Beatty employs on his scale are "Jet Black," with people like Billie Holiday and Malik El-Shabazz (Malcolm X), and Charles Barkley; "Flat Black," with people like Wynton Marsalis, Thurgood Marshall, Rosa Parks, and Charles Barkley; "Glossy Black," with people like Public Enemy, W. E. B. Du Bois, The Congressional Black Caucus, and Charles Barkley; and "Gray," with people like Bill Cosby, Clarence Thomas, Rae Dawn Chong—and Charles Barkley.[20] Clearly, as with much of Beatty's writing, one can see the humor at work here. And yet, one can easily see the political impulse at work, as well. Charles Barkley's presence on all four lists is certainly humorous, but also speaks to the fluidity of categorizations of blackness. After all, there is an important, telling asterisk attached to the title of the Scale itself: "*Degrees of Blackness are subject to change without prior notice."[21]

Obama skillfully executes his blaxploration gesture by figuratively locating these five students (including his earlier self) on what is tantamount to his own version of the Beatty Scale. Joyce, for instance, would certainly fall under Gray. "In his memoir," writes Zadie Smith, "Obama takes care to ridicule a certain black girl called Joyce—a composite figure from his college days who happens also to be part Italian and part French and part Native American and is inordinately fond of mentioning these facts."[22] Obama introduces Joyce as "a good-looking woman," possessing "green eyes and honey skin and pouty lips."[23] But when Barry asked her one day if she was going to the Black Students' Association meeting, she looked at him funny and then shook her head. "I'm not black," Joyce said to Barry, "I'm *multiracial*.... Why should I have to choose between them?" While I've been careful, here, to suggest that Barry's bicultural status plays a bigger role in his journey than simply being biracial, Obama's treatment of Joyce is one of the moments in his identity narrative that brings the question of genetic racial composition to the fore. On a single page early in his fifth chapter, Obama first states that he is "more like the black

[20]Paul Beatty, "What Set You From, Fool?," in *Next: Young American Writers on the New Generation*, ed. Eric Liu (New York: W. W. Norton, 1994), 47.

[21]Ibid., 47.

[22]Smith, "Speaking in Tongues," 25.

[23]Obama, *Dreams from My Father*, 99.

students who had grown up in the suburbs,"[24] and, continuing, says, "You could spot them right away by the way they talked, the people they sat with in the cafeteria. When pressed, they would sputter and explain that they refused to be categorized. They weren't defined by the color of their skin, they would tell you. They were individuals."[25] The next paragraph begins, "That's how Joyce liked to talk."[26]

Obama, then, explicitly links Joyce, the *multiracial* young woman, with the rhetoric of black individualism—even though he explicitly places "I'm not black" solidly in her mouth. Indeed, three-quarters of the way down the page, he writes that she got almost tearfully emotional as she complained, "[I]t's *black people* who always have to make everything racial. *They're* the ones making me choose. *They're* the ones who are telling me that I can't be who I am...."[27] His repetitive use of italicized emphasis only intensifies Joyce's outpouring. But his examination of Joyce, whether he intended it or not, emerges as a key blaxploration moment in his text, since he has seamlessly moved, textually, from comparing his biracial self to suburban blacks who call themselves "individuals," whom he then compares to Joyce, a woman who promptly *rejects* the very blackness that Obama says she resembles! To further complicate matters, at the bottom of the page, Obama, echoing his italicized use of "*They're*" above, begins the next paragraph with, "They, they, they. That was the problem with people like Joyce. They talked about the richness of their multicultural heritage and it sounded real good, until you noticed that they avoided black people."[28]

This entire short passage is unintelligible unless one looming reality is considered: in Barry's life, and in the complicated, post-soul, post-civil rights movement era in which he came of age, "black" means markedly different things to different people, whether they're black, biracial, or multiracial. It's during moments like this that his oft-quoted sentence from *Dreams from My Father* seems most apt: "I was trying to raise myself to be a black man in America, and beyond the given of my appearance, no one around me seemed to know exactly what that meant."[29] In the original context, "no one around me" refers to his white mother and grandparents. But it seems an appropriate quotation for the present context, as well: no one introduced, referenced or described on page ninety-nine seems to know "exactly" what it means to be black in America, either. His narrative-long search for where he fits is, indeed,

---

[24]Ibid., 99.

[25]Ibid., 99.

[26]Ibid., 99.

[27]Ibid., 99.

[28]Ibid., 99.

[29]Ibid., 76.

a journey that can't be told without the realization that his exploration is, as well, a blaxploration—an attempt to reveal, for perhaps a largely unknowing readership, the vast complexities of blackness.

Of the five characters Obama examines, "Tim" is perhaps the least closely described. Likely one of the suburban blacks Obama describes above, he's another composite who would easily show up as "Gray" on the Beatty scale:

> Tim was not a conscious brother. Tim wore argyle sweaters and pressed jeans and talked like Beaver Cleaver. He planned to major in business. His white girlfriend was probably waiting for him up in his room, listening to country music. He was happy as a clam, and I wanted nothing more than for him to go away.[30]

Tim asks to borrow an assignment from Barry, and leaves after receiving it. "Tim's a trip, ain't he," said Barry to some friends in a dorm room. "Should change his name from Tim to Tom."[31] He got some laughs after his cruel quip, but not from Marcus, who called Barry out on his comment: "Seems to me," replied Marcus, "we should be worrying about whether our own stuff's together instead of passing judgment on how other folks are supposed to act."[32]

Marcus, at first glance, is Jet Black. Obama describes Marcus as "the most conscious of brothers," saying, "He could tell you about his grandfather the Garveyite; about his mother in St. Louis who had raised her kids alone while working as a nurse; about his older sister who had been a founding member of the local Panther party; about his friends in the joint. His lineage was pure, his loyalties clear...."[33] In fact, Barry called Tim a Tom after the latter interrupted Marcus's latest pronouncement on his "authentic black experience."[34] (It certainly appears as if Barry, in that moment, was dancing closer to the "superblackness" pole of Trey Ellis's cultural mulatto construct.)

But while Marcus, at first, seemed comfortably black at Occidental, he was eventually revealed to be struggling, too: "He became more demonstrative in his racial pride," writes Obama. "He took to wearing African prints to class and started lobbying the administration for an all-black dormitory. Later, he became uncommunicative. He began to skip classes, hitting the reefer more heavily. He let his beard grow out, let his hair work its way into dreadlocks."[35] Finally, he left school. The last thing Obama says about Marcus is this: "I realized

---

[30]Ibid., 101–02.

[31]Ibid., 102.

[32]Ibid., 102.

[33]Ibid., 101.

[34]Ibid., 101.

[35]Ibid., 117.

that Marcus needed my help as much as I needed his, that I wasn't the only one looking for answers."[36] So while Joyce and Tim would likely rate as Gray on the Beatty scale, and Marcus originally seemed Jet Black, he ended up considerably less than that, ending up fronting "superblackness" after all.

So Barack Obama's construction of these five characters (with the other four as likely composites) features Barry Obama in the throes of his identity quest, quarreling with a quartet of college kids on the Quintessential African-American Blackness scale; when Joyce cried "multiracial," Barry said, "The truth was that I understood her, her and all the other black kids who felt the way she did. In their mannerisms, their speech, their mixed-up hearts, I kept recognizing pieces of myself. And that's exactly what scared me."[37] Similarly, Tim represented precisely the sort of the deracinated black male from which Barry desperately wanted to distance himself. It was "fear," he said later, that caused him to ridicule Tim in front of his friends. "The constant, crippling fear that I didn't belong somehow, that unless I dodged and hid and pretended to be something I wasn't I would forever remain an outsider, with the rest of the world, black and white, always standing in judgment."[38]

Poor Barry, then, was getting it from all sides. Desperate to avoid the Gray, he overcompensated, flirting with superblackness. "To avoid being mistaken for a sellout, I chose my friends carefully," writes Obama. "The more politically active black students. The foreign students. The Chicanos. The Marxist professors and structural feminists and punk-rock performance poets. We smoked cigarettes and wore leather jackets.... We were alienated."[39] Certainly that cohort included Jet Black Marcus, "lean and dark and straight-backed and righteous,"[40] representing everything Barry could imagine wanting in a "pure" black lineage.[41] But it surely also included Regina, Flat Black, wise, centered, and conscious, possessor of a checklist Chicago childhood that contained "the absent father and struggling mother," and the "South Side six-flat that never seemed warm enough in the winter and got [too] hot in the summer."[42] Obama's ability to cram these differing versions of blackness, plucked from the various aspects of the Beatty scale, into a cultural blender and hit "start" speaks to the vivid blaxploration occurring in Barry's world—and in Obama's narrative.

[36]Ibid., 118.

[37]Ibid., 100.

[38]Ibid., 111.

[39]Ibid., 101.

[40]Ibid., 107.

[41]Ibid., 101.

[42]Ibid., 104.

In the end, the events Obama relayed in chapter 5 of *Dreams from My Father* suggest that Regina was perhaps the most important student Obama came to know as an undergraduate. It was Regina, after all, who, after learning his first name, asked, "So why does everybody call you Barry?" She received his answer—"So I could fit in"—and then asked if she could call him Barack. As they got to know each other at that first meeting, her voice, writes Obama, "evoked a vision of black life in all its possibility, a vision that filled me with longing—a longing for place, and a fixed and definite history."[43]

These words are familiar to students of the post-soul aesthetic. "There was talk in 1986 of the arrival of a new way of looking at the world by young black artists," writes Lisa Jones in *Bulletproof Diva*. "This aesthetic ... was said to embrace, among other things, irreverence, profit-making, an elastic view of 'black' art, ideas of integration and nationalism, a yen for tradition (or at least the apparel), and the usual questions about who we are and where is our home."[44] The mature Obama's authorial perspective, from which he writes *Dreams from My Father*, both reenacts Barry's search as well as symbolically represents its' successful completion—to the extent that identity quests can ever be fully "completed," at any rate.

After Barry spoke at an antiapartheid rally, he told Regina, "I'm going to leave the preaching to you. And to Marcus. Me, I've decided I've got no business speaking for black folks." When he called her naïve for believing otherwise, she replied, "If anybody's naïve, it's you. You're the one who seems to think he can run away from himself."[45] It was indeed Regina's role, at least in Barack Obama's carefully constructed identity narrative, to help him understand that there was more than one way to be black, that difference can, indeed, be pleasurable and effective.

The Barry Era was a painful, uncertain time in the life of Barack Obama, but clearly a necessary one, as well. One curious, recurring narrative crutch that Obama uses to discuss the other four characters of the chapter seems to be a holdover from his youth. Visual and historical affectations seem to describe—and define—these characters in a way that recalls narrow adolescent observation. Tim's upscale clothing tastes (likely called "preppy" at the time), use of Standard English, and white girlfriend and the fact that she listens to country music; fatherless Marcus's Panther Party-sister, Marcus Garvey affiliations, and working mother; Joyce's Italian father and part-African, part-French, and part-Native American mother; and Regina's fatherlessness in Chicago, struggling mother, and familial, church-going childhood all seem, at first glance, like questionable narrative shorthand, a quick and easy way for Obama's readers

---

[43]Ibid., 104.

[44]Jones, *Bulletproof Diva*, 134.

[45]Obama, *Dreams from My Father*, 108.

to instantly "know" these characters based on our own sense of what it must mean, say, to be black and wear argyle socks and date a country-music-loving white woman. But while Barry might have seen the world that way, Obama's maturity—perhaps even as a writer—emerges over the course of *Dreams from My Father*.

As he metaphorically floats, moment-by-moment, from Jet Black to Flat Black to Glossy Black to Gray—and back again—he gains a gradual, fitful understanding that, as a post-civil-rights-movement "healthy" cultural mulatto, "difference as pleasure" is indeed the goal. And as he moves his readers through the rest of the memoir, he loses that narrative crutch, and begins to describe subsequent characters more fully, without cheap descriptive shorthand. Indeed, Obama ends his memoir by describing his cousin Abongo's maturation, a description that sounds as if he could well be referring to himself:

> His conversion has given him solid ground to stand on, a pride in his place in the world. From that I see his confidence building; he begins to venture out and ask harder questions; he starts to slough off the formulas and slogans and decides what works best for him. He can't help himself in this process, for his heart is too generous and full of good humor, his attitude toward people too gentle and forgiving, to find simple solutions to the puzzle of being a black man.[46]

Or, to put it another way, blaxploration is a valuable, never-ending practice, and ultimately, from within this "process" of identity-discovery, incisive presidential candidate Barack Obama emerged. Yes, he goes on to spend time in Chicago as an organizer, grappling with issues of "community"[47] in more ways than one. And yes, it was important for him to travel to Kenya and visit with his father's family to discover that black authenticity—like any other authenticity—is something to which one can aspire but can never quite completely attain.

Unquestionably, his journey is not close to complete as he leaves Occidental for Columbia and New York, but his experiences at Occidental do provide the core of his identity quest, and his authorial, blaxplorative rendering of his experiences solidly mark *Dreams from My Father* as a post-soul aesthetic text—and Barry Obama as a budding post-soul protagonist. His ultimate reconciliation of that essential, adolescent tension between lusting for a Marcus-like "authentic blackness," his fear of an unconscious, suburbanite persona like Tim's or his resistance to a Joycelike multiracialism—a reconciliation aided by the grounded Regina—finally launches him toward ending up as a man who

---

[46]Ibid., 441–42.

[47]Ibid., 278.

does, indeed, personify "difference as pleasure," a man who is so comfortable in his skin that he can embody both the codes of cultural whiteness *and* cultural blackness in a breathtakingly, almost unbelievably effortless fashion, thereby enabling a large part of the American voting public to believe he's "like them," whether the "them" is black or white or other. As a result of the success of his journey from "Barry" to "Barack," from "racially ambivalent status" to "healthy" cultural mulatto—and the success of his ability to render that journey in narrative fashion—Barack Obama, on January 20, 2009, was not just inaugurated as the first black president. Perhaps more importantly, he was inaugurated as the first post-soul president, as well.

"Let Us Not Falter Before Our Complexity": Barack Obama and the Legacy of Ralph Ellison

M. Cooper Harriss

"Who is Barack Obama?" became the signal question of the 2008 election cycle as opponents generated a barrage of legitimate and fabricated concerns about a charismatic yet relatively unknown candidate for president of the United States. Issues concerning the senator's mixed race (and thus ambiguous origins in the overwrought determinations of American racial identity), birthplace, cosmopolitan lineage, "funny" name (as the candidate himself frequently joked), and limited national track record were compounded by Internet-, talk radio–, and cable news–driven whisper campaigns designed to exploit ignorance and paranoia against Obama. That is what politicians and pundits do, of course, but the vagaries surrounding Obama's identity lent an especial sense of urgency to identifying and understanding this unprecedented candidate and the significance of his candidacy.

The question "Who is Barack Obama?" also occupied a number of thoughtful commentators, journalists, and intellectuals, many of whom turned to comparison in order to situate Candidate Obama within an identifiable intellectual or political tradition, to domesticate the unknown by filtering it through a known property. Gary Wills explored Obama's Lincolnesque oratory.[1] David Brooks devoted a *New York Times* column to Obama's international outlook in terms of Reinhold Niebuhr's theological tempering of American exceptionalism via neo-orthodox realism.[2] Detractors, too, drew comparisons, noting

---

[1] See Gary Wills, "Two Speeches on Race," *New York Review of Books* 55, no. 7 (May 1, 2008); http://www.nybooks.com/articles/archives/2008/may/01/two-speeches-on-race/.

[2] David Brooks, "Obama, Gospel and Verse," *New York Times*, April 26, 2007, http://select.nytimes.com/2007/04/26/opinion/26brooks.html?_r=1 (accessed August 12, 2010). Indeed, a quotation that Brooks attributed to Obama now serves as a blurb gracing the back cover of the 2008 reissue of Niebuhr's *The Irony of American History*: "I take away [from Niebuhr's works] the compelling idea that there's serious evil in the world, and hardship and pain. And we should be humble and modest in our belief that we can eliminate those things. But we shouldn't use that as an excuse for cynicism and inaction." See the back cover of Reinhold Niebuhr, *The Irony of American History* (Chicago: University of Chicago Press, 2008/1952).

(with foreboding) selected consistencies between Obama and former president Jimmy Carter—both relatively inexperienced candidates who emerged in the wake of strongly divisive presidents—auguring a return to the lean days of the late 1970s.[3]

These examples serve as a representative sample of a far broader phenomenon. Candidate Obama's public identity was both a cipher and an overwrought metaphor. Just as many could mold him to represent their own hopes and beliefs, others (for good and ill) found it impossible to ignore the indelible significance that marked his visage and the promise or the pain that it implied. Ultimately, such comparisons remain illuminating, if unsatisfying. Whereas they generally do justice to aspects of Barack Obama as a presidential candidate, and now, to a lesser extent, as president, they also fail to capture other vital essences of his persona. The essence on which this essay focuses is of the blazingly talented and ambitious individual who, while not one to deny the significance of racial identity (nor the viability of his own identity), does not fit easily into the established discourses available in the early twenty-first century for thinking about and discussing race—especially blackness—in the United States. I suggest that sustained engagement with how the constructed identity of "Barack Obama" as a 2008 presidential candidate bears resonance with aspects of the life and literary corpus of Ralph Ellison—while not constitutive of a one-to-one comparison—helps to frame a manageable portrait of "Obama," the man and the political sign, that illustrates how the first president of color, rightly celebrated for this remarkable achievement and the milestone that it represents, has been seen by many, paradoxically, to "transcend" race or otherwise to invoke a "postracial" America.[4]

Ralph Ellison and "The Blackness of Blackness"

Ralph Ellison (1913–1994) built his considerable literary reputation on the strength of one major novel (*Invisible Man* [1952]) and two collections of essays (*Shadow and Act* [1964] and *Going to the Territory* [1986]).[5] *Invisible Man* remains his masterpiece, influential in no small part for its evocative

---

[3]Steve Kornacki, "Turning Obama into Jimmy Carter," *New York Observer,* February 25, 2008, http://www.observer.com/2008/turning-obama-jimmy-carter (accessed August 12, 2010).

[4]Others have discussed correspondences between Obama and Ellison—most notably David Samuels, "Invisible Man: How Ralph Ellison Explains Barack Obama," *New Republic,* October 22, 2008. See also M. Cooper Harriss, "E Pluribus Obama," *Sightings,* November 13, 2008, http://divinity.uchicago .edu/martycenter/publications/sightings/archive_2008/1113.shtml (accessed August 12, 2010).

[5]Ellison devoted the second half of his life to a second novel that was never finished, although excerpts were edited and published posthumously as *Juneteenth* (New York: Random House, 1999). An unexpurgated version of the manuscript recently appeared. See John F. Callahan and Adam Bradley, eds., *Three Days Before the Shooting …* (New York: Modern Library, 2010).

metaphor—"invisibility." In the novel's prologue, Ellison's anonymous protagonist observes: "I am an invisible man, ... understand, simply because people refuse to see me. ... When they approach me, they see only my surroundings, themselves, or figments of their imagination—indeed, everything and anything except me."[6] The highly visible phenotypical distinction of blackness obscures the particular humanity of its individual agents. This wisdom is hard-earned by the protagonist, who encounters and endures lessons of this invisibility ranging from the violence of his Southern hometown, the ruthless paternalism of segregation, and his time spent as a laborer and a leftist political activist in Harlem's "Brotherhood." No one sees him as a human being—only as a problem, a cause, a category. By novel's end, the invisible man understands that his humanity had been rendered invisible even unto himself: "[M]y problem was that I always tried to go in everyone's way but my own. ... So after years of trying to adopt the opinions of others I finally rebelled. I am an *invisible* man."[7] He inhabits this invisibility, wielding it against those (white and black) who would use him for their own purposes, advancing their own agendas: "I learned in time though that it is possible to carry on a fight against them without their realizing it."[8] Humanity becomes a weapon against the categories of identity that efface his individuality.

Ellison and his corpus have maintained a difficult relationship with academic discourses of race since the very emergence of race as "viable" object of study nearly fifty years ago. Evidence of this nascent tension appears in the first reviews of *Invisible Man*. George Mayberry suggests in *The New Republic* that the novel is "shorn of the racial and political clichés that have encumbered the Negro novel."[9] In a review for *Harper's*, Katherine Gauss Jackson claims that *Invisible Man* is not the work of a "Negro novelist" but of an author "who happens to be a Negro."[10] "Negro novelists" wrote from a perspective of onto-logical blackness. Their literary output placed a premium upon the primacy of racial identity to artistic representation, much as Richard Wright did in his landmark novel *Native Son* (1940). As an ad hoc protégé of Wright, moving in the leftist political and artistic circles of 1930s Harlem, Ellison gained famil-iarity with Marxism and its broader critiques rooted in cultural materialism. He praised *Native Son* for its visceral realism in depicting the urban plight of dispossessed African-American people. Writing in 1941, Ellison suggests that

---

[6]Ralph Ellison, *Invisible Man* (New York: Vintage, 1995/1952), 3.

[7]Ibid., 573.

[8]Ibid., 5.

[9]George Mayberry, "Underground Notes," *New Republic*, April 21, 1952, 19.

[10]Katherine Gauss Jackson, "Books in Brief," *Harper's Magazine* 204, no. 1225 (June 1952): 105. Mayberry makes a similar point in "Underground Notes."

activist literature is capable of overcoming systematic oppression, that it can help the Negro "become conditioned in working class methods of organized struggle," thereby gaining ownership of "the conscious meaning of their lives."[11] In this context, it would come as some surprise eleven years later for informed readers to discover Ellison's anonymous protagonist in *Invisible Man* to bear closer resemblance to any number of characters from the bourgeois "classics" of the Western canon (reviewers specify Dante's Virgil, Bunyan's Pilgrim, Dostoevsky's Raskolnikov and Underground Man, Swift's Gulliver, and the Ulysses figure) than to Wright's Bigger Thomas.[12]

Thus we might understand *Invisible Man* to depict a version of African-American experience and identity characterized not by materialist dialectics but through an ironized cosmopolitan humanism, one that contextualizes identity and troubles the overtly political interpretations that had characterized African-American literature of recent decades. Ellison embraced the complexity of human identities and interactions. Ellison found the social sciences (whose research informed much of the political "protest" literature that became synonymous with "Negro literature" of his era) reductionist, tending to oversimplify the contributions that literature can make in the articulation of culture.[13] He preferred to explore the possibilities inherent in those human ambiguities that flummox the determinations of scientific inquiry—social or otherwise. In this way, Ellison believed, human experience can never be reduced to the statistics, trends, or categories that render human identity invisible. Human beings are capable of exceptional, unpredictable, and irrational acts. That is precisely what makes them so interesting, so *literary* on the Ellisonian view.

We do well to consider Barack Obama in these Ellisonian terms. Obama and Ellison are, in a sense, kindred iconoclasts, men who bear complex relationships both to the marginalized identities from which they emerge (and with which they self-identify) and the broader cosmopolitan acceptance to which they aspire (and into which, as President and "great" American novelist, respectively, they are accepted). While myriad connections pertain, this essay shall treat three categories of resonance between Obama and Ellison: (1) a geography of race that considers their respective locations in a narrative

---

[11]Ralph Ellison, "Recent Negro Fiction," *New Masses* 40 (August 5, 1941): 22–26.

[12]Wright Morris, "The World Below," *New York Times*, April 13, 1952, BR5; Mayberry, "Underground Notes," 19; Harvey Curtis Webster, "Inside a Dark Shell," *Saturday Review of Literature* 35, no. 22 (April 12, 1952); Worth Tuttle Hedden, "Objectively Vivid, Introspectively Sincere," *New York Herald Tribune*, April 13, 1952, BR5.

[13]The clear reference here would be to Richard Wright's (and others') contributions to, and gleanings from, Chicago School sociology—specifically the research and findings that would become St. Clair Drake and Horace A. Cayton, *Black Metropolis: A Study of Negro Life in a Northern City* (Chicago: University of Chicago Press, 1993/1945). Wright penned the introduction to this landmark volume.

of blackness; (2) a genealogy of race that situates them respectively within a specific lineage or inheritance; and (3) a civil religious sensibility through which, respectively, they articulate unique political and intellectual visions of the United States. In the end shall emerge an understanding that, despite resounding proclamations of Obama's "visibility" in the wake of his election, a more rigorous examination of the Ellisonian concept of "invisibility" reveals the reports of race's untimely conceptual and practical demise to be, indeed, exaggerated.

Geography

Ellison's and Obama's narratives of origin share significant geographical components. These "first things" are foundational to the ways they participate in broader African-American and American narratives of identity and cultural legitimacy. Both men were raised by single mothers, were bereft of fathers, and came of age in the African-American provinces: Obama in Kansas, Hawaii, and abroad, and Ellison in Oklahoma City—"the territory" as he was fond of calling it.[14] Ellison was born in Oklahoma less than six years after it became a state. Similarly, Obama was born in Hawaii two years after it gained statehood—a convergence that marks a shared valence of "frontier" experience in their respective youths. Significantly, these locations situate Ellison and Obama outside of the two major terminals of migration undertaken by African Americans in the first half of the twentieth century: the segregated South and the urban North. This trajectory—South to North—represents a continuum of blackness in historical American narratives of race.[15]

As natives of the African-American frontier, Ellison and Obama would adopt new homes within the geographical continuum of blackness in order to reinforce their racial *bona fides*. Ellison left Oklahoma to attend Tuskegee in Alabama, and despite confronting significant segregation growing up in Oklahoma City, he makes more frequent appeals to his time in Alabama under Jim Crow to mark his own legitimacy as an African American. From Tuskegee, Ellison migrated northward to Harlem. Through this movement, we observe Ellison, a son (and self-styled product) of "the territory," willfully adopting the broader African-American migratory patterns of his day,

---

[14]See Ralph Ellison, *Going to the Territory* (New York: Vintage, 1986), especially the title essay in which Ellison depicts the ontological impact of growing up in Oklahoma.

[15]See, among other sources, James R. Grossman, *Land of Hope: Chicago, Black Southerners, and the Great Migration* (Chicago: University of Chicago Press, 1989), Carole Marks, *Farewell, We're Good and Gone: The Great Black Migration* (Bloomington: Indiana University Press, 1989), and Joe William Trotter, ed., *The Great Migration in Historical Perspective: New Dimensions of Race, Class, and Gender* (Bloomington: Indiana University Press, 1991).

participating in a definitive African-American experience in the first half of the twentieth century.[16]

Like Ellison, Obama assumed a sense of racial legitimacy through the geographical alignment of his identity with a sense of place. Out of sorts as a student at Occidental College in Los Angeles, he transfers to Columbia University where, situated (like Ellison) on the outskirts of Harlem, he attempts to connect with his own blackness: "[I]f I had come to understand myself as a black American and was understood as such, that understanding remained unanchored to place. ... I figured if there weren't any more black students at Columbia than there were at [Occidental], I'd at least be in the heart of a true city, with black neighborhoods in close proximity."[17] Upon graduation, Obama moves to Chicago, where he adopts the geographical legitimacy afforded by the South Side. He famously serves as a community organizer, learns the ropes of Chicago politics, joins the fold of the rich African-American church tradition at Trinity United Church of Christ, and consummates this transformation by marrying into the community.[18] Significantly, this geographical trope cuts both ways for the biracial Obama. By emphasizing his Kansan mother, he frequently asserts his own inheritance of a Midwestern (read "white") "normality" and the wholesome values that are assumed to accompany it.[19] Though Obama (as biracial) diverges from Ellison's own pattern in this familial migration, we still may recognize an Ellisonian sense of purchase in Obama's attempts to solidify his African-American identity, to link it to tangible locales and institutions.

As native outsiders to the dominant continuum of blackness, ranging from the Jim Crow South to the urban North, Ellison and Obama also share a liminal racial identity. Such liminality leads critics to question the relative authenticity

---

[16]Ellison would eventually settle just on the outskirts of Harlem, on the banks of the Hudson, on Riverside Drive. Interesting in this regard, and in the broader terms of geography's ability to speak to a sense of identity, Ellison characterized *Invisible Man*, which I discuss earlier as "ironizing" earlier assumptions of racial identity, as a novel that was conceived and written both in Harlem and in midtown Manhattan. In this way, it emerges from two worlds, and gives some credence to the refrain about the novel itself's own racial identity—is it a Negro novel or a novel that happens to be about a Negro? Is it a Harlem novel or a novel that is about Harlem?

[17]Barack Obama, *Dreams from My Father: A Story of Race and Inheritance* (New York: Three Rivers Press, 1995), 115.

[18]See Ta-Nehesi Coates's "American Girl" in *The Atlantic* (January/February 2009) on Michelle Obama, http://www.theatlantic.com/doc/200901/michelle-obama/4 (accessed August 12, 2010). Coates writes: "A buddy of mine once remarked that Michelle 'makes Barack black.' But that understates things. She doesn't simply make Barack black—she makes him American."

[19]It is also through his Kansan mother that Obama connects with a broader American narrative of heroism, through his grandfather, who—Obama frequently reminds auditors—"marched with Patton's army." See, for instance, his national self-introduction—the 2004 keynote address at the Democratic National Convention, http://www.washingtonpost.com/wp-dyn/articles/A19751-2004Jul27.html.

of their blackness. Obama describes these categories as "too black" and "not black enough" in his Philadelphia address on race, delivered in the wake of the public kerfuffle over his minister, Jeremiah Wright.[20] Of particular concern for both Ellison and Obama is the charge of being not black enough, not conforming to or representing certain unwritten codes of "authentic" blackness as determined by a folk sensibility within given communities and worldviews, articulated by appropriate and recognizable modes of speech and action. Two anecdotes illustrate this confluence for Obama and Ellison.

Former Black Panther Bobby Rush's campaign leveled the "not black enough" charge against Obama when Obama challenged Rush for his congressional seat in the Democratic primaries of 2000. As a relative outsider to Rush's first congressional district (located in Chicago's South Side), and especially as a lecturer in constitutional law at the University of Chicago Law School (an association that can raise suspicious eyebrows across swaths of the first district), Rush easily succeeded in damaging Obama's credibility as "authentically" black.[21] He did not fit into the political conception of authentic blackness that was endemic to Rush's campaign, one rooted in the congressman's historical entrenchment in the South Side and among Chicago's marginalized neighborhoods. In this way, his qualifications to represent the district came under suspicion. Rush's constituency agreed, and Obama was summarily trounced in the primary, gaining a valuable political lesson in the process.

Similarly, around 1970, a patron asked a librarian at a black studies library at Southern Illinois University for help in locating a copy of *Invisible Man*. "Ralph Ellison is not a black writer," the librarian shot back, drawing sharp contrast between phenotypical and cultural definitions of racial identity.[22] The expectations of an "authentic" blackness, differentiated from one that is somehow compromised by associations with white institutions or legacies, emerged during a period in American history marked by increased frustrations and responding to long legacies of oppression in, and sanctioned by, the political and cultural institutions of the United States. Ellison's cosmopolitanism diverged from these conceptions of authenticity. Consequently, he became *persona non grata* among many political and aesthetic figures in the Black Power and Black Arts movements of the 1960s and 1970s.[23] They labeled him an Uncle Tom. His college

---

[20]See the text and video of this speech at http://my.barackobama.com/page/content/hisownwords/ (accessed August 12, 2010).

[21]Rush suggested that "Obama wasn't black enough and didn't know the black experience, the black community." See Ryan Lizza, "Making It," *New Yorker*, July 21, 2008, 59–60.

[22]Maryemma Graham and Amrijit Singh, eds., *Conversations with Ralph Ellison* (Jackson: University Press of Mississippi, 1995), 397.

[23]For more on these movements, see Lisa Gail Collins and Margo Natalie Crawford, eds., *New Thoughts on the Black Arts Movement* (New Brunswick, NJ: Rutgers University Press, 2006), Peniel

lectures became contentious affairs as student radicals challenged the nature of his work and a perceived lack of commitment toward political and social activism. Despite his adoption of Alabama and Harlem as geographical legitimators of racial identity, Ellison would frequently return to the idea of his frontier origins as a signal component of his intellectual and aesthetic project. His second collection of essays, *Going to the Territory,* sought in this way broadly to distinguish his own orientations from those of his opponents. His frontier origins explained his inability to fit into this new racial paradigm.

Earlier, we observed that Ellison, through *Invisible Man,* was distinguished from other "Negro novelists" such as Richard Wright by critics who designated him a novelist "who happens to be a Negro." Along similar lines, pundits distinguished Obama's candidacy from those of earlier African-American presidential candidates, including Jesse Jackson and Al Sharpton, by calling him a "serious" or "viable" candidate, thereby implying that Jackson and Sharpton, as activists associated with specifically racialized agendas, were neither serious nor viable.[24] One might say in this light that Barack Obama was perceived (and campaigned) not as an African-American candidate but a candidate who happens to be an African American. No small component of this hedging on identity among the broader public emerges directly from the influence of Obama's and Ellison's respective frontier origins situated outside of the primary racial paradigm of the late twentieth century and in how these origins situate both men within the racial narratives and expectations of their respective times.

Genealogy

We now turn to a second convergence: Ellison's and Obama's respective relationships to what I shall designate, somewhat clumsily, as the "Black Power generation." This generation rose to prominence in the wake of the Civil Rights Act of 1964 and the Voting Rights Act of 1965, when the freedom movements—having achieved their primary legislative goals—found themselves in disarray as they sought (and fought) to define their next course of action.[25]

E. Joseph, ed., *The Black Power Movement: Rethinking the Civil Rights–Black Power Era* (New York: Routledge, 2006), Peniel E. Joseph, *Waiting 'Til the Midnight Hour: A Narrative History of Black Power in America* (New York: Holt, 2007), Jeffrey O. G. Ogbar, *Black Power: Radical Politics and African American Identity* (Baltimore, MD: Johns Hopkins University Press, 2005), and James Edward Smethurst, *The Black Arts Movement: Literary Nationalism in the 1960s and 1970s,* John Hope Franklin Series in African American History and Culture (Chapel Hill: University of North Carolina Press, 2005).

[24]See Joshua Alston, "Post-MLK: Barack, Jesse, and Al," *Newsweek,* April 14, 2008, http://www.newsweek.com/id/130609 (accessed August 12, 2010).

[25]For more on these tensions between SNCC and the SCLC, especially as the context for the emergence of Black Power, see Taylor Branch, *At Canaan's Edge: America in the King Years, 1965–1968* (New York: Simon and Schuster, 2006).

Representatives of this generation continue to serve as leaders in local and national arenas today, well into their sixties, seventies, and beyond. Interestingly, separated as Ellison and Obama are in age by nearly fifty years (Ellison was born in 1913, Obama in 1961), both have found their more vociferous opponents in this generation that falls between them, a generation of African-American leadership that has tended to affirm essential terms of blackness, seeking to establish its power and beauty as primary concerns in opposition to more integrative approaches. "Black Power," a slogan coined by Stokely Carmichael in 1966, arose out of frustration with Martin Luther King, Jr.'s, insistence upon nonviolence. Carmichael and other representatives of this vanguard sought to escalate the terms and methods of resistance. Accordingly, Obama characterizes them as "Reverend Wright's generation" in the Philadelphia address, one for whom "the memories of humiliation and doubt and fear have not gone away," and who still remember "the anger and the bitterness" of their experiences.[26] Despite significant political and ideological differences, it is largely members of this generation who have questioned Obama's racial *bona fides*.[27] Likewise, Ellison frequently sparred with the likes of Amiri Baraka, Ishmael Reed, and other writers participating in, or active during, the "Black Arts" movement—organized as it was around aesthetic expressions of Black Power that promoted Afrocentric modes of consciousness. Activists interrupted Ellison's speaking and teaching engagements, seeking to question his commitment to "the cause." Ellison's attempts to separate himself from the literary and intellectual legacies of social protest served as a point of alienation from "Reverend Wright's" younger generation who understood its own voice to emerge by confronting the injustices that characterized the crucible of African-American social and political reality through art-as-activism. These differences have led some to speak in terms of a "generation gap"—a broader social phenomenon at play across American cultural divides during the 1960s.[28]

---

[26]See the "A More Perfect Union" speech.

[27]It is interesting to remember that such African-American political luminaries as James Clyburn, John Lewis, Andrew Young, and others initially endorsed Hillary Clinton, implicitly dismissing Obama's candidacy. See William Jelani Cobb, "As Obama Rises, Old Guard Civil Rights Leaders Scowl," *Washington Post*, January 13, 2008, B1. Consider, too, Jesse Jackson's July 6, 2008, off-camera (but on-mike) remarks about Obama at a Fox News broadcast: "I want to cut his nuts off. ..." There's an interesting parallel here with Ellison's *Invisible Man*, where in a dream, all of the antagonists confront the anonymous protagonist on a bridge and castrate him. The invisible man is asked, "HOW DOES IT FEEL TO BE FREE OF ILLUSION" (569–70).

[28]See Rick Perlstein, *Nixonland: The Rise of a President and the Fracturing of America* (New York: Scribner, 2008) for more on the notion of a generation gap. Also see Andrew Sullivan's *Atlantic* cover essay, "Goodbye to All That: Why Obama Matters," December 2007, http://www.theatlantic.com/doc/200712/obama (accessed August 12, 2010). Sullivan distinguishes what he takes to be Obama's relative civility from the tendency of the Clintons (and others of the Baby Boom generation—the broader umbrella that would roughly include members of "Reverend Wright's

That Ellison and Obama would find resonant conflicts with the same generation of black activists throws into relief a number of shared political and cultural assumptions. Ellison was a singularly ambitious novelist, aspiring to inscribe the cultural and social particularities of African-American experience in literature that rivaled Sophocles, Shakespeare, Cervantes, Dostoevsky, Melville—the Western literary canon writ large.[29] For Ellison, blackness was never diminished through this strategy—indeed, he understood race as the signal struggle of American culture.[30] Thus he insisted, at a time when "Negro" literature frequently protested openly against social injustice, that his own tragic relationship to skin color was in fact better represented by analogies in Western literature. He situated the complexity and ambiguity of a DuBoisean double-consciousness in the correspondences between aesthetic statements such as jazz and the blues with tragedy, the epic, the novel, and other literary forms. For this reason, we find a profound sense of racial symbiosis in Ellison's novelistic treatments of race in America—especially in the unfinished second novel, which concerns a racist white senator, mortally wounded on the senate floor, whom we first meet as a child preacher of indeterminate racial identity (passing for white), adopted by a black minister and raised by his Southern black congregation in the preaching tradition of black churches. This church incubates the very oratorical skills that ultimately facilitate his racist legislative agenda. Accordingly, instead of articulating race in America as a classic dialectic, Ellison ironizes the dialectic form. Struggle becomes a reciprocal art. Antagonism becomes a cooperative prospect because one's identity is forged within this very struggle. Ellison's second novel depicts stunning examples of betrayal and unconditional love, of the very intimacies that relate white and black, and their proximities, ambiguities, and indeterminacies in the United States.

Obama finds similar ambiguity in his white grandmother, whom he describes in the Philadelphia address as "a woman who helped raise me, ... a woman who loves me as much as she loves anything in this world, but a woman who once confessed her fear of black men who passed by her on the street, and who on more than one occasion has uttered racial or ethnic stereotypes that made me cringe."[31] The white grandmother—the warmth of her love and the sting of her exclusion—endows young Obama with the tools necessary to decipher and ultimately to embrace his black identity. In this way, he

---

generation" [as Obama describes them in the Philadelphia address]) to rely upon confrontation and partisan bickering—an attribute that Sullivan suggests is a hallmark of that generation. In this case, the generation gap, in a manner of speaking, "transcends" race.

[29]Ralph Ellison, "The Art of Fiction: An Interview," *The Collected Essays of Ralph Ellison*, John F. Callahan, ed. (New York: Modern Library, 1995), 210-24 (212).

[30]Harvey Breit, "Talk with Ralph Ellison," *New York Times*, May 4, 1952, BR26.

[31]See the "A More Perfect Union" speech.

deals in analogies that translate across racial lines in the Philadelphia address, analogies of conflict that reveal the cooperative nature of such antagonism. He juxtaposes Jeremiah Wright and his white grandmother; working-class racial frustration becomes more about the perception of privilege and unrecognized hard work than a function of phenotype. Obama himself becomes a microcosm of "America," embracing the Whitmanesque contradictions that comprise his identity (white and black; Kansas, Kenya, and Harlem; et al.) as the cooperative sum of its antagonistic parts.[32]

For Ellison and Obama, then, race becomes less a diagnosis of a problem, racism less a disease that plagues the American body politic, and more a symptom through which increasingly expansive social ills might be translated and communicated across interpersonal and intersubjective borderlines. Despite race's historical role in marking division, separation, and distinction, for Ellison and Obama, there remains the sense—and, moreover, the hope—that such a boundary may also serve as a point of convergence, a fracture that may yet mend to full strength. In this way we may understand Obama's Ellisonian ambition. If Ellison chafed against what he deemed to be the limitations of protest fiction and its categorical determinations of racial identity, aspiring instead to translate African-American experience into literature much in the same way that he understood Shakespeare or Dostoevsky to translate the particular experiences of their historical, social, and political occasions, we might understand Obama, too, to look beyond what he might believe to be the political limitations of Jacksonesque or Sharptonesque presidential aspirations—rooted as they were in a protest tradition that determined the role of the black candidate—and to aspire to the presidential pantheon of Lincoln, Roosevelt, Kennedy, and even Reagan.

Civil Religion

A third correspondence between Ellison and Obama reflects upon their masterful abilities to wield symbols of and allusions to American civil religion in order to characterize the particular urgency of the problem at hand. Both depict race as a fundamentally American issue; it defines the nation's inability to align the reality of the American experience with the promises of its founding documents. Slavery, then, for both Ellison and Obama, serves as the "American original sin," a point of identification upon which multiple understandings of the "American" ideal may converge.[33] Furthermore, on a very cursory level,

---

[32] As Walt Whitman famously wrote in the fifty-first stanza of *Leaves of Grass*: "Do I contradict myself? / Very well then I contradict myself. / (I am large, I contain multitudes)."

[33] See Obama's "A More Perfect Union" and Ralph Ellison, "Perspective of Literature," *Collected Essays*, 778.

we find that both Ellison and Obama express interest in talismans of civil religion: Ellison employs the Lincoln Memorial to great effect in the second novel, and elsewhere ruminates at length upon the founding documents of American independence.[34] Obama similarly announced his presidential intentions in front of the Old Capitol building in Springfield, Illinois—the same location where Lincoln announced his candidacy in 1860. He delivered the "A More Perfect Union" speech across the street from Independence Hall in Philadelphia where the Constitution to which his title referred was signed. In this speech, he acknowledges his "*faith* in the American people" to overcome racial divisiveness, and frames the perfection of the union like a good dissenting Protestant: "For we have a choice in this country. We can accept a politics that breeds division, and conflict, and cynicism. ... That is one option. Or, at this moment, in this election, we can come together and say 'not this time.'"[35] Obama's language is textbook Wesleyan theology adapted to an electoral context, one in which the choice in the voting booth corresponds to choices of eternal consequence. The political choice resonates with eschatological urgency. The salvation at stake does not belong to the individual but to the nation.

Martin Marty notes that American civil religion has become increasingly difficult to discuss in the present tense because a shift in American ontology, effected in the 1960s, transformed the American identity from a "centripetal" one (which means that all outlying properties are thrust toward a central point of identity) to a "centrifugal" one (wherein a central point of identification is fractured, thrusting common elements toward the periphery).[36] Whereas civil religion historically tended to imagine the sanctification of a unified nation, in recent decades it has served to demarcate particular nationalized communities organized around categories of identity that become sanctified at the expense of the remainder of the whole.

Marty's use of "centripetal" and "centrifugal" aligns with similar oppositional ideas that he finds held in tension by the unofficial motto of the United States: *E Pluribus Unum*, or "one from many."[37] Centripetal in this instance corresponds to the "one"; centrifugal corresponds to the "many." The idea of a central, unified American identity to which one's particular identity relates and through which it is filtered stands as an essentially foreign concept to contemporary discourse on race and identity. We tend to "celebrate diversity" and to shun the hegemonic

---

[34]See, for instance, Graham and Singh, *Conversations with Ralph Ellison*, 336.

[35]See the "A More Perfect Union" speech (emphasis mine).

[36]Martin E. Marty, *Modern American Religion, Vol. 3: Under God, Indivisible (1941–1960)* (Chicago: University of Chicago Press, 1996), 3.

[37]Martin E. Marty, *The One and the Many: America's Struggle for the Common Good* (Cambridge, MA: Harvard University Press, 1997), 3.

tendencies of cultural imperialism(s), those forces that thrust peripheral objects toward the center, which can obfuscate particularities of identity and impose artificial cohesion where little might pertain. Still, perhaps more than any other figure with whom we might sensibly compare Obama, he and Ellison share a significantly—and uniquely—centripetal orientation. On a sliding scale of "one" and "many," both men clearly favor the "one." Such oneness makes it possible to suggest that the object of political discourse geared toward race, or toward war, or toward some other potentially divisive proposition, is a matter of perfecting the union. In this way, it works toward a common good.

It is this common good that simultaneously seemed so anachronistic in Obama's campaign rhetoric and appealed to so many people across the diversity of the American populace. He succeeded in representing both a metaphorical and a literal return to a centripetal orientation of "America" by expanding the concept of nation to include a greater number of the "many" within the "one." And yet, whereas in the past such singular orientations have been exclusive, segregated, even jingoistic, the Obama effect represents an aspiration not to isolate oneness from the many, but to locate a oneness within this multitude. In this way— through the creative reorganization of older, exclusive definitions of nation and identity into a renewed democratic prospect—Obama represents the ideal Ellisonian figure. This new dispensation renovates older, "traditional" conceptions of nation, identity, and citizenship within a radically contemporary variation upon the American theme. Such prospects are fleeting; they require tremendous humility in order to be sustained. Yet the Obama campaign rhetoric in 2008's election resonated strongly with the following passage from Ellison's second novel—a passage at once heavily ironized and yet perfectly sincere, spoken—interestingly enough—by the race-baiting Sunraider on the Senate floor:

> So let us not falter before our complexity. Nor become confused by the mighty, reciprocal, enginelike stroking of our national ambiguities. We are by no means a perfect people—nor do we desire to be so. ... We do not seek perfection, but coordination. Not sterile stability but creative momentum. Ours is a youthful nation. ... [It] was designed to solve those vast problems before which all other nations have been proved wanting. Born in diversity and fired by determination, our society was endowed with a flexibility designed to contain the most fractious contentions of an ambitious, individualistic, and adventurous breed. Therefore, as we go about confronting our national ambiguities, let us remember the purposes of our built-in checks and balances....
>
> E pluribus unum![38]

---

[38]Ellison, *Juneteenth*, 20–21.

Speaking for Whom?

Days after the election, in an interview with the *Wall Street Journal*, Toni Morrison riffed curiously on the president-elect's Ellisonian cache, claiming that "if Ralph Ellison was alive," he would title his book *The Visible Man*.[39] This reversal became a bromide for reflecting upon the significance of Obama's election, but it rests on a misunderstanding of invisibility. Morrison likely intended to make a simpler joke than my overreading here permits, but if we understand Barack Obama, and particularly *President Barack Obama* (who stands, of course, as the people's endorsement of the campaign persona) as anything approaching an Ellisonian figure, we should understand absolutely that his election does not render him visible, but bespeaks his virtuosity at wielding his own invisibility within an American context.

Candidate Barack Obama became the forty-fourth president of the United States by virtue of his ability to recognize and capitalize upon the persistence of Ellisonian invisibility, the recognition that people see in Obama not *himself*, but *themselves*—what they want him to be. Cynics—who are often (unfortunately) correct—will claim that the Obama campaign's unique success in mobilizing unprecedented numbers of voters evinces only the twenty-first-century innovation of politics as usual. If invisibility means that people see what they want to see, an invisible candidate merely represents some fancy form of pandering, of telling different groups precisely what they want to hear rather than adhering to a consistent message or system of beliefs. Only the most naïve could deny, roughly halfway through his first term, that this may yet turn out to be the case—proving right the caricature of Obama as the Joker, a wild card, the roving sign.[40] But beyond such caveats, the Obama Effect, and particularly its Ellisonian genius as both a campaign strategy and political phenomenon, relies upon a capacity to acknowledge, understand, and marshal the concept of invisibility not simply for political victory, but also—at its best—to inaugurate a new American prospect. This prospect is not simple. The scrutiny of the American presidency in the twenty-first century makes the notion of an "invisible president" difficult to achieve—as Obama's early cabinet and court nominations, his legislative battles over health care, and the vociferous resistance of the "Tea Party" movement reveal.

---

[39]Jamin Brophy-Warren, "A Writer's Voice," *Wall Street Journal*, November 7, 2008, W5. Note that Morrison misstates the title's construction. Ellison's novel is *Invisible Man*, not *The Invisible Man*.

[40]Similarly, the word "socialism" that frequently appears below the "Joker" caricature carries ambivalence. Obama is not, of course, a socialist in any practical or theoretical sense of the word. The term, rather, deployed with negative intent, represents shifting, "invisible" categories of grievances that appeal simultaneously to various, diverse factions of resistance to Obama and his broader agenda.

A more hopeful reading of Obama's candidacy and its electoral endorsement suggests that because he contains and embodies such myriad contradictions of American identity, he may yet succeed in the elusive achievement of translating a singular oneness across the many iterations that comprise "America." In this way we do not inhabit, as some suggest, a "postracial" moment; race has not been, and cannot be, "transcended," representing as it does a definitive characteristic of "America." Rather, we find ourselves in a moment of ontological renovation. There may be reason to hope that Barack Obama, emblematic of the Ellisonian ideal and of the complexity of American identity, may yet point to a more perfect iteration of this national character. At the very least, he serves as a reminder of the possibilities that are driven by the antagonistic cooperation that resides between the one and the many, and at the core of an abiding American experiment.

The Obama Effect on American Discourse about Racial Identity: *Dreams from My Father* (and Mother), Barack Obama's Search for Self

Suzanne W. Jones

During the 2008 presidential campaign, Joseph Curl reported that the Obama organization "would not answer when asked why the biracial candidate calls himself black," replying only that the question didn't "seem especially topical."[1] Biracial ancestry and racial identity are still sensitive subjects in the United States, not suitable for sound bites. But they are perfect topics for the introspective musings of an autobiography, and Barack Obama must have thought he had answered this question in depth in *Dreams from My Father* (1995). In his introduction, Obama hesitates to use the term "autobiography" because it connotes, he says, "a certain closure";[2] however, *Dreams from My Father* does provide closure on his quest for identity, if not on his life story. In American literature, the racially mixed black–white figure, more than any other literary character, has embodied the promises and challenges of integration in a racially troubled society.[3] The same might be said about Barack Obama during the presidential campaign. While many supporters embraced his biracial ancestry as emblematic of America, his cosmopolitan, multicultural background as essential for the new century, and his self-described African-American identity as a step toward fulfilling Martin Luther King, Jr.'s, dream, many of his critics questioned his identification as an African American, his unconventional transnational upbringing, and even his Americanness.[4]

---

[1]Joseph Curl, "Who Decided to Call Obama a Black Man?," *Washington Times*, July 8, 2008, B1.

[2]Barack Obama, *Dreams from My Father* (New York: Three Rivers Press, 2004), xvi. Subsequent citations are indicated parenthetically in the text.

[3]Barbara Ladd, *Nationalism and the Color Line in George W. Cable, Mark Twain, and William Faulkner* (Baton Rouge: Louisiana State University Press, 1996), 140.

[4]See, for example, Adam Nossiter, "For Some, Uncertainty Starts at Racial Identity," *New York Times*, October 15, 2008, http://www.nytimes.com/2008/10/15/us/politics/15biracial.html (accessed January 10, 2009). Nossiter reported that when he was interviewing prospective voters

131

In a November 11, 2007, interview with Barack Obama on ABC news, Charlie Gibson quoted a provocative passage from *Dreams from My Father*: "I learned to slip back and forth between my black and my white worlds." Then Gibson asked what he termed a "simple question": "In which world do you really belong?" Obama's answer came quickly and assuredly: "I think it's both."[5] Gibson's question sounds simple, but the psychological, social, and historical reality of racially mixed people in the United States is complex, as *Dreams from My Father* reveals. While the autobiography explains why Obama feels comfortable in both worlds but identifies as African-American, the differences in the way Obama frames his search for self in his 1995 introduction and his 2004 preface to the reprint suggest changes both in his perspective on his autobiography and his hopes for its reception. The book is definitely a search for self, an "interior journey" focused, as he points out in the 1995 introduction, "on a boy's search for his father, and through that search a workable meaning for his life as a black American" (xvi). When he began *Dreams from My Father*, Obama did not view his life as representative of either the black experience or the American experience, although by 2004 he had come to feel it was representative of both.

---

in Mobile, Alabama (the deep South), and rural Virginia (also the deep South), the question of "whether Mr. Obama is black, half-black or half-white often seemed to overshadow the question of his exact stand on particular issues, and rough-edged comments on the subject flowed easily from voters who said race should not be an issue in the campaign." For example, Glenn Reynolds of Martinsville, Virginia, said that he does not trust Obama because he is biracial, claiming that the Bible forbids interracial marriage. Others Nossiter interviewed who perhaps resented Northern reporters expecting white Southerners to be prejudiced against Obama, revealed stereotypical views of African Americans even as they endorsed him for president. A white Obama supporter from Mobile, Alabama, Kimi Oaks, said, "He doesn't come from the African-American perspective-he's not of that tradition. ... He's not a product of any ghetto." (Nossiter mistakenly calls Martinsville, Virginia, "Martinsdale.") And some of Obama's African-American colleagues who should have been his comrades in the Illinois senate rejected the very qualities that drew Oaks to Obama. See, for example, Eli Saslow, "From Outsider to Politician," *Washington Post*, October 9, 2008, A1, A12. If Kimi Oaks was pleased that the first African American to have a shot at the White House was not "too black," members of the Black Caucus in the Illinois state legislature did not think Obama "black enough": "Ricky Hendon and Donne Trotter, fellow black Democrats from Chicago, dismissed him as cocky, elitist and, Trotter said, 'a white man in blackface.'" After reading *Dreams from My Father* for ammunition for their attempts to marginalize Obama, they teased him "for smoking marijuana as a teenager and for being raised by his white grandmother. Most frequently, they ridiculed Obama for his complex ethnicity. *You figure out if you're white or black yet, Barack, or still searching?*" The frosty relationship between Obama and Hendon ended in a shoving match before Hendon stopped teasing Obama and Obama started voting more often with Hendon. To this day, observers of their scuffle in the Illinois legislature wonder if Obama had reacted uncharacteristically, finally losing his temper, or acted characteristically in a calculated way to meet Hendon "on his own level," which won Obama Hendon's respect. Hendon was a lifelong resident of a poor, blighted neighborhood on Chicago's West Side. He supported Obama for president.

[5]Obama, *Dreams from My Father*, 82. Charles Gilson, Interview with Barack Obama, taped 11 November 2007. http://abcnews.go.com/Video/playerIndex?id=3808661 (accessed July 17, 2008).

Refusing to Be a "Tragic Mulatto"

In her analysis of autobiography, Julie Swindells points out that "the autobiographer's voice is often one which is oppositional, heretical, or radical in some way," and in such narratives, the story "moves beyond the life-story of the key individual, and focuses the use of autobiography as part of a political strategy to produce change."[6] If Obama hoped that *Dreams from My Father* would produce any kind of change in 1995, his introduction suggests that he wanted readers to know that a man of racially mixed ancestry could "affirm a common destiny" with black people no matter their nationality (xvi) and that his mixed ancestry did not mean that he was in any way a "divided soul, the ghostly image of the tragic mulatto trapped between two worlds" (xv). And yet the narrative he constructs in *Dreams from My Father* is a contemporary transnational version of that old American story of the "mulatto as existential man,"[7] struggling to find his identity in a society indelibly shaped by a racial caste system.

The first part of Obama's autobiography, "Origins," resembles the narratives of such early twentieth-century biracial writers as Jean Toomer and Nella Larsen who recount the trials of angst-ridden tragic mulattos who could not come to terms with their mixed ancestry or adjust to their social marginality. The second part, "Chicago," recalls the plots of earlier African-American writers who reserved heroic status for racially mixed characters who identified as black and became "race leaders." However, the outcome of Obama's identity quest, which also takes him to Kenya, followed a different narrative arc, which he emphasizes in his "Epilogue." Because times have changed, Obama has been able to forge a meaningful racial identity and a satisfying social role without confining his leadership to the black community or hiding his biracial ancestry. Although he identifies as African-American, he no longer suppresses his mother's race as he had done since puberty, when he suspected that by revealing it, he was "ingratiating" himself to whites (xv). And while he may have begun his career as a "race leader" of sorts, he has become a national leader with a vision for social change. As our forty-fourth president, he is intent on refashioning America's place in a global society and creating a more perfect union at home.

---

[6]Julia Swindells, "Conclusion: Autobiography and the Politics of 'the Personal'" in *The Uses of Autobiography*, 205.

[7]This is one of Judith R. Berzon's categories in *Neither White Nor Black: The Mulatto Character in American Fiction* (New York: New York University Press, 1978), 218–19. Berzon's other categories include the mulatto passing as white, as black bourgeois, and as race leader. Berzon argues that while being moved to positive action or active rebellion was positively regarded by African Americans, "both passing and the desire for acquisition have usually been regarded by blacks as forms of escapism and of denial of self" (219).

By the time *Dreams from My Father* was reissued in 2004—two weeks after the delivery of his electrifying speech at the 2004 Democratic National Convention—Barack Obama had begun to view his life story as an American story. Whether this perspective arose from political expediency, personal wisdom, changing times, or a complex combination of all three is difficult to discern. But Obama writes in the 2004 preface that he went to work on the book "with the belief that the story of my family, and my efforts to understand that story, might speak in some way to the fissures of race that have characterized the American experience, as well as the fluid state of identity—the leaps through time, the collision of cultures—that mark our modern life" (vii). Thus he subtly reframes both the book and his life story, making it a more broadly American story, not only a narrative about race relations and personal identity, but one about the fluidity of identity, cultural hybridity, and globalization—topics that gained currency in the decade since he first published his autobiography, but topics deeply embedded in the text.

Thus, in his interview with Charlie Gibson, Obama presented himself as the quintessential American: "What's interesting is how deeply American I feel. What is quintessentially American is all these different threads coming together to make a single quilt."[8] Not surprisingly, on the campaign trail, he presented himself as a unifier of a country divided by class, race, religion, and politics. Repeatedly emphasizing his biracial ancestry—the son of a white woman from Kansas and a father from Kenya—although never identifying as biracial, he became for his supporters a symbol of hope, occupying the political place that racially mixed figures currently hold in contemporary American literature. For some of his detractors, Obama became a symbol of apprehension, occupying the place that "mulattos" held for white Southerners at the turn of the previous century. Hesitant to play the race card directly, the opposition trotted out one representation after another of Obama as un-American, hoping something would stick.[9] But the majority of Americans decided that racial identity should not be the crucial concern, at least in the case of Barack Obama, whose message was inclusivity. Obama highlighted this message in his 2004 preface to *Dreams from My Father* when he summarized what

---

[8]Gibson, "Interview."

[9]The opposition argued that he wanted to end the war in Iraq or that he had a pastor who said "God damn America," making him unpatriotic; that he attended a Muslim school in Indonesia, making him un-Christian, and so un-American; and finally that his middle name was Hussein and that he "pals around with terrorists," making him anti-American. Later, Republicans claimed that his economic plan meant redistributing wealth, which made him either a communist or socialist, but in either case more European than American, and that his tax plan would remake America into a welfare state, a nod to race. Dark skin and that fist bump with his wife Michelle upon winning the Democratic primary race were just two visual signs to which Obama's detractors hoped all of these allegations would stick.

his life had taught him: the importance of insisting on a "set of values that binds us together" (x) and of rejecting "the hardening of lines, the embrace of fundamentalism and tribe" that "dooms us all" (xi).

Rethinking America's One-Drop Rule

That the racially mixed Obama did not take the path of Tiger Woods and identify as biracial has confounded some Obama supporters, particularly those who are not African-American, as letters to the editors of newspapers around the country attest. A Zogby International poll taken in 2006 asked voters how they saw Obama's race: 55 percent of whites and 61 percent of Hispanics considered him biracial, but only 22 percent of blacks saw him that way.[10] This disproportionate reaction, which persisted throughout the campaign, paradoxically reveals both the lingering effects of the country's racial history and its progress in race relations. Slavery and segregation shaped American understanding of the old "one-drop" rule, in which anyone known to have African ancestry was considered black. American laws have perpetuated this thinking: antebellum laws classified all children born to slave mothers as slaves; until 1989, hospitals assigned babies the racial status of the nonwhite parent; and the U.S. Census relied on hypodescent until 2000, when citizens were allowed to check any number of racial identifiers.[11] Recently, researchers of attitudes about mixed-race identity have discerned an interesting new paradox: As white Americans have become more willing to break the old one-drop rule, many black Americans have held firmly to it, even though they know that most African Americans have mixed ancestry. Their reasons are many and vary from the personal to the ideological.[12] While some, particularly black Americans,

---

[10]Andrew Bolt, "Obama Born to Cross the Colour Divide," *Australian Herald*, February 27, 2008, ED18.

[11]Maria P. P. Root, "The Multiracial Experience: Racial Borders as a Significant Frontier in Race Relations," in *The Multiracial Experience: Racial Borders as the New Frontier*, ed. Maria Root (Thousand Oaks, CA: Sage, 1996), xviii.

[12]I discuss these issues in Race Mixing: *Southern Fiction since the Sixties* (Baltimore: The Johns Hopkins University Press), particularly on pages 229 and 230 and throughout Chapter 5, "Rethinking the One-Drop Rule." In an ongoing struggle against white power and privilege and in an attempt to maintain cultural plurality, many African Americans do not want to dilute their numbers. Also, many do not know the identity of their nonblack ancestors, or if they do, want nothing to do with a kinship begun by rape or with white kin who refuse to acknowledge the family relationship. Others do not acknowledge mixed ancestry for ideological reasons-because they do not want to appear as if they, like some light-skinned African Americans in the past, are ashamed of a black identity. See C. Reginald Daniel, "Black and White Identity in the New Millennium: Unsevering the Ties That Bind," in Root's *The Multiracial Experience*, 132, and see Itabari Njeri's *The Last Plantation: Color, Conflict and Identity Reflections of a New World Black* (Boston: Houghton Mifflin, 1997), 37–38. Those who do identify as biracial or multiracial most often, like Tiger Woods, have parents who are socially recognized as belonging to different races. The present

still see biracial or multiracial identity as threatening racial unity or denying the reality of socially ascribed identity, others, particular racially mixed Americans and their parents, claim that such arguments deny people of mixed ancestry the basic human rights to honor both parents and to classify themselves, and thus to fashion a new American reality with regard to racial identification.[13]

America's thinking about the old one-drop rule has recently begun to change because of increased immigration and growing acceptance of inter-racial marriage as well as new ideas about multiculturalism and postmodern constructions of identity. Psychologist Charmaine Wijeyesinghe has pinpointed eight factors affecting contemporary racial identity formation in the United States: racial ancestry, early experiences and socialization, cultural attachment, physical appearance, social and historical context, political awareness, other social identities such as sexual orientation, and spirituality.[14] These variables help explain why biracial siblings, like Barack Obama and Maya Soetoro-Ng, identify differently, he as African-American and she as biracial. This difference mirrors the statistics of a mid-1990s survey conducted by the Bureau of the Census, which showed that those most likely to choose a multiracial identifica-tion were not African Americans but Asian Americans.[15] Rachel Moran argues that such identification allows lighter-skinned Asian Americans "to begin con-verting their racialized status into one that approximates an ethnic identity."[16]

---

desire of some racially mixed individuals to so identify has met with concern about how their offspring will identify, with worries that such attempts to solve anomalies may create others, and with questions about whether new classifications may worsen race relations or end racial classifica-tion prematurely. But in "Government Classification of Multiracial/Multiethnic People," in Root, *The Multiracial Experience* (29–32), Carlos A. Fernandez addresses important minority concerns, successfully arguing before the U.S. Congress that the issue of entitlement programs being directly tied to population numbers can be finessed by allowing racially and ethnically mixed people to indicate all classifications that apply to their identity, as was eventually done on the 2000 census. See Lawrence Wright, "One Drop of Blood," *New Yorker*, July 25, 1994, for an overview of how and why the Census Bureau has changed racial classifications in the last two centuries (46–55). He argues convincingly that "by attempting to provide a way for American to describe themselves, the categories actually began to shape those identities" (52). See also Farai Chideya's *The Color of Our Future* (New York: William Morrow, 1999) for an argument about how biracial and multiracial identification is closely tied to place; 2000 census figures bear out Chideya's assertion.

[13]Fernandez, "Government Classification," 29–32. See also Maria P. P. Root's "A Bill of Rights for Racially Mixed People" in her *Multiracial Experience* and Itabari Njeri's *The Last Plantation*.

[14]Charmaine L. Wijeyesinghe, "Racial Identity in Multiracial People: An Alternative Paradigm," in *New Perspectives on Racial Identity Development*, ed. C. L. W. and Bailey W. Jackson (New York: New York University Press, 2001), 138–43.

[15]Steven A. Holmes, "Panel Balks at Multiracial Census Category," *New York Times*, July 9, 1997, A12.

[16]Rachel Moran, *Interracial Intimacy: The Regulation of Race and Romance* (Chicago: University of Chicago Press, 2001), 167. Moran goes on to argue that "By converting from a racial to an ethnic identity, Asian Americans can sustain a symbolic recognition of ancestry, reflected in choice

But how to explain the different choices of Barack Obama and Tiger Woods, whose skin color is similar and who share African ancestry? Some would say that Obama exhibits racial pride and social realism in his self-identification, while Woods exhibits naiveté at best but at worst elitism or even self-hate. Wijeyesinghe would no doubt ask us to think of the two men as situated selves—products of particular times, places, and personal experiences. Each man publicly named his racial identity at a very different time in our nation's history. Barry became Barack in his college years during the heyday of Afrocentrism and the late-1970s anti-apartheid movement on college campuses. Well over a decade later, in the mid-1990s, Tiger Woods came out as "Cablinasian" on the *Oprah Winfrey Show*. Unlike Obama, Woods grew up with both parents, an Asian mother and an African-American father of mixed ancestry. Today, more young Americans of mixed ancestry are choosing the route Woods took, and quite a few, like Sundee Frazier, Elliot Lewis, and Rebecca Walker, are writing about the process.[17]

Becoming a Black Man

During the presidential campaign, a white woman in Detroit said that "she didn't approve of the way Mr. Obama tries to pass himself off as black despite being raised by a white mother and white grandparents."[18] Such comments expose a profound ignorance about the distinction between racial ancestry and racial identity, but also about the history of the one-drop rule, the social power of ascribed racial group membership, and the personal politics of identification. In the first section of *Dreams from My Father*, "Origins," Obama examines the factors that explain his racial identification. During his early childhood in Hawaii, growing up with his white mother and grandparents, he writes that he was too young to know that he "needed a race" (27), a verb choice laden with American history. During his elementary school years in Indonesia, when distinctions were made, he was often identified as American. But Obama emphasizes that his mother never ignored his black ancestry or African-American history. She supplemented his formal education with her own and his father's experience of shaping their own lives. She praised his

---

of foods or observation of holiday rituals without giving up the privileges of whiteness through intermarriage."

[17]See Frazier's *Check All That Apply: Finding Wholeness as a Multiracial Person* (Downers Grove, IL: InterVarsity Press, 2002); Lewis's *Fade: My Journeys in Multiracial America* (New York: Carroll & Graf Publishers, 2006), and Walker's *Black, White, and Jewish: Autobiography of a Shifting Self* (New York: Riverhead Books, 2001).

[18]Eileen Pollack, "The Top Banana," *New York Times*, October 19, 2008, http://www.nytimes.com/2008/10/19/opinion/19pollack.html?emc=tnt&tntemail1=y (accessed January 10, 2009).

father's brilliance, his drive, and his charm, as well as the resilience and talent of African Americans: "Every black man was Thurgood Marshall or Sidney Poitier; every black woman Fannie Lou Hamer or Lena Horne. ... More than once, my mother would point out: 'Harry Belafonte is the best-looking man on the planet'" (51).

If Obama's mother imparted a mostly heroic version of African-American history, she did warn him about racial bigotry and arm him with books about the civil rights movement and the speeches of Martin Luther King, Jr. Obama traces the growth of his self-confidence to this "stretch of childhood free from self-doubt." This period ended, however, when at age nine, he came across an article about a black man who tried to lighten his skin, an article which he says made him realize "there was a hidden enemy out there, one that could reach me without anyone's knowledge, not even my own."[19] For the first time, he questioned his mother's "account of the world" and his father's place in it (51).

Barry Obama met the "enemy" the next year, when he returned to Hawaii at age ten to live with his grandparents and enroll as a scholarship student at the exclusive private school Punahou. Although his classmates' socioeconomic backgrounds were homogeneous, their racial and ethnic ancestry was diverse (Anglo, Chinese, Hawaiian, Japanese) with the notable exception of African Americans. Obama details how some students laughed at his last name, and others taunted him with racist comments.[20] Obama's attempt to distance himself from the one black girl in his class and win white friends later made him feel guilty. His description of his painful first year at Punahou makes it clear that he did not simply "choose" to be black, as some reporters and pundits have suggested,[21] but that he began the process of becoming "black" when racial identity was thrust upon him. In a rare public statement about his racial identification, Obama told Steve Kroft in a February 2007 interview on *60 Minutes*, "I think if you look African American in this society, you're treated as an African American."[22]

---

[19]Obama, *Dreams from My Father*, 51. Obama remembered the article as appearing in *Life* magazine. The *Chicago Tribune* reported that no such article appeared in the magazine, and later when Obama was questioned about the veracity of the story, he said that it might have been Ebony. The *Tribune* then reported that *Ebony's* archivists could not locate such an article either. Much has been made of this discrepancy. But the important point here is one that Richard Cohen made in an editorial in the *Washington Post* (March 27, 2007): Where the article appeared and whether Obama remembered the source correctly is not as important as the impact of the article on a nine-year-old boy, the "emotional truth" of the incident (A13).

[20]See p. 80. One boy asked if his father was a cannibal, another called him a coon, and a girl wanted to touch his hair.

[21]See Eric Deggans, "Shades of Black," *St. Petersburg Times*, April 15, 2007, 1P; George F. Will, "Misreading Obama's Identity," *Washington Post*, December 30, 2007, B7; Gregory Rodriguez, "MLK Would Be Proud," *Los Angeles Times*, January 21, 2008, A17; Curl, "Who Decided ...?"

[22]See Rodriguez, "MLK Would Be Proud."

In his teens, Obama entered an uncertain period when he struggled to figure out what being "a black man in America" (76) meant. His description of this time of turmoil when he searched for a male role model makes for some of the most compelling and introspective passages in *Dreams from My Father*. Not surprisingly, Obama turned first to his absent father's letters, which he found disappointing because they "provided few clues" (76). There is no evidence that Obama discussed his identity struggle with his grandparents or his mother, although he clearly felt loved and cared for by them and "close" to his mother (75). In fact, Obama suggests that he purposefully kept the struggle from his white family, refusing to return to Indonesia with his mother when she did her fieldwork, preferring instead to concentrate on what he says was a purpose he could "barely articulate" (75).

To fashion his racial identity, Obama turned to popular culture and an older black teenager whom he calls Ray. From the images of pop culture, Obama writes that he learned to "cop a walk, a talk, a step, a style" (78), and he gives readers a playful reminiscence of his youthful swagger. But lest readers grow too fond of the persona, about which he obviously enjoyed reminiscing, Obama abruptly interrupts his tale of growing racial self-confidence with a retrospective analysis that calls into question his youthful definition of blackness: "I was living out a caricature of black male adolescence, itself a caricature of swaggering American manhood … the principal difference between me and most of the man-boys around me—the surfers, the football players, the would-be rock-and-roll guitarists—resided in the limited number of options at my disposal. Each of us chose a costume, armor against uncertainty" (79). Obama goes on to explain that from his friend Ray he learned anger at the white racism that fostered such limited options for black men. But he represents his relationship with Ray as sometimes tense because of Ray's certainty about his own "black" identity. For example, when Obama questioned Ray about his perceptions of white racism, Ray doubted Obama's blackness, thereby exacerbating Obama's insecurity and curtailing the dialogue that Obama says he needed in order to make sense of his own perceptions of white behavior. Obama shapes his youthful identity quest as a more lonely "interior struggle" (76) than his friends remember it,[23] with the result that he presents himself as a teenager very much like the lonely protagonists in the tragic mulatto narratives that he rejects in his introduction.

---

[23]In *Dreams from My Father*, Obama does not depict his friendship with "Ray" in the same way that Obama's actual close friend Tony Peterson remembers their relationship. Tony recalls instead a mutually supportive friendship, built on probing conversations about race relations and racial identity, especially the charge of "acting white" because of their interest in their studies. Whatever the truth of the relationship, the perceptions and/or memories are different. See Toby Harnden, "True Colors," *Daily Telegraph*, August 23, 2008 http://www.lexisnexis.com/us/lnacademic/results/docview/docview.do?docLinkInd=true&risb=21_T5504248128&format=GNBFI&sort=RELEVANCE&startDocNo=1&resultsUrlKey=29_T5504244136&cisb=22_T5504244135&treeMax=true&treeWidth=0&csi=8109&docNo=4 (accessed January 10, 2009).

Rejecting a Biracial Identity

For answers to his existential questions, Obama did not turn to writers who explored the biracial experience, but to writers like Baldwin, Du Bois, Ellison, Hughes, and Wright who analyzed race relations. Obama explains that he wanted to test Ray's "nightmare vision" (85) of white power and black powerlessness, of black self-doubt and the double bind of being labeled militant if one resisted. In all of these black authors, Obama sensed an "anguish" and a "doubt" that he wanted to avoid—"a self-contempt that neither irony nor intellect seemed able to deflect" (87). Obama finally found a model in Malcolm X's "repeated acts of self-creation," with his insistence on respect in the face of white racism (86). In Obama's own second attempt at self-creation, he left Hawaii for Los Angeles, where he sought and found a black community of sorts, a cluster of African-American students who formed what he terms a "tribe"—a significant word choice and a potent concept to which he returns with different connotations later. In college, Obama found that novels like Joseph Conrad's *The Heart of Darkness* finally helped him understand why white people feared black people. His reaction was to recreate himself as a more socially conscious black man, distancing himself from racially mixed students like Joyce who identified as "multiracial" but who had no black friends. Later, Obama admits that he rejected Joyce out of fear, because in her attempt to create her own identity, he recognized his own difficulty with "racial credentials" (100).[24] Interestingly, although Obama viewed Joyce as avoiding black people, she saw black people as avoiding her because she identified as "multiracial": "It's not white people who are making me choose. ... No—it's black people who always have to make everything racial. *They're* the ones making me choose. *They're* the ones who are telling me that I can't be who I am" (100). Obama writes that he "understood" Joyce's insecurity, but he clearly perceives her as "mixed-up" rather than making her own thoughtful choice in naming her identity, albeit a different one than his.[25]

---

[24]Psychologists view multiracial individuals in situations like Joyce's as having dual minority status: minority status within the larger society but also within the minority community, a position that can result in rejection, isolation, and stigmatization from both groups. See Ronald C. Johnson, "Offspring of Cross-Race and Cross-Ethnic Marriages," in *Racially Mixed People in America*, ed. Maria P. P. Root (Newbury Park, CA: Sage, 1992), 239.

[25]Obama, *Dreams from My Father*, 100. In *Fade*, Elliott Lewis reflects that the most offensive misconceptions others have of him are that he identifies as biracial because he is "attempting to avoid being 'stigmatized,'" that he views "being black as negative, bad, or distasteful," and that he is trying "to distance himself" from his black heritage (10). He would no doubt have understood Joyce's frustration. Biracial British writer Zadie Smith, who names biracial identification the "third bogeyman of black life" (the other two are the Uncle Tom and the House Nigger) emphasizes in her own analysis of *Dreams from My Father* that "it's the fear of being mistaken for Joyce" that ensures most biracial people will ignore "the box marked 'biracial' and tick the box marked 'black' on any questionnaire" they complete. See "Speaking in Tongues," *New York Review of Books* 56, no. 3 (February 26, 2009).

Later, in Kenya, when Obama meets his biracial stepbrother Mark (son of his father's third wife), whose physical resemblance to him is uncanny, Obama draws a sharp distinction between Mark's lack of interest in Kenya and their father and his own desire to know, using Mark, as he uses Joyce, to construct another cautionary tale about how not to deal with biracial ancestry. Although his sister Auma explains that being a mixed child in Kenya is not easy (which recalls Joyce's experience in the United States) and although Mark reveals that Obama Sr.'s drunkenness and lack of concern for his wife and children caused a rift between him and his father (behaviors that Barack never experienced firsthand), Barack Obama's own overwhelming desire "to affirm a common destiny" with black people whether in the United States or Africa (xvi) seems to limit (at least in 1995) his understanding of the formative significance of biracial people's different personal experiences. As a result, his autobiography obscures other legitimate ways of being biracial. Ironically, while Obama wants African-American definitions of blackness to be broad enough to include the unique individual he is, he does not go as far as Maria Root's call for emancipating racially mixed people and allowing them to name themselves, just as Tiger Woods (and maybe Joyce) had done.[26]

Obama actually took a rather conventional route to racial identification in the late 1970s and early 1980s when the one-drop rule still reigned supreme. To avoid being "mistaken for a sellout" (100), which he and others considered Joyce, Obama suppressed his mixed ancestry. He learned quickly that his college "tribe" considered a real black man to be "alienated" from white society and to show "loyalty to the black masses" (101). So Obama sought out the politically active black students and the foreign students. He admits that in his desire for acceptance, he confidently divided the "brothers" into those who were politically "conscious," like Marcus, and those who weren't, like Tim (101), who was too close for comfort to Obama's own middle-class upbringing. Not surprisingly, Obama envied black students like Regina, who grew up in a poor black neighborhood in Chicago, with no need to prove her racial authenticity. But Obama reveals that just when he was becoming more confident about exactly what constituted authentic blackness, Marcus upbraided him for calling Tim a "Tom" and Regina pulled him up short for romanticizing her impoverished life in Chicago. Obama's dialectic of certainty and then doubt structures the "Origins" section and works to undermine any certainty that readers, whether black or white, may have about what constitutes authentic blackness.

Listening to His White Mother Within

During this time of searching for "a workable meaning for his life as a black American" (xvi), Obama dreamed of his absent father, but discovered that his

---

[26]See Root, "A Bill of Rights."

core values are rooted in the teachings of his mother: honesty, fairness, straight talk, independent judgment—the very values that he stressed in his inaugural address.[27] He ends his 2004 preface to *Dreams from My Father* saying that had he known his mother would not survive cancer, he might have "written a different book—less a meditation on the absent parent, more a celebration of the one who was the single constant in my life. In my daughters I see her every day, her joy, her capacity for wonder. ... I know that she was the kindest, most generous spirit I have ever known, and that what is best in me I owe to her" (xii). But his mother is present in *Dreams from My Father* at crucial moments. Thoughts of her overwhelmed him and redirected him whenever he fell into the trap of racial authenticity or got caught up in the heady rhetoric of Black Nationalism or wallowed in pessimism about never finding himself. Significantly, he writes, "Sometimes I would find myself talking to Ray about *white folks* this or *white folks* that, and I would suddenly remember my mother's smile and the words that I spoke would seem awkward and false" (81). While Ray assured him that they would never talk this way in front of whites, Obama says he "recognized the risks in his terminology," "how words control thoughts" (81). But his adolescent uncertainty about his racial credentials would not allow him to voice these concerns. Images of his mother also flooded Obama's thoughts when he read Malcolm X's desire to expunge his "white blood" (86), for Obama knew that he could not respect himself if he turned his back on his mother and grandparents. And finally, in his senior year, when he began to suspect that hard work would never get a young black man very far in life, his mother was the one who pushed him on to college.

Obama places his moment of epiphany about his youthful performance of "black" identity at a time when his black friend Regina upbraided him as his mother might have for not striving to be his best self, for judging others too harshly, and for not being considerate of the college's Mexican housekeepers. Even as Regina first encouraged him to embrace his African first name, she judged him more interested in confirming his blackness than in genuine social activism. Obama realized that he had heard similar comments from his grandparents and his mother but stopped listening because they were white.[28] This realization made him understand that morality did not have "a color," causing him to turn his gaze away from "the imagined traps that white authority had set" and back onto himself. He determined that his fear of not belonging to the black community had made him into a "stunted and narrow and small" person

---

[27] Obama, *Dreams from My Father*, 49. President Obama's inaugural address, "What Is Required of Us Now Is a New Era of Responsibility," *Washington Post*, January 21, 2009, A34.

[28] "President Obama's Remarks at National Prayer Breakfast," *New York Times*, February 5, 2009, http://www.nytimes.com/2009/02/05/us/politics/05text-prayer.html (accessed May 17, 2009). At the National Prayer Breakfast, Obama said about his mother, "She was the one who taught me as a child to love, and to understand, and to do unto others as I would want done."

and that "a lack of imagination, a failure of nerve," had made him think that he had "to choose" between the black and the white people in his life (110–11). As a result, he momentously concluded, "My identity might begin with the fact of my race, but it didn't, couldn't end there," only to reflect with characteristic irony on his conclusion: "at least that's what I would choose to believe" (111). With such a qualification, Obama knew that others, black and white, would attempt to define him, but he vowed that he would do what he could to define himself, thus acting with the renewed determination that his mother had not wanted him to cede to either white racism or bad luck. Obama ends the chapter paying homage to the determination of his many "grandmothers" and their expectations of him: Regina's Chicago grandmother living in poverty, his Indonesian step-grandmother grieving as the Dutch burn her home, his white grandmother Toot boarding the bus at 6:30 a.m. for work (111). This racially mixed image stands out as the first time Obama is able to embrace his biracial ancestry and his multicultural upbringing and still think of himself as African-American. Obama begins the next and final chapter of "Origins" with a letter from his father, reminding him how important it is to know both "your people" and "where you belong" (114). Obama leaves Los Angeles for New York, eager to find that place, more certain of himself as a black American, but also convinced that he did not yet understand the real basis of black community.

Searching for a Black Community

In "Origins," Obama lays bare the social construction of race and the power of racial authenticity to conflict with an individual's desire for self-creation. Philosopher Charles Taylor has argued that "a basic condition of making sense of ourselves" is that "we grasp our lives in a narrative."[29] Just as the "tragic mulatto" narrative was not a script that Obama wanted to shape his life, neither was the black oppositional narrative of self-construction in the face of white racism suited to his family. And yet at the same time that Obama struggled to find a narrative useful to his own self-fashioning, he needed a black community to validate his identification with black people. Taylor describes the need for belonging this way: "On the intimate level, we can see how much an original identity needs and is vulnerable to the recognition given or withheld by significant others."[30] The tension Obama felt between his own individuality and the collective black identities he encountered as a young man exemplifies Taylor's argument that the self is dialogically constructed. Philosopher Anthony Appiah, whose mother is English and whose father is Ghanaian,

---

[29]Charles Taylor, *The Ethics of Authenticity* (Cambridge, MA: Harvard University Press, 1991), 40.

[30]Charles Taylor, "The Politics of Recognition" in *Multiculturalism: Examining*, ed. Amy Gutmann (Princeton, NJ: Princeton University Press, 1994), 36.

is not as sanguine about the available collective black identities as Taylor is, and thus raises two questions that Taylor does not: "how existing identities should be treated; and what sort of identities there should be." As a result, Appiah emphasizes that recognition can become imposition and limitation.[31] Although Obama represents any quest for racial authenticity as a delusion and self-identity based solely on race as a limitation, he represents finding a racial community to validate his own sense of self as necessary to emerge from his existential crisis. As a result, he transferred to Columbia University to be closer to urban black neighborhoods, but not until he moved to Chicago after college did he find the sense of black community that he sought.

Not surprisingly, Obama begins the "Chicago" section of his autobiography by saying, "I still had wounds to heal, and could not heal myself" (138). His biracial ancestry hovered at the forefront of his consciousness, even as once again he hid it from those he met. Significantly, he shows how his biracial ancestry intrudes on his thoughts in a setting where he feels confident about his blackness—the barbershop. As Obama shared in the excitement about Harold Washington's election as Chicago's first black mayor, he writes that he wondered if the men would still include him in their celebration if his white grandfather walked into the barbershop. Later, he confronted his own biracial ancestry more directly when he met two biracial girls and their white mother, who had been disowned by her parents and abandoned by her black husband. While Obama was friendly enough with Mary for her to share her tragic story with him, he pointedly refused to share his biracial family story with her, even when she encouraged him to open up. With Mary and her daughters, Obama stayed on the black side of the boundary, much as he did with Joyce at Occidental College.

But working as a community organizer in black neighborhoods in Chicago allowed Barack Obama to experience firsthand the organic sense of black community that he needed to validate himself as a black man and eventually simply to be himself: an intellectual and an athlete, a cosmopolitan man who needed roots. Through organizing, Obama was able both to align himself with the 1960s civil rights workers he admired and to gain another definition of black community, one that gave him hope of acceptance: "I saw the African-American community becoming more than just the place where you'd been born or the house where you'd been raised. Through organizing, through shared sacrifice, membership had been earned. And because membership was earned—because this community I imagined was still in the making, built on the promise that the larger American community, black, white, and brown, could somehow redefine itself—I believed that it might, over time, admit the uniqueness of my own life" (135).

---

[31]Anthony Appiah, *The Ethics of Identity* (Princeton, NJ: Princeton University Press, 2005), 108.

An important corollary lesson that Obama learned about community activism—that it is fueled by self-interest—resulted in his listening to the stories South Side Chicagoans told about their lives. Such close associations not only allowed him to determine what issues to pursue, but also enabled him to break out of the isolation that had engulfed him since his identity crisis in Hawaii. Listening to their stories gave Obama the courage to finally tell his own—"stories of Toot or Lolo or my mother and father, of flying kites in Djakarta or going to school dances at Punahou." His fear of "foreignness," of "disturbing expectations," gradually dissipated as the African Americans he met offered stories to "match or confound his" (190). Psychologist John Shotter's concept of social accountability pertains here; he argues that "one *ontologically* learns how *to be* this or that kind of person" in conversation with other people.[32] Obama suppressed such conversations in college, except with Regina, because he knew that his black bona fides would be called into question by young African Americans with their own insecurities. By the time he left Chicago for Harvard Law School, Obama realized that the African Americans who had come to know his life story did not question his racial identity or his black community membership, even though he was leaving to attend an elite white university: "No one expected self-sacrifice from me. ... As far as they were concerned, my color had always been a sufficient criterion for community membership, enough of a cross to bear" (278).

Before he left Chicago, Obama joined Reverend Jeremiah Wright's church, which cemented his membership in the black community. His lack of religious conviction and connection to a black church, an institution central to black cultural life, marked a crucial way in which Obama did not share in the black experience, one more reminder of his outsider status. Chronologically, he links his decision to join the church with Mayor Washington's unexpected death and unfulfilled promise, finding that the hope in Wright's message and the inclusivity of his congregation fostered "a powerful program ... more pliant than simple nationalism, more sustaining than my own brand of organizing" (268). The trajectory of Obama's identity quest reflects the central paradox of individuation; according to psychologist Jessica Benjamin, "at the very moment of realizing our own independence, we are dependent upon another to recognize it."[33] But even as Obama reveled in immersing himself in the black community in Chicago, he needed to resolve key questions regarding the black community and its relationship to the majority white society. These concerns also shape the "Chicago" section and determine its cast of characters: Does black pride

---

[32]John Shotter, "Social Accountability and the Social Construction of 'You,'" in *Texts of Identity*, ed. John Shotter and Kenneth J. Gergen (London: Sage, 1989), 138.

[33]Jessica Benjamin, *The Bonds of Love: Psychoanalysis, Feminism, and the Problem of Domination* (New York: Pantheon, 1988), 33.

depend on a racial loyalty that brooks no critique of African Americans? Can black people love themselves without hating white people? Is black nationalism really an effective strategy for building community? Can knowledge of African culture heal the community's social ills?

Moving beyond Tribalism/Nationalism/Afrocentrism

Much the way Obama selected scenes and situations in "Origins" to question received definitions of black identity, he chose encounters with a variety of community leaders in "Chicago" to resolve his questions about the best basis for black community. By observing the minimal success of Marty, the white community organizer who hired him, he learned early on that thinking in race-blind terms about poverty was not the way to understand African Americans in South Side Chicago or to find solutions for their deep-rooted social problems—from the lack of self-esteem to the prevalence of violence. At the same time, Obama ran into equally problematic African-American approaches to the problems. The first was a wall of blind racial allegiance erected when Harold Washington became mayor. Chafing at the refusal of one community leader, Reverend Smalls, to admit problems with the black policemen who inadequately patrolled their neighborhoods, Obama labeled himself a "heretic" because he refused such a racial allegiance that ignored the truth. Not wanting to be ostracized by the very community that he sought to help and that he needed to validate his blackness, Obama turned his attention to another problem—lack of jobs. But he represents the frustrating experience with Reverend Smalls as an example of both the psychological causes of racial loyalty and the social problems that misplaced allegiance can perpetuate: "[T]he men in the barbershop didn't want the victory of Harold's election—their victory—qualified. They wouldn't want to hear that their problems were more complicated than a group of devious white aldermen, or that their redemption was incomplete. … [I]n politics, like religion, power lay in certainty—and that one man's certainty always threatened another's" (163). Much like his rhetorical strategy in "Origins," Obama refuses to subscribe to such certainty. As a result, a chapter that begins by celebrating the camaraderie of a black barbershop ends by questioning a racial loyalty that distorts the truth and thus impedes social progress.

If in many respects Reverend Smalls stands in for an older generation of religious black leaders, Rafiq represents a younger generation's response. Advocating black ownership of businesses in a black community where Koreans are the shopkeepers, Rafiq employs black nationalism's affirming message "of solidarity and self-reliance, discipline and communal responsibility" (197) as a blueprint for racial uplift, and pairs this positive message with a blanket indictment "of everything white" (198). Obama uses Rafiq's lack of success to explain "how nationalism could thrive as an emotion and flounder as a program" (203). He observes that while Rafiq's "unambiguous morality tale" worked as a rallying cry because it was easily communicated (198), it failed as a program of action for two reasons: because white people could not be removed from the daily lives of most African Americans and because race-baiting and blind racial allegiance eroded African Americans' ability to hold themselves or members of their community "accountable" (203). Obama's experience with Rafiq links problems of nationalism and community back to his earlier conclusions about authenticity and identity: "that notions of purity—of race or of culture—could no more serve as the basis of the typical black American's self-esteem than it could for mine. Our sense of wholeness would have to arise from something more fine than the bloodlines we'd inherited" (204).

Asante, an Afrocentric school counselor took a cultural approach, particularly to the problem of black boys drawn to gangs and violence in order to prove their manhood. Concerned that the history they learn in school is not only "someone else's history" but the history of a culture that has denied their "humanity" (258), Asante exposed black students to African history, geography, and artistic traditions so as "to give them a different values orientation—something to counteract the materialism and individualism and instant gratification that's fed to them the other fifteen hours of their day." (259). Obama worked with Asante to set up a mentoring program, but not because of its Afrocentric focus. Both the school principal's inspiring practice of involving parents in their children's educations and Obama's own experience of having an absent father, whose African birthright he had researched to little effect as a boy in Hawaii, led Obama to believe that it was not so much African culture as Asante's presence that made a difference in the boys' lives. This chapter of *Dreams from My Father* begins and ends with Obama observing black gang members asserting their manhood, first with guns and finally with speakers blaring late at night. At first, Obama compares his teenage "assertion of self" with theirs, but then emphasizes an important difference. While most of the black boys he met did not know their fathers, Obama had a loving relationship with his white grandfather, which he contends contained his "unruly maleness" by fostering both guilt and empathy. As a result, he had a stake in the social order that the gang members did not, a difficult position to negotiate because that very social order made "them objects of fear or derision" (271). Obama's representation of his encounter with the unruly black youth is significant for several reasons. Most important, it signals the growing complexity of his understanding about race and community, evidenced by the way he employs the word "tribe" in this chapter. While Obama's skin color had placed him in the close-knit segregated "tribe" (98) of African-American college students at Occidental and at first leads him to align himself with the Chicago youth, his own position in the larger social order in Chicago locates him and these black boys in "different tribes, speaking a different tongue, living by a different code" (270–71). The knowledge of that difference led Obama to understand how their fathers' absence had affected the black boys and weakened the black community as well as the larger social fabric. Finally, although Obama does not point out the parallel, his reluctantly admitted fear of the black gang members calls to mind his grandmother's fearful reaction to a black man that had disturbed him as a teenager in Hawaii.

The word "tribe" appears frequently in *Dreams from My Father*. Obama's knowledge of how African tribes function, gleaned from his African half-siblings Auma and Roy and from his own trip to Africa, is evident in his analysis of group behavior throughout the text. When describing his feelings of teenage isolation, he focuses on the security a "tribe" can engender; when feeling more secure as a member of the black community in Chicago, he senses the problems tribal behavior can foster. Not surprisingly, in the "Chicago" section, Africa intrudes on Obama's meditation about black community. In the middle of the chapter detailing Asante's love of African culture, Obama describes his meeting with his African half-brother Roy, whose life had been shaped as much by his father's absence as his African upbringing. This view corroborates Obama's belief that caring human relationships, especially with male role models one knows, not those one reads about on a distant continent, are the true source of Asante's success with young black men. Following the chapter on black nationalism, Obama inserts a chapter about Auma, which reveals three significant pieces of information, one of which seems a direct commentary on the problems of tribalism no matter their origin. Auma asserted that tribalism in Kenya had led to government corruption and the loss of their father's job, when he began to speak out against the unethical and illegal behavior of the majority tribe in power.

A second revelation of the ups and downs of Auma's love affair with a German man leads Obama to share with his sister that he too has had an interracial love affair while in New York. Chronologically, he should have analyzed this love affair in "Origins," but he withholds this important revelation until halfway through his "Chicago" section. Did Obama want to make sure his readers no longer saw him as a "tragic mulatto" before revealing a piece of his personal history that some might use to label him so? In Bliss Broyard's interracial family history, *One Drop*, about her writer father Anatole, she asserts that the black community discerns the biracial person's racial loyalties by his or her choice of a life partner. Obama uses his termination of an interracial love affair as evidence of his commitment to the black community: "I realized that our two worlds, my friend's and mine, were as distant from each other as Kenya is from Germany. And I knew that if we stayed together I'd eventually live in hers. After all, I'd been doing it most of my life. Between the two of us, I was the one who knew how to live as an outsider" (211).

Perhaps most significant for Obama's own sense of self at this juncture of his life was the portrait Auma painted of their father, not the "brilliant scholar, the generous friend, the upstanding leader" his mother had drawn for him, but a man who serially abandoned his children, abused his wives, and drank too much, a man who ended his life a "defeated, lonely bureaucrat" (220). This new image of his father destroyed the "fantasy" that had kept Obama from despair, and it eventually sent him to Kenya in search of a way not only to reconcile the two portraits, but also to revise the narrative of his own life: "Where once I'd felt the need to live up to his expectations, I now felt as if I had to make up for all his mistakes. Only the nature of those mistakes still wasn't clear in my mind; I still couldn't read the signposts that might warn me away from the wrong turns he'd taken. Because of that confusion, because my image of him remained so contradictory—sometimes one thing, sometimes another, but never the two things at once—I would find myself, at random moments in the day, feeling as if I was living out a preordained script, as if I were following him into error, a captive to his tragedy" (227).

Locating his African Father

If Barack Obama's experiences in Chicago proved that he was not destined to follow the "tragic mulatto" script, his trip to Kenya showed him that he was not captive to his father's ill-fated script either and ultimately opened him up to a more racially integrated and multicultural community on his return to the United States. What he learned in Africa gave him the confidence to be the "cultural mulatto" that he already was and, ironically, to follow his father's earlier path. Except for the first chapter and several pages of the last, the "Kenya" section of *Dreams from My Father* is not as introspective as the first two sections. Often reading like a travelogue or a transcript of family oral history, this section, however, performs two very important functions. Obama's descriptions of Kenyan people and places both explain and revise the romantic views of Africa he encountered in Chicago as well as position conflicting views of his father in a cultural context that resolves that contradiction. In a sea of black faces, Obama experienced "the transformation that Asante and other black Americans claimed to have undergone after their first visit to Africa": "the freedom that comes from not feeling watched. … Here the world was black, and so you were just you; you could discover all those things that were unique to your life without living a lie or committing betrayal" (311). Obama reveled in this ease and basked in the added special "comfort" of effortless "belonging" that comes as strangers recognized his name and family connections. For the first time in his life, he says, "I felt the comfort, the firmness of identity that a name might provide, how it could carry an entire history in other people's memories" (305). However, Obama came to these conclusions in the first two days he was in Nairobi, as a tourist might. It took him several weeks to see Africa as a real place instead of "a new promised land" (302). As many an African-American tourist before him, he embraced Kenya's "ancient traditions and sweeping vistas, noble struggles and talking drums," but he was there long enough to observe what tourists might miss: tribal conflicts and gender inequities, collisions of ethnicities and lingering effects of colonialism, widespread poverty and extensive nepotism. Both through his sister Auma's ambivalent feelings toward Africa and the expectations placed on him there, he came to see that the family closeness he admired, which "conformed" to his "idea of Africa and Africans, an obvious contrast to the growing isolation of American life" (328) provided pleasure and joy, but also promoted dependency and demands that could engender guilt.

As Africa became more than an idea, Obama's father became more than a myth. In Kenya, Obama could better understand how his father was shaped by both his culture and his cosmopolitan experiences. His father's sister Zeituni saw his financial troubles as a product of extended family expectations that he provide for them all, his daughter Auma explained his dismissal from his government post as a failure to remember how tribalism worked, and his brother Sayid thought the African practice of having multiple wives produced distance between him, his wives, and his many children. In her family history, Granny, the woman who raised Obama's father, pointed out a family dynamic of brilliant, adventurous sons rebelling against strong fathers, of fathers pushing sons away, and of sons, who were open to other cultures and other ideas, reinventing themselves. The Kenya section, like the other two, concludes with Obama weeping. At the end of "Origins," his tears spring from loss. When he learns of his father's death, he realizes the profound effect that his father's absence has had on his life. At the end of "Chicago," his tears come from joy, at the gift of community he has gained by joining a church. At the end of "Kenya," weeping between the graves of his father and grandfather, he mourns the unfulfilled dreams of his father who failed because he had "clung to too much and too little" of his past: "Too much of its rigidness, its suspicions, it male cruelties. Too little of the laughter in Granny's voice, the pleasures of company while herding the goats, the murmur of the market, the stories around the fire" (428). Here Obama's tears are cathartic because his trip to Africa closed the "circle" on his understanding of self and gave him a sense of "wholeness" that had eluded his father (430).

Embracing the Fullness of His Identity

In the epilogue to *Dreams from My Father,* Obama reveals his new self understanding through two significant scenes. Even as he identifies as African-American, these scenes show him to be a twenty-first-century American: a cultural hybrid with racially mixed ancestry, a distinct individual at home in a diverse society. Before he left Africa, he visited with his sister Auma's history professor, Dr. Rukia Odero, and asked her if there is anything that's "truly African." She concluded her brief answer with an aside of more importance: "I'm less interested in a daughter who's authentically African than one who is authentically herself." (435). This is the hard-won conclusion that Barack

Obama's own introspective musings about race, culture, and identity had led him to, so it is not surprising that he places Dr. Odero's statement so prominently in his autobiography. Obama rapidly concludes his autobiography, jumping to his marriage six years later to Michelle Robinson, a native of South Side Chicago but a woman of a larger world, educated at Princeton and Harvard. The symbolism of the wedding celebration reveals Barack Obama's cultural and racial hybridity. Images of mixing and mingling permeate the final pages of *Dreams from My Father*. His African half-siblings are present for the wedding in Chicago, as is his Indonesian half-sister and his white mother and grandmother. Obama's black friends tell his mother what a good job she did raising him; his grandmother from Kansas embraces her grandson's African relatives.[34] Obama's toast is followed by the African custom of dribbling drinks onto the floor for the ancestors. That his toast "to a happy ending" (442) is positioned on the very last page of his narrative of existential angst suggests that Obama has successfully fashioned an identity that he is comfortable with (an African American willing to speak openly about his biracial ancestry) and a social role that brings him satisfaction (finding common ground among people with diverse backgrounds and ideologies).

After Barack Obama's inauguration as the forty-fourth president of the United States, African-American columnist Courtland Milloy wrote that because of the "racial politics that characterized the presidential contest," no one sung Obama's mother Ann's praises: "She was most often presented as Exhibit A in attempts to prove that Obama was biracial, not black. Or not black enough."[35] Despite its title, *Dreams from My Father* reveals that Barack Obama is the man he is because of dreams from both his father and his mother, as Milloy emphasized. His parents dreamed of an interconnected world beyond a narrow focus only on race or tribe. The breakup of their marriage, as Barack Obama points out, left him occupying "the place where their dreams had been" (27). His ability to be comfortable in many communities and to speak with many voices makes him most American. But because of our own tribal history, this is a lesson that Americans have been slow to learn, a lesson that *Dreams from My Father* powerfully teaches. If Barack Obama's reticence to discuss his racial identity formation during his presidential campaign was a missed opportunity, his very presence on the national stage is compelling Americans to talk more openly about how we define racial and national identity. Since the

---

[34]The diversity of the wedding celebration calls to mind the utopian idyll of Obama's African safari with its global cast of characters (a Kibuyu driver and his daughter, Barack and his sister Auma from the rival Luo tribe, an Italian man, and a British couple) with their history of African tribalism and British colonialism, but with none of these perils in the present. The way they get along, despite initial stereotyping, makes Obama wish for "that time before Babel" (356).

[35]Courtland Milloy, "A Mother's Lasting Values Shine through Obama's Words," *Washington Post*, January 21, 2009, A43.

election, a number of racially mixed Americans have spoken more openly about their racial identification (however they choose to define it), many Americans have grown more optimistic about race relations, and young African Americans have gained a new role model.[36] But as talk radio and Internet sites recycle the same old lies from the campaign, other Americans have grown fearful of the change Obama embodies.[37]

---

[36]Numerous newspaper articles from around the country, especially immediately following the election and the inauguration, verify these effects. Take for example these three from the *Washington Post*: Krissah Thompson's "In Obama's Run, Finding a Long-Sought Sense of Acceptance," January 11, 2009, C4; Michael Alison Chandler and Maria Glod's "Multiracial Pupils to Be Counted in New Groups," March 23, 2009, A1, A4; and DaNeen L. Brown's "To Teach, They Reach For Obama: President-Elect Viewed as a Role Model for Kids," December 13, 2008, C1, C7.

[37]Frank Rich's editorial, "The Obama Haters' Silent Enablers," in the *New York Times*, June 14, 2009, summarizes a minority of Americans' fearful reactions to Obama at a time when his popularity is quite high, both at home (65 percent) and abroad. That minority was quick to question Obama's Supreme Court nominee Sonia Sotomayor; interestingly, her gender was not nearly as much of a negative factor as her ethnic background; see Jon Cohen and Robert Barnes, "Most Americans Want Sotomayor on Court," *Washington Post*, June 28, 2009, A3.

Our First Unisex President?
Obama, Critical Race Theory,
and Masculinities Studies

*Frank Rudy Cooper**

During the 2008 Democratic presidential primaries and general election, there was a discourse in the media about Senator Barack Obama's femininity. When he faced Senator Hillary Clinton in the primaries, the head of a women's nonprofit said, "He's the girl in the race."[1] The magazine *Marketing* said, "In swept Barack Obama with what could be described as a classically feminine campaign.... The values he represented contrasted with Clinton in being more collaborative, more human, more feelings-led and people-focused."[2] While Clinton was tough and hawkish, Obama was empathetic and inclusive.[3] As Carol Marin wrote in the *Chicago Sun Times*:

> If Bill Clinton was once considered America's first black president, Obama may one day be viewed as our first woman president. While [Hillary] Clinton, the warrior, battles on, talks about toughness,

*Copyright © 2010 Frank Rudy Cooper, professor, Suffolk University Law School. I thank Ann C. McGinley, Angela Onwuachi-Willig, Andrew Perlman, Song Richardson, Jessica Silbey, Catherine Smith, and Devon Carbado's Critical Race Theory Colloquium class for incisive feedback. I also thank Ann Brown, Eddie Crane, Diane D'Angelo, Ami Dave, Lia Marino, and Lisa Parker for assistance with research and production. A version of this chapter was originally published in the *Denver University Law Review*. I welcome comments at fcooper@suffolk.edu. For more on masculinities studies, see *Masculinities and Law: A Multidimensional Approach*, ed. Frank Rudy Cooper and Ann C. McGinley (New York: New York University Press, forthcoming 2011)

[1]Amy Sullivan, "Gender Bender," *Time*, June 16, 2008, 36 (analyzing why Hillary Clinton did not win Democratic presidential primary) (quoting Marie Wilson).

[2]Philippa Roberts and Jane Cunningham, "Feminisation of Brands," *Marketing*, September 3, 2008, 26.

[3]Martin Linsky, "The First Woman President? Obama's Campaign Bends Gender Conventions," *Newsweek*, February 26, 2008, http://www.newsweek.com/id/115397/page/1 (accessed August 28, 2010) (arguing that Obama advocates conversation and collaboration while Hillary Clinton supports realism).

and out loud considers nuking Iran, it is Obama who is full of feminine virtues. Consensus. Conciliation. Peace, not war.[4]

For those reasons, a number of people (half-jokingly) refer to Obama as our first "female" president.[5]

In order to evaluate Obama's status as our first "female" president, we must ask, what does it mean to say that a presidential candidate acted in a "feminine" or "masculine" manner? Even someone who believes in a version of cultural feminism has to acknowledge that "masculine" qualities are hardly limited to men, and "feminine" qualities are not limited to women.[6] Cultural feminism posits that women tend to have certain cultural traits that are most prevalent among women, such as focusing on nurturing relationships.[7] Still, "masculine" and "feminine" qualities are nothing more than shared understandings about what it means to act like a man or woman.[8] They are not reflective of stable essences of man or woman as such.[9] Nonetheless, the popular media used these concepts to describe the presidential candidates. Accordingly, I will analyze what it meant that Obama displayed qualities the media called "feminine" during the campaign.

I argue that Obama was more feminine than most mainstream candidates because he is a black male.[10] I base this argument on my theory of the "bipolarity" of media representations of black men.[11] We are typically described as either the completely threatening Bad Black Man or the fully assimilationist Good Black Man. The Bad Black Man is a criminal you might see denigrated on the local news or a race-conscious black leader you might see criticized

---

[4]Carol Marin, "Thanks to Hillary for Being a Winner at Heart," *Chicago Sun Times*, May 11, 2008, A17.

[5]Lucy Berrington and Jeff Onore, "Bam: Our 1st Woman Prez?," *New York Post*, January 7, 2008, http://www.nypost.com/f/print/news/opinion/opedcolumnists/bam_our_st_woman_prez_gtyYtI3muhgCg8g7zrrfNK (accessed August 28, 2010) (noting Obama's feminine style); Linsky, "The First Woman President?"; Marin, "Thanks to Hillary," A17; Roberts and Cunningham, "Feminisation of Brands," 26.

[6]Nancy Ehrenreich, "Disguising Empire: Racialized Masculinity and the 'Civilizing' of Iraq," *Cleveland State Law Review* 52 (2005): 131–32 (noting both sexes can bask in reflected masculinity).

[7]Martha Chamallas, *Introduction to Feminist Legal Theory*, 2nd ed. (New York: Aspen Publishers, 2003), 53–60 (describing the rise of difference feminism).

[8]Michael S. Kimmel, "Masculinity as Homophobia," in *The Gender of Desire: Essays on Male Sexuality* (Albany, NY: State University of New York Press, 2005), 25, 26.

[9]Athena D. Mutua, "Theorizing Progressive Black Masculinities," in *Progressive Black Masculinities*, ed. Athena D. Mutua (New York: Routledge, 2006), 3, 12.

[10]Obama is half-black. Historically, however, one drop of black blood has made you black in the United States. Further, Obama's skin tone made it hard for him to emphasize his whiteness.

[11]Frank Rudy Cooper, "Against Bipolar Black Masculinity: Intersectionality, Assimilation, Identity Performance, and Hierarchy," *University of California at Davis Law Review* 39 (2006): 853.

during political shows.[12] The Good Black Man is a token member of the corporate world or a conservative postrace spokesman.[13] A prime stereotype of the Bad Black Man that Obama must avoid is the stereotype of the angry black man.[14] One way to counter this stereotype is to be unusually calm. Obama has that quality, as well as a penchant for negotiation. Together, those qualities seem to be the source of claims that he would be our first "female" president.[15]

Obama's calmness has roots in the general need of black men to be non-threatening in order to achieve mainstream success. As a youth, Obama learned to be calm in order to assimilate.[16] During the campaign, Obama's calmness in the face of attacks was strategic in order to prevent whites from associating him with the angry black man stereotype. Obama's feminine qualities were necessitated in part by his desire to avoid a stereotype of the Bad Black Man.[17]

Obama's feminization strategy was potentially dangerous, however, since femininity is denigrated in our male-dominated culture. Obama had to engage in a balancing act. He could not be too masculine because that would trigger the Bad Black Man image, but he could not be too feminine because that would have looked unpresidential. Obama seems to have resolved that conflict by being masculine enough to pass the Commander-in-Chief test yet feminine enough to make people comfortable with his blackness.[18] He tried to place himself more toward the middle of the general gender continuum as a means of showing that he was on the good side of the specific black masculinity continuum. The appropriate term for Obama's feminine-but-not-too-much-so style seems to be "unisex."[19]

---

[12]Ibid., 875–79. Jerry Kang argues that the local news is full of stories about violent crimes prominently featuring African Americans as the perpetrators. Jerry Kang, "Trojan Horses of Race," *Harvard Law Review* 118 (2005): 1489–90.

[13]Cooper, "Against Bipolar Black Masculinity," 879–86 (defining Good Black Man). An example of a conservative postrace spokesman is Shelby Steele.

[14]Courtland Milloy, "Maybe It's Time We Redefined Manliness," *Washington Post*, September 10, 2008, B1.

[15]Linsky, "The First Woman President?"

[16]David Remnick, "The Joshua Generation," *New Yorker*, November 17, 2008, 68, 71–77.

[17]I cannot definitively prove that Obama thought about being feminine as a means of avoiding the angry black man stereotype. There is some evidence of such thinking in Joe Klein's "Anger vs. Steadiness in the Crisis," *Time*, October 2, 2008, http://www.time.com/time/politics/article/0,8599,1846401,00 .html (accessed August 28, 2010). However, little that a presidential candidate does is unplanned.

[18]In this sense, Obama was engaged in what Carbado and Gulati call a "comforting strategy." Devon W. Carbado and Mitu Gulati, "Working Identity," *Cornell Law Review* 85 (2000): 1301–04.

[19]One could suggest that Obama's style was "metrosexual," but I do not believe that label fits. The term is "generally applied to heterosexual men with a strong concern for their appearance, and/or whose lifestyles display attributes stereotypically attributed to gay men." (Wikipedia, http://en.wikipedia.org/wiki/Metrosexual [accessed August 28, 2010]). Bernard E. Harcourt, in "Foreword: You Are Entering a Gay and Lesbian Free Zone: On the Radical Dissents of Justice

A unisex style is one that is "designed to be suitable for" either gender.[20] A unisex style can swing both ways, and Obama's style was unisex in that he moved from more masculine to more feminine depending on the context.

While there is some implication that a unisex style is one that lacks the characteristics of either sex, I am emphasizing the fact that a unisex style is one that a member of either gender can adopt.[21] Often the term applies to clothing that can be worn by either men or women.[22] A unisex style fits between the two genders, but not in the sense of being asexual. Obama was more feminine than most presidential candidates, but hardly nongendered, like "Pat" from the famous *Saturday Night Live* skit.[23] Obama's style ranged from his tough-guy acceptance speech at the Democratic convention[24] to playing feminist folk songs at his rallies.[25] Accordingly, I argue that Obama was not our first "female" presidential candidate, but our first unisex candidate.

I will make that argument in three stages. First, I will review some tenets of critical race theory and masculinities studies. Next, I will analyze how the discourse on Obama's femininity is related to both the bipolarity of black masculinity and the denigration of femininity within the hegemonic discourse on masculinity. Finally, I will conclude that Obama has deviated from the norm for presidential candidates and thereby left all of us a little more free to perform our race and our gender as we see fit.[26]

Scalia and Other (Post-) Queers. (Raising Questions about Lawrence, Sex Wars, and the Criminal Law)," *Journal of Criminal Law and Criminology* 94 (2004): 503, 516, defines "metrosexuals" as "generally heterosexual practicing males—sometimes hyper-heterosexual—who share aesthetic sensibilities with the more traditional stereotype of the gay male." Obama's style makes no such suggestion.

[20]*Shorter Oxford English Dictionary on Historical Principles,* 5th ed. (Oxford: Oxford University Press, 2002) (defining "unisex").

[21]Ibid. (defining "unisex").

[22]"Unisex" means different things for people with different identities. Hillary Clinton's version of going unisex was to wear pant suits with conservative blouses. Robin Givhan, "The Frontrunners: Fashion Sense," *Washington Post,* December 18, 2007, http://www.washingtonpost.com/wp-dyn/content/discussion/2007/12/16/DI2007121601778.html (accessed August 28, 2010).

[23]See Wikipedia, http://en.wikipedia.org/wiki/Pat_(Saturday_Night_Live) (accessed August 28, 2010) (describing the character).

[24]Carla Marinucci, "Obama Promises to Restore Promise of the U.S.," *San Francisco Chronicle,* August 29, 2008, A1 (describing Obama's speech as "tough" on McCain).

[25]Michael Scherer, "Hillary Is from Mars, Obama Is from Venus," *Salon.com,* July 12, 2007, http://www.salon.com/news/feature/2007/07/12/obama_hillary/print.html (accessed August 28, 2010) (noting Obama rallies sometimes play Indigo Girls music).

[26]I mean "free" only in the sense that, with one set of assumptions having been broken down, there seems to be more of a possibility that we can break down other assumptions. I agree with Judith Butler that "freedom" is actually obtained through the repetition with a slight difference of the

Theories of Identities

My methodology in this chapter is rather simple. I have reviewed the news stories on LEXIS/NEXIS that discuss Obama and femininity.[27] In order to analyze the significance of Obama's feminine side, I will turn to three theories of identity. Identity performance theory serves as a foundation, and states that people make choices about how to present themselves that position their identities against the backdrop of social expectations.[28] Critical race theory explores the ways that race is simultaneously non-existent and materially consequential.[29] Masculinities studies posits that assumptions about the meaning of manhood influence behaviors, ideologies, and institutions.[30] Together, these theories help us analyze how Obama's presidential campaign influenced popular understandings of femininity and of black male identity.

Shared Tenets of Critical Race and Masculinities Theories

A shared tenet of both critical race theory and masculinities studies is that race and masculinity are not natural but socially constructed.[31] Men do not act like men simply because they are biologically male.[32] Instead, all men must learn how to act out particular forms of masculinity through social training.[33] Because identity is socially constructed, part of what was at stake

---

process of citationality. Judith Butler, *Excitable Speech: A Politics of the Performative* (New York: Routledge, 1997).

[27]I used the following two searches under the terms and connectors method: "obama/s masculine or feminine" and "obama/s 'first female president,'" then supplemented those searches with a variety of searches for specific propositions.

[28]Frank Rudy Cooper, "Cultural Context Matters: Terry's 'Seesaw Effect,'" *Oklahoma Law Review* 56 (2003): 833, 843. For some recent thoughts on identity performance, see Holning Lau, "Identity Scripts and Democratic Deliberation," *Minnesota Law Review* 94 (2010): 897.

[29]Frank Rudy Cooper, "The 'Seesaw Effect' from Racial Profiling to Depolicing: Toward Critical Cultural Theory," in *The New Civil Rights Research: A Constitutive Approach*, ed. Benjamin Fleury-Steiner and Laura Beth Nielsen (Aldershot, UK: Ashgate, 2006), 139, 148.

[30]Frank Rudy Cooper, "Who's the Man?: Masculinities Studies, Terry Stops, and Police Training," *Columbia Journal of Gender and Law* 18 (2009): 671.

[31]On race as socially constructed, see for example, Angela Onwuachi-Willig and Mario Barnes, "By Any Other Name?: On Being 'Regarded As' Black, and Why Title VII Should Apply Even if Lakisha and Jamal Are White," *Wisconsin Law Review* (2005): 1283, 1296. On gender as socially constructed, see for example, Nancy Levit, "Feminism for Men: Legal Ideology and the Construction of Maleness," *UCLA Law Review* 43 (1006): 1037, 1051.

[32]Levit, "Feminism for Men," 1098.

[33]Ibid., 1062.

in the 2008 presidential election was what types of behaviors people would learn to expect of black men. Another shared tenet of both critical race theory and masculinities studies is that identities are multiple. Critical race theory's concept of intersectionality illustrates this point. Intersectionality refers to the fact that unique identities are formed at the places where categories of identities intersect.[34] Men who are black are stereotyped in different ways and have different senses of self than men who are white. Likewise, men who are black are subject to different stereotypes and have different senses of self than blacks who are also women. For the same reason, masculinities studies scholars agree that there is no such thing as a singular masculinity; instead, there are masculinities in the plural.[35] The plurality of masculine identities includes working-class white masculinity, gay black masculinity, and so on.[36]

A third shared tenet of critical race theory and masculinities studies is that there are hierarchies within categories of identity. The hierarchization of races in the West is so obvious that it does not bear further discussion.[37] Similarly, sociologists R. W. Connell and James Messerschmidt say that certain forms of masculinities are more honored and wield more power than others.[38] The masculinity traditionally associated with white, Christian, heterosexual, upper-class men has been installed as the ideal.[39] Alternative masculinities, such as those associated with black, Jewish, gay, and lower-class men, have been depicted as too masculine or too feminine, or both.[40] The tenets that identities are socially constructed, multiple, and hierarchized constitute a shared understanding of how identities work that grounds my explications of critical race theory and masculinities studies.

---

[34]Kimberlé Crenshaw, "Mapping the Margins: Intersectionality, Identity Politics, and Violence Against Women of Color," *Stanford Law Review* 43 (1991): 1241.

[35]Paul Smith, "Introduction," in *Boys: Masculinities in Contemporary Culture*, ed. Paul Smith (Boulder, CO: Westview Press, 1996), 1, 3.

[36]In keeping with multidimensionality theory's elaboration upon intersectionality theory, we can say "given the interconnectedness of patriarch/sexism and racism, among other oppressive systems, black men, as a single multidimensional positionality, are in some contexts privileged by gender and sometimes oppressed by gendered racism." Mutua, "Theorizing Progressive Black Masculinities," 6.

[37]Cornel West, *Race Matters* (Boston: Beacon Press, 1993), *passim*.

[38]R. W. Connell and James W. Messerschmidt, "Hegemonic Masculinity: Rethinking the Concept," *Gender & Society* 19 (2005): 829, 846. Still, hegemonic authority is exercised by co-opting portions of disparate points of view so as to make the dominant view palatable to a wide range of groups.

[39]Kimmel, "Masculinity as Homophobia," 25.

[40]Ibid., 37–38.

Some Tenets of Critical Race Theory

Critical race theory is an interdisciplinary field that draws heavily upon ethnic studies, history, and sociology, among other fields. The editors of the legal academy's most important anthology of critical race theory texts define this school of thought as "challeng[ing] the ways in which race and racial power are constructed and represented in American legal culture and, more generally, in American society as a whole."[41] Taken together, the principles of identity theories in general and the tenets of critical race theory in particular describe a perspective that can be brought to bear on the question of how black men are understood in popular culture.

In a critical review of scholarship on media representations of black men, I found that they

> depict us as either the completely threatening Bad Black Man or the fully assimilationist Good Black Man. The Bad Black Man is animalistic, sexually depraved, and crime-prone. The Good Black Man distances himself from black people and emulates white views. The images are bipolar in that they swing from one extreme to another with little room for nuanced depictions. Threatened with the Bad Black Man image, black men are provided with an "assimilationist incentive" to pursue the Good Black Man image.[42]

It may be helpful to emphasize some points about the bipolarity of black masculinity. First, similar phenomena play out with respect to other denigrated groups.[43] Second, I identify race consciousness as a trait of the Bad Black Man because the bipolarity of black masculinity has the purpose of forcing assimilation. The assimilationist model makes no room for race consciousness, let alone racial loyalty. Since the default position on black men is that we are bad, we must abandon race loyalty to gain mainstream acceptance.[44] While the criminal is the paradigmatic Bad Black Man, the race-conscious black man is also bad.

[41]Kimberlé Crenshaw et al., "Introduction," in *Critical Race Theory: The Key Writings That Formed the Movement*, ed. Kimberlé Crenshaw et al. (New York: New Press, 1995), xiii, xiii. For a more recent compilation of articles, legal cases, and other materials, see Juan Perea et al., *Race and Races: Cases and Resources for a Diverse America*, 2nd ed. (St. Paul, MN: Thomson/West, 2007).

[42]Ibid., 857–58; D. Aaron Lacy, "The Most Endangered Title VII Plaintiff?: Exponential Discrimination against Black Males," *Nebraska Law Review* 86 (2008): 552, 566; Devon W. Carbado, "(E)Racing the Fourth Amendment," *Michigan Law Review* 100 (2002): 946, 1034–43.

[43]Mahmood Mamdani, *Good Muslim, Bad Muslim: America, the Cold War, and the Roots of Terror* (New York: Pantheon Books, 2004).

[44]Carbado, "(E)Racing the Fourth Amendment," 968–69.

Because the default position on black men is that we fit the Bad Black Man stereotype, we are incentivized to demonstrate our assimilation.[45] A primary means for the Good Black Man to distinguish himself from the Bad Black Man is to respond to the assimilationist incentive by engaging in race-distancing acts.[46] Race-distancing acts, such as adopting the colorblind stance, are ways of responding to the assimilationist incentive. Such race-distancing is problematic, though, since it suggests that only blacks who "act white" deserve mainstream success.[47] As a mainstream candidate, Obama would seem to have been especially subject to the assimilationist incentive.

Some Tenets of Masculinities Studies

The first tenet of masculinities studies is that the principal message that masculinity norms send is that masculinity is to be privileged over femininity. For example, Deborah Brake has described the privileging of men in athletics.[48] Ann C. McGinley has discussed the privileging of masculinity in the very structure of work.[49] Valerie Vojdik has discussed male privileging in the rituals of all-male educational institutions.[50] Throughout Western civilization, men have generally been the leaders and have generally relegated women to subordinate roles.[51] Here, that privileging is seen in the fact that Obama was often denigrated for having feminine traits.[52]

---

[45]Cooper, "Against Bipolar Black Masculinity," 887.

[46]Ibid.

[47]Ibid., 893–95.

[48]Deborah Brake, "The Struggle for Sex Equality in Sports and the Theory Behind Title IX," *University of Michigan Journal of Law Reform* 34 (2001): 13, 92–93 (explaining masculinity and male dominance in male athletics).

[49]Ann C. McGinley, "Masculinities at Work," *Oregon Law Review* 83 (2004): 359.

[50]Valorie K. Vojdik, "Gender Outlaws: Challenging Masculinity in Traditionally Male Institutions," *Berkeley Women's Law Journal* 17 (2002): 71, 75.

[51]Lorna Fox, "Re-Possessing 'Home': A Re-Analysis of Gender, Homeownership, and Debtor Default for Feminist Legal Theory," *William & Mary Journal of Women and the Law* 14 (2008): 423, 437; Judith Koons, "'Just' Married?: Same-Sex Marriage and a History of Family Plurality," *Michigan Journal of Gender & Law* 12 (2005): 1, 11–12; Gila Stopler, "Gender Construction and the Limits of Liberal Equality," *Texas Journal of Women and the Law* 15 (2005): 43, 46.

[52]A related tenet of masculinities studies is that what makes this privileging of masculinity over femininity all the more insidious is the fact that it has been invisible. When I say masculinities have been invisible, I mean this in the way Barbara Flagg talks about "white transparency," wherein whites sometimes operate from perspectives that are widely shared by whites without acknowledging that they are using a particular perspective. Barbara J. Flagg, "Was Blind, But Now I See: White Race Consciousness and the Requirement of Discriminatory Intent," in *A Reader on Race, Civil Rights, and American Law: A Multiracial Approach*, ed. Timothy Davis et al. (Durham, N.C.: Carolina Academic Press, 2001), 33. Similarly, men may often operate from a male perspective while thinking they are operating from a neutral perspective.

A second tenet of masculinities studies is that men have a constant need to prove to other men that they possess the normative masculinity, which leads to an ongoing masculine anxiety.[53] That is so because the rules of the United States' hegemonic, or dominant, form of masculinity[54] are unrealizable.[55] Manhood is a relentless test of how close you are to the ideal.[56] Men must constantly re-prove that they possess the hegemonic form of masculinity.[57] We are thus placed in a state of constant anxiety over our masculinity.[58]

For example, in the 2000 and 2004 elections, individual men's anxieties over their masculinity seemed to have been rooted in Republican-created anxiety over the lack of masculinity of Democratic presidential candidates Al Gore and John Kerry.[59] Nancy Ehrenreich's theory of reflected masculinity is instructive. She says,

> [M]embers of both sexes can obtain a validating sense of masculinity (of strength, moral merit, and the like) from the reflected masculinity of their country. Concomitantly, many individuals (of both sexes) may feel emasculated (that is, may feel a humiliating loss of power) when their sense of strength and "maleness" of their country is threatened—such as by the events of September 11, 2001.... American masculinity invites citizens to bask in the reflected glare of state virility, improving their own sense of self-worth through identification with the aggressive actions of their government.[60]

The damning effect of feminizing presidential candidates thus seems to stem both from the fact that masculinity is privileged over femininity and from anxiety over our nation's masculinity.[61] The need to prove one's own masculinity

---

[53]Kimmel, "Masculinity as Homophobia," 33.

[54]Kimmel's rules of hegemonic masculinity are (1) never act feminine, (2) accrue power, success, wealth, and status, (3) always hold your emotions in check, and (4) always exude an aura of daring and aggression. Ibid., 30–31.

[55]Ibid., 31.

[56]Ibid.

[57]Ibid., 36.

[58]Ibid., 37.

[59]Maureen Dowd, "Who's Hormonal? Hillary or Dick?," *New York Times*, February 8, 2006, A21; David Nitkin, "Clinton Voters Disappointed More than Words Needed to Unite Party, Many Say," *Baltimore Sun*, June 8, 2008, A2.

[60]Ehrenreich, "Disguising Empire," 132.

[61]Note that "masculinity" is not just a proxy for describing being in a position of dominance. Rather, it is a particular style of acting. One can wield power by gently persuading others, but that would not be deemed masculine.

is the principle source of the anxiety some men (and some women) feel over the nation's reflected masculinity.

A third tenet of masculinities studies is that norms of masculinity constrain men's performances of identities. The first constraint on men's identity performances is the need to denigrate contrast figures. As legal theorist Athena Mutua says, "[T]he central feature of masculinity is the domination and oppression of others; namely women, children, and other subordinated men."[62] Since the idealized figure of the powerful white male is the model for hegemonic masculinity, demonstrating that you fit the hegemonic pattern of U.S. masculinity involves a repudiation of that model's contrast figures, most notably, women, gays, and racial minorities.[63] This tenet, like the tenet of masculine anxiety, helps explain why the Republicans' recent strategy of feminizing Democratic presidential candidates had been so effective prior to Obama's election. To feminize the candidate is to make him seem less manly, and thus, less presidential.[64] According to Glen Greenwald,

> Central to the right-wing myth-making machine is the depiction of [Republican] male leaders as swaggering tough guys in the iconic mold of an American cowboy and brave, steadfast warrior....
>
> Vital to this masculinity marketing campaign is the demonization of Democrats and liberal males as weak, sniveling, effeminate, effete cowards....[65]

Greenwald's statement seems to capture accurately the way President George W. Bush was able to portray himself as more masculine than Democratic candidates Al Gore and John Kerry.

A second constraint on men's identity performance stems from the first: a competitiveness reflected in a need to dominate other men. Behaviors that seek to express dominance over other men, such as aggression, are part of the project of establishing that one possesses the hegemonic form of U.S. masculinity.[66] Given that hegemonic masculinity is associated with economic success, it might seem strange that a lowbrow quality like aggression is so prized. As Jewel Woods notes, however,

[62]Mutua, "Theorizing Progressive Black Masculinities," 5.

[63]Ibid., 24–25.

[64]Rick Pearson, "Obama, McCain Clash on Security; Rivals Fire from Afar on Mideast Policy," *Chicago Tribune*, May 17, 2008, C1.

[65]Glen Greenwald, "Book News and Media Campaign Coverage," *Salon.com*, April 2, 2008, http://www.salon.com/opinion/greenwald/2008/04/02/book_news (accessed August 28, 2010).

[66]Patricia Hill Collins, "A Telling Difference: Dominance, Strength, and Black Masculinities," in *Progressive Black Masculinities*, 73, 86.

Despite the economic trend away from blue-collar jobs, many of the most powerful expressions of masculinity within contemporary American society continue to be associated with blue-collar imagery. . . .

At the very same time society is becoming less reliant on male brawn, the dominant cultural images of masculinity are largely derived from the "traditional" ideas of maleness.[67]

So, there is a nostalgia for blue-collar aggression. The expectation that a man will display an aggressive demeanor is so pervasive that it stands as a second constraint on men's performances of their identities. This fact was reflected in the many criticisms of Obama for not striking back more aggressively when attacked by Hillary Clinton or Republican presidential nominee John McCain.[68]

Analyzing Obama's Femininity

As sociologist Michael Kimmel has noted, "From the founding of the country, presidents of the United States have seen the political arena as a masculine testing ground."[69] It is thus appropriate that an editorial in the *Orlando Sentinel* presented the 2008 presidential general election as a referendum on whether we wanted masculine leadership or feminine leadership. It said, "Now that the actual presidential campaign is under way, we have the traditionally 'masculine' style, embodied by John McCain, emphasizing experience, toughness, feistiness, stubbornness, grit, exclusivity, etc., and the newly emergent 'feminine' managerial style practiced by Obama and emphasizing communication, consensus, collegiality and inclusivity."[70] Prior to that editorial, the *New York Post* ran an editorial suggesting that Obama would be "our first woman president."[71]

---

[67]Jewel Woods, "Why Guys Have a Man-Crush on Obama; Sure Women Swoon, But Modern Men Seem Weak-Kneed, Too," *Chicago Sun-Times*, July 24, 2008, 25.

[68]Maureen Dowd, "Where's His Right Hook? Barack Obama Seems Refreshingly Decent. Can He Survive Hardball Politics?," *Pittsburgh Post-Gazette*, March 5, 2007, B7; Milloy, "Maybe It's Time," B1; Amy Alkon, "The Self-Help President," *Advice Goddess Blog*, August 26, 2008, http://www.advicegoddess.com/archives/2008/08/26/the_selfhelp_pr.html (accessed August 28, 2010). The expectation of aggression can be thought of as stemming from our "culture of honor." Dov Cohen and Joe Vandello, "Social Norms, Social Meaning, and the Economic Analysis of Law," *Journal of Legal Studies* 27 (1998): 567; Cooper, "Who's the Man?"

[69]Michael Kimmel, "Integrating Men into the Curriculum," *Duke Journal of Gender Law & Policy* 4 (1997): 181, 183.

[70]Robert Carter, "The Macho Factor," *Orlando Sentinel*, September 1, 2008, A18.

[71]Berrington and Onore, "Bam."

Obama was called feminine because of his restraint, calm demeanor, collaborative style, and finely honed language.[72] Those characterizations of Obama as feminine, while melodramatic, did seem to capture real differences between Obama and his opponents. The media has recognized that Obama has "an unusual blend of traditionally masculine and feminine skills at work in him."[73] Further, there is reason to believe Obama's feminization was conscious.[74] Obama's feminine style was unlikely to be accidental given the meticulous planning that goes into every move of a presidential candidate.[75] The media's gendered framing of Obama thus had some basis in Obama's actions.

The identity theories that I outlined in the first part of this chapter will prove helpful in analyzing Obama's feminine style. First, this election gave us a chance to observe the processes of the social construction of the meanings of black masculinity and of femininity in action. Since the presidency is a bully pulpit that influences how people think about themselves and others, I expect that Obama's election will influence people's expectations for performances of race and gender. Second, we see both the multiplicity and the hierarchy of masculinities in the different constraints (and privileges) placed on Obama because he is a black male. McCain could be angry, but Obama could not.[76] Ironically, Obama's status as a minority male may have given him more leeway to feminize himself than McCain because of the assumption that black men are already overly masculine.[77] With those general identity theory insights in mind, I now turn to specific critical race theory and masculinities studies analyses of Obama's femininity.

Critical Race Theory and Obama as a Good Black Man

Does the bipolar black masculinity thesis that I described above apply to the 2008 election? It seems that it does. The media has sometimes acknowledged

---

[72]Goodman, "Trading Places: Obama Is the Woman," *Pittsburgh Post-Gazette*, February 22, 2008, B7.

[73]Christi Parsons, "Women Lean toward Obama; But McCain to Fight for Clinton Backers," *Chicago Tribune*, June 18, 2008, C1.

[74]Linda Valdez, "We Need a President with Both Masculine, Feminine Values," *Arizona Republic*, May 8, 2008, 4.

[75]Obama may have found it strategic to demonstrate a feminine side to the disproportionately female Democratic electorate.

[76]Steve Chapman, "John McCain, Reveling in Anger," *Chicago Tribune*, October 14, 2008, C33.

[77]Kimmel, "Masculinity as Homophobia," 38. Ann C. McGinley reminds me that McCain faced his own identity constraints, as his age threatened to demasculinize him. McGinley, "Masculinities at Work," 376.

Obama's bipolarity problem. In an article in the *Washington Post*, journalist Courtland Milloy says, "You can walk a fine line between being too black for whites and not black enough for blacks."[78] That is the basic problem Obama faced, even though he largely had blacks locked into voting for him given that McCain was not seen as a viable alternative. I suspect that many whites would have been less interested in Obama if he had been seen as an inauthentic black man or downright collaborator with white supremacy. Obama thus had to navigate between poles of blackness and whiteness.

David Frank and Mark Lawrence McPhail illustrate the way Obama has been positioned as a Good Black Man.[79] They note that at the 2004 Democratic Convention, the media contrasted Obama as the Good Black Man against Reverend Al Sharpton as the Bad Black Man.[80] Sharpton was a Bad Black Man because he was race-conscious rather than race-distancing. Observers agree that during his presidential run, Obama distanced himself from both race in general and past racial-minority candidates in particular.[81] He could thus be characterized as playing the Good Black Man role.

As the Good Black Man image would dictate, Obama consistently downplayed his race and avoided racial issues.[82] For instance, David Axelrod, a significant Obama campaign official, said, "[W]e're focusing not on his race but the qualities of leadership that he would bring to this country."[83] Such statements are problematic because they suggest that he was engaging in the type of race-distancing acts that the Good Black Man model calls for.[84] That conclusion is supported by the fact that Obama seemingly tied himself

---

[78]Milloy, "Maybe It's Time," B1.

[79]David A. Frank and Mark Lawrence McPhail, "Barack Obama's Address to the 2004 Democratic National Convention: Trauma, Compromise, Consilience, and the (Im)possibility of Racial Reconciliation," *Rhetoric & Public Affairs.* 8 (2005): 571.

[80]Ibid., 576–77, 583–85.

[81]Indiana University, "Two Elephants in the Room," *IU News Room*, April 10, 2008, http://newsinfo.iu.edu/news/page/normal/7542.html (accessed August 28, 2010).

[82]Cooper, "Against Bipolar Black Masculinity," 887.

[83]Christi Parsons and John McCormick, "Obama, Huckabee Strike First with Iowa Victories; Edwards Ekes by Clinton for 2nd Amid Huge Turnout," *Chicago Tribune*, January 4, 2008, N1; Susan Page and William Risser, "Beyond Black and White; Obama's Rise Spotlights Gains in Race Relations and How Ethnicity Remains a Dividing Line on Some Issues," *USA Today*, September 23, 2008, 1A; Joseph Williams, "Changing of the Guard; New Generation Replaces Past Civil Rights Leaders," *Boston Globe*, August 28, 2008, A1.

[84]"EUR Political Analysis: Obama Hit for not Mentioning Dr. King's Name during Acceptance Speech," *Electronic Urban Report*, September 2, 2008, http://www.eurweb.com/ (accessed August 28, 2010).

to colorblindness,[85] another characteristic of the Good Black Man.[86] Obama often said things like, "There's not a black America and white America and Latino America and Asian America—there's the United States of America."[87] As others have noted, Obama cultivated a "postracial" image.[88] While Obama did explicitly mention race during the controversy over his former pastor, Jeremiah Wright, he only did so because race became unavoidable. In a post-election *New Yorker* article, journalist David Remnick said, "The speech in Philadelphia did more than change the subject."[89] But changing the subject was the speech's primary goal.

The bigger problem for Obama, though, was his need to reject linkage with the Bad Black Man. This explains why he publicly denigrated black fathers and repudiated Wright. First, in his Father's Day speech to a black audience, Obama scolded black fathers specifically for being "missing in action."[90] It is hard not to believe that such statements were meant to distance Obama from the Bad Black Man image. As civil rights leader Julian Bond told Remnick, "Jesse [Jackson, Sr.] had the feeling that Obama played to white Americans by criticizing black Americans, for not doing enough to help ourselves...."[91] When Jackson had to apologize for the crude form of such a criticism, it gave Obama the opportunity to distance himself from a famously race-affirming black man.[92]

Second, Obama repudiated Wright because Wright is a symbol of the Bad Black Man by virtue of his race-affirming rather than race-distancing acts. Specifically, Wright has said, "[T]he government gives (black men) drugs, builds bigger prisons, passes a three-strike law and then wants us to

---

[85]Frank and McPhail, "Barack Obama's Address," 583–84.

[86]Cooper, "Against Bipolar Black Masculinity," 884.

[87]John Aloysius Farrell, "Obama Revives MLK's Dream," *Denver Post*, August 1, 2004, A25; Peter Wehner, "Why Republicans Like Obama," *Washington Post*, February 3, 2008, B7.

[88]Matt Bai, "Post-Race," *New York Times*, August 10, 2008, MM8, http://www.nytimes.com/2008/08/10/magazine/10politics-t.html (accessed August 28, 2010).

[89]Remnick, "The Joshua Generation," 79.

[90]Michael McAuliff, "Bam Slams AWOL Fathers," *New York Daily News*, June 16, 2008, 8; Julie Bosman, "Obama Calls for More Responsibility from Black Fathers," *New York Times*, June 16, 2008, A15; Juliet Eilperin, "Obama Discusses Duties of Fatherhood," *Washington Post*, June 16, 2008, A7; Abdon M. Pallasch, "Obama Urges Fathers to Step Up," *Chicago Sun-Times*, June 16, 2008, 2.

[91]Remnick, "The Joshua Generation," 79; Gregory Scott Parks and Jeffrey J. Rachlinski, "A Better Metric: The Role of Unconscious Race and Gender Bias in the 2008 Presidential Race," Cornell Legal Studies Research Paper No. 08-007 (2008), 23–24, http://ssrn.com/abstract=1102704 (accessed August 28, 2010).

[92]Remnick, "The Joshua Generation," 79.

sing 'God Bless America.'"[93] As Remnick says, the Obama campaign worried that whites were wondering if "[u]nderneath his welcoming demeanor, was he [Obama] like a cartoon version of Wright, full of condemnation and loyal only to his race?"[94] The loyalty question is key, as black men are presumed to be completely race-loyal.[95] Obama needed to sever his connections to such a speaker more than a white politician would have had to sever ties to a white supremacist because the bipolarity of black masculinity makes such associations a sign of a completely bad character. If white masculinity were represented in such a bipolar fashion, McCain could have been subjected to claims that he had a completely bad character. But the media hardly mentioned McCain's ties to Reverend John Hagee, who said that Hitler "was fulfilling God's plan for Jews."[96]

We can now see that Obama's postracial Good Black Man approach is related to his feminine style. The best example of this is the fact that, as a black man, Obama had to soften his approach or be deemed an angry black man. During the campaign, Milloy said that Obama was being called on to prove he was man enough for the presidency, but "without coming off as an angry black man."[97] That stereotype may be related to the image of black men as overly masculine since anger is an extreme form of the aggressiveness expected of men; people fear that black men will easily lose their tempers and become out of control.[98]

I speculate that Obama's preternaturally calm demeanor originated in his need to counter the stereotype of the angry black man. Anecdotes from Obama's autobiography, *Dreams from My Father*, support that view. Remnick

[93]Marie Szaniszlo, "Race for White House Impacted by Freedom of Preach," *Boston Herald*, March 16, 2008, 14. Frankly, Wright's statement might be true. The government has long been accused of having helped send drugs into the black community. See Patricia A. Turner, *I Heard It Through the Grapevine: Rumor in African-American Culture* (Berkeley: University of California Press, 1993), 181–83; Regina Austin, "Beyond Black Demons and White Devils: Antiblack Conspiracy Theorizing and the Black Public Sphere," *Florida State University Law Review* 22 (1994): 1021, 1023; Kenneth B. Nunn, "Race, Crime, and the Pool of Surplus Criminality: Or Why the 'War on Drugs' Was a 'War on Blacks,'" *Journal of Gender, Race & Justice* 6 (2002): 381, 425.

[94]Remnick, "The Joshua Generation," 78.

[95]Cooper, "Against Bipolar Black Masculinity," 891.

[96]Eric Ressner, "Associations: Tit for Tat," *St. Louis Post-Dispatch*, October 19, 2008, B2; Frank Rich, "If Terrorists Rock the Vote in 2008," *New York Times*, June 29, 2008, WK12; Michael Scherer, "Still Prepping for Prime Time," *Time*, June 9, 2008, 28.

[97]Milloy, "Maybe It's Time," B1.

[98]U.S. Federal Glass Ceiling Commission. *Good for Business: Making Full Use of the Nation's Capital.* Washington, DC: GPO, 1995, 71. On stereotyping of black males, see generally Floyd D. Weatherspoon, *African-American Males and the Law: Cases and Materials* (Lanham, MD: University Press of America, 1998).

concludes that as an undergraduate, "What Obama [learned] was the strategic benefit of a calm and inviting temperament."[99] Obama learned that people like a calm black man; it was "such a pleasant surprise to find a well-mannered young black man who didn't seem angry all the time."[100] Remnick's statements are consistent with what we know about how young black men are raised. We are often warned to be nonthreatening in order to avoid police brutality, which is disproportionately visited upon young black males.[101] Obama was certainly aware that black men are often viewed as threatening since he mentioned his grandmother's fear of black men during his campaign speech on race.[102]

My argument is not that Obama hid his anger during the campaign. Rather, Obama became a calm black man much earlier in life because he learned that angry black men are not acceptable in elite mainstream environments. Further, the reason angry black masculinity is unacceptable is because it is associated with a race-affirming position. For example, even when Obama wanted to infuse race into the conversation, he found that whites would not allow him to do so; the campaign noted a decline in Obama's poll numbers after he repeatedly stated that he did not look like the other presidents on U.S. currency.[103] Consequently, Obama's refusal to get angry even in the face of attacks, which contradicts hegemonic masculinity's call for aggressiveness and is a primary basis for his being called feminine, should be deemed to be the result of special constraints on the performance of black male identity. The principal reason Obama was more feminine than other presidential candidates was to avoid a pervasive stereotype, the Bad Black Man. However, that feminization strategy came with risks.

Masculinities Studies and the Dangers of Obama's Feminization

Obama's conundrum was that he had to feminize himself in order not to be seen as an angry black man. But, many people do not fully believe that women can lead or that feminine styles can show strength.[104] Despite his masculine traits,

[99]Remnick, "The Joshua Generation," 71.

[100]Ibid.

[101]Carbado, "(E)Racing the Fourth Amendment," 953–54.

[102]Michael McAuliff and Michael Saul, "Bam Jam Over 'Typical White' Folk Talk in Philly," *New York Daily News*, March 21, 2008, 9.

[103]Remnick, "The Joshua Generation," 78.

[104]Laura Padilla, "A Gendered Update on Women Law Deans: Who, Where, and Why Not?," *American University Journal of Gender, Social Policy & the Law* 15 (2007): 443, 485; Mary Radford, "Sex Stereotyping and the Promotion of Women to Positions of Power," *Hastings Law Journal* 41 (1990): 471, 490–91; Deborah Rhode, "The Difference 'Difference' Makes," *Maine Law Review* 55 (2003): 15, 17.

such as being an avid sports fan[105] and his seemingly traditional relationship with his wife Michelle,[106] Obama had a feminine style. Estelle Freedman fleshed out Obama's gender problem: "Some of the criticisms of Obama as being too aloof, or not going after red meat enough, or not being aggressive enough, are really questioning his masculinity in some ways."[107] Obama's restrained style could have proven unacceptable to voters because it was a break with the masculine style associated with the presidency.

The masculinities studies tenets I noted earlier elucidate the aspects of Obama's feminine style that proved problematic. First, the privileging of masculinity is clearly seen in the denigration of Obama for his feminine style. For example, MSNBC talk show host Joe Scarborough called Obama "prissy."[108] That denigration of Obama's perceived feminine qualities was consistent with hegemonic masculinity's privileging of masculinity. The persistence of associations between the presidency and masculinity suggests that we still have a long way to go on gender.

Second, we see masculine anxiety in the hand-wringing about the possibility that an Obama presidency might be a feminized presidency. Recall that a need to prove that one is sufficiently masculine is built into the structure of the hegemonic form of masculinity. Recall further that many people implicitly expect to be able to bask in the nation's reflected masculinity. Obama's style was risky; it could fail to satisfy people's needs to soothe their anxiety over our nation's masculinity. His openness to negotiating rather than imposing his will made some people worry he was not tough enough to be president.[109] That anxiousness was gendered.

Third, the criticism of Obama's lack of manliness reflects hegemonic masculinity's constraint of requiring the denigration of contrast figures. In contravention of the dictate that masculinity is achieved by not "acting like a woman,"[110] Obama did not attempt to distance himself from his feminine

---

[105]Jonathan Martin, "First Fan Obama Takes Aim at the BCS," *Politico.com*, January 11, 2009, http://www.politico.com/news/stories/0109/17313.html (accessed August 28, 2010).

[106]Christi Parsons, "Is Michelle Obama Really in the Kitchen?," *L.A. Times*, February 23, 2009, A9, http://www.latimes.com/news/nationworld/nation/la-na-michelle-obama23-2009feb23,0,2585916.story (accessed August 28, 2010). Of course, this is also about Barack Obama's heteronormativity, which is an important subject that I do not address in this chapter.

[107]Milloy, "Maybe It's Time," B1.

[108]*Morning Joe*, MSNBC television broadcast, March 31, 2008, http://mediamatters.org/items/200803310007 (accessed August 28, 2010).

[109]Linda Killian, "Obama's Tough Talk Falls Short," *Politico.com*, August 2, 2007, http://www.politico.com/news/stories/0807/5222.html (accessed August 28, 2010).

[110]Angela Harris, "Gender, Violence, Race, and Criminal Justice," *Stanford Law Review* 52 (2000): 777, 785.

tendencies.[111] Given the need to denigrate contrast figures that inheres in hegemonic masculinity, Obama put his masculinity in question when he was inclusive rather than exclusive. The hegemonic form of U.S. masculinity calls on men to reject femininity; Obama's failure to do so may explain why he was often criticized as unmanly.

Fourth, a further constraint on Obama's performance of his identity is that his empathetic style is antimasculine. This was reflected in the calls for Obama to be tougher in responding to attacks. The title of one editorial captures the spirit of this criticism: "Where's His Right Hook?"[112] That attitude was reflective of the expectation that men will maintain an aggressive demeanor. Calls for Obama to be more aggressive were also reflective of Democrats' desires to "fight the last war" by not having their candidate get "swift-boated."[113] But the intensity of the calls for aggressiveness suggests that gender, and not just political effectiveness, was at issue.

Finally, we might note that despite the dangers that Obama's feminization presented for him, his ability to feminize was bolstered by certain stereotypes. As a man, Obama had more room to feminize without seeming too feminine than female politicians. Moreover, the stereotypes of black men as overly masculine meant people still took Obama to be sufficiently masculine. In contrast, Hillary Clinton clearly felt the need to out-macho Obama during their Democratic primary contests. As professor Georgia Duerst-Lahti says, "The first woman has to out-masculine the man, kind of like Margaret Thatcher did. … Men have a lot more latitude."[114] As a man, and a black man in particular, Obama had more room to negotiate a partly feminized masculinity.[115]

Obama Had to Be Unisex

So, why do I suggest that Obama is our first "unisex" president? Because Obama could not be too masculine, even as he had to prove he was not too feminine. Perhaps, then, Obama's masculinity problem is really a refracted version of his

---

[111]Obama did denigrate his female opponent, Hillary Clinton—"You're likable enough"—but that is not the same thing as denigrating femininity. Steve Huntley, "Despite Divisions, Dems on Top," *Chicago Sun-Times*, February 10, 2008, A27.

[112]Dowd, "Where's His Right Hook?," B7; Alkon, "The Self-Help President"; Milloy, "Maybe It's Time," B1.

[113]E. J. Dionne, "Finally, Jinxed Month of August Is Almost Over," *Charleston Gazette*, August 23, 2008, 4A.

[114]Scherer, "Hillary Is from Mars."

[115]For examples of how Hillary Clinton and other prominent women had their identity performances constrained during the 2008 campaign, see Ann C. McGinley's excellent essay on this topic. Ann C. McGinley, "Hillary Clinton, Sarah Palin, and Michelle Obama: Performing Gender, Race, and Class on the Campaign Trail," *Denver University Law Review* 86 (2009): 709.

bipolar black masculinity problem. Just as Obama had to navigate between the shoals of blackness and whiteness, he had to position himself as feminine, but not too much so. He had to be unisex.

Use of the term *unisex* is especially appropriate in this context because it captures the performative nature of race and gender. He sometimes chose to be more feminine than other presidential candidates in order to be racially palatable. He sometimes chose to be more masculine in order to project the ability to be Commander-in-Chief. The overall effect was to place him toward the middle of the gender continuum rather than well into the more masculine end, which is where we usually expect to find presidential candidates.

Obama was relatively unisex for the context of a presidential campaign. That his gender performance must be contextualized helps us see that all identity performance is limited by what is intelligible and acceptable to the relevant audience. As Ann C. McGinley points out, Hillary Clinton, Sarah Palin, and Michelle Obama each performed their identities differently because of ways that aspects of their identities, such as age, ideology, and race, made certain identity stances more or less available to them.[116] For Obama, identity factors impelled him toward a certain unisex style.

Conclusion: The Possibilities of a Unisex Presidency

I did not imagine I would live to see a black president (and I am not especially old). Nor did I expect to see anything but a macho man (or woman) win the presidency in our recent climate. Given the symbolic power of the presidency, one would expect Obama's election to influence how people think about race and gender. In this concluding part of the chapter, I speculate about the impact of Obama's unisex style.

The potential for Obama to change what is an intelligible performance of black masculinity has been recognized by black men:

> For African-American men, Obama has accomplished something even more extraordinary. He has arguably single-handedly transformed the black public sphere. In their eyes, it is no longer "easy" to view black men solely through the lens of deficiencies, bad behavior, their bodies or even their relationship to black women.[117]

In the simplest sense, then, black male identity has already been reconstructed by Obama's success since it is now possible to imagine a black man as president. In addition to that opening, Obama will create new images of black masculinity

---

[116]Ibid.

[117]Woods, "Why Guys Have a Man Crush," 25.

that will help to construct the future expectations of black men. This is the racial payoff of Obama's success.[118]

The gender payoff of Obama's success is that it could remove some of the stigma from femininity. Taken together, the tenets of masculinity describe a privileged but anxious status that may constrain men nearly as much as it empowers them. This is why men, who are clearly privileged as a group, sometimes feel disempowered as individuals.[119] This creates a tension in masculinity whereby masculinity is both something people expect you to demonstrate and something some people might want to escape. This may be the genius of Obama's feminization: It allows us to have it both ways on masculinity. While Obama is hardly effeminate, he seems unusually nonanxious about his masculinity. As *MS. Magazine* put it on their cover, perhaps Obama is "what a feminist looks like."[120] There is some basis for believing that Obama could be a harbinger of a move toward "progressive black masculinities" that are not based on the denigration of femininity.[121] As a result, the potential is there for Obama's example to allow all men greater movement along the gender continuum.

In a small way, but at a fundamental level, Obama's refusal to accept that a presidential demeanor requires a hypermasculine style challenges the assumptions of the hegemonic form of masculinity. If the president can be both black and unisex, maybe we are all more free to perform our identities as we see fit than we had imagined.[122]

---

[118]A remaining concern, however, is that Obama may be framed as a special case that proves nothing about the abilities and characters of black men in general.

[119]Kimmel, "Masculinity as Homophobia," 40.

[120]http://msmagazine.com/ (accessed August 28, 2010).

[121]Mutua, "Theorizing Progressive Black Masculinities," 7.

[122]Again, I do not mean that we are free in a transcendental sense. I mean only that, after the election of a black and unisex president, it is easier to imagine that we can break down other assumptions.

Section IV: Publics

Oprah and Obama: Theorizing Celebrity Endorsement in U.S. Politics

Rebecca A. Kuehl

"That's exciting. ... Let's face it, Oprah is Oprah. She's pretty amazing."[1]
—Michelle Obama, about Oprah Winfrey's fund-raising event for her husband

Michelle Obama had many reasons to be excited about Oprah Winfrey's endorsement of her husband's presidential candidacy. Considering that many Americans see Oprah as one of the most influential women in America, an endorsement by Oprah would seem to be a slam-dunk for the Obama campaign. Columnist Jennifer Hunter writes about Oprah's pop-culture influence:

> Oprah has clout beyond any other media star. Her syndicated show has been consistently the highest-rated talk program in U.S. television history ... Many of the book selections from Oprah's Book Club sell in the millions ... [and] the items Winfrey doles out on her "Oprah's Favorite Things" episodes—a Burberry quilted jacket, a Movado watch—become must-haves.[2]

Oprah's status as an American pop-culture icon seems well-established. Although many political scholars recognize the importance of endorsement for politicians, few account for the significance of *celebrity* endorsement and its role in politics.[3] But consumption of celebrity media is widespread, and an increasing number of celebrities attach themselves to political causes. In a report published by the Pew Research Center for the People and the Press,

---

[1]"Oprah's Fund-Raiser Brings in Big Bucks for Obama," *Jet*, September 24, 2007, page 6.

[2]Jennifer Hunter, "Can Oprah Really Push Obama to New Heights? Celebs, Politics Often Don't Mix, but This Could Be Different," *Chicago Sun-Times*, September 11, 2007, page 14.

[3]David J. Jackson and Thomas I. A. Darrow, "The Influence of Celebrity Endorsements on Young Adults' Political Opinions," *Harvard International Journal of Press/Politics* 10, no. 3 (2005): 81.

the authors note that although people do not admit that they follow celebrity stories, their knowledge of this topic seemingly contradicts that statement:

> [O]ur knowledge data suggests that the public knows more about these types of stories than it does about virtually any other category of news. On average the public answered 60% of the questions dealing with scandal, entertainment and crime correctly.[4]

People's interest in celebrities, and the desire for celebrities' wealth, fame, and social status, seems most important to young people. In fact, 51 percent of eighteen-to-twenty-five-year-olds surveyed by the Pew Research Center said that being famous is their generation's most important or second most important life goal.[5] What celebrities do—and have—seems important to individuals' goals and opinions.

However, there is a disconnect between this attraction to celebrity news and people's belief in celebrity influence. For example, one survey found that 69 percent "say that if they heard Winfrey was supporting a presidential candidate it would not influence their vote."[6] However, a staggering 60 percent of those polled believed her support for Obama would actually help his candidacy in *other* Americans' decision-making in 2008.[7] Besides an indication of the third-person effect at work, this statistic indicates that celebrity endorsement deserves scholarly attention. People tend to *underestimate* the influence of persuasive messages on themselves and *overestimate* the influence on others.[8] How and why does celebrity endorsement rhetorically influence potential voters?

Despite Oprah's iconic status in the realm of popular culture, coverage of her endorsement of Obama within U.S. media indicated that her political significance is not as established. Martha T. Moore explains this skepticism of Oprah's political influence:

---

[4]Pew Research Center for the People and the Press, "Ten Years of the Pew News Interest Index" http://people-press.org/report/107/ten-years-of-the-pew-news-interest-index (Washington, D.C.: Pew Research Center, 1997).

[5]Sharon Jayson, "Generation Y's Goal? Wealth and Fame," *USA Today*, January 10, 2007, (online version of *USA Today*: http://www.usatoday.com/news/nation/2007-01-09-gen-y-cover_x.htm).

[6]Pew Research Center for the People and the Press, "The Oprah Factor and Campaign 2008: Do Political Endorsements Matter?" http://people-press.org/report/357/the-oprah-factor-and-campaign-2008 (Washington, D.C.: Pew Research Center, 2007).

[7]Ibid.

[8]Paul Bryant, Michael B. Salwen, and Michel Dupagne, "The Third-Person Effect: A Meta-Analysis of the Perceptual Hypothesis," *Mass Communication & Society* 3, no. 1 (2000): pages 57–85; W. Phillips Davison, "The Third-Person Effect in Communication," *Public Opinion Quarterly* 47, no. 1 (1983): pages 1–15; Edwin Diamond, *Good News, Bad News* (Cambridge: Massachusetts Institute of Technology Press, 1978).

Oprah Winfrey can get people to read Tolstoy, sell millions of magazines.... To get Americans to vote for her favorite presidential candidate, Democrat Barack Obama, though, she'll have to twice prove conventional wisdom wrong: once with voters who repeatedly say endorsements don't make a big difference, and once with politicos who say they can—but that those by celebrities usually don't matter.[9]

Reporters and campaign strategists shared this ambivalent stance on Oprah. Even when national polls indicated that Oprah's endorsement had not yet had much of an influence on public opinion, one article explains how Oprah's endorsement might play a role in Democratic candidate Joe Biden's campaign: "[Larry] Rasky, [Democratic Sen. Joseph] Biden's strategist, questions whether a celebrity has what it really takes to win votes.... 'There's no history of celebrity endorsements meaning much. But I'm certainly not going to dismiss Oprah.'"[10]

While dismissing celebrity endorsement generally, Rasky simultaneously indicates that *Oprah's* endorsement might be influential.[11] Likewise, another reporter quotes political scientist Franklin D. Gilliam, Jr., on Oprah's potential significance as an endorsement: "When it comes to competing celebrity endorsements, 'I don't know if anybody stands equal with Oprah,' Gilliam said."[12] Media coverage suggested that Oprah's potential influence should not be dismissed.

Theorizing Celebrity Endorsement: Social Comparison Theory and Celebrity Politics

To theorize celebrity endorsement in politics, I connect social comparison theory with scholarship on celebrity politics. Through this combination of theory, I posit different functions of celebrity endorsement. I begin with social comparison theory to demonstrate how individuals make decisions by looking for heuristics, often through comparing themselves to others.

---

[9]Martha T. Moore, "Oprah Becomes Test of What an Endorsement Means; Such Backing Can Draw Attention, but Doesn't Always Lead to Votes," *USA Today*, October 22, 2007, page A1.

[10]Ibid.

[11]Oprah did take on a more active role by traveling to Iowa, New Hampshire, and South Carolina to campaign for Obama during the primary campaign season. See Diane Francis, "Is Oprah for Obama or against Hillary?," *National Post*, December 1, 2007, (online version of *National Post*).

[12]Michael R. Blood, "With Black Votes in Play, Obama Gets Oprah and Hillary Gets Magic," *Associated Press*, September 15, 2007, (AP newswire, but printed in *The Washington Post* online: http://www.washingtonpost.com/wp-dyn/content/article/2007/09/15/AR2007091500 619.html).

Social Comparison Theory and Its Role in Political Decision-Making

Social comparison theory tries to explain how individuals make decisions by comparing themselves to other individuals in their social group.[13] According to David R. Mettee and Gregory Smith, this theory is about "our quest to know ourselves, about the search for self-relevant information and how people gain self-knowledge and discover reality about themselves."[14] In making any decision, individuals compare their potential decision to the decision of others in their social group.[15] In the case of a presidential election, voters compare their political decision to that of their peers, which can include celebrities.

Social comparison theorists have largely neglected celebrities, however, in their theorization of how individuals compare themselves to others. Although scholars acknowledge that social comparison varies among individuals (e.g., some individuals care more than others about how they compare to other people within their social group),[16] the influence of celebrities on many people's lives is widespread and significant. For example, in considering the theory of parasocial interaction, individuals forge personal relationships with celebrities, relying on their opinions and admiring their social status.[17] Through parasocial relationships, individuals consider their relationships with celebrities to be quite interpersonal, despite the fact that most of the interactions between individuals and celebrities are in fact mediated.[18] Upward social

---

[13]Leon Festinger, "A Theory of Social Comparison Processes," *Human Relations* 7 (1954): pages 117–140.

[14]David R. Mettee and Gregory Smith, "Social Comparison and Interpersonal Attraction: The Case for Dissimilarity," in *Social Comparison Processes: Theoretical and Empirical Perspectives*, ed. Jerry M. Suls and Richard L. Miller (Washington, D.C.: Hemisphere Publishing Corporation, 1977), 69–70.

[15]Abraham P. Buunk and Frederick X. Gibbons, "Social Comparison: The End of a Theory and the Emergence of a Field," *Organizational Behavior and Human Decision Processes* 102 (2007): 3.

[16]Abraham P. Buunk, Hinke A. K. Groothof, and Frans W. Siero, "Social Comparison and Satisfaction with One's Social Life," *Journal of Social and Personal Relationships* 24, no. 2 (2007): 199; Kenneth J. Hemphill and Darrin R. Lehman, "Social Comparisons and Their Affective Consequences: The Importance of Comparison Dimension and Individual Difference Variables," *Journal of Social and Clinical Psychology* 10, no. 4 (1991): pages 372–394.

[17]Donald Horton and R. Richard Wohl, "Mass Communication and Para-Social Interaction: Observations on Intimacy at a Distance," *Psychiatry* 19 (1956): 215.

[18]Ibid.; Peter Gregg, "Parasocial Relationships' Similarity to Interpersonal Relationships: Factor Analyses of the Dimensions of Parasocial Interaction," (Minneapolis, MN.: University of Minnesota, 2005); Edward Schiappa, Mike Allen, and Peter Gregg, "Parasocial Relationships and Television: A Meta-Analysis of the Effects," in *Mass Media Effects: Advances through Meta-Analysis*, ed. Barbara Gayle Ray Preiss, Nancy Burrell, Mike Allen, and Jennings Bryant (Mahwah, NJ: Lawrence Erlbaum, 2007); Edward Schiappa, *Beyond Representational Correctness* (Albany, NY: State University of New York Press, 2008), 97.

comparison is quite common with celebrities; individuals compare themselves to members of a higher-status group and strive for such social status in their own lives.[19]

Understanding social comparison theory is crucial in theorizing celebrity endorsement. Social comparison theory explains one important reason why individuals compare themselves and their decisions to others: to reduce uncertainty about their individual decision. Thomas Ashby Wills and Jerry Suls expand on this view of uncertainty:

> At times, people don't necessarily want to know what their relative position is but want reassurance that their position is a good one. From this perspective, the self-enhancement processes ... may not reduce uncertainty per se, but instead strengthen an already established belief.[20]

When individuals compare their voting choice to a celebrity's endorsement of a politician, individuals use the social comparison to reduce their own uncertainty about the decision. More importantly, individuals also use social comparison to strengthen their *current* beliefs or decision. Although a celebrity may not be able to persuade a Republican to vote for a Democratic candidate, the celebrity's endorsement might *reinforce* a Republican's decision to vote for a Republican candidate.

Celebrity Politics and Celebrity Endorsement

In addition to social comparison theory, the area of celebrity politics also relates to questions of political decision-making, because celebrity status increases a famous person's access to rhetorical and political opportunities. Liesbet van Zoonen explains the need to understand politics' connection to culture: "Politics has to be connected to the everyday culture of its citizens; otherwise it becomes an alien sphere, occupied by strangers no one cares and bothers about."[21] Celebrity politics attempts to revitalize the political sphere and political decision-making for citizens by connecting politics to celebrity, which is an important part of "everyday culture" for most citizens who have become fans of entertainment celebrities.

---

[19]Douglas J. Brown, D. Lance Ferris, Daniel Heller, and Lisa M. Keeping, "Antecedents and Consequences of the Frequency of Upward and Downward Social Comparisons at Work," *Organizational Behavior and Human Decision Processes* 102 (2007): 59–60.

[20]Jerry M. Suls and Thomas Ashby Wills, eds., *Social Comparison: Contemporary Theory and Research* (Hillsdale, NJ: L. Erlbaum Associates, 1991), 404.

[21]Liesbet van Zoonen, *Entertaining the Citizen: When Politics and Popular Culture Converge, Critical Media Studies* (Lanham, MD: Rowman & Littlefield, 2005), 3.

Following political scholars Darrell M. West and John Orman,[22] I suggest four areas where the line is blurred between celebrity and politics: (1) where politicians become celebrities, which results in us treating our politicians like tabloid celebrities (e.g., the Kennedys); (2) where celebrities are treated as politicians (e.g., Michael Moore); (3) where celebrities endorse candidates, raise money, and try to pass on their luster to the candidate (e.g., Madonna endorsing Wesley Clark in the 2004 U.S. presidential race); and finally, (4) where the celebrity bypasses the political system and takes on a specific political issue (e.g., Sting and protecting rainforests). Although West and Orman cite celebrity endorsement as one of the areas in which celebrity and politics interact, they fail to articulate an actual theory of how and why celebrity endorsement matters. In this project, I extend their work to account for these questions.

Although little research has focused on celebrity endorsement within *politics*, David J. Jackson and Thomas I. A. Darrow explain that "much research has been done by marketing scholars on the impact of celebrity endorsements of products, and political scientists have examined the influence of 'experts' and other authority figures on public opinion."[23] Although this research does lend some insight into why celebrities have persuasive capabilities when it comes to selling products (some factors include expert status, credibility, likeability, and attractiveness),[24] it does not answer questions about why and how celebrities may have persuasive capabilities when it comes to endorsing *politicians*.

---

[22]Darrell M. West and John Orman, *Celebrity Politics*, ed. Paul S. Herrnson, *Real Politics in America* (Upper Saddle River, NJ: Prentice Hall, 2003).

[23]Jackson and Darrow, "The Influence of Celebrity Endorsements on Young Adults' Political Opinions," 81. For more information on the "celebrity expert," see also: Tania Lewis, "Embodied Experts: Robert Hughes, Cultural Studies and the Celebrity Intellectual," *Continuum: Journal of Media & Cultural Studies* 15, no. 2 (2001): pages 233–247. Lisa Slawter, "Robert F. Kennedy Jr.'s Environmental Advocacy: Discursive Tensions of the Celebrity Expert," in *National Communication Association's 91st Annual Convention* (Boston, MA: 2005); Rachel Smolkin, "Star Power," *American Journalism Review* 25, no. 8 (2003): pages 42–46.

[24]For more information on the relationship between celebrity and product endorsement, see the following essays: Sami Alsmadi, "The Power of Celebrity Endorsement in Brand Choice Behavior: An Empirical Study of Consumer Attitudes in Jordan," *Journal of Accounting: Business and Management* 13 (2006): pages 69–84; Abhijit Biswas, Dipayan Biswas, and Neel Das, "The Differential Effects of Celebrity and Expert Endorsements on Consumer Risk Perceptions," *Journal of Advertising* 35, no. 2 (2006): pages 17–31; Michael A. Kamins, Meribeth J. Brand, Stuart A. Hoeke, and John C. Moe, "Two-Sided versus One-Sided Celebrity Endorsements: The Impact on Advertising Effectiveness and Credibility," *Journal of Advertising* 18, no. 2 (1989): pages 4–10; Grant McCracken, "Who Is the Celebrity Endorser? Cultural Foundations of the Endorsement Process," *The Journal of Consumer Research* 16, no. 3 (1989): pages 310–321; R. Bruce Money, Terence A. Shimp, and Tomoaki Sakano, "Celebrity Endorsements in Japan and the United States: Is Negative Information All That Harmful?," *Journal of Advertising Research* 46, no. 1 (2006): pages 113–123.; David H. Silvera and Benedikte Austad, "Factors Predicting the Effectiveness of Celebrity Endorsement Advertisements," *European Journal of Marketing* 38, no. 11/12 (2004): pages 1509–1526.; Carolyn Tripp, Thomas D. Jensen, and Les Carlson, "The

In theorizing celebrity endorsement, one must realize the importance of the endorser as a kind of celebrity politician. Bono, lead singer of the Irish rock band U2, is probably one of the best examples of this phenomenon. Bono is not a traditional politician, yet he is granted political recognition and rhetorical opportunity by influential world leaders. He has become an expert in debt relief and poverty through studying with leading world economists.[25] Jack Ewing articulates the negative aspect of celebrity activism, however: "No question that Bono's intentions are good. But celebrity-led relief efforts still make some people uneasy. Star power generates publicity, but it's not so clear what the lasting effect is."[26] Even though Bono has expertise, his status as a celebrity threatens to overpower his status as expert.

In addition, race also factors into how celebrity politicians are perceived. One might ask why it is easier for Bono, a white Irishman, to be a spokesperson for Africa than it is for the scores of black celebrities before him who tried to focus world attention on Africa. A large part of this is due to Bono's status as a white European man. Oprah was criticized for endorsing Obama by many reporters, and part of this criticism is about race. Some critics implicitly and explicitly cited race in their response to her endorsement.[27] Many of Oprah's viewers as well as critics saw Oprah's endorsement of Obama as choosing race over gender.[28]

Oprah's race was also a factor in endorsing Obama because of the race of her audience. Oprah's audience is not only overwhelmingly female; it is also mostly *white* females. In the past, Oprah has been chastised for not using her show to address racial politics. Dana L. Cloud explains this reluctance to talk about race relations on Oprah's show:

> For no matter whether "Oprah" or her biographers or publicists are the agents of persona construction, "Oprah"'s identity is articulated

---

Effects of Multiple Product Endorsements by Celebrities on Consumers' Attitudes and Intentions," *Journal of Consumer Research* 20 (1994): pages 535–547.

[25]Stephen McGinty, "Bono Still Hasn't Found What He Is Looking For: Debt Relief," *The Scotsman*, September 25, 2004, page 26.

[26]Jack Ewing, "For Bono, Star Power with Purpose," *Business Week Online* published online January 30, 2006, page 4; (2006) (accessed August 28, 2010).

[27]Irene Monroe, "By Dissing Palin, Oprah Hurts Obama," *LA Progressive*, September 17, 2008, accessed August 28, 2010; Earl Ofari Hutchinson, "White Women Are Punishing Obama, Not Oprah," *American Chronicle*, May 29, 2008, online version of the *American Chronicle*: http://www .americanchronicle.com/articles/view/63447); Tony Allen-Mills, "Women Turn on 'Traitor' Oprah Winfrey for Backing Barack Obama," *Sunday Times*, January 20, 2008, (online version of the *Sunday Times*: http://www.timesonline.co.uk/tol/news/world/us_and_americas/us_elections/ article3216586.ece).

[28]Allen-Mills, "Women Turn on 'Traitor.'"

within a liberal frame that guarantees continued high ratings and profits ... [A]rticulation of difference remains at the level of identity and does not imply political opposition or activity against the system that produces racism and sexism.[29]

Scholars and critics suggest she stays away from race to ensure her good ratings with white viewers and commercial sponsors.[30] When Oprah suddenly endorsed an African-American candidate, some polls as well as numerous critics suggested her likability rating with white viewers suffered.[31] Earl Ofari Hutchinson explains: "It's also true that celebrities who get too political can tick off a lot of their fans. It's also an undeniable fact that Oprah has slipped in the ratings and the slip can be directly traced to her Obama support."[32]

Race is one characteristic that inflects the status of a celebrity politician. Like Bono, Oprah acts as a kind of celebrity politician. Unlike Bono, Oprah's race matters differently in her enactment of celebrity politics. By endorsing Obama and agreeing to support him through her media enterprise, Oprah acted as a celebrity politician in support of a "real" politician. In short, Oprah *performed* celebrity politics, and her race (and gender) became a part of this performance and an object of controversy. In a vein similar to John Street and Liesbet van Zoonen, I suggest that the connection between celebrity and politics necessitates a rethinking of politics in terms of *performance*.[33] Van Zoonen explains the importance of the politician as a kind of "actor performing a relevant 'persona': a self as revealed to others."[34] By endorsing Obama, Oprah demonstrated her "celebrity persona" to others as one who is interested in political change. Like Street and van Zoonen, I am interested in *how* celebrity politicians, such as Bono or Oprah, are able to participate in the political realm through celebrity endorsement of politicians. How are their celebrity status and involvement in politics a useful rhetorical resource in endorsing a particular candidate?

---

[29]Dana L. Cloud, "Hegemony or Concordance? The Rhetoric of Tokenism in "Oprah" Winfrey's Rags-to-Riches Biography," *Critical Studies in Mass Communication* 13 (1996): 132.

[30]Ibid.: 126; 31–32.

[31]Monroe, "By Dissing Palin"; Allen-Mills, "Women Turn on 'Traitor.'"

[32]Hutchinson, "White Women Are Punishing Obama."

[33]John Street, "The Celebrity Politician: Political Style and Popular Culture," in *Media and the Restyling of Politics*, ed. John Corner and Dick Pels (London: SAGE Publications, 2003), 97; Zoonen, *Entertaining the Citizen*, 72.

[34]Zoonen, *Entertaining the Citizen*, 72.

The Functions of Celebrity Endorsement:
Oprah's Endorsement of Barack Obama

Building on the work reviewed above, I describe four functions of celebrity endorsement for an American audience. My conjectures about celebrity endorsements' influence on audiences will need to be refined by audience research.[35] Importantly, these functions are described for optimal conditions, in which individuals do judge their own decisions in relation to celebrities' opinions.

I posit four functions of celebrity endorsement: (1) it increases awareness/publicity for the candidate, (2) it transfers optimal investment from the celebrity to the candidate, (3) it influences undecided and independent voters to (re)consider the candidate, and (4) the endorsement has more rhetorical force if the celebrity is a first-time endorser (what I call the "uniqueness factor"). After discussing each of these functions and illustrating them with Oprah's endorsement of Obama, I suggest future directions and potential limitations of theorizing celebrity endorsement.

Endorsement Increases Awareness/Publicity

Celebrity endorsement has the ability to increase voter awareness and the publicity of a presidential candidate, thereby bolstering political support for a candidate. Before any candidate receives votes, that candidate must be familiar to voters, at least on the level of name recognition. Although most people would not vote for a candidate based on the celebrity's endorsement alone,[36] certainly the publicity for a candidate that is brought by a celebrity endorsement does not hurt that candidate. Surely, the hundreds of news articles about Oprah's endorsement of Obama lend support to this hypothesis.

Oprah also has the capacity to draw a larger crowd to events such as political rallies. This was crucial for Obama right before the Iowa caucus; he attracted much larger crowds with Oprah than he did without her.[37] The celebrity factor seems more important in a primary situation when there are a bunch of candidates battling for attention than in a two-way race. In such a situation, name recognition is crucial to differentiating the candidate from the crowd of other candidates. Oprah's endorsement distinguished Obama from the rest of the crowd.

Although voters had heard Hillary Clinton's name in the news for over a decade, Barack Obama had only recently emerged on the national political

---

[35]Schiappa, *Beyond Representational Correctness*, 56.

[36]"'O' Is for Oprah," *National Journal*, September 22, 2007.

[37]Scott Martelle and Louise Roug, "Oprah, Obama Team up in Iowa," *Los Angeles Times*, December 9, 2007.

scene at the 2004 National Democratic Convention.[38] Whereas Obama was often portrayed as the "inexperienced" newcomer in the presidential race for the Democrats, Hillary Clinton was often viewed as the "experienced" candidate, largely due to her lengthy political presence, albeit not in official roles. Clinton's name was clearly recognized by the electorate.

Based on this discrepancy of name recognition between Clinton and Obama, Oprah's political endorsement increased his name recognition among voters, as well as increased general awareness of his role as a candidate and contributed to publicity surrounding Obama. Although pundit Susan Estrich argues that Obama did not need this name recognition as badly as other Democratic candidates, she notes that *if he did*, Oprah's endorsement would most certainly have given him that recognition.

> If name recognition were Obama's problem, Oprah could give it to him, almost instantly. If sizzle and charisma were what he was lacking, Oprah could provide a healthy dose of it with her magic touch. If the issue were [*sic*] his personality, his being too cool or distant or ruthlessly ambitious, Oprah could warm him up.[39]

Oprah's endorsement of Obama demonstrates the first function of celebrity endorsement: increased public awareness of the candidate.

Endorsement Transfers Optimal Investment

Celebrity endorsement also transfers optimal investment from a celebrity to the endorsed candidate. Building off Grant McCracken's theory of "meaning transfer,"[40] I suggest that the meanings associated with celebrity appeal and the credibility of the celebrity transfer to the endorsed candidate.

McCracken explains his theory of "meaning transfer" and how it connects a celebrity to a consumer good and eventually to the consumer:

> The argument is that the endorsement process depends upon the symbolic properties of the celebrity endorser. Using a "meaning transfer" perspective, these properties are shown to reside in the celebrity and to move from celebrity to consumer good and from good to consumer.[41]

---

[38]"Barack Star," *American Journalism Review* 29, no. 1 (2007): 14.

[39]Susan Estrich, "Obama Gets a Little Help from Oprah," *Corpus Christi Caller Times*, September 13, 2007, page 9.

[40]McCracken, "Who Is the Celebrity Endorser?"

[41]Ibid., 310.

If we apply this premise to presidential candidates, celebrity endorsement transfers the meanings, celebrity appeal, and status associated with the celebrity to the political candidate. In a method similar to how celebrity endorsers persuade an individual to invest in a consumer good, celebrity endorsers are able to extend this notion of investment to the political candidate, persuading individuals to invest in the candidate through the action of voting.

The race of both celebrity and candidate, however, plays a role in the transfer, and can complicate an endorsement, sometimes in negative ways. Race can derail or complicate optimal investment, often putting the candidate in a position where he or she tries to dismiss or deny the endorsement.[42] For example, black hip-hop star Ludacris wrote a song about Obama, and Obama distanced himself from the lyrics' provocative racial critiques of Hillary Clinton and John McCain. In the media, the Obama campaign suggested that Ludacris "should be ashamed" of the song's lyrics.[43] Instead of embracing an African American's celebrity endorsement, the Obama campaign distanced itself from the racial overtones of the rap artist and his music for fear that the endorsement would transfer negative feelings to the Obama campaign. This move by the Obama campaign was not too surprising, in part because of the controversial role of the rap community in provoking discussions of race relations in the United States.[44] Race also played a role in Oprah's endorsement, but because of her predominantly white audience, it may have played a more positive role in optimal investment than in the case of Ludacris's majority black audience. Reflecting on Cloud's critique, Oprah is seen as a "safe" black woman, and possibly a woman who has "transcended" race, by her primarily white audience. Through optimal investment, Oprah transfers her racial safety to Obama, which is one reason why Obama would accept her endorsement, in contrast to the endorsements by those in the hip-hop community.

Importantly, Oprah indicated that her endorsement of Obama meant that she would *not* welcome other presidential candidates on her show.[45] Even on the level of keeping other candidates away from her influential television show,

---

[42]For example, many hip-hop stars endorsed Obama and wrote songs about him; some of these stars were criticized by the press: "Obama Rejects Ludacris Rap Lyrics," *BBC News*, July 31, 2008, (*BBC News* online version: http://news.bbc.co.uk/2/hi/entertainment/7534736.stm); "Obama Campaign Denounces Ludacris Song," in *Music News*, National Public Radio, July 31, 2008); Azi Paybarah, "Obama's Hip-Hop Admirers," *New York Observer*, March 4, 2008, (*New York Observer* online version: http://www.observer.com/2008/obama-s-hip-hop-admirers).

[43]"Obama Rejects Ludacris Rap Lyrics." (*BBC News* online version: http://news.bbc.co.uk/2/hi/entertainment/7534736.stm).

[44]Tricia Rose, *Black Noise: Rap Music and Black Culture in Contemporary America* (Hanover, NH: University Press of New England, 1994), 99, 102.

[45]"Oprah's Backing a Big Boost for Obama," in *NPR: Morning Edition*, National Public Radio, September 10, 2007.

Oprah's endorsement of Obama demonstrated that she hoped to persuade her audience to invest in Obama like they have invested in the numerous other products she has endorsed. By offering Obama exclusive access to the millions of viewers of her television show (and the crucial segment of women over the age of fifty, a voting segment for which both Clinton and Obama were vying), she simultaneously increased these voters' awareness of Obama (the first function of celebrity endorsement) while transferring optimal investment of her own celebrity appeal and status to that of Obama.

Endorsement Influences Undecided and Independent Voters

Although a celebrity's appeal and status may not be enough to change the minds of a dedicated Republican or Democrat, the appeal may be influential to the undecided and independent voters. As social comparison theory explains so well, one of the reasons why we look toward others in making a decision is that we hope to reduce our own uncertainty about that decision. We look to experts—including celebrities—for their opinions so that we have more information to make our own decisions.

Most authors and political writers did not believe that Oprah's political knowledge would change people's current opinions; however, few of these writers addressed the fact that Oprah might have had some influence among the undecided and independent voters. Because Oprah has millions of viewers a day, of which 75 percent are women,[46] her endorsement of Obama may have influenced these voters—many of which were undecided and independent voters—to consider Obama as a presidential candidate. For example, in the 2004 presidential race, women composed 58 percent of undecided voters and 54 percent of swing voters nationwide.[47] One author asserted Oprah's influence in what became known as the "Oprah bounce":

> During the 2000 campaign George Bush appeared on Oprah at a time when he was struggling in the polls. A week later he had turned a 10% deficit [with women voters] into a 2% lead over the Democratic candidate, Al Gore, a turnaround many attributed to the "Oprah bounce."[48]

---

[46]"Newscast: Oprah Winfrey Hosts Fundraiser for Barack Obama," in *NBC News: Sunday Today*, NBC, September 9, 2007.

[47]*Welcome to Votes for Women* (Communications Consortium Media Center in Washington, D.C., 2004 [cited December 3, 2007]), http://www.equality2020.org/gender.htm (accessed August 28, 2010).

[48]Dan Glaister, "For Obama It's the Promised Land—Oprah's Endorsement," *The Guardian*, September 8, 2007, (*The Guardian* online version: http://www.guardian.co.uk/world/2007/sep/08/barackobama.uselections2008).

Eight years later, according to a poll of Iowa voters by the *Des Moines Register*, Obama became the frontrunner in that caucus, with a significant increase in women voters:

> In the new poll, Obama leads with support from 31% of women likely to attend the caucuses, compared with 26% for Clinton. In October, Clinton was the preferred candidate of 34% of women caucus goers, compared with 21% for Obama.[49]

Although there is no way to determine definitively whether Oprah's support helped cause this turnaround for Obama, certainly her endorsement and popularity among women did not hurt Obama's cause. Even if Oprah's influence is more in the realm of elite conjecture and third-person effects, it still shapes discourse about candidates.

The importance of race emerges in this example of the "Oprah bounce." If Oprah was able to give a white man (George W. Bush) a bounce in 2000, but was questioned about the validity of her endorsement of a black man (Barack Obama) in 2008 by many reporters and critics, what does that tell us about the role of race in celebrity endorsement? In addition to complicating optimal investment (in both negative and positive ways), race also plays a role in helping voters to (re)consider a political candidate. Oprah's racial "safety" among her white audience seems important in persuading them to reconsider voting for a black man over a white woman. At the very least, Oprah's endorsement helped to reduce uncertainty about this important political decision, while simultaneously filling that void of uncertainty with important knowledge and bolstering support of Barack Obama as the best presidential candidate.

Endorsement and the "Uniqueness Factor"

The final function of celebrity endorsement is that the endorsement has more rhetorical force if the celebrity is a first-time endorser, what I refer to as the "uniqueness factor." A variety of political strategists indicate that celebrity endorsement is unimportant because in the past, these celebrities have endorsed candidates with seemingly little influence on people's opinions.[50] Because many of these celebrities consistently support politicians, especially financially, year after year, their influence seems to become diluted over time. The novelty of Oprah's status as an official endorser seems important in theorizing celebrity

---

[49]Thomas Beaumont and Jonathan Roos, "Huckabee, Obama Take Lead in Iowa Polling," *USA Today*, December 2, 2007, (online version of *USA Today*: http://www.usatoday.com/news/politics/election2008/2007-12-02-iowapoll_N.htm).

[50]"Profile: Impact of Oprah Winfrey Endorsing Barack Obama; Politico Editor in Chief John Harris Speaks About Celebrity and Politics," *CBS News: The Early Show*, CBS Worldwide, Inc., September 7, 2007.

endorsement. Most of the articles written about her endorsement of Obama focused on this "uniqueness" factor. Because Oprah had never endorsed a political candidate before, her views and opinions of Obama were novel and seemingly had more rhetorical force.

Oprah became involved with Obama's campaign with nothing to gain and with the risk that she could actually *lose* viewers because of her involvement with politics. Some critics asserted that Oprah *did* lose viewers through endorsing Obama, in part because her audience saw Oprah's endorsement as choosing race over gender.[51] One television broadcast articulated the risks involved for Oprah:

> With her daily talk show, Oprah can put books on the best seller list, start fashion, diet and exercise crazes, but she's also been talking to and with Americans about the most intimate aspects of their lives. So the possibilities are intriguing, but so are the risks.... Now Oprah could be inextricably linked to Obama and any stumbles that he makes on the campaign trail could reflect back on her.[52]

Because Oprah engaged in a calculated risk, her credibility and motives as to *why* she endorsed Obama seemed to be more genuine. In media discourse about Oprah's motives for endorsing Obama, she consistently stated that Obama was the first candidate she truly believed in: "For me, this was the moment to step up,' [Oprah] said in a recent radio chat with friend Gayle King."[53] Because of Oprah's novelty in choosing Obama as her first presidential endorsement, I suggest that the "uniqueness factor" plays an important role in understanding how and why celebrity endorsement has rhetorical force for many voters.

Concluding Thoughts on Theorizing Celebrity Endorsement

Because my theory is mostly bolstered with evidence from press reports and audience surveys about Oprah's endorsement of Barack Obama, I invite other scholars to extend my theory to other examples of celebrity endorsement, as well as explore a variety of methodological approaches, including that of audience research. By theorizing how celebrity endorsement functions, I do not explore the economic component of celebrity, and the fact that celebrity

---

[51]Monroe, "By Dissing Palin"; Allen-Mills, "Women Turn on 'Traitor.'"

[52]"Profile: Impact of Oprah Winfrey."

[53]Matthew Mosk, "Campaign 2008: Winfrey Looking to Step up Role in Obama Campaign/ Analysts Ponder Impact Her Media Empire Could Have in the '08 Election," *Washington Post*, September 6, 2007, page 5.

is a position of privilege to which very few Americans ever have access. One limitation to theorizing celebrity endorsement is this problem of access and the myth of the American dream: Upward social comparison necessitates a view that upward social mobility is possible for *all* Americans, and as other studies have suggested,[54] this is not the case for many Americans who face structural inequalities on a daily basis.

A second limitation involves a common critique of celebrity politics: What happens when people only blindly follow the celebrity because of the celebrity's status and not necessarily because that celebrity has political expertise? My response to this critique of celebrity politics focuses on a recentering of politics within the notion of democracy. Do celebrities sometimes endorse seemingly "wrong" candidates? Absolutely. However, do Americans in general also seem to choose "wrong" candidates for the country? Again, absolutely. Because we live in a democracy, we are all free to assert our political beliefs and support for different political candidates, regardless of whether such candidates are necessarily the best. We must remember that celebrities are Americans, too, regardless of their economic and social clout. American citizens are *not* cultural dupes. Even though they may listen to celebrities' endorsements and political beliefs, in the end, Americans as democratic citizens will be the ones in the voting booths.

And Americans did go to the voting booths on November 4, 2008. On that historic evening, Barack Obama was elected as our forty-fourth president of the United States. On the night of Obama's win, as well as during his inauguration on January 20, 2009, Oprah was positioned as a special guest in media coverage. Television cameras continually featured Oprah's face in Grant Park on election night, and commentators made mention of her early support for Obama.[55] Oprah was seen as a guest of honor on election night, and at the inauguration, where she received an honored place on the stage.[56] Given this continued coverage of Oprah's relationship to Obama's success, I see further support for my theory of celebrity endorsement. Although no one would make the argument that Oprah caused Obama's success, the different functions of celebrity endorsement show us *how* Oprah's endorsement provided Obama with different rhetorical resources and media opportunities.

---

[54]Sut Jhally and Justin Lewis, *Enlightened Racism: The Cosby Show, Audiences, and the Myth of the American Dream, Cultural Studies Series* (Boulder, CO: Westview Press, 1992).

[55]"'Yes We Did,' Obama Crowd Chants at Rally," *CNN.com*, (http://www.cnn.com/2008/POLITICS/11/04/obama.celebration/), November 5, 2008.

[56]John Bingham, "Barack Obama Inauguration: Hollywood out in Force for Real-Life Epic," *Telegraph*, January 20, 2009, (online version of *Telegraph*: http://www.telegraph.co.uk/news/worldnews/northamerica/usa/barackobama/4299955/Barack-Obama-inauguration-Hollywood-out-in-force-for-real-life-epic.html).

The Obama Mass: Barack Obama, Image, and Fear of the Crowd

Robert Spicer

As the Democratic Party convened in Denver in August 2008, an ailing but nevertheless boisterous Edward Kennedy stood before a mass of blue signs bearing his family name. As the television feed cut to a wide-angle shot, the audience watching the spectacle at home saw the large, blue video monitors with the Kennedy name writ large with a halo-like faded glow. And with this image we are confronted with the reality of what the Obama candidacy and presidency tell us. To truly address the effect of Obama on American politics and vice versa, we must discuss the name that has defined Democratic presidential politics for a half-century: Kennedy. One couldn't help feeling that the ghost of JFK was floating above the 2008 convention. Or perhaps it is better to say that the ghost was conjured by the audience. Could it be that Obama was tapping into political forces not contained within supernatural imagery, but instead in the collective desires of the American liberal atmospheric?

The locus of Obama in the history of liberalism is rooted in the Kennedy legacy in three ways: (1) iconography of the two presidents' images; (2) the relationship between the two presidents and the new-media forms of their respective eras; and (3) lionization. The final element is more the result of the first two; this is the evolution from lionization to religiofication, deification, and demonization. This chapter draws a line from the Kennedy legacy through the Obama candidacy and into his presidency. The Kennedy legacy, as a lens through which Obama is viewed, engages American liberalism in a process of lionization of Obama.

This Kennedy shadow that looms large over liberalism and Democratic presidential politics is liberalism's state of Freudian melancholy. The lionization of Barack Obama during the campaign was part of an attempt to move from melancholy to mourning and beyond, to a new, reinvigorated liberalism in American politics. However, we may also find it not only in the liberal imagination but the American mind more generally. We see this in the media coverage of the election-night festivities and the inauguration of President Obama.

The lionization of Obama leads to a critical point of problematization of Obama throughout the course of the 2008 campaign, a critique termed here the "Obama success flaw." At various points in the campaign, Obama's popular support was framed as a threat to the body politic, thus transforming the audience into a point of counterattack on the campaign itself. In this sense, the audience is something more than a group of people listening to a speech; they represent a singular object to be feared. This fear of the collectivity was expressed via images of campaign rallies, especially those found at the conservative news portal the *Drudge Report*.

Obama and the Kennedy Family

In "A President Like My Father," Caroline Kennedy wrote, "All my life, people have told me that my father changed their lives.… Sometimes it takes a while to recognize that someone has a special ability to get us to believe in ourselves.… In those rare moments, when such a person comes along, we need to put aside our plans and reach for what we know is possible.… We have that kind of opportunity with Senator Obama."[1] It is difficult to see Caroline Kennedy's invocation of her father as just another endorsement. Even if it was not intended to, this endorsement spurred the shift from liberal melancholy to mourning and beyond, by way of situating Obama as the natural political heir to the Kennedy legacy.

The news media have also alluded to this legacy in both subtle and overt ways. Throughout the 2008 campaign and the inaugural ceremonies, there were broader drawings of the Obamas as a twenty-first-century Camelot, seen in comparisons of Michelle Obama to Jacqueline Kennedy.[2] Upon announcing Obama's victory, Brian Williams noted that "[t]here will be young children in the White House for the first time since the Kennedy generation."[3] Images of President Obama himself have also contributed to this phenomenon. One in particular accompanied a *Washington Post* article on the Kennedy family's support for Obama. Figure 13.1[4] features a bust of Robert F. Kennedy foregrounding then-Senator Obama. The bust of RFK also partially obscures Senator Edward Kennedy. This image

---

[1] Caroline Kennedy, "A President Like My Father," *New York Times*, January 27, 2008.

[2] Helen Andrews, "Michelle O: Suited to be Jackie's Successor," *Politico*, January 31, 2008, http://www.politico.com/news/stories/0108/8221.html (accessed October 8, 2008). Shelly Branch, "Michelle O Meets Jackie O," *Wall Street Journal*, March 1, 2008, http://online.wsj.com/public/article/SB120433199073503697.html?mod=(_pageid_)_topbox (accessed October 8, 2008).

[3] Brian Williams, NBC election night coverage, November 2, 2008.

[4] This image of Obama and Kennedy was part of a photograph slideshow of various images of Obama and Kennedy family members that appeared on the *Washington Post* Web site. It can be found at http://www.washingtonpost.com/wp-dyn/content/gallery/2008/01/28/GA2008012801291.html?sid=ST2008012900890.

FIGURE 13.1 Then-senator Obama with Senator Edward Kennedy, who is obscured by a bust of his brother Robert F. Kennedy (Photograph by Alex Wong/Getty Images)

makes a powerful statement beyond being a simple presentation of the two senators sitting together. Here, Senator Kennedy is obscured by the bust of his deceased brother, just as he is also overshadowed by the very legacy he is using to promote Obama; he sits behind this legacy as he wields its political power.

The interpretation of the picture will depend largely on the political perspective of the "reader" of the image. Images of a candidate will "affect individuals differently depending on their prior attitude toward the figure in question."[5] For example, a more liberal-minded "reader" of the image might see it as poetic, as the Kennedy legacy transferring to a new generation. For a more conservative-minded "reader," this image may resurrect tales of Chicago's mayor Richard Daley stealing the 1960 election for Kennedy. Senator Kennedy's face is half-hidden and he is pointing, directing Obama's attention toward something. In this, one might see Edward Kennedy as a *Wizard of Oz*–type figure, pulling the strings of a potential future president by bestowing upon the person the use of the Kennedy legacy toward winning election to the presidency.

---

[5]Paul Waldman and James Devitt, "Newspaper Photographs and the 1996 Presidential Election: The Question of Bias," *Journalism and Mass Communication Quarterly* 75, no. 2 (1998): 302–11.

The connection between Barack Obama and the martyred Kennedy brothers, and the state of left melancholy in America, combine to create the prospect of religiofication. Eric Hoffer defines "the art of 'religiofication'" as "the art of turning practical purposes into holy causes."[6] Religiofication is a potent tool for harnessing the energy of the body politic, for turning the disconnected individual into the citizen, the citizen into the voter, the voter into the activist, and the activist into the "true believer." This serves a purpose for the aspiring president and the public crusader, as well as for his or her enemies. Religiofication motivates supporters, yet can also scare away or inspire resistance to power.

Throughout the 2008 presidential campaign, Obama's supporters demonstrated a level of emotional attachment that is not present for many political candidates. As one blogger put it, "Obama volunteers speak of 'coming to Obama' in the same way born-again Christians talk about 'coming to Jesus.'"[7] This frames support for Obama as borderline deification. The distinction between deification and lionization is an important one. Where deification carries with it the implications of the supernatural, lionization is more analogous to the idolization of a celebrity; while the figure is greatly admired, there is still an acknowledged mortal quality. Both terms are wrapped up in the modeling of Obama after John F. Kennedy. They were reinforced by news reports of supporters fainting at Obama rallies; the reports seem to imply that supporters were overly emotional and irrational rather than affected by heat and overcrowding. This perception of the irrational supporter was codified in the term "Obamamania," which likened support for Obama to a mental illness.

This problematization of Obama's supporters was not new. The way in which Obama's conservative critics employed it is akin to what Hofstadter,[8] Schlesinger,[9] and others have characterized as the "paranoid style." The paranoid style is not necessarily used because the opponent sees the "domestic Other" as a dangerous mass movement that is out of touch with the mainstream, but because the opponent is afraid that "otherwise normal political actors will be drawn *away from* the moderate center and into more radical forms of politics."[10] So it is not just the crowd in and of itself, but rather its

---

[6]Eric Hoffer, *The True Believer* (New York: Harper Collins, 1966), 6.

[7]Kathleen Geier, "Barack Obama Is Not Jesus," *Talking Points Memo*, February 5, 2008, http://tpmcafe.talkingpointsmemo.com/2008/02/05/barack_obama_is_not_jesus/#more (accessed February 6, 2008).

[8]Richard Hofstadter, *The Paranoid Style in American Politics* (New York: Vintage, 1967).

[9]Arthur Schlesinger, *The Vital Center: Our Purposes and Perils on the Tightrope of American Liberalism* (Cambridge, MA: Riverside Press, 1962).

[10]Jack Z. Bratich, *Conspiracy Panics* (New York: State University of New York Press, 2008), 34–35.

ability to lend credibility to a perceived radical movement that others would otherwise avoid for a more "reasonable" option.

Accurate or not, the focus of this critique during the 2008 campaign simultaneously demonstrated the perceived power of Obama's rhetorical skills and represented, for his opponents, a tool for undermining Obama's appeal to those undecided moderate voters. Conservative opponents tried to reframe one of Obama's strengths—his capacity to inspire supporters—as a weakness. During the campaign, Obama was criticized for both the enthusiasm and the size of crowds. One might find this to be counterintuitive on the part of Obama's critics. However, "[t]here are no masses; there are only ways of seeing people as masses."[11] But this critique is not solely about the masses; it is about political affect and the employment of the fear appeal as a tool for political persuasion.

The Obama Affect

Walter Lippmann argued that "beside hero-worship there is the exorcism of devils. By the same mechanism through which heroes are incarnated, devils are made."[12] Obama embodies Lippmann's concept of the "symbolic personality." Through our media, political figures are transformed from mere human beings into images, messages, ideas consumed by multiple publics. In these cases, the candidate's handlers are in a constant struggle to manage the image of both the candidate and the opponent, an ongoing contest to define one another and the cultural and political parameters of the debate. While the candidates and their campaigns are the central actors in this exchange, journalism is equally combative, not just mediating but participating in the fight. More than the campaigns themselves, journalism helps to create and perpetuate the parameters of debates. As Mendelson argues, "[j]ournalistic symbols appearing iconologically—repeated in patterns over time—become mythic. Myths are constantly told and retold within a culture."[13] This conceptualization of a "culture's grand narratives"[14] conjures Lippmann's pseudoenvironment in which oversimplified perceptions of a complicated world are established and maintained as a shorthand for the real world.[15] Journalism and punditry assist in this process of reinforcing myths and fostering new ones. Visual representation

---

[11]Raymond Williams, *Culture and Society* (London: Random House, 1961), 20.

[12]Walter Lippmann, *Public Opinion* (New York: Free Press, 1997), 7.

[13]Andrew Mendelson, "Slice-of-Life Moments as Visual 'Truth': Norman Rockwell, Feature Photography, and American Values in Pictorial Journalism," *Journalism History* 4 (Winter 2004): 166–78.

[14]Ibid., 169.

[15]Lippmann, *Public Opinion*, 10–11.

is one part of media influences on public opinion, acting as a summary for a belief system. It is important to note that the visual can begin to blur the line between mere representation and idolatry.[16]

In the case of the Obama campaign, this was also the line between Caroline Kennedy's picture of Obama as inspirational and his opponents' deployment of fear appeals. Moriarty and Garramone argue that candidate representation in the media has more to do with their personal presentation than choices made by the media.[17] While candidates manipulate media imagery, partisan media and rival campaigns can be just as skilled at visual manipulation as the candidates themselves. No matter how skilled a candidate's handlers may be, they never fully have control of the image; the affective connection is never fully under the control of any campaign.

As Sarah Ahmed argues, "affect does not reside positively in the sign or commodity, but is produced only as an effect of its circulation."[18] Thus, a dual affect of Barack Obama was created through the campaign by political allies and opponents via their relationships with audiences both in person and through media. Here it is most useful to think of affect defined by Seigworth and Gregg as "*forces or forces of encounter*" that are "born in-between-ness"[19] and "can serve to drive us toward movement, toward thought and extension."[20] These forces are tapped into, connecting different actors at different times (or simultaneously), coming out as forces that drive inspiration, fear, political action, or apathy.

For Obama's supporters, the affective connection "in-between" is in the Kennedyesque call to action, to civic duty. It is in Caroline Kennedy's description of a political figure's "special ability to get us to believe in ourselves."[21] This ability does not simply reside within the politician; the ability is only given meaning when "we" as a people or political body act on it. Likewise, our ability

---

[16]Appadurai employs a concept similar to Lippmann's pseudoenvironment in his discussion of the "multiple worlds which are constituted by the historically situated imaginations of persons and groups spread around the globe." He argues that individuals and groups are "able to contest and sometimes even subvert the 'imagined worlds' of the official mind." In other words, the public is able to play with representations and take the meanings they want from them. Arjun Appadurai, "Disjuncture and Difference in the Global Cultural Economy," *Theory, Culture, and Society* 7 (1990): 295–310.

[17]Sandra Moriarty and Gina Garramone, "A Study of Newsmagazine Photographs of the 1984 Presidential Campaign," *Journalism Quarterly* 63 (1986): 728–34.

[18]Sarah Ahmed, "Affective Economies," *Social Text* 79, vol. 22, no. 2, (2004): 117–39.

[19]Gregory J. Seigworth and Melissa Gregg, "An Inventory of Shimmers: Affect, For Now," in *The Affect Theory Reader*, ed. Gregory J. Seigworth and Melissa Gregg (Durham, NC: Duke University Press, 2010), 2.

[20]Ibid., 1.

[21]Kennedy, "President Like My Father."

to "believe in ourselves" is given meaning through the inspirational oratory of an Obama (or a Kennedy). The essential point is that the affective relationship between the audience and candidate activates their power.

Obama's opponents were also tapping into this political affect, but in this case, the "in-between-ness" was transformed into an affect of fear; in this case, note that fear *is* affect, *not* emotion. As Ahmed presents it, fear is particularly potent in a political campaign because it "responds to that which is approaching rather than already here."[22] Political campaigns are all about that which is approaching or *potentially* approaching. In politics, affect and emotion are not concerned with the present, but with what may someday be faced or even an imagined and idealized past.

The challenge of fear functioning as a form of political capital, motivating or moving bodies, is that it has the potential to weaken political movements.[23] Fear must create in the political imagination a perception of the approaching object as an imminent threat,[24] but also a sense that the object of fear is not insurmountable.[25] In other words, "fear works to restrict some bodies through the movement or expansion of others."[26] For Ahmed, the affective energy of fear brings about, in one subject, an active response and in another impotence; fear is not just being passed to and fro, it is continuity, happening between and connecting subjects. The next section of this chapter will focus on the "circulation of the signs of fear"[27] by Obama opponents, especially in visual representations of "the Obama crowd."

The Implicit Form of Barack Obama

Seeing a photo is not a totally objective experience; the photograph is a doubling of the subjectivities of sight. The photographer frames the shot, and editors create captions and decide what images to include. In another sense, however, seeing *is* believing, because the political audience will believe in what it wants to see and see what it wants to believe. By seeing an image in a certain way, they bring beliefs into being and by the prepossession of beliefs, they

---

[22]Ahmed, "Affective Economies," 125.

[23]Here this notion of fear as capital is borrowed from Ahmed, who links the movement of capital in Marx with "the movement between signs." Ibid., 120.

[24]Michael William Pfau, "Who's Afraid of Fear Appeals? Contingency, Courage, and Deliberation in Rhetorical Theory and Practice," *Philosophy and Rhetoric* 40, no. 2 (2007): 216–37.

[25]Ibid., 229.

[26]Ahmed, "Affective Economies," 127.

[27]Ibid.

bring an image into representing a certain thing for them.[28] Political campaigns and media outlets, especially partisan media outlets, frame images to influence audience perceptions.

One partisan outlet that has become influential in the Internet age is the *Drudge Report*. Matt Drudge has been cited as a significant part of the modern, insular, conservative media culture that has been evolving since the rise of Rush Limbaugh.[29] Indeed, Drudge was credited as being the launching pad for the Swift Boat Veterans for Truth.[30] Immediately relevant to the present discussion is Drudge's editorial decisions for photographic images of Barack Obama. Over the course of the Democratic primary and into the general election, Drudge repeatedly used photographs of Obama that featured a common thread: the "Obama crowd." The *Drudge Report*, on multiple occasions, chose images of Obama that presented him blending in with, or being visually overwhelmed by, an audience. The underlying purpose of these choices is to problematize support for Obama with a visual equivalent to the term Obamamania and to play on conservative discomfort with mass movements and collectivism.

Figure 13.2 is the first example of this thread in the *Drudge Report*. What makes it especially interesting is its placement alongside a photograph of Obama's rival, Hillary Clinton. There is a marked contrast between the two photos and the subtext of what they are saying about the two campaigns. Taken together, the two images present both Obama and Clinton as leaders of mass movements, but in very different ways.

In Figure 13.3, we see that Hillary Clinton is the only subject in the photo. This is especially significant when seen beside the image of Obama, who is surrounded by supporters. Clinton appearing larger-than-life in the photo sends the message that the critique of her campaign is about her, whereas the critique of Obama's campaign, as it appears in Figure 13.4, is about him *and* his supporters.

What connects the images to one another is the implication about the creation of a mass movement. In the case of Clinton, it is a movement built around the glorification of a leader; with Obama, it is the image of the uncontrolled mob. In Figure 13.4, Obama is almost lost in the crowd. He is the charismatic

---

[28]For just one example on the subjectivity of photography, see Susan Sontag, *On Photography* (New York: Picador, 1973).

[29]Kathleen Hall Jamieson and Joseph Cappella, *Echo Chamber: Rush Limbaugh and the Conservative Media Establishment* (New York: Oxford University Press, 2008).

[30]The *Drudge Report* carried headlines promoting the book *Unfit for Command* on July 28, July 29, and August 4, 2004. The book claimed that Kerry had lied about his military service in Vietnam. Drudge's Web site was seen as a key outlet for the promotion of the book. "Drudge Report Sets Tone for National Political Coverage: Book Compares Online Newsman to Walter Cronkite," *ABC News*, October 1, 2006, http://abcnews.go.com/WNT/story?id=2514276&page=1 (accessed June 16, 2010).

THE 48 HOUR BLITZ
DRUDGE REPORT

FIGURE 13.2 A headline and image appearing on the *Drudge Report*, February 2, 2008

FIGURE 13.3 Hillary Clinton during the 2008 Democratic presidential primary, appearing on the *Drudge Report*, February 2, 2008

FIGURE 13.4 Barack Obama at a rally, featured on the *Drudge Report*, February 2, 2008

leader, but the movement itself is of a higher purpose than one personality and more to be feared than the leader himself.

Figure 13.4 is also compelling because of the feeling of movement. Obama stands in front of a large crowd and is pointing forward. Partly because the subjects' legs are framed out of the photo, and given the index vector[31] created by Obama's hand pointing, one gets the feeling that Obama, and the crowd, are literally marching toward the camera. Obama is lost in the crowd, but that does not matter because he *is* the crowd and they are part of him. In other words, the phrase "we are the ones we've been waiting for" is something to be feared here. This conservative photographic discourse parallels Bratich's discussion of the vulnerable and reactive audience. Within this framework, audiences "were considered easily provoked, mobilized, and even excited.... [A]udiences were identified via their highly charged capacity to be activated."[32] In this image, Obama is presented as the trigger for that reactivity.

This returns us to the affective in-between as being essential to the critique. Where Caroline Kennedy's rhetoric essentializes the relationship between the inspiration of a political figure and the audience members' ability to "believe in themselves," Drudge's photographic critique does the same between the political figure's charisma and the audience members' states of automatonamous action. Here, hope and fear act as opposing sides of the same affective coin. In both cases, Obama is situated in relation to the audience's "capacity to be activated." For Caroline Kennedy, it is a hopeful activation of democratic action; for Drudge, it is a frightening crowd with the potential to lose control or, more important, take control.

Figure 13.5 presents a similar image, but with a slight variation: the absence of Obama's face. Again, Obama is potentially lost in the crowd, as in Figure 13.4, but it is doubly problematic because his back is turned to the camera. Obama is *in* the audience and *of* the audience. In these images, the crowd exists as unification where the lines separating the individuals become blurred. This rhetorical approach to Obama's audiences echoes Butsch's statement, "The speaker or focus of the crowd was simply the trigger to unify it into one mind, making it more powerful."[33]

In Drudge's photographic critique of Obama, one could imagine a blank outline in place of Obama's body. Again, what is important to both Drudge

---

[31]Zettl defines index vectors as being "created by something that points unquestionably in a specific direction" leading the viewer's eyes. Herb Zettl, *Video Basics 5* (Belmont, CA: Thomson Higher Education, 2007), 97.

[32]Jack Z. Bratich, "Amassing the Multitudes: Revisiting Early Audience Studies," *Communication Theory* 3 (2005): 242–65.

[33]Richard Butsch, *The Citizen Audience: Crowds, Publics, and Individuals* (New York: Routledge, 2008), 36.

THE FRONTRUNNER

DRUDGE REPORT

FIGURE 13.5 A headline and photo of Obama shaking hands at a rally from the *Drudge Report*, February 13, 2008

and Caroline Kennedy is *what Obama does to the crowd*, not necessarily Obama himself. This, in a sense, is the greatest lionization of all, because Obama ceases to be a tangible human being and becomes something more; he embodies without having or needing a body. The irony is that a common conservative critique throughout the campaign was to portray Obama as having a messiah complex and his followers as mistaking him for Jesus.[34] Drudge's images conjure this complex more than anything Obama's supporters said during the campaign.

The Obama-as-messiah meme is furthered in Figures 13.6 and 13.7. The word choice, alongside the image, in Figure 13.6 is especially interesting. Beneath a crowd stretching for what feels like miles is the "Obama Mass," with the dual meaning of *mass*, implying both greatness in size and religious ceremony. Most of all, it suggests to viewers the idea of the dangerous crowd, a great mass of naïve automatons following the commands of a totalitarian figure. The image of Obama is just one of many different ways in which he and his supporters were presented as being engaged in a manipulation. Obama was often presented as cultish or having a messiah complex. In one overt example of this, the McCain campaign created a Web ad entitled *The One*. In this ad, lines

---

[34]Amy Sullivan, "An Antichrist Obama in McCain Ad?," *Time*, August 8, 2008, http://www.time .com/time/politics/article/0,8599,1830590,00.html (accessed August 10, 2008).

FIGURE 13.6 Obama rally in Oregon from the *Drudge Report*, May 19, 2008

are drawn that some interpreted as being subtle attempts at calling Obama the Antichrist.[35] This video was an attempt at "dog-whistle" politics, using references to the Book of Revelation that would, theoretically, be understood by conservative Christians.

There was also the ongoing strategy to portray Obama as a mere celebrity. In Figures 13.6 and 13.7, the critique is, again, directed more at Obama supporters than Obama himself. It implies that his supporters are somehow overly emotional or irrational; they can't be trusted and so their voting choice also can't be trusted. It's a critique of the candidate through his supporters. Thus the audience became a weapon, and one of Obama's strengths was transformed into a flaw, something to be worried about.

These images are a reinforcement of the use of the term *Obamamania*. The term is especially relevant to the accompanying headline that reads "FIRED UP AND FALLING DOWN" in capital letters and red text, thus making it even more inflammatory. Here the audience is not just irrational in their support for Obama, they are reduced to the equivalent of young girls at a Beatles concert. Obama is also, once again, placed on the level of a cult leader. Obamamania is like Beatlemania, which was seen as "an affliction, an 'epidemic,' and

---

[35]Ibid.

FIRED UP AND FALLING DOWN: String of Crowd Fainting Incidents Hits Obama Rallies...

FIGURE 13.7 A headline and photo from the *Drudge Report*, February 17, 2008

the Beatles were only the carriers."[36] So the Beatles, and Obama, are carriers of a disease that afflicts the crowd, which in turn is transformed into the carrier of a critique of Obama. Obama does not have to proclaim himself "more popular than Jesus"; the image suggests it for him.

Figure 13.8, appropriately enough, is reminiscent of photos of ecstatic Beatles audiences. Again, there is implied movement in this single photographic frame and, like Figure 13.2, it presents an interesting contrast of two images, this time between Obama and John McCain. Rather than being in a static pose, Obama appears to be running past the crowd, stopping to shake as many hands as possible, as quickly as possible. As in the previous examples, the crowd is more of a blurred mass of bodies than a collection of individuals. They have a look of excitement similar to girls screaming for the Beatles, underlining the "celebrity" critique the McCain campaign leveled at Obama. The photo of McCain, in which he appears to lurch forward, starkly contrasts with the apparently rapid movement of Obama. The portrayal of movement is reinforced by the captions; "She can't catch us" fits the movement of Obama's image. McCain being "fired up" seems to be a cut at his less-than-vibrant personality; the caption mocks the visual.

While this chapter has thus far presented the affective relationship between Obama and liberalism as one of a positive or hopeful nature and his relationship to conservative perceptions as couched in fear, it is important to

---

[36]Barbara Ehrenreich, Elizabeth Hess, and Gloria Jacobs, "Beatlemania: Girls Just Want to Have Fun," in *The Audience Studies Reader*, ed. Will Brooker and Deborah Jermyn (New York: Routledge, 2003), 180–84.

FIGURE 13.8 Headlines featuring Obama and McCain from the *Drudge Report*, February 13, 2008

note the more negative feelings at play in liberalism and how the hope aspect of Obama's campaign was, and his presidency is, tied to them. In doing so, the critique can come full circle to where this chapter began, with the connection between perceptions of Obama and the Kennedy legacy.

The Kennedy Shadow, Obama and American Left Melancholy

Over the course of five decades, the *idea* of John F. Kennedy and the Kennedy legacy have loomed large over Democratic presidential processes. Jimmy Carter's loss to Ronald Reagan was at least partially caused by Edward Kennedy's primary challenge. There is Lloyd Bentsen's infamous rebuke of Dan Quayle: "Senator, you're no Jack Kennedy." Michael Dukakis became the embodiment of the "Massachusetts liberal," code for Kennedys. Finally, Bill Clinton represented the rebirth of liberalism's hopes for that legacy. The visual presentation of this was demonstrated with very little subtlety through a widely distributed photograph of a young Clinton shaking hands with JFK. Even in liberalism's fictional representations of the presidency, Kennedy is inescapable. On NBC's *The West Wing*, Martin Sheen, who once played Kennedy, plays Jed Bartlett, a politician clearly styled after Kennedy.

Kennedy creates a challenge for liberalism generally and Obama specifically on multiple levels. First is the level of the image and the imaginary. Kennedy occupies a space in the liberal imagination that makes him unavoidable in presidential politics. He is the image of a new form of media, television, truly coming into its own and taking hold of the American imagination. This "creation of media" image of Kennedy is made apparent in the oft-repeated anecdote of differences in public perception of Kennedy and Nixon. There is reciprocity: Kennedy creating television and television creating Kennedy.

Kennedy is intertwined with the rising power of image most of all in his assassination. As Joshua Meyrowitz presents it, one legacy of the violent imagery of Kennedy's death is the creation of the grim presidential "death watch" where "nothing will happen to the chief executive without full media coverage."[37] Kennedy's death left not just liberalism but the nation as a whole with a general anxiety about violence and the presidency. This reiterates Ahmed's discussion: "[F]ear's relationship to the potential disappearance of an object is more profound than simply a relationship to the object of fear."[38] This is the legacy of the spectacle of the Kennedy assassination. It is within those moments, captured in the Zapruder film, that there is a reverberation of anxiety through American culture; alongside that is liberalism left in a state of Freudian melancholy.

Kennedy and Obama: Melancholy, Mourning, and Beyond

As members of the Kennedy family threw support behind Obama as Camelot 2.0, supporters could read the text of the situation as the "passing of the torch"; critics saw an attempt on the part of the Kennedy family to remain relevant. An alternative reading of the political/presidential drama would be to see the endorsement as the Obama turn, an officially recognized moment when the reins of power were handed down. As the *Washington Post* reported on the Kennedy endorsement in January, the "political and social legacy of the late president—Camelot, the Big Myth, the story of American royalty, a sense of Americans being awestruck by themselves—was gift-wrapped by the Kennedy family yesterday and given to Sen. Barack Obama, a political gift with remarkable and remarkably strange baggage."[39] The turn from Kennedy to Obama was also the beginning of the turn from melancholy to mourning and beyond for American liberalism.

As Freud defines it, mourning is "regularly the reaction to the loss of a loved person, or the loss of some abstraction which has taken the place of one."[40] The problem occurs when people instead find themselves trapped in a state of melancholy. Melancholy is distinct from mourning in that in a state of "grief

---

[37]Joshua Meyrowitz, *No Sense of Place* (New York: Oxford University Press, 1986), 169.

[38]Ahmed, "Affective Economies," 125.

[39]Neely Tucker, "Barack Obama, Camelot's New Knight," *Washington Post*, January 29, 2008, http://www.washingtonpost.com/wp-dyn/content/article/2008/01/28/AR2008012802730.html?sid=ST2008012900890 (accessed January 30, 2008).

[40]Sigmund Freud, *General Psychological Theory* (New York: Collier Books, 1963), 164.

the world becomes poor and empty; in melancholia it is the ego itself."[41] One would not be hard-pressed to see liberalism's "self-reviling" over the last few decades. There has been the transformation of the very word "liberal" from its perception as the leading political elite consensus to a reviled term. In a post–Reagan Revolution world, the word "liberal" can be the kiss of electoral death.

This state of liberal melancholy is at the very least an indirect result of the Kennedy assassination and, to use Barbara Biesecker's words, "the loss of an impossible object," a "doubled fabrication of loss."[42] Biesecker referred to a loss of principles of democracy post-9/11. We find a similar state of affairs in the loss of Kennedy. The difference is that the *ideal* of Kennedy, while it existed pre-assassination, existed in a state no different from the idealization of any political leader in his or her own time. The post-assassination ideal is the "doubled fabrication of loss."

It is no small problem that the *ideal* is just that. The reality of the object, in this case Kennedy, is never truly possessed. As Zizek argues, lack is discernible in loss. Through loss, we are made aware that "what melancholy obfuscates is that the object is lacking from the very beginning, that its emergence coincides with its lack, that this object is nothing but the positivization of a void or lack, a purely anamorphic entity that does not exist in itself."[43] Kennedy as imagined is the "anamorphic entity," and after the assassination, liberalism no longer had even that. Or, perhaps, it is wrong to even use the words "no longer." Following Zizek, what melancholy shows us is that liberalism never "possessed" Kennedy in the first place. Yet even the *ideal* of Kennedy was not fully there before his assassination. No less a progressive than Eleanor Roosevelt questioned Kennedy's "readiness for the presidency"[44] during the 1960 Democratic presidential primary. In the absence of the object, there is both lack and longing, longing for something that never truly was.

Freud says that "when the work of mourning is completed the ego becomes free and uninhibited again."[45] Thus it should be the goal of liberalism as a movement to go beyond the melancholic morass. Unfortunately, as Zizek argues, liberalism is unable to escape its Kennedy-induced melancholy because "[m]ourning is a kind of betrayal, the second killing of the (lost) object, while the melancholic subject remains faithful to the lost object, refusing to renounce his or her attachment to it."[46] Conservative writer James Pierson argues that the liberal intelligentsia was unprepared to react appropriately to the Kennedy

[41]Ibid., 167.

[42]Barbara Biesecker, "No Time for Mourning: The Rhetorical Production of the Melancholic Citizen-Subject in the War on Terror," *Philosophy and Rhetoric* 1 (2007): 147–69.

[43]Slavoj Zizek, "Melancholy and the Act," *Critical Inquiry* 4 (2000): 657–81.

[44]Robert Dallek, *An Unfinished Life: John F. Kennedy 1917–1963* (Boston: Little Brown, 2003), 233.

[45]Freud, *General Psychological Theory*, 166.

[46]Zizek, "Melancholy and the Act," 658.

assassination. The liberal frame could not be properly arranged to make a place for this event.[47] The assassination stalled American liberalism "by undermining the confidence of liberals in the future" and "changing their perspective from one of possibility and practical reform to one of grief, loss and frustrated hopes."[48] Obama's candidacy becomes poetic in this context. Kennedy's assassination symbolizes hope frustrated; Obama symbolizes an attempt to reinvigorate that "confidence in the future."

The collective affective state of melancholy gave rise to conspiracy theories about the assassination, a refusal to accept the Warren Report (exemplified in *JFK*). There is also a sense of something left unfinished, thus the refusal to move from melancholy to mourning. Kennedy as object is gone; but as a figure, he was left incomplete; he cannot truly be mourned because he was taken before being completed. This affective state is blocking political energies for liberalism. Instead of focusing on movement toward the future, liberalism is left in a mindset characterized as a "conservative, backward-looking attachment to a feeling, analysis, or relationship that has been rendered thing-like and frozen in the heart of the putative leftist."[49]

Situating Obama within the melancholy of the liberal imagination as the natural heir to the Kennedy legacy serves a specific purpose. This placement is the doing of multiple actors in the theater of presidential politics. Not least among them, the Kennedy family themselves have played a part in this. Again, we find in this a parallel between JFK and Obama in their implicit forms, their effective presences; JFK's reverberation through history is to be embedded within Obama, to have his ideals imposed upon Obama, in some ways for Obama's sake and in others for the sake of liberalism. The aforementioned *Washington Post* article presents the best characterization of the reverberating affect of JFK and the Kennedy name as "remarkable and remarkably strange baggage."[50]

Conclusion: "We're Still Here; We're Just Watching Along with You."

On the first day of the Obama Effect conference, journalist Desiree Cooper asked if it would be possible for Obama to "just be president."[51] Does he have to be something more than that? A difficult question, to be sure, but part of the

[47]James Pierson, *Camelot and the Cultural Revolution* (New York: Encounter Books, 2007), x.

[48]Ibid., x.

[49]Wendy Brown, "Resisting Left Melancholy," *Boundary 2*, no. 3 (1999): 19–27.

[50]Tucker, "Barack Obama, Camelot's New Knight."

[51]Desiree Cooper, "Reflections on Covering the Campaign" (University of Minnesota, Minneapolis, MN, October 23, 2008).

problem is that many observers do not want him to be "just president." Through the campaign, on election night, and on the day of the inauguration, there was always an aura of "something more."

The NBC coverage of the inauguration, for example, had a very interesting flow that presented a few disconnected audiences as one. At certain moments, they would dissolve from Obama to the crowd in front of him in Washington, D.C. There would then be a dissolve to a crowd outside Rockefeller Center in New York, then a dissolve to an auditorium full of students. The dissolve is an effective editing tool for reducing disconnection between subjects. Here the "Obama crowd" reappears in a different context with a very different purpose. NBC employed the video dissolve to create the feeling of one single audience and reconnecting Obama to that audience, dissolving the two together. The frames of video presented a portrait of racial diversity and a presidency that illustrated the idealized multiculturalism that liberalism wants to make real.

A common conservative complaint throughout the campaign and into the Obama presidency has been to accuse the media of fawning over Obama. This is where the line from Kennedy to Obama makes a brief stop at Ronald Reagan. King and Schudson argue that Reagan's policies did not have the public support the press portrayed them as having. One explanation for this disconnect is that the political establishment in Washington, D.C. and the American public in general did not want another failed presidency.[52] From the Kennedy assassination to Watergate to Carter's American malaise, people needed Reagan to succeed not just for the typical reasons that a nation needs a president to succeed. Obama is in a similar position. From Clinton's impeachment to George W. Bush's leaving office with the public perception that his presidency was a failure, Obama needs to succeed not just for the typical reasons that a nation needs a president to succeed.

Media coverage of election night and the inauguration echoed coverage of Reagan's presidency. As King and Schudson characterize it, reporters became enamored with Reagan.[53] Journalists turned themselves into the audience, just as they did through the coverage of election night in 2008. One particularly fitting moment came on NBC. After announcing Obama's victory in the election, there was two full minutes of nothing but the sound of the crowds cheering, and then Brian Williams announced, "We're still here; we're just watching along with you."[54] Just as with the inauguration coverage, NBC showed video of audiences in various, separate places, but used the dissolve

---

[52]Elliot King and Michael Schudson, "The Press and the Illusion of Public Opinion: The Strange Case of Ronald Reagan's 'Popularity,'" in *Public Opinion and the Communication of Consent*, ed. Theodore L. Glasser & Charles T. Salmon (New York: Guilford Press, 1995), 142.

[53]Ibid., 148.

[54]Brian Williams, NBC election night coverage, November 2, 2008.

and cut effects to erase geographic distance. The crowds were blended into *a crowd*, the Obama crowd. When Brian Williams began talking again, he noted that Obama won the election "with the coalition you've been watching on the screen."[55] Problematic for the notion of the watchdog press is the fact that they were "watching along with" us, becoming part of the Obama crowd.

Maybe the final answer to this question—Can he "just be president"?—is complicated by the fact that Barack Obama, like every other man who has held the office, does not want to be *just* president. The Reagan comparison is pertinent here because Obama himself made it at one point during the 2008 Democratic presidential primary. During a campaign rally, he said that Reagan "was able to tap into the discontent of the American people."[56] Obama was alluding to the transformative nature of the Reagan presidency. If Obama is aiming for the same goal, building a lasting coalition that will give the Democratic Party a foundation for electoral success for decades after he is gone, if he wants to be Reagan or Kennedy, then he cannot just be president and nothing more. And, if that is what he is working toward, he, his supporters, *and his critics* have put him well on his way.

---

[55]Ibid.

[56]Katharine Q. Seelye, "Obama, Reagan, and the Internet," *New York Times*, January 21, 2008, http://www.nytimes.com/2008/01/21/us/politics/21web-seelye.html (accessed January 21, 2008).

Mothers Out to Change U.S. Politics:
Obama Mamas Involved and Engaged[1]

Grace J. Yoo, Emily H. Zimmerman, and Katherine Preston

In October of 2008, a mother driving a carpool of five-years-olds to school heard them fighting in the backseat, like this:

"I'm Obama, and you're McCain," declared one of the children.

"I don't want to be McCain! I want to be Obama!" someone protested.

"No, I'm already Obama."

"No, I'm Obama!"

"No, I'm Obama! But you don't have to be McCain. You can be Biden!"

A few days later, these children got a chance to vote for president of the United States. Results tallied by their San Francisco Bay Area kindergarten teacher showed 15 for Obama, 2 for McCain, and 3 abstentions. In the excitement of the 2008 presidential race, it seems even many five-year-olds knew whom to root for. Most likely, they caught the contagion of their parents' enthusiasm. As it happened, mothers' influence played a special role in supporting Barack Obama's presidential candidacy, and not only through capturing their children's imaginations. Organizing within Obama's groundbreaking and innovative campaign, mothers numbered among a whole generation of diverse women, young and old, whose energy fueled the presidential race. Historically, 2008 marked a banner year for women's White House ambitions, as two major female candidates ascended to the national stage—Hillary Clinton, a viable contender for the Democratic nomination, and Sarah Palin, the

---

[1]The authors would like to thank the participants of this survey who were so willing and generous in sharing their thoughts about and hopes for the Obama presidential campaign.

Republican Party's first female running mate. Yet while Clinton and Palin both had firsthand knowledge of motherhood, the "Obama Mamas" looked beyond similar life experiences as women to more compelling reasons for staking their children's future on Barack Obama's promise to bring change.

During the 2008 Democratic Presidential primaries, some mass media depicted women voters as if they were a unified block eager to support Hillary Clinton wholeheartedly and thus diminish Obama's chances. Contrary to this oversimplified perception, Obama's presidential campaign actually inspired and jumpstarted the political involvement of countless women who played an instrumental role in spreading the campaign's message, raising funds, and persuading voters. Among Obama's supporters, mothers who joined the campaign had particular interests at stake. Pollsters overlook the importance of mothers during a political campaign, even as the popular sound bite "soccer moms" multiplied in recent decades. In reality, mothers regularly influence their multiple social worlds, whether through their workplaces, their communities, their children's classrooms, or their families. In past presidential elections, however, the true political influence and voices of mothers have gone comparatively unrecognized by both scholars and politicians, let alone by the mass media. This paper, therefore, attempts to fill some of this gap in understanding by documenting the efforts of those mothers who became particularly energized, engaged, and active in their support for Barack Obama's 2008 presidential campaign. The aims of this national study include (1) examining reasons why mothers became supporters of Barack Obama, (2) identifying how mothers involved themselves in the Obama campaign, (3) understanding how mothers engaged others, including their children, in their support of Obama, and (4) understanding their concerns for their children and the hopes they placed in the Obama presidency.

Data collection commenced during Mother's Day weekend from May 9 to May 31, 2008. Prospective participants were e-mailed a letter inviting them to take part in surveys. Themselves identified as Barack Obama supporters, the investigators registered with the Barack Obama Web site and then, through the Web site, sent an invite letter to several e-mail networks including thirty-four Obama Mama networks, seven Women for Obama networks, two Parents for Obama networks, and four more general and ethnic-specific networks. Those who expressed interest in participating clicked on a designated link to the SurveyMonkey.com survey. From the outset of the survey, the voluntary nature of the study was stressed, and participants were told they had the right to refuse to participate in the study. The survey then took about ten minutes to complete. The survey consisted of questions about demographic background, reasons why participants supported Obama for President, their involvement in the campaign, their top three concerns as mothers, the impact of Obama as president on their children's future and the impact of Obama as president on the nation. Three hundred fifty-six women responded to the survey over a four-week period.

The sample included 356 women between the ages of 22 to 75 with a mean age of 42 years (see Table 14.1). The top ten states where mothers resided and responded from included first California, followed by Pennsylvania, Illinois, North Carolina, Florida, New York, Texas, Minnesota, Oregon, and Maryland. Survey respondents included mothers from all 50 states.

TABLE 14. 1

Demographic Background of Obama Mamas (N = 356)

What are the ages of your children? Please check all that apply	Response Frequency	Response Count
0–4 years old	39.8%	140
5–11 years old	35.8%	126
12–18 years old	28.7%	101
Over 18 years of age	33.0%	116
What political party do you identify with?		
Democrat	85.9%	298
Republican	4.0%	14
Independent	9.5%	33
Decline to State	0.6%	2
Other (please specify)		13
What is your martial status?		
Single	8.0%	28
Married/Partnered	74.6%	261
Divorced/Separated	15.1%	53
Widowed	2.3%	8
How do you self-identify racially and ethnically?		
White	64.6%	221
African American	23.1%	79
Latina	4.1%	14
Asian American	2.3%	8
Mixed Race	5.8%	20
Other (please specify)		14
What is your highest level of education?		
High school graduate	3.7%	13
Some college	25.6%	90
College graduate	27.9%	98
Post graduate education	42.7%	150

The sample consisted of women with 1 to 12 children, with a mean of 2 children. The children were of various ages: 40 percent under the age of 4, 36 percent between the ages of 5 and 11, 29 percent between the ages of 12 and 17, and 33 percent over the age of 18. In terms of party affiliation, 86 percent were registered as Democrat, 10 percent Independent, and 4 percent Republican. The majority of the women (75 percent) were married, followed by 15 percent divorced, 8 percent single, and 2 percent widowed. The majority of respondents identified as white (65 percent), followed by African American (23 percent), mixed race (6 percent), Latina (4 percent), and Asian American (2 percent). In addition, the majority of respondents reported a high level of education, including a majority with postgraduate education (43 percent), followed by college graduates (28 percent), those with some college (26 percent) and those with a high school education (4 percent).

Mothers Deciding to Support Barack Obama for President

In supporting Barack Obama for President, his central theme of change was an important factor for mothers, with over 90 percent reporting that this was important to extremely important in their support for his presidency (see Table 14.2). When asked why they became Barack Obama supporters, most women answered that they were tired of the traditional way politics was done in this country and the lack of accountability to the will of the people. A mother of three and a registered Republican from New York writes, "I am tired of the old attack and … spin politics which I think Hillary and Bill really represent."

Mothers in this study overwhelmingly believed that presidential candidates Hillary Clinton and John McCain represented the traditional way politics got done in Washington. Mothers were seeking a different, better way for the U.S. government to demonstrate leadership and gain respect throughout the world, and they hoped Obama would provide this. A thirty-one-year-old mother of a young child from Florida who became a supporter during the presidential campaign writes:

> For too long, we have been a divided nation with leadership that has been inattentive to the needs and opinions of citizens. Obama will mark a distinctive change in how Washington responds to both Americans and other countries, with honesty, open-mindedness, compassion and wisdom.

Mothers talked about how Barack Obama inspired them and how as mothers they felt he would make the United States safer for their children. A thirty-seven-year-old mother of two young children in Florida writes:

TABLE 14. 2

Importance of Change: Mothers' Support of Barack Obama

In your support of Barack Obama for President, how important was the theme of CHANGE?

	Response Percent	Response Count
Not important	0.6%	2
Somewhat important	4.9%	17
Important	10.9%	38
Very Important	28.0%	98
Extremely Important	55.7%	195

"He is inspiring and positive, something that gives me hope that my children will be handed a better world in which to live."

Although the media has suggested that Obama's racial identity has influenced voters, over 91 percent of mothers in this sample stated that race did not influence their decision to support Barack Obama. Asked if Hilary Clinton's divisive campaign politics encouraged their support for Barack Obama, only 14 percent suggested that it did.

Again, the key factor explaining why mothers supported Obama was desire for change: their perception that he represented a diversion from traditional politics-as-usual, including the way in which he would smooth the progress of diplomatic relations, even with our enemies. A forty-one-year-old mother from New Jersey who became a supporter during the presidential primaries writes:

> We need to talk to our enemies. I want a president who will hear both (or more) sides to an issue. I want a president to look at the data (or campaign reports or war reports) and admit the reality, even if it means he was wrong in the first place.

Respondent after respondent echoed similar themes of how diplomacy in the twenty-first century needs to be for the greater good of the U.S. society but also the world. A thirty-two-year-old mother from Ohio who became a supporter during the presidential primaries writes,

> I envision a place where we take responsibility for our actions and sacrifice for the greater good. I want to be proud of my country— how we treat our own citizens as well as the citizens of other countries—once again.

Involving Self and Family in Supporting Barack Obama for President

Unlike other political campaigns in U.S. history, mothers in this presidential campaign took on many tasks. Over 95 percent of the mothers in this sample were engaged to extremely engaged in this presidential campaign (see Table 14.3). Mothers were split in terms of the timing of their support for Barack Obama for president: 52 percent had become supporters prior to the start of the presidential primaries, while 48 percent emerged as Barack Obama supporters during the presidential primaries.

In their enthusiastic support of Barack Obama, mothers found numerous ways to involve themselves in their support for his candidacy: 76 percent of these mothers donated online with a mean donation of $324, while 92 percent encouraged family and friends to vote for Obama and 56 percent encouraged others to donate to the Obama campaign; 40 percent participated in phone banks, and some women also mentioned volunteering through assisting with voter registration, hosting fundraisers, displaying bumper stickers and yard signs, canvassing and walking precincts, organizing rallies, and blogging (see Table 14.4).

The level of involvement also became contagious among their family members. Women educated, informed and engaged their children in this campaign. A forty-nine-year-old mother with five children from Texas writes, "All of my boys watch CNN and never missed any of Obama's speeches. I record them and we watch at an appropriate time." Furthermore, women with young children find ways to involve themselves and their children. A thirty-six-year-old mother of two young children from Minnesota states: "My kids made shirts, my son's said 'Obama Rocks!' and my two year old daughter's said 'O is for Obama!'" A twenty-four-year-old mother with one child from Oregon writes: "[Our son] watches debates with us and we talk with him about why we are praying for this. He also attended the rally in Salem with us and he loves to

TABLE 14.3

Level of Engagement with Presidential Campaign

How engaged and energized are you about this year's presidential primary?

Answer Options	Response Percent	Response Count
Not engaged	0.3%	1
Somewhat engaged	2.3%	8
Engaged	9.5%	33
Very Engaged	31.2%	109
Extremely Engaged	56.7%	198

TABLE 14. 4

Support for Barack Obama and Level of Involvement

When became supporter?	
Before the start of presidential primary campaign	52.3%
During the presidential primary campaign	47.7%
How involved?	
Donated by Mail	12.1%
Donated Online	75.9%
Encouraged Family/Friends to Vote for Obama	91.7%
Encouraged Family/Friends to Donate to Obama Campaign	56.3%
Involved in Phone Banks for Obama	40.5%
Range of Amount Donated	$324 mean ($1–$4600 range)

wear his Obama shirt!" A thirty-eight-year-old mother with three children in Pennsylvania relates how all three children volunteered at an Obama campaign office: "The baby brought donuts, my 8-year-old put labels on forms, and my 11-year-old did anything he was asked."

Even mothers with older children discuss ways that they involved themselves in the campaign. A divorced forty-one-year-old mother with four children from Washington, D.C. states:

> My 14-year-old son has been traveling with me to other states to volunteer for the campaign. He said when he turns 18, he wants the first president he votes for to be Obama for his second term. Everyone in my family wants Obama to win so he can end this war and bring my daughter home.

Mothers' Concerns and Hopes in the Barack Obama Presidency

The five top concerns among mothers in this sample included: (1) education, (2) the economy, (3) ending the war in Iraq, (4) the environment, and (5) health care (see Table 14.5). The mothers in this study engaged in their support for Barack Obama because they felt strongly that his presidency will have an impact on their children's future (100 percent of respondents). Women believed that because Obama had young children, education would be a priority for him. Many were concerned about the quality of schools and wanted their children to receive the best education

TABLE 14. 5

Top Concerns of Mothers

Concern	N (%)
Education	209 (59.0)
Economy	200 (56.0)
War	167 (47.0)
Environment	163 (46.0)
Health Care	142 (40.0)

possible. Others were concerned whether college would be affordable for their children. Many were concerned about the economy, including unemployment and how that would impact their families. In addition, many women cited the need for health-care reform and universal health-care coverage, and expressed general concerns about their children's health and well-being. Moreover, mothers talked about Barack Obama's serving as a role model for children in his ability to move away from partisan politics and work across differences; 90 percent believed that Barack Obama as president would make our world a bit safer.

When asked, "Write in your own words how you imagine Obama's presidency will impact the issues that you have for your children," many mothers imagined multiple scenarios for positive change, where Obama's new leadership could possibly shape their children's future for the better. Some women commented explicitly on dimensions of identity politics, exulting in a changed political environment, where we need no longer expect all U.S. presidents to be white men. For women of color, and black women especially, Obama's race and ethnicity carried momentous historic import for their children's perception of a more promising future. An African-American woman with three children from Pennsylvania states:

> NO matter what, this election has already made history!! IT is the first election that we have had a woman or an African-American run for office ... what's more important - he's a man of multi-ethnicity!!! Even 30 years ago no one could have imagined that! so really that is history-making! I'm very encouraged to talk to my son about this and all the misconceptions about each of the candidates ... and how important it is to know the facts ... for truth is in the facts.

Similarly, a forty-one-year-old mother with three children from California mentions:

> My children are mixed race and for them to see a president who looks like them, to me, would be outstanding. My husband and I already tell

them they can do whatever they put their minds to, but how extraordinary to see a man who's actually done that become president.

Also commenting on this historic import, a twenty-three-year-old mother of two children from Utah says:

It will show our children that the U.S. is ready to turn a page in its history and move to a more Perfect Union.

Many other respondents expressed confidence in salient aspects of Obama's personal character, viewing him as a person of integrity who could be trusted to keep his word if at all possible. As a devoted parent, moreover, they felt he could be expected to feel the same range of human emotion and motivation to protect his children's future as any parents would normally feel. A twenty-seven-year-old registered Republican mother from Pennsylvania states:

Because given the chance to make change and allowed to make change I believe he will try his best to live up to his promise because he has small children who will be affected by this world and without change for the world there will be no change for them!!!!!

Still others underscored their belief that Obama possessed the self-assurance and necessary skill and capacity to handle the enormous and complex challenges of serving as president. Some remarked on Obama's competence and creativity as an eloquent communicator and brilliant politician, capable of weighing alternatives and achieving tricky diplomatic negotiations. A thirty-eight-year-old mother of two from Oregon states:

Mr. Obama's ability to reason with others will help pass legislation that will address many issues of my concern. That same ability is that which he will bring to the international table for discussion on possible solutions, not just seeing force as the answer.

With similar hopeful general confidence in Obama's capabilities, others viewed Obama as all-purpose national problem-solver, able to lead the country in the right direction on multiple fronts, both militarily and economically. In this regard, Obama would serve as wise allocator of resources, in terms of both money and military might. A twenty-nine-year-old mother of one from Missouri writes:

Hopefully he will remove the possibility that my husband will be sent to Iraq, for one. Second, I would like to see our efforts focused on getting ourselves out of debt so my children aren't forced to shoulder our debts in addition to their own. Last, and tied in with the others is the importance of global competition. We need to focus not just our money, but our time and resources into education. Including ways to make college attainable for the middle class. (my family)

Many also responded affirmatively to the question of whether they thought the election of Barack Obama would make the world a safer place. A thirty-seven-year-old with two children from Texas says:

> The world will be a safer place because we will have a leader who is willing to negotiate between enemies, which promotes our interests and those of our allies. We will have a President who will not rush us into an unnecessary war. We will have a President who will not threaten and antagonize other countries and thus create new enemies.

Conclusion

Unlike other U.S. presidential elections, mothers took an active role in engaging and involving themselves in this election. Notably, Internet technology enabled more women to get involved in ways that were not available to them in elections past. E-mails, blogs, donating online, and telephoning voters from home were all ways women participated without having to be away from their children. Women able to get out in the field also canvassed, hosted house parties, and volunteered in myriad ways with the Obama campaign, often bringing their children along to join in appropriate aspects of this historic grassroots campaign.

The findings of this survey capture the work of mothers in this presidential election, but also their hopes and dreams for this country and the next generation. A key theme throughout these surveys is the importance of change on multiple levels. Despite the entrance of two women candidates into this race, presidential candidate Hilary Clinton and vice presidential nominee Sarah Palin, the women surveyed were more interested in practical, substantive issues likely to pave a more hopeful path for their children's future. Gender, although important, was not the main driving force for many of these women.

The issues of education, the economy, war, and the environment were much more salient. Mothers wanted their children to grow up knowing that a college education could be within their reach. Moreover, many stated their concerns about the future, and where the country was heading. The shaky state of the economy worried many mothers, who wondered how their families would survive unemployment and uncertain or grim economic times. Meanwhile, mothers and wives of American servicemen hoped for a leader who could bring an end to a controversial war. Some mothers were extremely worried about the environment and climate change and the failure of U.S. leadership to address these critical issues, and felt change was imperative. Finally, mothers in general longed to see a new face on world leadership, someone they could trust to protect their children's future—someone with a more open, global, and cross-cultural outlook, a fresh and alert mindset more likely to secure peace and a safer, stabler future for their children.

Section V: Representations

For the Love of Obama: Race, Nation, and the Politics of Relation

Aimee Carrillo Rowe

The rhetorical production of "Obama" gains meaning within the slippery politics of race, class, gender, and sexuality in the United States. This context might be understood as a color-blind racial formation.[1] It emerges in the wake of the civil rights movement, the formation of identity politics, and institutional gains for minoritized publics. We find ourselves in the midst of a backlash against these gains, marked by white appropriations of identity politics (white victimage) and the dissolution of race and gender as salient categories for claims to victimization (postracism and postfeminism). This context is also organized by the post-9/11 mobilization of anti-Muslim sentiment, xenophobia, and the ongoing "war on terror." These post-9/11 forces seek to unify Americans under a banner of benign multicultural inclusion *against* a threatening outside world. America is imagined through its exceptionalism—a status forged through the moral authority it accrues through demonstrations of minority inclusion. Queers, women, people of color, the poor, the differently-abled, the elderly— all, allegedly, have a legitimate place at the American table. This imperative of inclusion, however, masks a host of exclusions based on these same categories of difference. This dynamic generates a fundamental paradox, a foundational lie—the slippery seat of the nation-state. The secret of this contradiction is housed within the language of color-blind racism.[2]

---

[1]I draw upon Michael Omi and Howard Winant's (*Racial Formation in the United States: From the 1960s to the 1990s* [New York: Routledge, 1994]) concept of "racial formation" to account for the ways in which racial meanings shift across historical moments. Color-blind racism, as a constitutive force of this "postracial" historical moment, extends Omi and Winant's theorization to account for the slipperiness of the contemporary moment through which racial politics are negotiated in the United States.

[2]Eduardo Bonilla-Silva (*Racism without Racists: Color-Blind Racism and the Persistence of Racial Inequality in the United States* [Lanham, MD: Rowman and Littlefield, 2003]) marks the emergence of this color-blind rhetoric as emerging and gaining dominance in the late 1960s. While Jim Crow racism worked through the assertion of the overt inferiority of people of color, color-blind racism compels "whites [to] rationalize minorities' contemporary status as the product of market dynamics, naturally occurring phenomena, and blacks' imputed cultural limitations" (2).

Color-blind racism created a paradox for presidential candidate Barack Obama. While he could not escape "race," his candidacy strategically figured "race" through color-blind rhetorics that contained the threat of a black presidency. In spite of his campaign's efforts to avoid his racialization, "Obama" was alternately racialized and deracialized through his affective ties. On one hand, Obama was a threat to the nation because he was figured as "too black," or too "un-American"—not because the media or the conservatives who oppose him explicitly said so, but because he was *affiliated* with U.S. civil rights and transnational articulations of blackness. The Obama campaign and other media sources, alternately, produced images of the candidate's affinity to whiteness—not to claim that he is white, but to represent his close relations to white familial ties.

This chapter rethinks how we theorize racial formation within the context of a "postracist" racial formation in the United States. I draw on and extend the argument I make in my earlier work[3]—that subjectivity is coalitional. I call this framework a *politics of relation*. Extending this argument, I examine popular representations of Obama's presidential campaign. The media's preoccupation with Obama's mixed heritage, his friendship with his preacher and Bill Ayers, and his partnership with Michelle Obama tell us something about how race is constructed in contemporary popular culture. It's not necessarily Obama's blackness or his whiteness—as identities that could be located on his body—but rather his belongings, his affiliations, his affective investments that became the contested terrain of his (de)racialization. My argument gestures toward a methodology for reading popular culture within the contemporary hegemony of color-blind racism. Attending to the affinities through which mixed-race figures get (de)racialized provides a different point of entry to study racial formation as more fluid, less essentialized, than identity categories can contain. A politics of relation provides a postessentialist theorization of identity in which racial formations are located not first and foremost in identity categories, but within alliance formations.

I attend to the layers of the (de)racialization of Obama through such a relational framework. I trace the ways in which his (de)racialization is negotiated through the cultural production of intimacy. Extending the work of critical race scholars, who study the meanings associated with racialized

---

[3]In *Power Lines: On the Subject of Feminist Alliances* (Durham, NC: Duke University Press, 2008), I argue that "who we love is who we are becoming" in an effort to intervene in the race/gender divide within U.S. feminism. This move from identity to belonging allows for us to attend to the various ways in which exclusions are structured through the norms of community formation, as opposed to essentialized identities. Thus, a politics of relation strives for a collection notion of "location," not one founded in the individual, but rather forged through how the subject is shaped by his or her belongings. This means that feminists of privilege are freed to move beyond the guilt associated with their identities, but also that they must be held accountable for how they position themselves within community.

identities, I interrogate the meanings associated with racialized *identifications*. This approach is attuned to the complexities of a postracial racial formation in which U.S. racial politics emerge less through overt, Jim Crow racial domination and segregation, but rather through subtler mobilizations of benign multiculturalism. The new face of America is figured through diverse belongings, through the language of inclusion and equality. Within such a context, white supremacy is leveraged through the inclusion of tokenized people of color, who are often framed as overly privileged against beleaguered whiteness. Yet sometimes racial inclusion truly is transformative. So how do we assess the politics of the multiracial image?

Within a postracial historical moment, the politics of belonging become a particularly important point of entry into theorizing power relations. Mixed-race intimacies are both a potential alibi for benign multiculturalism *and* a potential site for authentic connection across power lines. Racial politics become less fixed and more fluid, less essentialized and more contingent, less about identity and more about identification. This is not to suggest that they are any less dangerous. Rather, the tools cultural workers use to leverage critique and envision alternatives must be sensitive to the subtleties of postracial politics. The presidential campaign of Barack Obama, with its heavy reliance on affinity to do the work of (de)racialization, provided a productive site in which to examine the politics of relation within postracism. An investment in color-blind cultural scripts permeated the campaign coverage; commenting explicitly on Obama's "black identity" seemed "racist." To maintain the postracial secret, both sides of the campaign figured race through Obama's affiliations.

I trace two key moments of the intimate trajectory of Obama's production as a presidential candidate. The first section outlines what is at stake for postracism for Obama's mixed-race genealogy. I explore the tension between conflicting investments in individualism and belonging, which is at the heart of his figuration as a sign of postracial accomplishment. The second section considers the ways in which Obama was rendered out-of-bounds through his affiliations with sites, locales, communities, and geographies imagined as "un-American." On one hand, Obama's blackness was produced as a threat to American whiteness through his affiliation with civil rights "radicals." When this tack failed to gain traction within the post-9/11 historical moment, Obama was figured through his "cosmopolitan" attachments, his body remapped and his affiliations scattered across various disparate and "un-American" sites around the globe. This analysis reveals the temporal and spatial dimensions of belonging through which postracism gains rhetorical traction. The temporal dimensions circulate through tropes of birth and ancestry as markers of a new future—the haunting of an essentialized blackness that reanimates past racial struggles in the present, threatening to unravel color-blind logics of racial harmony. The spatial dimension emerged through this temporal dimension as Obama's ancestry was mapped onto various nonwhite and Muslim places around the globe, deterritorializing his American body and suturing it to a threatening transnational blackness.

Genealogy as Point of Entry

"The first thing I ever heard about Barack Obama," writes Shelby Steele, in his *Time* magazine essay, "The Identity Card," "was that he had a white mother and a black father."[4] Steele notes that Obama's parentage was always cited, matter-of-factly, as "the way we Americans had to introduce Obama to each other. For some reason, knowledge of his racial pedigree had to precede even the mention of his politics—as if the pedigree inevitably explained the politics."[5] "Obama" emerges, in Steele's account, as an intelligible figure through the repetition[6] of his "pedigree": a constellation of gender, race, class, and heterosexual meanings, distilled within his ancestral origin story. This frame guides readers to attend to Obama's parentage and its peculiar racial blending to serve as a screen, or grid of intelligibility, through which America would come to "know" the anomalous presidential figure of Obama. Indeed, this pedigree is necessary as the racial and sexual terrain of Obama's body is a contested site—not clearly identifiable as black or white.

The rhetorical work of postracial belongings becomes visible if we juxtapose Obama's introduction with that of other new candidates, such as Sarah Palin. Palin's uncontested whiteness presumes and naturalizes her white parentage, so her genealogy never comes into question. This absence marks the unstated terrain of racial belonging in America in its *presumed* affective segregation; Palin need not be introduced to America through her "pedigree" because she is white. Thus, her "parentage" is not open to scrutiny. Yet America needs to be introduced to Obama through his "mixed" parentage precisely because "America" is produced through an unspoken, yet powerfully compelling, investment in affective segregation. Thus, to introduce Obama to the nation through his mixed-race genealogy reveals a whole host of racial negotiations. The color line has already been bent, transgressed, and thus reconfigured by virtue of his birth. This point of entry for the collective imagination of "Obama" would, in turn, provide a host of racial contestations, destabilizations, and reinscriptions of American exceptionalism over the course of his campaign. The taken-for-granted purity of whiteness could no longer be assumed.

---

[4]Shelby Steele, "The Identity Card," *Time Magazine*, November 30, 2007, 46.

[5]Steele, "The Identity Card," 46.

[6]The repetition of the pronouncement of Obama's parentage recalls Judith Butler's *Bodies That Matter: On the Discursive Limits of 'sex'* (New York: Routledge, 1993) performative refrain, that gender performance becomes stabilized through repetition. But here it is not gender performance, or not *just* a gender performance, that is repeated.

The implicit transgression of his parentage creates a host of challenges and possibilities—not only for his campaign, but also for the nation. The question would be how America would make sense of this confounding genealogy.

Steele offers the trope of "transparency" of color to render Obama safe. The metaphor harkens back to Martin Luther King's invocation that we focus on the content of one's character over the color of one's skin. If Obama is transparent, readers can see right through him, enabling them to judge, without mediation, the content of his character. Steele's account is symbolic of a broader cultural formation that fetishizes Obama's genealogy. The presence of the mixed-race Obama is claimed to achieve an "almost perfect transparency in which color is indeed no veil over character—where a black, like a white, can put himself forward as the individual he truly is."[7] Steele thus figures Obama as a transparent body that holds the potential to achieve a whiteness of blackness. Because whiteness is imagined as invisible, transparent, and "unmarked,"[8] Steele invites readers to apprehend Obama not through "the veil of color," but rather through his "almost perfect transparency."

This depiction, however, is contingent upon Obama's individuation. Obama's exceptionalism enables readers to distinguish him from an overwhelming mass of cultural blackness, wrought over the centuries through a host of stereotypes: mammy, rapist, and Hottentot, the absent father and the overbearing mother. Steele's assertion that Obama "can put himself forward as the individual he truly is" functions to *disarticulate* the spectacle of his mixed-race figure and that of the black male aggressor.

Thus, Obama's pedigree is deployed through a fundamental contradiction. On one hand, Steele invites his readers to view Obama through his familial belongings. On the other hand, he wants us to read him as an individual. This framing draws upon relationality, as Obama's identity is only intelligible if we understand—indeed, become preoccupied with—his relations to his parents: his abandonment by his black father, his devotional mother, and his close affinities to his white grandparents. And yet this relationality is said to stand in for his individuality, and by extension, for a certain meritocracy that discourses of individualism produce. The repetition of his genealogy, then, may be understood to function as a guarantee for democratic "transparency" in which color

---

[7]Steele, "The Identity Card," 46.

[8]See Ruth Frankenberg, *White Women, Race Matters: The Social Construction of Whiteness* (Minneapolis: University of Minnesota Press, 1993); Richard Dyer, *White* (New York: Routledge, 1997); Jane Lazarre, *Beyond the Whiteness of Whiteness: Memoir of a White Mother of Black Sons* (Durham, NC: Duke University, 1996); George Lipsitz, *Possessive Investments in Whiteness: How White People Benefit from Identity Politics* (Philadelphia: Temple University Press, 1998); Thomas Nakayama and Judith Martin, eds., *Whiteness: The Communication of Social Identity* (Thousand Oaks, CA, London, New Delhi: Sage, 1999); Mason Stokes, *The Color of Sex: Whiteness, Heterosexuality, and the Fictions of White Supremacy* (Durham, NC: Duke University Press, 2001).

lines fade, commingle, and intermix—providing readers unmediated access into the content of Obama's character as unmediated by his skin color. This genealogy is offered as a racial grid through which readers are to decode the countless close shots of Obama's face (often depicting a solemn, vulnerable expression) to which the media continuously treats us. This genealogy serves as a promise that we can see *through* the expression to get to the character behind the face; to *know* the individual, the man behind the sincere expression.

We might apprehend this contradiction as a constitutive force of a postracial lexicon. It marks this historical moment as a point of departure for a new racial politics that become distilled within the "transparent" body of Obama. This pre-occupation with Obama's birth and his individuation mark a temporal shift to a new postracial historical moment. Steele identifies with Obama's mixed-race heritage, his preoccupation with "black authenticity," his desire to belong to black communities. These desires are described as a function of losing his father at a young age. Such longings pose a potential threat to white voters. His mother's attention and discipline, alternately, account for Obama's success. His affiliation with ancestral whiteness assuages the concerns over his affiliations with black-ness. As such, Obama recasts the racial boundaries of "American apartheid," hence rewriting "the mulatto's tragic exile standing as a cautionary tale meant to keep people 'with their own kind.'" This alchemy of birth and belonging, Steele concludes, means "today's mixed-race person is 'fresh,' a word that trails Obama like a nickname."[9] The "freshness" assigned to the historical shift Obama's origin signifies for U.S. racial formation marks it as a new moment. Obama's birthright as a mixed-race child—estranged from his black parentage and yet seeking to restitute his black belongings, safely located within the white American family by virtue of his white mother's own virtue as mother—constitutes Obama as a "sacred child"[10] whose very existence gestures toward a viable American future.

"The Violent, Leftist Weather Underground": Reviving Black Nationalism

Obama emerged as a contested figure over the course of his presidential campaign through two prevalent efforts to racialize him. First, Obama was racialized through his relationships with dangerous U.S. blackness, distilled

---

[9]Steele, "The Identity Card," 46.

[10]Lee Edelman (*No Future: Queer Theory and the Death Drive* [Durham, NC: Duke University Press, 2004]) argues that the figure of the "sacred child" comes to stand in for a certain kind of future organized through heterosexual imperatives and contingent upon queer death. Obama's family lineage and references to his childhood position him as a sacred child, who comes to embody hopes for a postracial American future. This preoccupation with his parentage presumes and naturalizes his heterosexual origins, thus revealing the ways in which postracism is organized through compulsory heterosexuality.

in the figures of racial others—in particular, Jeremiah Wright, Bill Ayers, and Michelle Obama. The "danger" produced through these figures is marked as a temporal reversion; they mark Obama not as a new figure of postracism, but rather as deeply rooted in American black radicalism. This effort to racialize Obama, however, proved less rhetorically compelling than the figure of Obama as America's postracial future. Hence, a second effort emerged to racialize Obama, by transnationalizing and deterritorializing his blackness. A host of affective ties did not locate Obama firmly within the U.S. national territory, but rather dispersed his location across the globe.

Obama was racialized through his African-American affinities, designed to evoke the specter of Black Nationalism and separatism. These tropes of blackness threaten the spatial territory of the United States as the very notion of Black Nationalism suggests a separate place and set of sovereignty practices under which African Americans could organize, cohere, and leverage control over the terms of national belonging and the boundaries of American inclusion. Thus, to figure his blackness through his affiliations to Black Nationalist icons positions Obama in a vexed relationship to the spatial integrity of the U.S. nation-state. Here I consider the example of Obama's relationship to Bill Ayers and other black male figures to render visible the efforts to racialize his masculinity through black homosocial affinity. This reading signals the ways in which postracial discourse precludes charging Obama overtly with being a "Black Nationalist," because such a charge would seem to essentialist and "racist." However, figuring Obama's blackness through his affiliations with radical activists from the past—such as Ayers and Wright, and even Michelle Obama (recall the *New Yorker* cover in which she was depicted, fist raised, sporting an Angela Davis 'fro)—drew on threatening tropes of black nationalism that were located in the past. As such, this rhetoric recirculated unsettling essentialisms and affixed them to black bodies that were linked to outdated politics. It marked Obama's blackness through his choice to align himself with those figures and the racial formation they came to embody.

A *Time* magazine article describes Obama as a "clever wooden offering of the Greeks to Trojans: something that appears to be a gift on the outside but is cunningly dangerous within."[11] Against Steele's reading of Obama's "transparent" mixed-race heritage, this figuration troubles the idea that Obama is anything like he seems. Rather, he is a Trojan horse that projects a benign exterior while hiding something dangerous in his interior. This risky interiority, as with his previous transparency, is located in his intimate ties to leftist friends and mentors:

> Obama has worked on education issues in Chicago with William
> Ayers and has visited the home of Ayers and his wife Bernadette
> Dohrn. Both were leaders of the violent, leftist Weather Underground.

---

[11]David Von Drehle, "The Five Faces of Barack Obama," *Time Magazine*, August 21, 2008.

> But the indictment of Obama is framed by his affiliation with a black
> man who told Obama that a true friendship with his white grandfather
> wasn't possible. The man's name was Frank Marshall Davis, and in the
> 1930s, '40s and early '50s he was a well-known poet, journalist and
> civil rights and labor activist. Like his friend Paul Robeson and others,
> Davis perceived the Soviet Union as a "staunch foe of racism" (as he
> later put it in his memoirs), and at one point he joined the Communist
> Party. "I worked with all kinds of groups," Davis explained. "My sole
> criterion was this: Are you with me in my determination to wipe out
> white supremacy?"[12]

Obama's ties are leveraged to racialize his figure through his dangerous
affinities to black radicals. Obama's affiliation with Ayers is mapped through
a spatial intimacy. Obama enters the radical private sphere, symbolized in his
visit to Ayers's home and a reference wife, Bernadette Dohrn. His move into a
domestic sphere metonymically provides the reader access into Obama's secret
interiority; it invites the reader to identify his private landscape through the
"violence" associated with Ayer and Dohrn.

The "indictment" circulating in this piece locates Obama geographically
outside of the continental United States. It evokes his often-cited growing up
in Hawaii, where he built a "true friendship" with an older black man, Frank
Marshall Davis. Davis's distance from whiteness is marked through his affective
segregation; he is racialized through his rejection of Obama's white grandfather—because he is white. Davis's rejection works against color-blind affective
economies that circulate within postracist culture. Racism is reversed as Davis
is depicted as intolerant. Alternately, Obama is often deracialized through
his father's absence and his close ties to his mother and white grandparents.
Yet he is re-racialized through frequent references to various "father figures"
(all of them black) he is reported to seek out. Obama is figured through an
oedipal search for his black father. This desire frames his masculinity through
the blackness associated with those dangerous black men who stand in for his
absent African father. Obama's search for a black father troubles his relationship to whiteness, affiliating him with a black ancestry—both of birth and of
choice.

His racialization is leveraged not through an explicit claim (that Obama
is a black radical), but rather through an indictment of Davis. The affinity that
binds these men is figured as dangerous blackness through Davis's affiliation
with Black Nationalism: civil rights and labor activism, the Soviet Union, com-
munism, and a staunch critique of white supremacy. In moments such as these,
dangerous black masculinity emerges as a compilation of interchangeable black
men, whose blood or paternal love are mapped onto Obama's interiority.

---

[12]Von Drehle, "Five Faces of Barack Obama."

"He's Not American Like the Rest of Us": Deterritorializing Obama

These efforts to racialize Obama through his ties to Black Nationalism were not entirely successful. But they ushered in an impulse to define him as un-American by transnationalizing his affinities. Obama's affinities, imagined as scattered across the globe, map his body in a host of threatening global places. These dispersed mappings deterritorialize Obama from his location within the U.S. nation-state. Obama has been depicted as maintaining a "cool head" in the face of the efforts to racialize him. As if a "cool head" were incongruent with black masculinity, this move, coupled with counterrepresentations of his 'familial whiteness, have undercut the moves to affix his black masculinity through tropes of aggression. As a result, the media seek to render the candidate transparent by mapping his affinities to both his psyche and to geographical space. One *Time* article frames Obama through a litany of spatially dispersed affective ties: "the polygamous father, the globe-traveling single mother, the web of roots spreading from Kansas to Kenya, friends and relatives from African slums to Washington and Wall Street, and intellectual influences ranging from Alexander Hamilton to Malcolm X."[13] While this excerpt does not explicitly charge him with being "un-American," Obama is racialized relationally through a "web of roots" that strays from the territory of the heartland to that of Africa. Moves such as these deterritorialize his body from the homeland and reterritorialize it in diverse and often threatening locations.

This affiliative racialization is mapped onto globalization in ways that render Obama "un-American." For instance, one report notes that the *National Review* online "demanded" that Obama produce his birth certificate to dispel rumors that he "was actually born in Kenya and therefore would be constitutionally ineligible to be President; that his middle name is not Hussein but Muhammad; and that his mother is actually named him Barry."[14] Such "rumors" gained traction through the globalization of Obama's "cosmopolitan" figure, woven like a web across the globe—from Africa to Iraq, from Kansas to Kenya, from Hawaii to Indonesia, a conglomerate global placements that dislocate Obama's identity from a fixed American locale. Obama's writing also figures his positionality through a globalized affect. He describes himself as "the son of a black man from Kenya and a white woman from Kansas" with "brothers, sisters, nieces, nephews, uncles and cousins, of every race and every

---

[13]Ibid.

[14]Karen Tumulty, "Will Obama's Anti-Rumor Plan Work?," *Time Magazine*, June 12, 2008.

hue, scattered across three continents."[15] This globalization of Obama's affect is imagined as providing readers with access to his interior.

While Obama may seek to convince audiences of his worldliness, this same quality is also leveraged to position him as "not American like us." His affiliations with markers of Muslim-ness position Obama as a potential terrorist lurking beneath his ambiguously racialized exterior:

> There is another Trojan-horse interpretation just below the radar. It is the idea that a man named Barack Hussein Obama might be hiding a Muslim identity. Obama has tackled this dozens of times. His Kenyan grandfather was indeed a Muslim; his father espoused no faith; Obama attended a Muslim school in Indonesia for a time as a boy because that's where he lived—Indonesia is a Muslim country. He believed in no religion until he moved to Chicago as a grown man and was baptized Christian by Wright.[16]

This excerpt globalizes Obama's affinities, citing his various foreign growing-up places to account for the suspicion that he "might be hiding a Muslim identity."

This anxiety about Obama's diverse affective and geographical affinities marks a shift in contemporary racial formation from a preoccupation with national inclusion to a unifying suspicion of international difference. This move is captured in the question posed by one *Time* reporter, "Is Barack Obama American Enough?"[17] He argues that:

> The racial wedge issues of the 1970s and '80s—busing, crime, welfare, affirmative action—have all but disappeared. When pollsters compile lists of Americans' top concerns, those barely register. What is on the rise is anxiety about globalization. Support for unregulated free trade has cratered on the Democratic left. Hostility to illegal immigration is red hot on the Republican right. And beyond the partisan divide, it's the same demographic that is most upset about both: working-class whites.[18]

Obama's body is mapped onto and historicized according to the shifting terrain of contemporary American politics. The cartography moves from outdated, divisive, essentialist politics to a color-blind, unified, national politics mobilized through a xenophobic mistrust of all things un-American. The "concerns" of

[15]Excerpt from his "More Perfect Union" speech, Philadelphia, Pennsylvania, March 18, 2008, cited in Lisa Rogak, *Barack Obama in His Own Words* (Philadelphia, PA: Running Press Miniature Editions, 2009), 114.

[16]Von Drehle, "Five Faces of Barack Obama."

[17]Peter Beinart, "Is Obama American Enough?," *Time Magazine*, October 9, 2008.

[18]Beinart, "Is Obama American Enough?"

Americans are produced through a new globality in conjunction with an elision of American-born racism. Current racial politics are divided from previous racial struggles. These past struggles are presumed to be resolved (busing, crime, welfare, affirmative action), which, in turn, mobilizes a new set of fears. In a post-9/11 moment, the nation is unified through the erasure of internal difference, where difference is displaced onto a host of global others: Third World workers taking "our jobs," illegal immigrants, and the specter of terrorism.

This postracist move of national unification is contingent on two interrelated moments: the alleged resolution of civil rights struggles and the evocation of another, more dispersed site of difference contained in the bodies of foreign others. Thus, the question of Obama's Americanness aligns him outside of the boundaries of the U.S. nation-state. As the nation is imagined as united within a postracial frame, the charge of un-Americanness becomes the new racial epithet. This label gets attached to Obama through his global affiliations, which threaten to divide his loyalties from those of other Americans. The preoccupation with his childhood time, spent in foreign locales and with relatives who hail from unfamiliar parts of the world, maps Obama's body and his genealogy around the globe. It becomes difficult to locate him in a seamless Midwestern childhood; rather, his location is rendered through sites and affinities difficult to imagine.

Conclusion

The cultural production of Obama remains caught in postracism's color-blind discursive and affective economies; race is simultaneously evoked and elided. Even as readers are invited to gaze into Obama's transparent figure—imagined through the convergence between his mixed-race parentage and his postracist politics—they are continually disappointed by the failure of this promise to transparency. This failure, however, is built into this postracial discourse as it presumes and indeed relies upon a foundational individualism—one in which Steele invests and through which he imagines Obama as a "transparent" figure. Yet this individualism is simultaneously undercut as Obama's figure is continually mapped through his often affectively dangerous affiliations.

This paradox returns me to the importance of a relational critical reading practice within a postracist discursive economy. My reading attends to the cultural production of Obama through an exploration of the ways in which his figure is racialized, or deracialized, through the second-level racialization of these related figures. "Obama" is produced as dangerous to the nation from within (Ayers) or from abroad (his African relatives). The racialization of Obama is not leveraged through an attack on his individual identity, but such essentialisms are attached to such secondary figures. Obama's racialization is leveraged not through his essential blackness, but through his affinities to essential blackness.

Obama's affective ties are mapped onto local and interior geographies (home) and disparate and foreign geographies (the world). This preoccupation with the local and the global, with home and the world, are mapped onto his body—frequently through the depiction of extreme close-ups of Obama's face. The politics of relation through which Obama is racialized are also bound up in temporalities of U.S. national identity. While the emphasis on his family, birth, and origin story frame Obama as embodying a certain kind of postracial future for the nation, his affective ties to Black Nationalism link him to an outdated racial politics grounded in old essentialisms. These temporal structures imagine the nation's future as one that is, in many ways, ruptured from the past.

Within the post-9/11 historical moment, U.S. national identity is imagined through the promise of racial harmony, which serves as the basis of American exceptionalism; radical or separatist politics must be bound to the past, rendered incompatible with this investment in a color-blind future. This future is imagined in juxtaposition to that which resides outside of the nation, particularly the Muslim other. This outside is both a spatial and a temporal constellation that animates Obama's belongings. His belongings are hitched to foreign places, which are, in turn, imagined as regressively lagging behind America.

A later issue of *Time*—the one in which Beinart[19] asks if Obama is American enough—featured Obama's face in two halves: half revealing his "natural" color, half painted white. The visual rhetoric positions Obama as both a figure of division and of unification, or as an ironically divided subject upon whose hopes for unification readers are invited to project. In moves such as these, Obama's belongings, his affective ties, the love of Obama, are simultaneously mapped onto his most intimate exterior. It exposes the production of America's investment in Obama's "true" interior and the complexities of the dance between the assertions and disavowal of racialization as the nation is mapped within a new global economy. Obama's body vacillates between the past and the future, between the here and multiple and disparate theres, as a contested site of belonging. He belongs to whiteness *and* to blackness, to America *and* to the globe. Through the meanings rendered within the realm of the popular, these interstices become the vexed terrain of U.S. nation formation.

---

[19]Ibid.

Framing a First Lady: Media Coverage of Michelle Obama's Role in the 2008 Presidential Election

Kimberly R. Moffitt

She endured commentary and critiques regarding her hair, fashion sense, church affiliation, and political stances—and she was not even a candidate in the U.S. presidential election of 2008. But she was the first African-American woman with a real chance to be First Lady of the United States as the wife of first-term senator and presidential candidate Barack Obama of Illinois. To say the least, Michelle Obama's pathway to becoming First Lady was a rocky one.

Michelle Obama is seen by many as the classic "American Dream" story, for she is the product of working-class stock, with dedicated parents who provided educational opportunities that would ensure her occupational success. The Princeton and Harvard graduate attained both professional and personal aspirations by practicing law with a firm in her hometown of Chicago, Illinois, and creating a family with a community organizer who desired to help others in the neighborhoods of her native South Side Chicago.

Because the 2008 U.S. presidential election was a landmark year for women and blacks in terms of candidacy for the highest political offices in the country, this chapter explores the media's framing of Michelle Obama through the lens of gender stereotypes of prospective First Ladies as well as an exploration of the role of race in the news coverage. Specifically, I intend to address the question, "What media frames are constructed for Michelle Obama as a prospective First Lady?"

Black Women Stereotypes

Historically, black women's images in popular culture relegated them to subservient and often demeaning roles in American society. We need only consider the early roles of black women in film as mammy (e.g., Hattie McDaniel in *Gone with the Wind*) or jezebel (e.g., Nina Mae McKinney in *Hallelujah*) to illustrate the point. These women represented the extreme polarities of the popular imagination—both asexual and sexual. The mammy

233

exhibited the role of primary caregiver to children on behalf of white women and a willing acceptance of her subordination in antebellum America, while the jezebel displayed unbridled sexual passion and eroticism that may often be experienced by white men. Some scholars argue that these two stereotypes can be found in contemporary roles of black women in film.[1]

Patricia Hill Collins extends the discussion to include images that are applicable to this investigation. The "Bad Black Mother" (BBM) is described by her "unregulated sexuality and uncontrolled fertility."[2] The BBM is a single mother who maintains her family with the support of social programs, may use drugs, is seen as lazy because she does not work for pay, and rarely establishes a positive, loving relationship with a man or the father of her child(ren). She is a "baby mama"—a label "echoing the 1965 Patrick Moynihan report that pathologized black families."[3]

The "Black Lady" creates a space for middle- and upper-middle-class African-American women who are successful professionals often presented with the task of balancing both work and family responsibilities.[4] She enters the workforce in order to maintain her middle-class standing, and also juggles to fulfill her roles of wife and mother. Claire Huxtable, the female lead on the 1980s television sitcom *The Cosby Show*, exemplifies the Black Lady best. She was seen as a smart, beautiful, hardworking lawyer who provided and cared for her husband and five children. Her character performed *all* of her tasks dutifully and gracefully, substantiating to the American viewers that black mothers were just like white mothers.

The "Angry/Strong Black Woman" is a stereotype exhibited in all African-American women, regardless of class. This trope reflects the binary of weak black man and strong black woman that historically has plagued our understanding of gender roles in society. Gender ideology proposes that men are masterful and controlling, while women should be submissive and demure. This naturalized truth about gender seems "normal" in white partnerships, but lacking and dysfunctional in black partnerships. Jean Wyatt notes:

---

[1]Donald Bogle, *Toms, Coons, Mulattoes, Mammies and Bucks: An Interpretive History of Blacks in American Films* (New York: Continuum, 2001). Also see Shawna V. Hudson, "Re-Creational Television: The Paradox of Change and Continuity within Stereotypical Iconography," *Sociological Inquiry* 68, no. 2 (May 1998): 242–57. Specifically, for example, Jean Wyatt, "Patricia Hill Collins's Black Sexual Politics and the Genealogy of the Strong Black Woman," *Studies in Gender and Sexuality* 9 (2008): 52–67; and Gina Athena Ulysse, "She Ain't Oprah, Angela, or Your Baby Mama: The Michelle O Enigma," *Meridians: Feminism, Race, Transnationalism* 9, no. 1 (2009): 174–76.

[2]Patricia Hill Collins, *Black Sexual Politics: African Americans, Gender, and the New Racism* (New York: Routledge, 2005), 130.

[3]Ulysse, "She Ain't Oprah," 175.

[4]Hill Collins, *Black Sexual Politics*, 138–40.

Because black women have customarily supported the family financially, as well as acting as the primary caretakers of children, they have acceded to a position of authority within the family. To succeed in bearing the double burden of principal breadwinner and principal nurturer within a world structured by racial discrimination a woman has to have extraordinary strength, endurance, and resilience.[5]

These assumed roles situate the black woman in a space of "anger" in which she begins to question the role of her male partner as well as continuing to struggle with the effects of racism. The early manifestation of this trope was the Sapphire, a term coined after the female character, Sapphire Stevens, of the *Amos and Andy Show*. Sapphire is known "for telling people off, and spouting her opinion in an animated loud manner [with] intense expressiveness and hands-on-hip, finger-pointing style."[6] Her wrath is often pointed with the intent to emasculate black men in particular, but anyone in the vicinity "runs for cover" as her sassy verbosity ensues. She also uses this "anger" to unleash the pent-up frustrations experienced by her (and her family) as a result of the social and political history that often impacts African Americans negatively. Various forms of these stereotypes were used in news coverage of Michelle Obama.

Coverage of First Ladies

Several studies have explored the role of a president's wife in relation to his administration, her ability to create fashion, her task as mother and spouse, and her role as host to the world's leaders and dignitaries.[7] These studies raise key findings as to how the public perceives the First Lady and how the media portray her. Often, these studies reveal that media are most interested in the First Family's courtship, their early life together, and how the First Lady fulfills the traditional roles of a woman. In recent years, those studies have also revealed to us that the more politically engaged the First Lady is, the more

---

[5]Wyatt, "Patricia Hill Collins's Black Sexual Politics . . .," 57.

[6]K. Sue Jewell, *From Mammy to Miss America and Beyond: Cultural Images and the Shaping of US Social Policy* (London: Routledge, 1993), 45.

[7]James G. Benze, "Nancy Reagan: China Doll or Dragon Lady?" *Presidential Studies Quarterly* 20 (Fall 1990): 777–80. Also see Betty Houchin Winfield, "The First Lady, Political Power and the Media: Who Elected Her Anyway?" in *Women, Media, and Politics*, ed. Pippa Norris (Oxford: Oxford University Press, 1997), 166–79. For additional examples, Lewis Gould, "Modern First Ladies and the Presidency," *Presidential Studies Quarterly* 20 (Fall 2000): 677–83; and Erica Scharrer and Kim Bissell, "Overcoming Traditional Boundaries: The Role of Political Activity in Media Coverage of First Ladies," *Women and Politics* 21 (Winter 2000): 55–83.

negative coverage she receives, which suggests that we are interested in keeping her in the "traditional role of a woman."[8]

Only a few studies have considered the media's coverage of a prospective First Lady. Betty Houchin Winfield and Barbara Friedman's study, for example, on the four women whose husbands were vying for the top jobs in the 2000 presidential election was an extension of an earlier work.[9] In 1997, Winfield explored the media frames journalists apply to First Ladies. Those frames included: (1) escort to the president; (2) fashion trendsetter; (3) supporter of charities; and (4) policy adviser in husband's administration.[10] In the aforementioned 2003 study, the authors employed these same frames to investigate how they might apply to prospective First Ladies. These media frames were apparent in the coverage of Tipper Gore and Laura Bush, as well as Hadassah Lieberman and Lynne Cheney. As an extension of the "escort" frame, the authors noted that the media framed the women as "defenders" or advocates of their husbands, while also highlighting their reluctance (and sacrifice) to join in the political spotlight with their spouses. An additional media frame noted in this study, the "anti-Hillary," remarked how different these women were from Hillary Rodham Clinton.[11] The media clearly were suggesting that the strong-willed antics of Clinton were no longer the country's desire and that either of these women would be a "welcome change."[12]

> One reporter wrote, "in manner and bearing, (Tipper) is an anti-Hillary." Similarly, a political commentator said, "People who do not like Hillary Clinton are going to be very happy to meet Laura Bush. She does not push a big political agenda."[13]

Media Framing

According to William A. Gamson and Andre Modigliani, a media frame is "a central organizing idea or story line that provides meaning to an unfolding strip of events and weaves a connection among them."[14] Shanto Iyengar further posits that

---

[8]Betty Houchin Winfield and Barbara Friedman, "Gender Politics: News Coverage of the Candidates' Wives in Campaign 2000," *Journalism & Mass Communication Quarterly* 80, no. 3 (Fall 2003): 548.

[9]Ibid., 549.

[10]Winfield, "The First Lady," 166–79.

[11]Winfield and Friedman, "Gender Politics," 556–57.

[12]Kenneth T. Walsh, "The Families Are Just Plain Folks," *US News & World Report*, August 28, 2000, 25.

[13] Rita Braver, "Running Mate: Laura Welch Bush," CBS Sunday Morning, July 30, 2000.

[14]William A. Gamson and Andre Modigliani, "The Changing Culture of Affirmative Action," in *Research in Political Sociology*, ed. R. G. Braungart and M. M. Braungart (Greenwich, CT: JAI Press, 1987), 143.

media frames draw upon preexisting cultural understandings[15] that then construct narratives seen as "reflective of common sense" to the audience.[16] This framework enables one to explore the power associated with the media's presentation of an individual. For example, in a study by Katie Gibson on Katie Couric as the first woman to anchor the evening news, the media frames of sexualization and personalization were found.[17] Specifically, Gibson noted that Couric was still confined to traditional understandings of a woman's role in society. The news coverage objectified her body, while reifying stereotypes that "emphasize women's emotions, weakness, and dependency."[18] She further concluded that the media framed criticism of the CBS evening newscast as "a consequence of Couric's gender" and "re-demarcated the news industry as a male space."[19]

Even in a study of the 2008 presidential election and its two women candidates, similar results were found. The iron-maiden frame that focused on the double bind, as explored by Kenji Yoshino, suggested that women must be both feminine and competent or equal to their male counterparts, especially in positions of power.[20] For Hillary Rodham Clinton and Sarah Palin, that meant they would have to enhance their femininity and exhibit their ability to handle the job as president or vice president. According to Donny Deutsch of *CNBC*, Palin had noted that in ways Clinton had not:

> She's certainly got experience, life gravitas experience, but she's still young enough to have that physical appeal. That perfect ingredient to sell a woman in power. She's a lioness. Look, she gave you the brand icon logo, the pit-bull with lipstick. Who wouldn't want a lioness protecting their cubs? She's funny, she's real, she's rock solid, she's feisty, she's smart. If I need to sell Woman in Power to the American public, that's what I'm putting in my cereal. Hillary Clinton's cereal maybe only has two or three of those ingredients. So the huge lesson here is: Before you can sell the candidate … you gotta first sell her as a woman. This is the new feminist ideal.

[15]Shanto Iyengar, *Is Anyone Responsible? How Television Frames Political Issues* (Chicago: University of Chicago Press, 1991).

[16]Robert M. Entman, "Framing: Toward Clarification of a Fractured Paradigm," *Journal of Communication* 43, no. 4 (1993), 231–42.

[17]Katie L. Gibson, "Understanding Katie Couric: The Discipline Function of the Press," *Women and Language* 32, no. 1 (2009): 51–59.

[18]Ibid., 55.

[19]Ibid., 56.

[20]Diana B. Carlin and Kelly L. Winfrey, "Have You Come a Long Way, Baby? Hillary Clinton, Sarah Palin, and Sexism in 2008 Campaign Coverage," *Communication Studies* 60, no. 4 (September–October 2009): 326–43. Also see Kenji Yoshino, *Covering: The Hidden Assault on Our Civil Rights* (New York: Random House, 2005).

... [T]here is the new creation that the feminist woman has not figured out in forty years ... that men can take in a woman in power and women can celebrate a woman in power.[21]

Deutsch's approach did not shield either of these women from continued criticism, however. It should be noted that Carlin and Winfrey found the iron-maiden trope to hinder both women, who were not seen as conforming to those traditional stereotypes for women.[22]

When exploring race-related issues in the news, media frames are said to be salient in reinforcing notions of race. In a study of the Hurricane Katrina aftermath, Donald P. Haider-Markel, William Delehanty, and Matthew Beverlin's findings revealed that the "African American 'face' of victims ... [helped blacks] to more closely identify with the victims, and therefore, be more negative toward government response" more so than nonblacks.[23] And when considering the images used of the Katrina victims, blacks were presented more negatively than whites.

> In one well-publicized example, the Associated Press wire service distributed two stories on August 30, 2005. In one, a white couple is shown wading through floodwater and the caption reads "Two residents wade through chest-deep water after finding bread and soda from a local grocery store ..." In the other image, a young black man is shown in nearly the exact same situation but the caption reads "A young man walks through chest-deep floodwater after looting a grocery store in New Orleans ..."[24]

These frames suggest that white victims of Katrina *found* food while black victims *stole* food. And as a result, according to Leonie Huddy and Stanley Feldman, these racialized frames may have led to whites being less sympathetic to the largely black population of victims.[25]

Analysis of Michelle Obama's media coverage between June 3, 2008 (when Barack Obama was declared the presumptive Democratic presidential nominee), and November 4, 2008 (election day), was selected. I specifically

---

[21]Donny Deutsch, "Squawk on the Street," CNBC, http://thinkprogress.org/2008/09/05/cnbc-host-praises-palin-for-putting-a-skirt-on-i-want-her-laying-next-to-me-in-bed/ (accessed August 14, 2009).

[22]Carlin and Winfrey, "Have You Come a Long Way, Baby?," 328.

[23]Donald P. Haider-Markel, William Delehanty, and Matthew Beverlin, "Media Framing and Racial Attitudes in the Aftermath of Katrina," *Policy Studies Journal* 35, no. 4 (2007): 596.

[24]Ibid., 590.

[25]Leonie Huddy and Stanley Feldman, "Worlds Apart: Blacks and Whites React to Hurricane Katrina," *DuBois Review* 3, no. 1 (2006): 97–113.

analyzed the text of twenty-seven news-related articles, located by a search of EbscoHost, in which Michelle Obama was featured centrally. Although this database is certainly not exhaustive, it provided a fair sampling of news content for this investigation. The stories included news features, personality profiles, editorials, and campaign updates. As noted by Carolyn Bronstein, textual analysis is an effective means of exploring the connections between media frames and latent meaning.[26] This method of close reading required me to account for details, themes, and nuances that may influence the interpretation of news content. The analysis revealed that there is no established lexicon for a woman like Michelle Obama who was a presidential candidate's wife but also an African American. As a result, the news coverage relied upon recycled stereotypes of African-American women to discuss her, unless referencing her as a mother.

Just Another Prospective First Lady

Michelle Obama seemed to exude two of the major frames of prospective First Ladies as outlined by the earlier studies on presidential candidates' wives.[27] Her role as "escort" to Barack is exemplified in the shared admiration the two have for one another. *USA Today* quotes Michelle: "[I'm] a wife who loves my husband and believes he will be an extraordinary president."[28] And Barack, when discussing his wife's upcoming speech at the Democratic National Convention (DNC), remarked, "It is a great way to kick off the convention with the star of the Obama family, Michelle Obama...."[29] Although she speaks with fondness about her husband, Michelle struggled with the idea of Barack's entering the presidential campaign, responding to his request with an emphatic, "Absolutely not! Please don't do this!"[30] Even prior to his announcement and earlier in his political career, she often commented on his extended time away from home with words such as, "I never thought I'd have to raise a family alone."[31] But believing in her spouse, they embarked on a journey that has entailed sacrifice, including taking leave during the campaign from her executive position at the University of Chicago Medical Center.[32]

---

[26]Carolyn Bronstein, "Representing the Third Wave: Mainstream Print Media Framing of a New Feminist Movement," *Journalism & Mass Communication Quarterly* 82, no. 4 (2005): 783–803.

[27]Winfield, "The First Lady," 166–79; Winfield and Friedman, "Gender Politics," 548–66.

[28]Martha T. Moore, "Michelle Obama Shows Off 'Star' Power," *USA Today*, August 26, 2008, 4A.

[29]Ibid., 4A.

[30]Amanda Paulson, "Michelle Obama's Story," *Christian Science Monitor* 100, no. 190 (2008): 1.

[31]See "Obama, Michelle," *Current Biography* 69, no. 10 (October 2008): 69–76.

[32]Harriet Cole, "The Real Michelle Obama: Who Is This Woman ..." *Ebony* 63, no. 11 (September 2008): 72–84.

Michelle also took the public by storm with her own fashion sense. She has been both revered and ridiculed for her wardrobe choices. "Just as some have compared her husband to JFK, others have likened her to Jacqueline Kennedy."[33] Flattered by the direct comparison to Jackie O., Michelle insists that,

> I do think that what you wear is a reflection of who you are. I love to look glamorous when there's a wonderful, purposeful event that is appropriate. But when I'm in Iowa campaigning with the girls, I am in Gap shorts and a T-shirt.[34]

American women seemed drawn to her personal sense of style and her willingness to get "dressed on her own"[35] without the assistance of a stylist. In fact, the $148 dress worn during her appearance on the television show *The View* sold out within a day after viewers learned that the dress was purchased at a White House/Black Market store.[36] But she has also experienced tremendous backlash for her perceived unwillingness to conform to the expectations maintained by former First Ladies. Her motto: "Wear what you like."[37] When Barack claimed his position as the presumptive Democratic presidential nominee, Michelle upstaged him momentarily with her "sleeveless purple silk crepe sheath" and her long legs minus the skin-toned pantyhose.[38] She was seen as out of uniform and unfit to hold the position, even though *Vanity Fair* included her on the 2008 list for best-dressed international figures and dubbed her "Queen of Sheath."[39] Recent musings about the cardigan sweater worn during a meeting with Queen Elizabeth of England and the shorts worn while disembarking Air Force One for a vacation stint in the Grand Canyon are continued critiques about Michelle's wardrobe and its suitability for 1600 Pennsylvania Avenue.[40]

---

[33]Ibid., 82.

[34]Ibid., 82.

[35]Guy Trebay, "She Dresses to Win," *New York Times*, June 8, 2008, 1.

[36]Jonathan Kaufman and Monica Langley, "With Monday Speech, Michelle Obama Seeks Reintroduction," *Wall Street Journal*, August 26, 2008, A4.

[37]Jill Lawrence, "Michelle Obama's Busy Summer," *USA Today*, June 30, 2008, 4A.

[38]Trebay, "She Dresses to Win," 1.

[39]"Obama, Michelle."

[40]Michelle Malkin, "And Now for Some Hard-Hitting Reporting on Michelle Obama," http://michellemalkin.com/2009/08/21/and-now-for-some-hard-hitting-reporting-on-michelle-obama/ (accessed September 4, 2009).

The New Millennium Jackie O.

Additional comparisons to Jackie O. also exist because of Michelle's youthfulness and her small children. Yet Michelle has demonstrated routinely that she is her own person and does not desire to emulate someone even as graceful as Jackie O. Michelle has stated, however, that the association flatters her because of Kennedy's ability "to raise some pretty sane and terrific kids in the midst of a lot of drama and difficulty."[41] Her desire to mother her children was a consistent media frame of the prospective First Lady. In fact, her primary task in the White House as "Mom-in-Chief" was confirmed when she told a group of 800 Women for Obama supporters,

> My girls are the first thing I think about when I wake up in the morning and the last thing I think about when I go to bed. When people ask me how I'm doing, I say, I'm only as good as my most sad child.[42]

This frame supports our culture's desire to maintain women in the traditional role as mothers. Michelle was presented as though she was an average woman committed to caring for her family. Even in the midst of a busy schedule of stumping, Michelle maintained control of her daughters' every movement, indeed comforting to the presidential candidate. One friend remarked, "[Michelle's] got this. This is her thing."[43] As several articles acknowledged, Michelle is devoted to her children and made all attempts to provide them a sense of normalcy that included play dates, soccer and dance practice, and weekend movies.

This task of mothering could seem overwhelming to someone who is also an executive with a major organization. The work/life balance that many working mothers strive toward today resonated strongly with Michelle. She discussed the tensions of her marriage in earlier years when Barack was away from home as a result of his political work. "I came into our marriage with a more traditional notion of what family is. It was what I knew growing up—the mother at home, the father works, you have dinner around the table [together]."[44] This notion was vastly different than that of her husband's, yet they sought ways to ensure their children's needs were fulfilled. "Stumping for her husband two or three days a week while almost always making it home in time to tuck her daughters in bed at night is no joke."[45]

---

[41]Cole, "The Real Michelle Obama," 82.

[42]Kerry Eleveld, "It's Not Just about the Hair," *Advocate*, September 23, 2008, 30–34.

[43]Cole, "The Real Michelle Obama," 82.

[44]"Obama, Michelle."

[45]Cole, "The Real Michelle Obama," 84.

And although she initially rejected her husband's desire to run for president, she eventually supported the idea because of her interest in *all* working mothers:

> ... [T]he last thing in the world I wanted was to turn my girls' lives upside down.... But then I took a step back, and I thought about the world I want my girls to grow up in—a world where they'll be paid fairly for their work.... Where they won't have to choose between their kids and their careers.[46]

Michelle eventually left her executive position as vice president for community and external affairs at the University of Chicago Medical Center to campaign full-time for her husband and care for daughters, Malia and Sasha. Seen critically by some feminists as the perpetual sacrifice of women's work for that of their spouse's, "the Obama marriage was a kind of professional symbiosis, a partnership between two passionately ambitious people who found they could rise higher in the world together than alone."[47]

An interesting twist to the mother media frame focused on Michelle's statuesque (and fit) five-foot-eleven-inch build. In an era where health disparities impact women and African Americans at alarming rates, it seemed reassuring to have a prospective First Lady express interest in the state of her health. Expectations for a "good bill of health" are placed upon presidential candidates, and commentary has been offered about previous First Ladies' thin (and not-so-thin) figures or Geraldine Ferraro's small dress size;[48] however, never was such attention given to a prospective First Lady's healthy physique. During an interview with Michelle, Jill Lawrence asked about her workout routine. Michelle proclaimed, "Nobody's asked that.... This is a scoop," and then proceeded to share specifics about the ninety-minute/four-day-a-week workout that includes cardio exercises, free weights, and the treadmill.[49]

So when posed similar questions about "being fit" in an *Ebony* magazine interview months later, Michelle maintained,

> [Being fit] has become even more important as I've had children, because I'm also thinking about how I'm modeling health to my daughters.... I'm trying to teach my daughters moderation and constancy [and] that exercise is not a luxury, it is a necessity.[50]

[46]Eleveld, "It's Not Just about the Hair," 30–34.

[47]Jodi Kantor, "Michelle Obama, Now a Softer Presence, Adopts Twin Agendas," *New York Times*, August 26, 2008, 14.

[48]Carlin and Winfrey, "Have You Come a Long Way, Baby?," 340.

[49]Lawrence, "Michelle Obama's Busy Summer," 4A.

[50]Cole, "The Real Michelle Obama," 78.

Her commitment to herself and as a role model for her children remains consistent to the mother media frame. She is fulfilling what she believes is necessary to care for her family. This new interest in a prospective First Lady's physical state highlights the added pressures that continue for women as they embark on public platforms that have little to do with their physical appearance. Clearly an aspect of womanhood embraced by Michelle, it still poses concerns for other women who want to be recognized as political forces or "escorts" for their husbands and not consumed by their body image.

The Michelle Obama Factor

Where Michelle Obama deviates the most from past or even prospective First Ladies is her race. Here, I note three distinct media frames that inform us how Michelle is discussed in the news. Interestingly enough, because of the significant support given to Barack by several media pundits, oftentimes there appears to be a constant binary pertaining to Michelle. The media never know exactly how to "handle" her. At any given point, she is seen as elitist or down-to-earth; anti-American or exemplifier of the American Dream; angry black woman or transcending race. As a result, the media never seem comfortable with a place for Michelle, and her coverage hence remains confined to that which is familiar.

I'm Proud to Be an American

One major gaffe set the tone for how many Americans viewed Michelle Obama: During a stump speech in Wisconsin, Michelle stated, "For the first time in my adult life, I am really proud of my country."[51] Conservative pundits pounced upon the opportunity to cast her as un-American, unpatriotic, and insincere in her interest in improving our great nation. Although she defended her remark almost immediately, many American voters maintained their concern for her commitment to the United States. Michelle clarified that "all she meant was that she'd never been prouder," but she seemed unable to ever atone for that sin.[52] An *Economist* editorial posited,

> Mrs. Obama's speeches rarely accentuate the positive. America, to her, is a "downright mean" country where families struggle to buy food, where mothers are terrified of being fired if they get pregnant and where "life" for regular folks has gotten worse over the course of [her] lifetime.[53]

---

[51]Nancy Gibbs and Jay Newton-Small, "The War Over Michelle," *Time* 171, no. 22 (June 2, 2008): 28–29.

[52]Melinda Henneberger, "Standing Tall: What Michelle Means," Commonweal, September 12, 2008, 8.

[53]"Michelle Obama's America," *Economist* 388, no. 8587 (July 5, 2008): 44.

Michelle maintained her stance throughout the campaign, yet the remark continued to haunt her. In fact, she found herself substantiating her American-ness even though as "a descendant of slaves and a product of Chicago's histori-cally black South Side," history was clearly on her side.[54] Teresa Heinz Kerry experienced similar admonishment in the 2004 presidential election because of her South African heritage; however, she was never asked to prove her American-ness. Attention was paid to her tremendous gaffes—like when she stated in *Elle* magazine, "I don't give a shit," and then was labeled "'the ungag-gable Teresa Heinz' in the *Washington Post* and 'Salty Tongue' in the *New York Post*"[55]—more often than to her status as an American.

In several articles, nonetheless, we see the binary in which Michelle is por-trayed as exemplifying the American Dream while also having to address the infamous "first time" statement. For example, Martha T. Moore, in a *USA Today* article, paraphrases Michelle by writing, "She and the candidate value strong family ties, a belief in hard work and upward mobility and a determination to create 'the world as it should be.'"[56] It only takes a few short lines, however, for the author to raise the controversy. While serving as guest host on *The View*, Michelle was asked to address the issue of patriotism; she once again clari-fied, "Of course I am proud of my country.... Nowhere but in America could my story be possible."[57] By sharing stories about her working-class parents and their commitment to her educational aspirations, viewers were then able to hear her reiterate her position on the controversial statement while she also (re)confirmed her traditional American values of hard work and perseverance.

In an attempt at satire, the *New Yorker* featured on its July 2008 cover both Barack and Michelle Obama as Muslim extremists occupying the White House. And what seemed to bind them together in their sinister plot was the "terrorist jab," a phrase coined by Fox News anchor E. D. Hill.[58] The terminol-ogy stuck, and news articles were written to suggest that the questions of loy-alty to America remained unanswered. Calvin Trillin, the "Deadline Poet" for *The Nation* also joined in the discussion with his "A Smear-Cheer for Michelle Obama" that referenced her elitism and "witch-like" demeanor, as well as her seemingly unpatriotic behavior (i.e., "terrorist jab").[59] A simple gesture of

---

[54]Michael Powell and Jodi Kantor, "After Attacks, Michelle Obama Looks for a New Introduction," *New York Times*, June 18, 2008, 1.

[55]K. Emily Bond, "Who's Afraid of Michelle Obama," *Bust* 53 (October–November 2008): 56–59.

[56]Moore, "Michelle Obama Shows Off," 4A.

[57]Alessandra Stanley, "Michelle Obama Highlights Her Warmer Side," *New York Times*, June 19, 2008, 19.

[58]Gail Russell Chaddock, "At Convention, Michelle Obama Melds Personal Ideals with Her Family's History," *Christian Science Monitor* 100, no. 192 (2008): 2.

[59]Calvin Trillin, "A Smear-Cheer for Michelle Obama," *The Nation*, July 14, 2008, 6.

affection toward her husband drew calls of concern about her American-ness. As explained on *The View*, she acknowledged the famous fist-bump as "the new high-five" that she had learned from young staffers on the campaign.[60] However, this incident was raised several times after her explanation on the June 8 show and during the time period selected for this study. In Patrick Healy's article, while acknowledging Michelle's role in generating support for her husband in the final days of the campaign, he suggested that Michelle was seen as a political target, namely for her "terrorist jab."[61]

Just Another Angry Black Woman

In addition to the fist-bump, the *New Yorker* cover also caricatured Michelle Obama as a modern-day Angela Davis type who donned an Afro, military fatigues, and an AK-47—the twenty-first century's "angry black woman." Not mutually exclusive of the media frame mentioned earlier, Michelle's comments, including the "first time" remark, maligned her to a familiar trope for black women. The "angry black woman" is "divisive, outspoken, and problematic"[62] and often bitter regarding the circumstances of blacks in America. Conservative pundits used her senior thesis from Princeton, entitled "Princeton-Educated Blacks and the Black Community," to argue the point that she "indulged in the luxury of experiencing alienation, instead of being grateful for the opportunity [at Princeton]."[63] Her findings suggested that these graduates excelled in white society, yet found themselves distanced further from the larger black community as a consequence of their time at Princeton. Michelle seemed to struggle internally with these findings, noting, "My experience at Princeton has made me far more aware of my 'Blackness' than ever before."[64] This sociological exploration served, then, as the basis for much angst toward Michelle. It was suggested that such ruminations were clearly those of an "aggrieved 'anti' who loves victimhood"[65] and was "once influenced by black separatism."[66]

The recycled trope of the "angry black woman" (most often accepted and expected of black women) is a frame in which Michelle Obama does not fit. However, in an attempt to understand her further, media continued to seek

---

[60]Stanley, "Michelle Obama Highlights Her Warmer Side," 19.

[61]Patrick Healy, "New to Campaigning, but No Longer a Novice," *New York Times*, October 28, 2008, 16.

[62]Cole, "The Real Michelle Obama," 78.

[63]Henneberger, "Standing Tall," 8.

[64]Paulson, "Michelle Obama's Story," 1.

[65]Henneberger, "Standing Tall," 8.

[66]Powell and Kantor, "After Attacks," 1.

categories in which to place her. She is seen as "[Barack] Obama's bitter half" and "angry, abrasive, and didactic"[67] because of her willingness to offer candid remarks separate from those of Barack's. *National Review* twice featured her on its cover, with the titles "Mrs. Grievance" and "America's Unhappiest Millionaire."[68] According to Mark Steyn, "Every time the candidate's wife speaks extemporaneously she seems to offer some bon mot consistent with [a] bleak assessment [of America]."[69] Although rarely acknowledged, race is clearly situated at the center of the angst toward Michelle, but without much substantiation. Michelle's upbringing locates her in the traditional black experience in which racial discrimination, hatred, and harm were present, and suspicions loomed as to whether she would use this public platform as an opportunity to shed light on black injustices. But as friend Verna Williams stated, "She doesn't fit [popular culture standards of] what it means to be an African-American woman"[70]— hence the reliance on media frames to construct her as "angry." Michelle, often seen as a modern-day Claire Huxtable, is representative of black women who

> account for 67 percent of all bachelor's degrees, 71 percent of all master's degrees, and 65 percent of all doctoral degrees awarded to black students. The concept of success among black women like Michelle and her peers, however, is still perceived as somehow extraordinary or even abnormal.[71]

These are not the black women often seen in our weekly television sitcoms or nightly news. Instead, these women are represented as welfare mothers or "baby mamas" and "angry." "I'm probably the first person of my kind the nation has seen out there,"[72] Michelle has said, recognizing her presence as counter to the stereotypes of black women.

Role Model Extraordinaire

One frame seen as more affirming of Michelle Obama is that of role model. The Ivy League–educated, successful executive, doting wife and mother, is counter to the representations often seen of black women in America. The black press (*Essence* and *New York Amsterdam News*) provided news articles that highlighted Michelle's accomplishments and the potential effect of her presence as the First

---

[67]Paulson, "Michelle Obama's Story," 1.

[68]Bond, "Who's Afraid of Michelle Obama," 56–59.

[69]Mark Steyn, "Mrs. Obama's America," *National Review* 60, no. 7 (April 21, 2008): 34–36.

[70]Powell and Kantor, "After Attacks," 1.

[71]Bond, "Who's Afraid of Michelle Obama," 56–59.

[72]Curtis Sittenfeld, "Michelle's Gift," *Time* 172, no. 14 (October 6, 2008): 42–44.

Lady of America. Michelle confirmed for many black women what they saw in themselves, motivated by determination, commitment to family, and dignified elegance under societal pressures.[73] Dr. Joy Angela DeGruy stated,

> Rarely have we seen an individual with such intelligence, poise, dignity, and yet [she's] humble. And what that produces is a feeling of vicarious esteem, a vicarious self-efficacy, meaning that the two of them produce a feeling that says, "I can effect something because I see you." I think this will impact the mental health of the country.[74]

The hope was expressed for young black children who then may accept the possibilities before them with the first black president and his black wife serving in the White House. Ted Wilson, poet and author, believed that "[t]he very fact that an African-American couple is at this level of attainment opens the door for our children to benefit enormously."[75]

Michelle, in her own manner, made efforts to acknowledge her racial history without appearing radical. Offering tidbits in her speeches about her working-class roots, she made the added point of her South Side surroundings that included the second floor of a bungalow in a neighborhood with gang-bangers, block associations, and basketball courts. During her speech at the DNC, she further honored that history with the remark,

> I stand here today at the crosscurrents of that history, knowing that my piece of the American Dream is a blessing hard won by those who came before me, all of them driven by the same conviction that drove my dad to get up an hour early each day to painstakingly dress himself for work.[76]

These words confirmed her recognition as a black woman in this country. And although met with resistance, her story "brought a new American story to the national consciousness."[77] Overtly lacking in critiques of Michelle Obama, these news outlets presented a media frame rarely observed in other news venues. Several articles mentioned Michelle's educational background; however, it was often in the context of justifying her credentials for the position of First Lady and not to highlight her personal accomplishments.

---

[73]Erin Aubry Kaplan, "Woman of the Year Michelle Obama," *Essence* 39, no. 6 (October 2008): 157.

[74]Daa'Iya L. Sanusi, "Michelle Obama—The Next First Lady?" *New York Amsterdam News*, August 28, 2008, 1, 30.

[75]Ibid., 1, 30.

[76]Ibid., 1, 30.

[77]Kaplan, "Woman of the Year," 157.

A New Paradigm?

Media frames of Michelle Obama were often consistent with the findings of earlier studies.[78] She was written about as a escort to her husband and acknowledged for her sense of style. The frames least noted in her coverage concerned her charity work or potential influence as a policy adviser. These frames appeared more frequently in the 2000 presidential election in which both Laura Bush and Tipper Gore were recognized for their personal causes, as well as their subtle influence in the presidential candidates' stances.[79]

Michelle seems to add to the media frames created for prospective First Ladies. She is the Jackie O. of the new millennium for her youthfulness, role as mother to young children, and her concern for self (as a means of caring for her family). Because voters think of the First Lady as the American standard for motherhood, it becomes important for this role to be highlighted in the media. Michelle fulfilled that frame while also extending upon it as a working mother who believed in fitness. Her exposed arms and bare legs were often mentioned to draw attention to her physique, not sexually, but as an exemplar of health. Only time will reveal if this frame is continued for future First Ladies or exclusively reserved for Michelle Obama and/or one of her age and stature.

The portrayals of Michelle Obama and what they mean for other African-American women and the larger society are best summarized by Melissa Harris-Lacewell:

> Black women are recognizable in American culture only if they are cast as the hypersexualized Jezebel, the Mammy figure (the "black best friend" role popularized in cinema and TV sitcoms), or the ABW (angry black woman).... When Fox ran the "Baby Mama" banner, which carries the connotation of a mother and father who've never been married, she became the Jezebel. Her softer and gentler appearance on *The View* described as her "reintroduction" to the American public in the *New York Times*, sought to transform her into everybody's best friend, thus casting her as Mammy for a day. And her early pronouncements on issues as varied as race relations and work-life balance made her the ABW, a stereotype that has trailed her incessantly and is all too familiar among her peers.[80]

---

[78]Benze, "Nancy Reagan," 777–80; Winfield, "The First Lady, Political Power and the Media," 166–79; Gould, "Modern First Ladies and the Presidency," 677–83; and Scharrer and Bissell, "Overcoming Traditional Boundaries," 55–83.

[79]Winfield and Friedman, "Gender Politics," 54–56.

[80]Bond, "Who's Afraid of Michelle Obama," 56–59.

The media have not been expected nor required to know a black woman in depth prior to Michelle Obama. Never before has a black woman held such a role or presence in national American politics. And now she is a force to be reckoned with. Unfortunately, that has meant relying upon old tropes that categorized African-American women narrowly, hence her rocky road on the campaign trail.

We have a unique opportunity with the presence of First Lady Michelle Obama. Media will continue to write about her, and such explorations as this one will continue to be published. The hope is the media will more carefully examine their journalistic practices and face the reality of the role of race in their "objective" reporting. Michelle Obama has created a potential new space for future First Ladies that, in turn, broadens society's view of black women in this country. As political parties gear up for midterm elections as well as the 2012 presidential election, new media frames will be necessary to discuss the candidates' spouses, which is certain to include Michelle Obama.

The Feminist (?) Hero versus the Black Messiah: Contesting Gender and Race in the 2008 Democratic Primary

Enid Lynette Logan

Senator Barack Obama's matchup against Senator Hillary Clinton during the Democratic primary raised important questions pertaining to the contrasting ways in which race and gender function in the post–civil rights, "postfeminist" era. U.S. scholars of "intersectionality" have argued that in order to understand how race works in any given context, we must consider the role of other social variables as well. Race, gender, class, and sexuality do not act independently of one another, but interrelate and are experienced simultaneously.[1] One of the most fascinating aspects of the 2008 presidential election was that as race came ever more to the forefront, questions of class, age, gender, religion, and nation were dragged right into the middle as well.

Two sets of questions are addressed in this chapter. First, I ask, What kinds of debates did the primary stir up about the salience, or weight, of gender and race in American society? What kinds of ideological, generational, and racial divisions did the contest reveal among Democrats—especially women—and why? Here I examine statements by the powerful second-wave white feminists who backed Clinton, angry responses from the mostly younger, mostly white feminists who supported Obama, as well as frustrated perspectives offered by progressive women of color, as found variously in the mainstream media and the blogosphere. Arguments voiced for and against the candidates revealed fundamental disagreements about what it meant to be a feminist in the twenty-first century, and the importance of gender relative to other social divides. The debates further show that despite decades of discussion about multiculturalism and inclusiveness, conceptions of "womanhood" among many prominent feminist activists remain tied to notions of whiteness.

---

[1]Winifred Breines, "Struggling to Connect: White and Black Feminism in the Movement Years," *Contexts Magazine* 6, no. 1 (February 2007): 18–24; Patricia Hill Collins, *Black Feminist Thought: Knowledge, Consciousness and the Politics of Empowerment* (Boston: Unwin Hyman, 1990); Audre Lourde, *Sister Outsider* (Trumansberg, NY: The Cross Press, 1984); Kum-Kum Bhavnani, ed., *Feminism and "Race"* (Oxford: Oxford University Press, 2001).

In the second part of the chapter, I inquire into the roles that race and gender played in the *outcome* of the election. Just how relevant were gender and sexism in explaining why Hillary Clinton lost, and why Barack Obama won? In what ways did race help Obama or hinder Clinton? And why was it that Obama's candidacy was always assumed to be more potentially transformative, significant, and historic for the nation, despite the fact that the United States had never before had either a female or a black president? In this section of the chapter, I rely on evidence from the print and online media, as well as quotes from a subsample of the 125 in-depth interviews I conducted with college students in the weeks preceding the election. I find, first, that the Clinton camp attempted to mobilize whiteness in her favor through the use of "dog-whistle" tactics, designed to appeal to the latent racism of white Americans. Yet, I argue, these maneuvers ultimately backfired, because the Obama was able to neutralize the more potentially "problematic" aspects of blackness, and because of the centrality of nonracism to the identity of liberal whites and to the 2008 campaign in particular. Obama's gender did work in his favor, in part because of the "naturalness" of the link between masculinity and leadership and because of his "movie-star good looks." However, I conclude, it was not so much Obama's reliance upon his gender privilege, as it was his successful mobilization of the powerful trope of race—as redemptive, and as revolutionary—that was key to his victory.

Divided Sisterhood

The 2008 Democratic primary might have been a moment of shared euphoria that the party had put forth its first serious female and black candidates in the same election. But instead it engendered bitter polarization around the issues of race and gender. The divide was particularly acute, and particularly painful, among women. As one journalist observed:

> There's a delicious irony in the 2008 Democratic presidential campaign: Liberal women who usually vote as a bloc are split. It has come down to a black man and a white woman, and no less than history hangs in the balance. The race has pitted friends against friends, sisters against sisters, and mothers against daughters …[2]

The intense infighting among feminists received substantial coverage in the press. While women under forty supported Obama, many older, "second-wave" feminists ferociously supported Hillary Clinton. As Clinton's lock on the nomination began to appear less than secure, numerous accusations were hurled across the ideological and generational divides.

---

[2]English, Bella. 2008. "The diversity bloc is divided." *Boston Globe*. February 15. Accessed March 18, 2008. http://www.boston.com/news/local/articles/2008/02/15/the_diversity_bloc_is_divided/

Prominent feminist supporters of Clinton took special aim at the women they felt were betraying the cause. Those who sided with Obama were accused of being fickle, naïve, romantically infatuated, and stupid.[3] The most serious charge, perhaps, was that they had capitulated to the patriarchal status quo. Gloria Steinem claimed from the pages of the *New York Times*, "[S]ome women, perhaps especially younger ones, hope to deny or escape the sexual caste system." Former Planned Parenthood president Gloria Feldt wrote in the *Huffington Post* that it was women's historic "responsibility" to vote for Clinton. And Robin Morgan (publisher of *Sisterhood Is Powerful*) charged that many who supported Obama were "eager to win male approval by showing [that] they're not feminists." They were unable to identify with Clinton, she continued, "because she is unafraid of *eeueweeeu* yucky *power*," and for "fear that their boyfriends might look at them funny."[4]

Angered and offended, many of the accused responded that they would not be subject to an ideological litmus test by the feminist thought police. As journalist Adele M. Stan wrote in the *Washington Post*, "I take no issue with the feminism of women who disagree with my choice [to back Obama]. I do, however, take issue with those who disparage my character as their explanation for my choice."[5] Still others argued that supporting Clinton did nothing to advance the cause of feminism. Megan O'Rourke wrote, "the more Clinton's campaign floundered ... the more masculine and hard-nosed she made herself out to be." And, in an article entitled "Why Women Hate Hillary," professor Susan Douglass wrote that Hillary Clinton aimed to be "like a man in her

---

[3]Hirschman, Linda. 2008. "For Hillary's Campaign, It's Been a Class Struggle." *Washington Post*. March 2. Accessed March 18, 2008. http://www.washingtonpost.com/wp-dyn/content/article/2008/02/29/AR2008022902991.html; Shriver, Kyle-Anne. 2008. "Women Voters and the Obama Crush." *The American Thinker*. March 11. Accessed April 25, 2008. http://www.americanthinker.com/2008/03/women_voters_and_the_obama_cru.html; Allen, Charlotte. 2008. "We Scream, We Swoon, How Dumb Can We Get?" *Washington Post*. March 2. Accessed March 18, 2008. http://www.washingtonpost.com/wp-dyn/content/article/2008/02/29/AR2008022902992.html

[4]Steinem, Gloria. 2008. "Women are Never Frontrunners." *New York Times*. January 8. Accessed January 8, 2008. http://www.nytimes.com/2008/01/08/opinion/08steinem.html; Feldt, Gloria. 2008. "Why Women Need to Learn History's Election Power Lesson." *Huffington Post*. February 18. Accessed March 18, 2008. http://www.huffingtonpost.com/gloria-feldt/why-women-need-to-learn-h_b_87218.html; Morgan, Robin. 2008. "Goodbye To All That (#2)." *Women's Media Center*, February 2. Accessed March 18, 2008. http://www.womensmediacenter.com/ex/020108.html

[5]Stan, Adele M. 2008. "The Feminist Case for Obama." *Washington Post*. March 4, 2008. Accessed March 4, 2008. http://www.washingtonpost.com/wp-dyn/content/article/2008/03/04/AR2008030401240.html; Martin, Courtney. 2008b. "More Than a Mother-Daughter Debate." *The American Prospect*. April 21. Accessed July 14, 2008. http://www.prospect.org/cs/articles?article=more_than_a_motherdaughter_debate

demeanor and politics, leaving some basic tenets of feminism in the dust....
[S]he is like patriarchy in sheep's clothing."[6]

Though they chafed at the scolding of the Clintonistas, Obama's feminist
supporters were alarmed by the misogynistic overtones of the criticism directed
at Hillary Clinton. As Rebecca Traister, a self-described "loud feminist and
longtime Clinton skeptic," wrote on *Salon.com*,

> I [began to get] e-mails from men I didn't know well who ap-
> proached me as a go-to feminist to whom they could express their
> hatred of Hillary and their anger at her. ... One of my closest girl-
> friends, an Obama voter, told me of ... a politically progressive
> man who made a series of legitimate complaints about Clinton's
> policies before adding that when he hears the senator's voice, he's
> overcome by an urge to punch her in the face.

Similarly, in "Dear Hillary: A Letter from an Obama Feminist," writer
Courtney Martin thanked Clinton "for weathering this storm of anxious masculinity and outright sabotage, but even more, for creating a moment where the
kind of subtle sexism that women experience everyday [*sic*] ... was brought to
undeniable light."[7]

Again Invisible: Women of Color and the Oppression Sweepstakes

In addition to reviving tensions within the predominantly white, middle-class
feminist movement, the election also battered the tenuous alliance between
mainstream feminists and progressive women of color. During the feminist
"third wave" (1980s to 1990s), dozens of essays were written promulgating the
ideas that feminism must be inclusive, that opposing race and class injustice

---

[6]O'Rourke, Megan. 2008. "Death of a Saleswoman: How Hillary Clinton lost me—and a generation of young voters." On the blog *Salon.com*. June 5. Accessed July 18, 2008. http://www
.slate.com/id/2192827; Kissling, Frances. 2008. "Why I'm still not for Hillary Clinton." *Salon.com*.
January 10. Accessed March 18, 2008. http://www.salon.com/news/opinion/feature/2008/01/10/
kissling_clinton; Douglass, Susan. 2008. "Why Women Hate Hillary." *In These Times*. April 27.
Accessed May 13, 2008. http://www.inthesetimes.com/article/3129/why_women_hate_hillary/;
Bravo, Ellen. 2008. "Why So Many Feminists Are Deciding to Vote for Barack Obama."
Huffington Post. February 1. Accessed March 18, 2008. http://www.huffingtonpost.com/ellen-
bravo/why-so-many-feminists-are_b_84482.html

[7]Traister, Rebecca. 2008. "Hey, Obama boys: Back off already!: Young women are growing increasingly frustrated with the fanatical support of Barack and gleeful bashing of Hillary." Salon.com.
April 14. Accessed April 14, 2008. http://www.salon.com/life/feature/2008/04/14/obama_
supporters;Martin,Courtney.2008a."DearHillary:ALetterfromanObamaFeminist." *TheAmerican
Prospect*. June 9. Accessed June 10, 2008. http://www.prospect.org/cs/articles?article=dear_hillary

should be central to its mission, and that movement leaders should cease to write as if "all the women are white and all the blacks are men." These were defining principles of the third wave, widely proclaimed to part of the painful, but necessary evolution of the moment. From the start of the 2008 primary, however, it seemed that these ideas had been all but abandoned.

Academics, journalists, and bloggers of color were alternately amazed and infuriated to see Clinton's feminist supporters render their experiences tangential distractions to "core" women's issues. This tendency was found implicitly in discussions of how "women" felt about Hillary Clinton that excluded the quite possibly very *different* feelings of women of color.[8] On *Salon.com*, Kim McLarin wrote that after being "confused" that "so many white women could be so shocked that sexism still exists," she had finally figured out that the angry debate was "a family fight between older white women and their daughters," and "me and my mother and my sisters are not even in the conversation." "What a relief," she concludes. "Ya'll carry on."[9]

A more explicit claim that race and class justice were not feminist issues was found in the Linda Hirshman's, "Looking Forward, Feminism Needs to Focus." In the *Washington Post*, Hirshman called for feminists to unite around the singular cause of gender oppression, leaving distractions like "intersectionality" aside. She wrote, "The Clinton campaign has, perhaps unwittingly, revealed what many in the movement know—that if feminism is a social-justice-for-everyone (with the possible exception of middle-class white women) movement, then gender is just one commitment among many. And when the other causes call, the movement will dissolve."

Numerous young feminists were offended by Hirshman's article. Jill at *Feministe* protested Hirshman's separation of "authentic 'feminist issues,'" from "those 'other' issues that those 'other' women are trying to integrate into feminism." She wrote, "It's a question of who feminism belongs to, and who is entitled to set out its goals and concerns." One Latina blogger argued on *La Chola*: "This is not a movement. I repeat, this is not a movement. It's an exclusive networking club. And no woman, of color or otherwise, owes her allegiance to an exclusive networking club simply because she has a vagina and the ... club members have vaginas."[10]

---

[8]Saslow, Eli. 2008. "To Women, So Much More Than Just A Candidate." *Washington Post*. March 4. Accessed March 4, 2008. http://www.washingtonpost.com/wp-dyn/content/story/2008/03/03/ST2008030303087.html; Donna. 2008. "White Women Feminism - There They Go Again." *The Silence of Our Friends*. March 6. Accessed March 7, 2008. http://the-silence-of-our-friends.blogspot.com/2008/03/white-women-feminism-there-they-go.html

[9]"McLarin, Kim. 2008. "Family Fight." *XX Factor*. June 7. Accessed June 7. http://www.slate.com/blogs/blogs/xxfactor/archive/2008/06/07/family-fight.aspx

[10]Jill. 2008. "Has Feminism Lost Its Focus?" *Feministe*. June 9. Accessed August 3, 2008. http://www.feministe.us/blog/archives/2008/06/09/has-feminism-lost-its-focus/; Brownfemipower. 2008.

Many women of color were also disappointed by the resolute blindness of mainstream feminists to what they perceived to be the numerous racial insults inflicted by the Clinton campaign. As Patricia Hill Collins was quoted as saying in *The Nation*, "It is such a distressing, ugly period. Clinton has manipulated ideas about race, but Obama has not manipulated similar ideas about gender."[11] Relatedly, black women complained about the deafening silence of white feminists who failed to rally to the defense of Michelle Obama during the months in which she faced widespread attacks from the media. As blogger Rikyrah wrote: "One has to wonder, as Michelle Obama is being labeled unpatriotic, bitter, mean, angry. Where are those feminists who saw sexism lurking around every corner with Hillary Clinton? *Where.are.they?*"[12]

Many argued that debates about the primary seemed to have devolved into an "oppression sweepstakes." In a May 2008 interview with the *Washington Post*, Senator Clinton herself had stated, "You can go to places in the world where there are no racial distinctions except everyone is joined together in their oppression of women. The treatment of women is the single biggest problem we have politically and socially in the world." Also in May, writer Lynette Long argued that one of the painful lessons that "women" had learned from the primary was that "in the world of presidential politics, race trumps gender." And Gloria Steinem, again, in her *New York Times* op-ed piece, claimed that "gender is probably the most restricting force in American life."[13]

"OOOh, look a thoughtful intelligent analysis of intersectionality!" *La Chola*. June 9. Accessed June 9, 2008. http://brownfemipower.com/; Ashley. 2008. "This Just In! Feminism Must Focus on White Ladies." *SAFER*. June 10. Accessed June 15, 2008. http://www.safercampus.org/blog/?p=466

[11]Reed, Betsy. 2008. "Race to the Bottom." *The Nation*. May 1. Accessed May 2, 2008. http://www.thenation.com/article/race-bottom-0

[12]Rikyrah. 2008. "When It Comes to Michelle Obama, Where Are the Feminists?" On the blog *Jack and Jill Politics*. June 23. Accessed June 23, 2008. http://www.jackandjillpolitics.com/2008/06/when-it-comes-to-michelle-obama-where-are-the-feminists/; Curtis, Mary C. 2008. "The Loud Silence of Feminists." *Washington Post*. June 21. Accessed June 23, 2008. http://www.washingtonpost.com/wp-dyn/content/article/2008/06/20/AR2008062002209.html; Stanard, Alexa. 2008. "Michelle Obama, radically awesome." *Michigan Messenger*. July 16. Accessed August 8, 2008. http://michiganmessenger.com/1574/michelle-obama-radically-awesome

[13]Mitchell, Greg. 2008. "Full Transcript of Hillary Claiming Sexism Worse than Racism in Campaign." *Huffington Post*, May 20. Accessed May 20, 2008. http://www.huffingtonpost.com/ greg-mitchell/full-transcript-of-hillar_b_102716.html; Romano, Lois. 2008. "Clinton Puts Up A New Fight: The Candidate Confronts Sexism On the Trail and Vows to Battle On." *Washington Post*. May 19. Accessed May 19, 2008. http: //www.washingtonpost.com/wp-dyn/content/article/2008/05/19/AR2008051902729.html; Long, Lynette. 2008. "Painful lessons: Primary reveals obstacles facing women in politics." *Baltimore Sun*. May 18. Accessed May 18, 2008. http://articles.baltimoresun.com/2008-05-18/news/0805160266_1_obama-women-voters-white-women; Long, Lynette. 2008. "Obama is a Megalomaniac." *Lynette Long: Truth, Justice and the American Way*. July 25. Accessed August 4, 2008. http://www.lynettelong.com/my_weblog/2008/07/

Women of color responded to these arguments with particular frustration. As "Jenn," (who describes herself as "an angry Asian-American woman") wrote on the blog *Reappropriate*,

> Where do we fit when we're being asked to choose between Obama and Clinton as a metaphor for race versus gender? And how are we supposed to react when an incorrect choice labels us as "less radical"? ... The juxtaposition [of race and gender] is disingenuous, divisive, overly simplistic, and ultimately harmful ...[14]

Seeking to bridge the growing, acrimonious divide, a coalition of black and white feminists met over breakfast in February 2008. Present at the meeting were Beverly Guy-Sheftall, Johnnetta B. Cole, Kimberlé Crenshaw, Eleanor Smeal, Mab Segrest, Laura Flanders, Gloria Steinem, and others. Reflecting upon the bitterness of the previous months, they asked

> How ... did a historic breakthrough moment for which we have all longed and worked hard, suddenly risk becoming marred by having to choose between "race cards" and "gender cards"? ... What happened ... to the last four decades of discussion about tokenism and multiple identities ...?[15]

Despite the group's commitment to continue to work toward a "collective better future," and other statements from feminists urging unity, the debate over "who has it worse" continued throughout the primary.[16]

A Black President: A Uniquely American Achievement

Analyses of the 2008 election that pit "women" against "blacks" are counterproductive, and tend to erase women of color from the equation altogether. Yet it is clear that, for a number of reasons, race worked for Obama

obama-is-a-mega.html; Steinem, Gloria. 2008. "Women are Never Frontrunners." *New York Times*. January 8. Accessed January 8, 2008. http://www.nytimes.com/2008/01/08/opinion/08steinem.html

[14]Jenn. 2008. "Pitting Race Against Gender in Election '08: Why the battle of electoral identity politics is bad for all of us." Reappropriate. January 8. Accessed January 12, 2008. http://www.reappropriate.com/?p=949

[15]"Morning in America: A Letter from Feminists on the Election." 2008. *The Nation*. March 17. Accessed March 18, 2008. http://www.thenation.com/article/morning-america

[16]See, for example, comments by blogger Donna Darko: "There was sexism in the campaign but also racism. YEAH BUT THERE WAS A HELLUVA LOT MORE SEXISM IN THE CAMPAIGN THAN RACISM,".... and "Sexism gave Obama the nomination and race was only used to his advantage." From Darko, Darko. 2008. "The race trumps gender theme." *Donna Darko*. July 30. Accessed August 5, 2008. http://donnadarko.wordpress.com/2008/07/30/working-my-last-nerve/

in a way that gender did not work for Hillary Clinton. First, while pundits were fascinated by the idea that the country might select a man classified as black to be president, much less discussion was devoted to what it would mean for the United States to choose a woman. There was a clear sense, from the beginning, that Obama's candidacy was somehow more potentially transformative for the nation than was Clinton's.

Such sentiments were reflected in many of the interviews that I con-ducted with college students ages eighteen to twenty-nine in the weeks before the general election.[17] When asked if the selection of our first black president or our first woman president would be more meaningful, the vast majority of students chose the former, even if they could not explain exactly why they felt that way. Consider for example the words of Scott, a twenty-year-old white male: "I'd be more inclined to say African American just because ... I don't know, I just feel like African-American people are more substantial for some reason?" Or as Aileen, a twenty-two-year-old white female, stated:

> I think it would be more historic if it would be our first black president, because I don't know ... [O]bviously we started off as a country with ... really horrible race relations and we had black people enslaved and now we have the potential for a black man to be running things.

As the quote above suggests, the explanation for the difference, lies in the subconsciously understood—if not fully articulated—role of "race" in our nation's history. It is the line between blacks and whites that most acknowledge to be the country's deepest divide, and most enduring symbol of shame. As Howard Winant writes, "Racial conflict is the very archetype of discord in North Amer-ica, the primordial conflict that has in many ways structured all others."[18] While Barack Obama was an extraordinary candidate whose success was due to a num-ber of factors, his race—or specifically, the fact of his blackness—was central among them. As journalist Benjamin Wallace-Wells suggested in late 2006:

---

[17]In September and October 2008, my team of research assistants and I conducted over 125 in-depth interviews with undergraduates about what they perceived to be roles of race and gender in the 2008 presidential election and in the wider society. This study generated tremendous inter-est on the part of the students to whom we spoke. We were able to achieve remarkable depth with regard to the racial diversity of those interviewed (about 60 percent of whom were nonwhite), which was a key goal of the sampling strategy. The present chapter draws upon responses to a small subset of the questions that were asked. Detailed discussion of sample design and data collection, as well as a more extensive analysis of the interviews, will be found in forthcoming articles.

[18]Howard Winant, *Racial Conditions: Politics, Theory, Comparisons* (Minneapolis: University of Minnesota Press, 1994), 23.

[R]ace can work better ... for Barack than gender for Hillary, because most Americans want to believe that the culture has moved past its racial problems.... Whatever racism remains in this country, it coexists with a galloping desire to put that old race stuff behind us.... [T]he election of a black man ... would be a particularly American achievement, an affirmation of American ideals.[19]

In a nation seeking to restore its honor in the aftermath of a long and unpopular "war on terror," the prospect of choosing a black president was especially appealing. Furthermore, in the post–civil rights era, *thinking of one's self* as nonracist, and being *perceived by others* to be nonracist are important to the self-concept of liberal white Americans in a way that opposing sexism simply is not.[20]

While blackness worked in Obama's favor in many respects, it was his specific deployment of blackness that was key. Obama positioned himself as a "next-generation" or "postracial" black candidate, carefully avoiding the appearance of anger, victimhood, or "grievance." At a number of key moments in the election, he crucially differentiated himself from the tactics of other black public figures that many whites (and nonwhites) had come to dislike strongly. Thus he was able to neutralize the "problematic" aspects of blackness while highlighting the redemptive ones. As one young white female (Fiona, age nineteen) said to my interviewer, the genius of Obama was that he "uses the motivation and excitement," of men like Jesse Jackson and Malcolm X in ways that seem "less harmful, aggressive," and "offensive."

Though the terms have been used in ways that many find problematic, I believe that there is a certain truth to claims that Obama is both a "magical Negro," and a kind of "black Messiah." It was from his blackness, after all, that Obama derived his purported ability to heal and redeem the nation. Through

---

[19]Wallace-Wells, Benjamin. 2006. "Is America too Racist for Barack? Too Sexist for Hillary?" *Washington Post*. November 12. Accessed November 12. http://www.washingtonpost.com/wp-dyn/content/article/2006/11/10/AR2006111001387.html

[20]There is, however, a critical distinction between being *nonracist* (having a commitment to the abstract ideals of equality, tolerance, and colorblindness) and being *antiracist* (actively working against racial injustice). In fact, adherence to what scholars such as Gallagher and Bonilla-Silva have termed the "colorblind racial ideology" prevents many whites from acknowledging the privileges they receive and how they themselves may help to reproduce racial inequality. Eduardo Bonilla-Silva, *Racism Without Racists: Color–Blind Racism and the Persistence of Racial Inequality in the United States* (Lanham, MD: Rowman & Littlefield, 2003); Charles Gallagher, "Colorblind Privilege: The Social and Politics Functions of Erasing the Color Line in Post-Race America," *Race, Gender & Class* 10 (2003): 22–37. Insights about antiracism found in Eileen O'Brien, "The Personal Is Political: The Influence of White Supremacy on White Antiracist's Personal Relationships," in *White Out: The Continuing Significance of Racism*, ed. Ashely W. Doane and Eduardo Bonilla-Silva (New York: Routledge, 2003), 253–70; and Barbara Trepagnier, *Silent Racism* (Boulder, CO: Paradigm Publishers, 2006).

speeches declaring that "only in America is [his] story possible," Obama for-warded the notion that in voting for him, whites demonstrated their "core goodness," and the United States proved itself to be a place of opportunity and tolerance. The promises of rebirth and renewal were also strongly reinforced via Obama's characterization of himself as the candidate representing "change," rather than the status quo. Voting for Clinton, who ran on a platform of "expe-rience," offered no redemptive blackness, and her ambivalence about the issue of gender provided no such psychological payoff.

Say What? Sexism?

Given these observations, it is perhaps unsurprising that the racial innuendoes designed to undermine Obama received much more analysis and condemnation from the press than the sexist rhetoric directed at Clinton. The *Washington Post* ran a July 2007 story on Clinton's "plunging neckline," in which her cleavage was said to "stir up the same kind of discomfort that might be churned up after spotting Rudy Giuliani with his shirt unbuttoned." Like "catching a man with his fly unzipped," the author continued, it's best to "[j]ust look away!"[21] In addition to her looks, journalists and bloggers often made disparaging comments about Clinton's voice. Her laugh was repeatedly referred to a "cackle," as in this from the *Boston Globe*: "Hens cackle. So do witches. And, so does the front-runner in the Democratic presidential contest." One *Washington Post* writer argued in January 2008 that Clinton "needs a radio-controlled shock collar so that aides can zap her when she starts to get screechy." A Fox News commentator stated that same month, "[W]hen Hillary Clinton speaks, men hear 'Take out the garbage.'"[22] And in February 2008, television commentator Tucker Carlson hosted Roger Stone, founder of the anti-Clinton 587 group Citizens United Not Timid, or C.U.N.T., on his program.[23]

[21]Ghivan, Robin. 2007. "Hillary Clinton's Tentative Dip Into New Neckline Territory." *Washington Post.* July 20. Accessed July 21, 2007. http://www.washingtonpost.com/wp-dyn/content/article/2007/07/19/AR2007071902668.html

[22]Vennoci, Joan. 2007. "That Clinton Cackle." *Boston Globe.* September 30. Accessed September 30, 2007. http://www.boston.com/news/nation/articles/2007/09/30/that_clinton_cackle/; Achenbach, Joel. 2008. "End of the Clinton Era?" *Washington Post.* January 6. Accessed January 15, 2008. http://voices.washingtonpost.com/achenblog/2008/01/end_of_the_clinton_era.html

[23]Wines, Heather. 2008. "Clinton responds to seemingly sexist shouts." *USA Today.* April 14. Accessed May 19, 2008. http://www.usatoday.com/news/politics/election2008/2008-01-07-clinton-iron-emotion_N.htm; Venezia, Todd. 2007. "Nut Buster: Wacky Hillary Gizmo is a Reall Easy Shell." *New York Post.* September 7. Accessed September 30, 2007. http://www.nypost.com/p/news/national/item_4eiLSEWHjAzDpC5vy7YTOJ;jsessionid=32B13AD893967D731268627A3CBE3AA8; Linkins, Jason. 2008. "MSNBC Hosts Founder Of Anti-Hillary Group 'C.U.N.T.'" *Huffington Post.* February 19. Accessed February 19, 2008. http://www.huffingtonpost.com/2008/02/19/msnbc-hosts-founder-of-an_n_87356.html

This coverage received relatively little discussion or outrage from the mainstream media. No angry rant from Keith Olbermann. Feminist bloggers were incensed, but few others seemed to notice. The students I interviewed confessed to having little awareness of insults directed at Clinton because of her gender. Even for those who described themselves as feminists, the notion that Clinton had been subject to systematically biased treatment in the media, or that sexism had anything to do with why she lost, were not very credible. Consider this exchange with Avery, a twenty-five-year-old female, who considered herself a "black feminist":

> Interviewer: Some Clinton supporters say that she could possibly have lost because of sexism. What do you think of that?

> Avery: That's ridiculous. You're less likely to lose from sexism than racism. Just historically, I mean, it's very funny.... I remember being irritated when her campaign started talking about sexism.

Students were especially unsympathetic to reports that Clinton had misted up in a speech before the New Hampshire primary.[24] In the words of Dwayne, a twenty-two-year-old Caribbean-American male who had once considered himself a Hillary supporter, "I think that she is a little too sensitive to run the country.... I mean, maybe she's not *built* for it. That's what I would say. She has some great ideas ... [but] she's not "Built Ford Tough" to be president.... Not at all." When Julia, a twenty-year-old biracial female was asked why she thought Clinton had lost the primary, she stated, "Umm, I remember hearing a lot of talk about her crying during a speech or something like that.... I think she needs to have better control of her emotions."

Dog-Whistle Racism and Black Anger

Clinton's general avoidance of the issue of gender, and posturing that many considered to be "masculine," caused her to lose the support of many feminist-identified women who might have otherwise come to her defense, but instead saw her as a less-than-ideal role model. Furthermore, her reliance on what several writers referred to as "dog-whistle" racism (designed to appeal to the latent racism of lower-income, less-educated whites) alienated her from another core constituency: black Americans.[25]

---

[24]Breslau, Karen. 2008. "Hillary Tears Up: A Muskie moment, or a helpful glimpse of 'the real Hillary'?" *Newsweek*. January 7. Accessed January 7, 2008. http://www.newsweek.com/2008/01/06/hillary-tears-up.html

[25]Cohn, Jonathan. 2008. "Why Obama Should Ignore Ferraro." *The New Republic*. March 12. Accessed March 18, 2008. http://www.tnr.com/blog/the-plank/why-obama-should-ignore-ferraro;

Through code words and innuendo, Clinton and her surrogates cast Obama as the *problematically* (rather than redemptively) "black candidate." We were told, variously, that Obama could only get black votes (Clinton pollster Sergio Bendixen and Bill Clinton), that he was anti-white (the Reverend Wright controversy), anti-patriotic (the flag pin controversy), possibly a drug seller (BET co-founder Bob Johnson), and married to an angry, ungrateful black woman. Though he had managed to "shuck and jive" his way through the presidential campaign (Andrew Cuomo), Hillary had to stay in the race in case he was assassinated (like RFK). Like other affirmative-action babies, he only got where he was because of his race (Geraldine Ferraro), and yet, being a latté-sipping elitist ("Bittergate"), he deigned to look down upon "hardworking white Americans" (Hillary)! Far from being postracial, the message was, Obama was *overdetermined* by his race.

While such messaging may have gained Clinton some white votes, it also contributed to the perception that her campaign was actively seeking to stir up white racial resentment. A particularly interesting perspective came from former Bill Clinton advisor and current Republican strategist Dick Morris. In a January 2008 *Real Clear Politics* article, he argued that the ex-president had deliberately raised the issue of race before the South Carolina primary in order to provoke a white backlash against Obama.

> Why is he making such a fuss over a contest he knows he's going to lose? ... If Hillary loses South Carolina and the defeat serves to demonstrate Obama's ability to attract a bloc vote among black Democrats, the message will go out loud and clear to white voters that this is a racial fight.... That will trigger a massive white backlash against Obama and will drive white voters to Hillary Clinton.[26]

In response, many African Americans, who had once warmly referred to Bill Clinton as America's "first black president," expressed a mixture of "seething, barely contained rage" and "revulsion" when discussing the Clintons. As journalist Terence Samuel wrote in April 2008:

Neiwert, David. "Blowing The Dog Whistle." *FiredogLake*. April 14. Accessed May 8. http:// firedoglake.com/2008/04/14/blowing-the-dog-whistle/; Calabresi, Massimo. 2008. "Obama's 'Electability' Code for Race?" *Time Magazine*. May 6. Accessed June 3, 2008. http://www.time .com/time/politics/article/0,8599,1737725,00.html; Spaulding, Pam. 2008. "White dog whistles no more." On the blog *Pam's House Blend*. May 8. Accessed May 8, 2008. http://www.pamshouseblend .com/showDiary.do?diaryId=5311; Conason, Joe. 2008. "Was Hillary channeling George Wallace?" *Salon.com*. May 9. Accessed June 15, 2008. Accessed June 15, 2008. http://www.salon.com/news/ opinion/joe_conason/2008/05/09/clinton_remarks

[26]Morris, Dick. 2008. "How Clinton Will Win the Nomination by Losing S.C." *Real Clear Politics*. January 23. Accessed January 23, 2008. http://www.realclearpolitics.com/articles/2008/01/ how_clinton_will_win_the_nomin.html

[T]he Clintons do not seem to understand that the kind of revulsion they are generating in what was once the heart of their base is not your garden-variety political frustration.... The idea that Obama, having played by all the rules and won by all the traditional measures, could lose the nomination because of Clinton's argument that he is unelectable because he is black, is profoundly revolting to many black people. [27]

In the end, the kinds of racial innuendoes used by the Clinton campaign gained her little mileage, as Obama succeeded in defining the 2008 campaign as referendum on the goodness-cum-racial tolerance of the nation. In this context, a hypervigilant liberal media, many white Democrats, and many more African Americans were repelled by what they perceived to be clear attempts by the Clintons to appeal to the baser, more racist instincts of the general population.

The Obama Crush

In addition to analyzing the role that whiteness played in Clinton's campaign, we must also consider the ways in which gender helped, or hurt, Obama. While he has been primarily described in terms of his race, it is also crucial to remember that he was running for president as a man. And as a man, Obama automatically commanded a kind of authority and legitimacy in his quest to become the president of the United States that a woman could not. But the senator's masculine appeal went deeper than this. Obama was uncommonly attractive, and known for his white-collar masculine swagger. Regularly described as handsome, dashing, cool, and "swoon-worthy," the American press corps and women everywhere were said be to "in love" with the senator. See, for example, this item from the *Washingtonian* magazine:

> When Barack Obama speaks, people listen. But we're also taken by his movie-star looks.... He's got a great physique, too.... This past summer, HottestUSSenator.com ran an online contest for the "Hottest U.S. Senator Not Counting Obama." Obama was omitted before the voting even began because of his "extreme hotness."[28]

[27]Samuel, Terence. 2008. "On the 2008 Primary and Black Anger." *The American Prospect*. April 25. Accessed April 25, 2008. http://www.prospect.org/cs/articles?article=on_the_2008_primary_and_black_anger

[28]Forrest, Kim and Brooke Lea Foster. 2006. "25 Beautiful People: Barack Obama." *Washingtonian Magazine*. March 1. Accessed January 5, 2008. http://www.washingtonian.com/articles/people/2295.html; "Obama love." 2008. John McCain Campaign Ad. July 22. Accessed August 5, 2008. http://www.youtube.com/watch?v=u6CSix3Dy04

Infatuation with Obama was not limited to the female sex. As male writer Jewel Woods commented in July 2008, "Sure, women swoon, but have you ever noticed that guys, too, seem almost weak-kneed over the senator with mad skills and a million-dollar smile?"[29] The August 2008 cover of *Ebony Magazine* (featuring a photo of Obama emerging from a limousine) described him as one of the "Coolest Brothers of All Time." During coverage of the Potomac Primary, MSNBC anchor Chris Matthews famously stated that after hearing Obama speak, "I felt this thrill going up my leg." He continued, "I don't have that too often."[30]

Even Obama's detractors commented upon his cool factor. As part of the Clinton/GOP characterization of Obama as an arrogant elitist, Karl Rove stated in June 2008, "Even if you never met him, you know this guy.... He's the guy at the country club with the beautiful date, holding a martini and a cigarette that stands against the wall and makes snide comments about everyone who passes by."[31] As many gender scholars have noted, there is something attractive about power in men that is simply not attractive in women.

When it became clear that Clinton would lose the contest, the residual anger that her supporters directed at Obama seemed to be rooted in the perception that while he may not himself have been overtly sexist, Obama was certainly willing to benefit from the sexism directed at Hillary Clinton.[32] For some, Michelle Goldberg wrote in the *New Republic*, Obama became "like every arrogant young man who has ever edged out a more deserving middle-aged woman." One blogger charged for example, that Obama had "[stood] silently, ... [supporting] the disgracefully sexist, blatantly anti-feminist attack on a well-respected woman of the same party ... with the cold reserve of ambition."[33]

---

[29]Woods, Jewel. 2008. "Bringing Sexy Back: Barack Obama & The "Triumph" of White-Collar Masculinity." On the blog *Jewel Woods*. July 18. Accessed July 18, 2008. http://jewelwoods.com/node/8

[30]"Chris Matthews: 'I Felt This Thrill Going Up My Leg' As Obama Spoke." 2008. *Huffington Post*. February 13. Accessed February 13, 2008. http://www.huffingtonpost.com/2008/02/13/chris-matthews-i-felt-thi_n_86449.html

[31]"Rove: 'Obama Is The Type Of Guy Who Hangs Out At Country Clubs.'" 2008. Talking Points Memo. June 23. Accessed July 15, 2008. http://tpmelectioncentral.talkingpointsmemo.com/2008/06/rove_obama_is_the_type_of_guy.php

[32]Kantor, Jodi. 2008. "As Clinton's hopes dim, gender issue lives on." *New York Times*. May 19. Accessed May 19. http://www.nytimes.com/2008/05/19/world/americas/19iht-19women.13000387.html

[33]Goldberg, Michelle. 2008. "3 A.M. for Feminism: Clinton dead-enders and the crisis in the women's movement." *The New Republic*. June 6. Accessed June 13, 2008. http://www.tnr.com/article/politics/3-am-feminism; Watson, Tom. 2008. "The Sexist Media Mugging of Hillary Clinton." January 7. Accessed January 7, 2008. http://tomwatson.typepad.com/tom_watson/2008/01/the-sexist-medi.html

But views about the role of sexism in Hillary's loss and about her legacy for women are widely contradictory. While some held Clinton to be a feminist hero, others found her political maneuvers to be repugnant and antifeminist at their core.[34] And though Clinton's camp did seem to try to manipulate ideas about race in her favor during the primary, it is also true that she was continually subjected to an undercurrent of gender-based slurs from the conservative and liberal press. How do we disentangle "simple dislike" for Hillary Clinton from hatred directed at her specifically because she was a woman stepping outside of her socially ascribed "place?"[35] How do we parse out the role of sexism from the other factors that led to her loss? As Jonathan, a nineteen-year-old Latino male told one of my interviewers, "A lot of people were turned off by her … because she was too shrewd, manipulative, you know I'm trying to not use curse words, but you know, the B-word." In the end, he opined, what hurt Clinton was not her gender but "the fact that she was Hillary."

While Obama likely benefitted from both the positive associations between masculinity and leadership, and from the subtle and blatant ways that Clinton was disparaged because of her sex, it does not logically follow—as some have argued—that his gender privilege simply "canceled out" or "trumped" the issue of race in his campaign. For me, the 2008 primary was less a story about Obama relying on sexism or gender to get over, and more about him "doing race" right. Simply put, Obama deployed the concept of race better, more appealingly, and more strategically than Clinton did gender. While she was the candidate of the status quo (who could be just as tough as the boys), he was "your cool black friend"—and the candidate of change.[36] Capitalizing upon the

[34]Milligan, Susan. 2008. "Clinton's Struggle Vexes Feminists." *Boston Globe*. February 9. Accessed February 12, 2008. http://www.boston.com/news/nation/articles/2008/02/19/clintons_struggle_vexes_feminists/; Fortini, Amanda. 2008. "The Feminist Reawakening: Hillary Clinton and the fourth wave." *New York Magazine*. April 13. Accessed April 13, 2008. http://nymag.com/news/features/46011/; Wilson, Marie C. 2008. "Commentary: Clinton started a new political movement." On *CNN.com*. June 6. Accessed June 15, 2008. http://www.cnn.com/2008/POLITICS/06/06/wilson/index.html; Robinson, Sara. 2008. "Standing at the Nexus of Change." *Ornicus*. July 10. Accessed July 15, 2008. http://www.dneiwert.blogspot.com/2008_07_06_archive.html; Kissling, Frances. 2008. "Why I'm still not for Hillary Clinton." *Salon.com*. January 10. Accessed March 18, 2008. http://www.salon.com/news/opinion/feature/2008/01/10/kissling_clinton; O'Rourke, Megan. 2008. "Death of a Saleswoman: How Hillary Clinton lost me—and a generation of young voters." On the blog *Salon.com*. June 5. Accessed July 18, 2008. http://www.slate.com/id/2192827; Douglass, Susan. 2008. "Why Women Hate Hillary." In These Times. April 27. Accessed May 13, 2008. http://www.inthesetimes.com/article/3129/why_women_hate_hillary/

[35]Liddle, Rod. 2008. "Hillary, they just don't like you." *The Sunday Times* [London]. June 8. Accessed June 8, 2008. http://www.timesonline.co.uk/tol/comment/columnists/rod_liddle/article4087544.ece/

[36]Zeitlin, Matt. 2008. "Barack Obama Is My Imaginary Hip Black Friend." On the blog *Matt Zeitlin: Impetuous Young Whippersnapper*. January 12. Accessed August 26, 2009. http://whippersnapper.wordpress.com/2008/01/12/barack-obama-is-my-imaginary-hip-black-friend/

"galloping" desire in this country to say that we have overcome our racial problems once and for all, and deploying the tropes of renewal, redemption, and rebirth, Obama tapped into the revolutionary potential of his candidacy in a way that Clinton simply did not. As Alyssa E., a twenty-one-year-old women's studies major, said to an interviewer:

> I definitely loved Hillary Clinton. But I don't think it was because of sexism that she lost. I think there were some really ugly, really sexist things that happened. But she was, you know, very far ahead at one point, and I don't think that *suddenly* we became sexist. I think that she could have had this really revolutionary candidacy; but it wasn't quite right. She wasn't talking about change.

Epilogue

Konrad Ng

"...[R]econstructing a multiethnic narrative from the ground up will entail the steadfast labor of a generation of scholars."

—*Scott Kurashige,* The Shifting Grounds of Race:
Black and Japanese Americans in the Making of Multiethnic Los Angeles

When Obama officially announced his bid for the presidency on a cold day in Springfield, Illinois, no one really knew how the campaign would play out. By his own admission, Obama was an improbable candidate for president, and the doubts about his chances were well-known. There was a strong field of candidates that included an accomplished, well-known woman, a Latino-American governor, and a former Democratic vice-presidential candidate. Obama had no money and no existing fundraising structure. He had no national campaign experience, no "executive" experience, and only two years of experience as a U.S. senator—and, it was frequently noted, the last sitting U.S. senator to be elected president was John F. Kennedy in 1960. Furthermore, his biography appeared to be a handicap. Obama was born in Hawaii, a place generally considered far too exotic to produce someone central to U.S. politics. He had a funny name that resembled the name of a notorious terrorist and—it was either whispered or stated bluntly—he was black, or close enough, and that was still a negative to many in this country. Would the promise of his candidacy, characterized by a youthful, grassroots, new media–savvy message of hope and change, be all flash and no substance? Would Obama reach the Iowa caucus? Perhaps he would continue to compete through the primaries and caucuses in New Hampshire, Nevada, and South Carolina, but many believed that the campaign would then end in defeat, and possibly in debt, on "Super-duper" Tuesday. The pundit postmortem would explain that Obama's failure supported rather cynical beliefs about American politics: new media is overrated; young people do not vote; women and minorities split the vote; money, the life blood and influence of a campaign, comes from elite high-rollers, lobbyists, and political action committees; and Bill Clinton was the first, and only, black president.

Obama did not think it was useful to fixate on the long odds. Exhibiting his characteristic calmness, confidence, and focus, he was certain that his campaign would be competitive. The mood of the electorate was restless, and

266

he had assembled a talented and dedicated campaign team. Aside from timing and competitiveness, both of the Obamas saw the campaign as an important opportunity to bring attention to key issues often lost in a political culture prone to smallness, pettiness, and feelings of disconnection with elected officials and political institutions. The Obamas knew that the campaign could be a profound force for social change; if they could offer more than "politics as usual," make politics a more thoughtful enterprise, the path to the presidency would work itself out.

The election of the once-improbable candidate has challenged conventional thinking about American politics and suggests that the contours of the American political map may have changed permanently. If the election of Obama points to different conditions of possibility for the present, what does it mean to conduct scholarship in the era of Obama and treat Obama as a field of research and object of study? Since the inauguration, there has been a steady stream of popular publications by journalists detailing their experiences of the election, reasons behind its outcome, and rough character sketches of the man and woman behind it all.[1] Academia is beginning to experience an Obama bump in scholarship. The fifty-eight-year-old American Studies Association notes in its June 2009 newsletter that "[t]he election of Barack Obama prompted arguably the largest number of submissions [to the annual conference] on the work and meaning of a single individual in the recent history of the organization."[2] And there is *The Obama Effect: Multidisciplinary Renderings of the 2008 Presidential Election Campaign*, of course, which showcases scholarship presented at a conference held during the election. What drew me to this project was the intellectual grace of its organizers, Heather Harris, Kimberly Moffitt, and Catherine Squires, and their collective desire to capture the dynamics and effects of an event that, at the time, remained in progress. The contemporaneity of their aim appealed to me for how it linked the uncertainty of a period with the lived experience of people in that time. This association lends a unique authority and open-endedness to the insight, and this dimension is crucial, I suggest, for scholarship conducted during a time when the nation is undergoing a fundamental transformation in its demography.

The contributors to *The Obama Effect* are both witness and accomplice to an America that is becoming more Asian, Native Hawaiian, Pacific Islander,

---

[1]Recent publications include Chuck Todd and Sheldon Gawiser's *How Barack Obama Won: A State-by-State Guide to the Historic 2008 Presidential Election* (New York: Vintage, 2009); Gwen Ifill's *The Breakthrough* (New York: Double Day, 2009); and Richard Wolffe's *Renegade: The Making of a President* (New York: Crown, 2009). Books are expected from *The New Yorker* editor David Remnick and correspondent, Ryan Lizza, and political journalist Robert Draper.

[2]Joanna Brooks, Melani McAlister, and Barry Shank, "2009 Interim Report of the Program Committee," *American Studies Association Newsletter* 36, no. 2 (June 2009). Washington, D.C.: Office of the Executive Director American Studies Association.

American Indian, Alaskan Native, black, Latino, and mixed in attitude and makeup. The U.S. Census Bureau projects that over the next fifty years, minorities will make up more than half of children born by 2023; by 2050, America's minority communities will become the numerical majority.[3] If we imagine this demographic trajectory alongside new media innovations, the study of American life will begin to be a showcase of sites, screens, and events that will have been previously seen as unconventional, unseen, and unlikely. My point is not to arrive at some Pollyanna notion of a diverse and networked America, nor to say that the election of Obama was the direct consequence of this emerging society. Rather, Obama offers a chance to acknowledge a new America in our cultural and political scholarship and realize that the demographic conditions of the present demand different narratives, methods, and ideas to address the nation's transformation. There are no assurances about the progressiveness and potential of Obama's America, but I am certain that projects like *The Obama Effect* provide important originary tales and starting points that will guide how a future generation of Americans will make sense of their more diverse and networked society.[4]

When I think back on the 2008 election and the Obama effect, a *New York Times* profile printed shortly after Obama secured the nomination comes to mind. At the end of the article, author Michael Powell asks Obama for his thoughts on profiles written about him. Powell cites a writer's description of Obama as someone who "comes across as someone who stored away for future consideration practically everything that was ever said to him, and who had a talent for watchfulness, part of the extraordinary armor he developed at an early age." Obama's response is instructive:

> Mr. Obama nods. That's intriguing. But he prefers his own riff, which not incidentally trains the eye not on him but on his crowds. "I love when I'm shaking hands on a rope line and"—he mimes the motion, hand over hand—"I see little old white ladies and big burly black guys and Latino girls and all their hands are entwining. They're feeding on each other as much as on me."
> He shrugs; it's that distancing eye of the author.
> "It's like I'm just the excuse."[5]

---

[3]U.S. Census Bureau, "An Older and More Diverse Nation by Midcentury," U.S. Department of Commerce, August 14, 2008, http://www.census.gov/Press-Release/www/releases/archives/population/012496.html (accessed August, 14 2008).

[4]I thank Scott Kurashige for his work on Los Angeles as a site of Afro-Asian collaboration. In *The Shifting Grounds of Race: Black and Japanese Americans in the Making of Multiethnic Los Angeles* (Princeton, NJ: Princeton University Press, 2007), Kurashige contends that multiethnic cities such as Los Angeles are important sites of inquiry for how they reflect the trend of an increasingly multiethnic America (p. 286).

[5]Michael Powell, "Barack Obama: Calm in the Swirl of History," *New York Times*, June 4, 2008, http://www.nytimes.com/2008/06/04/us/politics/04obama.html (accessed June 4, 2008).

Epilogue

For my part, the excuse was made clear on January 20, 2009, when I found myself sitting a few feet behind Obama as he delivered his inaugural address. Like many people, I have been suspicious about the possibilities of politics. But, as I listened closely to Obama's inaugural address on that cold winter day, I looked at the sea of people bearing witness to something that was once considered unlikely. Rising from the colorful crowd was a cityscape of monuments that marked key moments in American history. I realized that it would be a waste to avoid studying this moment or the experience of the campaign. That is, like the contributors and editors of this book, my hope is that we recognize this time as an important juncture for offering contemporaneous stories that will go on to build future methods. We will recognize, as Obama did in his St. Paul, Minnesota, speech when the Democratic primary season concluded, "This was the moment, this was the time when ..."[6]

---

[6]Barack Obama, "Remarks of Senator Barack Obama: Final Primary Night," http://www.barackobama .com/2008/06/03/remarks_of_senator_barack_obam_73.php (accessed June 4, 2008).

List of Contributors

Bertram D. Ashe, Ph.D. (College of William and Mary), is Associate Professor of English and American Studies at the University of Richmond. Dr. Ashe's work focuses on African-American culture and politics. He is the author of From within the Frame: Storytelling in African-American Fiction (Routledge 2002) and is a regular contributor to African American Review.

Michael Cheney is a senior fellow at the Institute of Government and Public Affairs, and a Professor of Communication and an Associate Professor of Economics at the University of Illinois at Springfield. Prior to his affiliation with IGPA and the University of Illinois at Springfield, Cheney taught at Rutgers College from 1977 to 1981 and at Drake University. In 1988, he became the Dean of the School of Journalism and Mass Communication at Drake University. Cheney currently focuses his research on political campaigning through the Internet.

Desiree Cooper is an award-winning author and journalist. A graduate of the University of Maryland, Cooper has worked as a columnist for the *Detroit Free Press*, has appeared as a frequent commentator on National Public Radio's *All Things Considered*, and was co-host of American Public Media's *Weekend America*. She is the author of many short stories and memoirs, which have been included in collections such as *Detroit Noir* (Akashic Books 2007), *Children of the Dream* (Atria 2000) and *Other People's Skin* (Atria 2007). Ms. Cooper lives in Detroit, Michigan, with her husband and two children.

Frank Rudy Cooper, J.D. (Duke University), is Professor of Law at Suffolk University. During law school, he was a staff editor of the *Duke Journal of Gender Law and Policy*. Professor Cooper writes in the areas of critical race theory, law and cultural studies, and constitutional criminal procedure. Recent book chapters include "The Seesaw Effect: From Racial Profiling to Depolicing: Toward a Critical Cultural Theory," in *New Civil Rights Research: A Constitutive Approach* (Benjamin Fleury-Steiner and Laura Beth Nielsen, eds., 2006) and "Where the Rubber Meets the Road: The CRA's Impact on Distressed Communities," in *Public Policies For Distressed Communities* (F. Stevens Redburn and Terry Buss, eds., 2002).

Kenneth D. Day, Ph.D., is Professor of Communication at the University of the Pacific, where he teaches courses in media theory, new communication technology, and intercultural communication. His current research and consulting practice involve the use of new communication technology in education, marketing, and cultural preservation. He is also a developer in virtual worlds and the use of mobile communication.

Raman Deol is an independent researcher. She received her master's degree in communication with an emphasis on rhetorical analysis at the University of the Pacific.

Qingwen Dong, Ph.D. (Washington State University), is Associate Professor of Communication at the University of the Pacific. Dr. Dong's research interests include media representations of race and ethnicity, Internet use, and media effects. Dr. Dong's work has appeared in *Critical Studies: Communication and Culture—China and the World Entering the 21st Century, Human Communication, Journal of Broadcasting & Electronic Media,* and *The Journal of Family & Economic Issues.*

Dina Gavrilos, Ph.D. (University of Iowa), is Assistant Professor in the Department of Communication and Journalism at the University of St. Thomas in Saint Paul, Minnesota. Professor Gavrilos conducts research that addresses how media construct racial, ethnic, national, and other identity categories in particular communities. She has recently published articles in the *Journal of Communication Inquiry,* including "Arab Americans in a Nation's Imagined Community: How News Constructed Arab American Reactions to the Gulf War" (2002). She regularly presents work at the annual meetings of the International Communication Association, the Cultural Studies Association, and the Association for Education in Journalism and Mass Communication.

Heather E. Harris, Ph.D. (Howard University), is Associate Professor of Business Communication at Stevenson University. Dr. Harris's research focuses on cultural studies, representations of Africana women in media, and women in romantic relationships. Her work has appeared in edited volumes and journals. She has presented numerous papers at regional, national, and international conferences.

M. Cooper Harriss is a Marty Martin Dissertation Fellow at the University of Chicago's Divinity School. His dissertation concerns the viability of religious thought in understanding Ralph Ellison's writings and worldview. He has served as managing editor of the journal *ETHICS* (University of Chicago Press) and holds an M.A.R. from Yale Divinity School.

Suzanne W. Jones, Ph.D. (University of Virginia), is Professor of English at the University of Richmond. Jones studies literature of the American South, and how literature can be used to help readers understand race relations and other complex social issues. She is interested in all aspects of the contemporary South, "particularly how it is sometimes given a one-dimensional portrait in the media," she says. She has published many articles on Southern literature, and her book, *Race Mixing: Southern Fiction Since the Sixties*, was published in March 2004 (Johns Hopkins University Press). *Choice* listed *Race Mixing* as "essential" for "all academic and public libraries." She is also the editor of *Crossing the Color Line: Readings in Black and White* (University of South Carolina Press).

Rebecca A. Kuehl is a doctoral student in the University of Minnesota's Department of Communication Studies. Kuehl's research focuses on rhetoric and politics, particularly the ways in which people are persuaded to become politically engaged.

Enid Lynette Logan, Ph.D. (University of Michigan), is Assistant Professor of Sociology at the University of Minnesota, Twin Cities. Her research interests include U.S., Latin American, and Caribbean race relations; intersectionality (race, class, and gender); cultural sociology, and sociology of the media. Her recent publications include "The 1899 Cuban Marriage Law Controversy: Church, State and Empire in the Crucible of Nation" in the *Journal of Social History*, and "The Crack Baby Panic," in *Deviance: The Interactionist Perspective*, 9th ed. (E. Rubington and M. Weinberg, eds., 2005).

Sarah McCaffrey is a doctoral candidate in the Department of Communication Studies at the University of Washington, Seattle.

Kimberly R. Moffitt, Ph.D. (Howard University) is assistant professor in the Department of American Studies at University of Maryland, Baltimore County (UMBC). Dr. Moffitt conducts research in the areas of mediated representations of marginalized groups as well as sports icons. Her recent work is a co-edited volume entitled *Blackberries and Redbones: Critical Articulations of Black Hair and Body Politics in Africana Communities* (Hampton Press 2010). In addition to the introduction, she wrote a chapter on the images of physically disabled black men in urban films. Her latest project is a qualitative study exploring the reactions of Baltimore residents to the now-defunct yet overwhelmingly popular, HBO original program *The Wire*. Dr. Moffitt has a forthcoming edited volume entitled, *The 1980s: A Critical and Transitional Decade?* (Lexington Books). She has published in *Black Issues in Higher Education and the Journal of Black Studies*.

Konrad Ng is the Acting Director of the Smithsonian Asian Pacific American Program (www.apa.si.edu) and a professor of creative media at the University of Hawaii at Manoa (www.hawaii.edu/acm). He has a long history of working in Asian and Asian American cultural institutions, programs, and organizations, and has published scholarly and popular articles on Asian and Asian American film, politics, and culture. Ng serves on the Board of Directors for the Global Film Initiative and the Center for Asian American Media. From 2007 to 2008, he assisted with constituency and new media outreach for the Obama for America campaign. Ng earned his Ph.D. from the University of Hawaii.

Crystal Olsen is a grant-writing assistant in the Civic Leadership Program at the University of Illinois at Urbana-Champaign. Olsen is an M.A. candidate in the Department of Political Science, and is co-authoring a book on the role of social media in the 2008 election.

James T. Petre is a doctoral candidate in the Department of Speech Communication at Southern Illinois University.

Aimee Carrillo Rowe, Ph.D. (University of Washington), is Associate Professor of Rhetoric at the University of Iowa. Dr. Rowe's teaching and writing address the politics of representation and feminist alliances, Third World feminism, and whiteness and antiracism. Her book, *Power Lines: On the Subject of Feminist Alliances* (Duke University Press 2008), offers a coalitional theory of subjectivity as a bridge to difference-based alliances. Her writing appears primarily in interdisciplinary outlets such as Hypatia (summer 2007), *Radical History Review* (summer 2004), and *NWSA Journal* (summer 2005).

Robert Spicer is a doctoral candidate in the Department of Communication and Theater at Millersville University.

Catherine Squires, Ph.D. (Northwestern University), is the inaugural John and Elizabeth Bates Cowles Professor of Journalism, Diversity, and Equality at the University of Minnesota. Her first book, *Dispatches from the Color Line* (SUNY 2007), analyzed news coverage of people of multiracial descent. She has written about African Americans and the media in her recent book, *African Americans and the Media* (Polity Press 2009), and in journals such as *Communication Theory, The Harvard International Journal of Press/Politics*, and *Critical Studies in Media Communication*. Her work has been included in collections such as *Counterpublics and the State* (SUNY 2001) and *Say It Loud! African American Audiences, Media and Identity* (Routledge 2002). Squires's research concerning race, gender, and media has been published in *The Black Scholar, The Journal of Intergroup Relations*, and *Signs*.

Grace J. Yoo, Ph.D. (University of California, San Francisco), is a medical sociologist and professor of Asian American Studies at San Francisco State University. Her work focuses on the experiences of Asian Americans with state agencies and constructions of Asian identities in media and public policies. Recent publications include "The Not-So-Forgotten War: Memories of Older Korean Immigrant Women," *Peace Review* (2004), and "Constructing Deservingness: Federal Welfare Reform, Supplemental Security Income, and Elderly Immigrants," *Journal of Aging and Social Policy* (2002).

Index

275

Index

Index